The Way We Lived

Volume II
1865–Present

The Way We Lived

Essays and Documents
in American Social History
Fourth Edition

Frederick M. Binder

City University of New York, College of Staten Island

David M. Reimers

New York University

Houghton Mifflin Company   Boston   New York

Editor-in-Chief: Jean Woy
Sponsoring Editor: Colleen Kyle
Associate Project Editor: Amy Johnson
Associate Production/Design Coordinator: Jodi O'Rourke
Senior Manufacturing Coordinator: Sally Culler
Senior Marketing Manager: Sandra McGuire

Cover Design: Wing Ngan/Stoltze Design
Cover Painting Detail: William J. Glackens, *The Soda Fountain*. Courtesy of the Pennsylvania
Academy of Fine Arts, Philadelphia. Joseph E. Temple and Henry D. Gilpin funds.

Photos: p. 3, Former slaves picking cotton (The Valentine Museum, Richmond, Virginia); p. 22,
The Chrisman Sisters, 1886 (Solomon Butcher Collection/Nebraska State Historical Society);
p. 42, Students at the Carlisle School in Carlisle, Pennsylvania (National Archives); p. 63, 19th
century office scene (Idaho State Historical Society, neg. #77-45); p. 83, "Breaker Boys"
(Pennsylvania Historical & Museum Commission/Bureau of Historic Sites & Museums/
Anthracite Museum); p. 99, "A Triumph for White Supremacy" cartoon (Historical Picture
Service/Stock Montage, Inc.); p. 115, WWI doughboys (Library of Congress); p. 139, KKK ceremony (The Granger Collection, NY); p. 156, 1920's bathing beauties (Archive Photos/Ameri-
can Stock); p. 173, Depression family (Library of Congress); p. 195, WWII homefront—female
workers (Library of Congress); p. 213, 1940's suburban family and their new home (Archive
Photos/Camerique); p. 234, Civil Rights demonstrators (George Gardner/The Image Works);
p. 255, Anti-Vietnam protestors taunting military police, 1967 (Corbis/Bettmann/UPI)
#U1571850>36; p. 276, Women's rights parade in Houston, Texas, ca. 1977 (Steve Northup);
p. 294, Cafe Cubano in Miami's "Little Havana" (Susan Greenwood/Gamma Liaison).

Printed in the U.S.A.

Library of Congress Catalog Number: 99-72018

ISBN: 0-395-95961-6

23456789-CS-03 02 01 00

Contents

Preface

History courses have traditionally emphasized the momentous events of our past. Wars and laws, technological advances and economic crises, ideas and ideologies, and the roles of famous heroes and infamous villains have been central to these studies. Yet what made events momentous is the impact they had on society at large, on people from all walks of life. Modern scholars' growing attention to social history is in part a recognition that knowledge of the experiences, values, and attitudes of these people is crucial to gaining an understanding of our past.

America's history as reflected in the everyday lives of its people provides the focus of these volumes. In preparing a work of selected readings, we have had to make choices as to which episodes from our past to highlight. Each of those included, we believe, was significant in the shaping of our society. Each of the essays is followed by original documents that serve several purposes. They provide examples of the kinds of source materials used by social historians in their research; they help to illuminate and expand upon the subject dealt with in the essays; and they bring the reader into direct contact with the people of the past—people who helped shape, and people who were affected by, the "momentous events."

Our introduction to each essay and its accompanying documents is designed to set the historical scene and to call attention to particular points in the selections, raising questions for students to ponder as they read. A list of suggested readings follows after each of the major divisions of the text. We trust that these volumes will prove to be what written history at its best can be—interesting and enlightening.

We are pleased to note that favorable comments by faculty and students as well as the large number of course adoptions attest to the success of our first three editions. Quite naturally, we thus have no desire in our fourth edition to alter the basic focus, style, and organization of *The Way We Lived*. Those essays that we and our readers consider to have been the earlier editions' very best remain intact. We believe that the new selections will identify and clarify significant issues in America's social history even more effectively than those they replaced.

F. M. B.

D. M. R.

Part I

*The Emergence of an Urban,
Industrial Society
1865–1920*

Chapter 1

Reconstruction and Free Plantation Labor

The Civil War eliminated slavery but left undecided the question of what agrarian labor system would replace it in the devastated South. Peter Kolchin's essay "Free Plantation Labor" describes how Alabama freedmen (former slaves) and their erstwhile masters established relationships to maintain the productivity of the land. As you read, consider the aspirations, fears, and misunderstandings that governed the behavior of blacks, Southern whites, and Southern-based representatives of the federal government working for the Freedmen's Bureau. Although salaried agricultural labor and tenant farming made an appearance on Alabama plantations, it was sharecropping that came to dominate agriculture in that state and much of the rest of the South. Sharecropping ultimately proved an unproductive system of land management, crushing black farmers and their families under a yoke of debt and poverty for generations to come. Yet, as Kolchin's essay points out, both blacks and whites initially found the system attractive. Why?

The first document is a letter from a freed slave to his former master. The letter speaks eloquently of the conditions and humiliations that he had endured in the past and also of the better life that he has built for himself. How would you describe the general tone of the letter?

Although even the most tenacious plantation owners recognized that slavery was finished and that the South needed a new system of labor, few white Southerners could accept the freedmen as social and political equals. In 1865–1866 Southern politicians established Black Codes to ensure white supremacy. The second document is the Black Code of St. Landry's Parish, Louisiana. To what extent does this document support the claim of some Northern Radical Republicans that the Black Codes amounted to nothing less than the continuation of slavery? The code explains part of the motivation for the passage of the Reconstruction amendments and laws by the Republican-controlled federal government. It also provides clues to the fate in store for Southern blacks after 1877, when the last federal troops left the South and Reconstruction ended.

The third document consists of letters from two Northern schoolteachers, who were among the hundreds who traveled south after the war under the auspices of the Freedmen's Bureau and several private philanthropic agencies. What do these documents and the Kolchin essay indicate about the goals of the newly freed blacks? What actions did the freedmen take to achieve their objectives?

Beginning in the 1890s, the freedmen lost the rights and opportunities they had won during the ten years following the Civil War, as Southern whites began systematically to disfranchise blacks and to institutionalize segregationist and discriminatory practices. Whites prohibited blacks from voting, segregated them in public life, denied them justice in the courts, and placed their children in underfunded "colored schools." Although blacks never accepted these conditions as permanent, over half a century would pass before their march toward full equality resumed with the promise of significant success.

ESSAY

Free Plantation Labor

Peter Kolchin

I

Despite the migration of Negroes to Alabama's towns and cities, the most important question to blacks in 1865 concerned the role of the rural freedmen. The end of the Civil War found general confusion as to their status.

SOURCE: *First Freedom: The Responses of Alabama Blacks to Emancipation and Reconstruction*, 30–48, by Peter Kolchin. Copyright © 1972 by Greenwood Press. Reproduced with permission of Greenwood Publishing Group, Inc., Westport, CT.

"You have been told by the Yankees and others that you are free," one planter declared to his Negroes in April 1865. "This may be so! I do not doubt that you will be freed in a few years. But the terms and time of your ultimate freedom is not yet fully and definitely settled. Neither you nor I know what is to be the final result." Even if free, the Negroes' position in society remained to be determined. Presumably they would continue to till the land, for agriculture, especially cotton, was the mainstay of the state's economy and would continue as such for years. But it was not clear under what new system the land would be cultivated.

In the spring of 1865, before the arrival of Freedmen's Bureau officials, Union officers played the greatest role in establishing the new order. Throughout the state, they informed whites that the Negroes really were free and gathered blacks together to tell them of their new rights. "All persons formerly held as slaves will be treated in every respect as entitled to the rights of freedmen, and such as desire their services will be required to pay for them," announced Lieutenant Colonel C. T. Christensen in a typical statement from Mobile.

The army also served as the precursor of the Freedmen's Bureau in establishing the new agricultural labor system, according to which freedmen were to work under yearly contracts with their employers, supervised by federal officials. Varieties of this contract system had already been tested in certain Union-occupied portions of the South before the end of the war, and in April Thomas W. Conway, general superintendent of freedmen for the Department of the Gulf, arrived in Montgomery to inaugurate it in Alabama. But it was late summer before the Freedmen's Bureau was fully established throughout the state, and until then the task of supervising relations between planters and freedmen rested primarily with the army. Officers advised blacks to remain on their plantations "whenever the persons by whom they are employed recognize their rights and agree to compensate them for their services." Similar circulars, although not always so friendly in tone, were issued from other parts of the state. Brevet Major General R. S. Granger ordered that all contracts between freedmen and planters must be in writing. He added bluntly that "[t]hose found unemployed will be arrested and set to work." But officers were usually vague in recommending what the compensation of the freedmen, or their working relations with planters, should be. Conditions varied widely from one location to another during the first few months after the war as individual army officers, Freedmen's Bureau officials, and planters exercised their own discretion.

Observers generally noted a demoralization of labor during the spring and summer of 1865, which they frequently associated with the early migration of freedmen. Upon his arrival in Montgomery, Conway noted a "perfect reign of idleness on the part of the negroes." Other Bureau officials joined planters in declaring that blacks either would not work or would at best make feeble symbolic gestures toward work. Southern whites, and some Northern ones as well, complained that Negroes refused to work and were "impudent and defyant." In one piedmont county, the commander of the local militia warned that "[t]he negroes are becoming very impudent and unless something is done very soon I fear the consequences." White Alabamians frequently confused black "impudence" with outright revolt, but organized violence did occasionally occur.

Events on the Henry Watson plantation, a large estate in the blackbelt county of Greene, illustrate the behavior of freedmen during the first few months after the war. "About the first of June," wrote John Parrish to his brother-in-law Henry Watson, who was vacationing in Germany, "your negroes rebelled against the authority" of the overseer George Hagin. They refused to work and demanded his removal. As Parrish was ill at the time, he induced a friend of Watson's, J. A. Wemyss, to go to the plantation and attempt to put things in order. "He made a sort of compromise bargain with the negroes," Parrish reported, "agreeing that if they would remain he would give them part of the crop, they should be clothed and fed as usual, and that Mr. Hagan [*sic*] should have no authority over them. . . . All hands are having a good easy time, not doing half work." Six days later Parrish reported that "they have again rebelled." When Wemyss informed them firmly that they must submit to the overseer's authority, at first they "amiably consented," but soon they once again objected—"their complaints were universal, very ugly"—and seventeen of them left for nearby Uniontown, where a federal garrison was stationed. Meanwhile, a Freedmen's Bureau agent had arrived in Greensboro. Parrish brought him to the plantation, where he "modified the contract in the negroes['] fav[or] & made them sign it with their marks." The modified contract granted the laborers one-eighth of the crop.

When Watson finally returned from Germany to take charge of matters himself, he was totally disgusted with what he found. The Negroes "claim of their masters full and complete compliance on their part," he complained, "but forget that they agreed to do anything on theirs and are all idle, doing nothing, insisting that they shall be fed and are eating off their masters." Finding such a state of affairs more than he could tolerate, he decided to rent the plantation to overseer Hagin and "have nothing to do with the hiring of hands or the care of the plantation." Hagin, in turn, later broke up the plantation and sublet individual lots to Negro families.

II

Southern whites, long accustomed to thinking of their slaves as faithful and docile servants, were quick to blame outsiders for any trouble. As early as April 1862, a north Alabama planter had noted that the Union soldiers "to a great extent demoralized the negroes. . . . The negroes were delighted with them and since they left enough can be seen to convince one that the Federal army[,] the negroes and white Southern people cannot inhabit the same country." After the war, planters continued to complain about the harmful influence of the army. The presence of black troops was especially unpalatable to former slave owners. "[N]egroes will *not work* surrounded [by] black troops encouraging them to insubordination," complained one outraged resident of a blackbelt community.

Although Alabama whites were deeply humiliated by the presence of Yankees and black troops in their midst, there was little foundation to the complaints about outside agitation. Indeed, federal officials often cooperated directly with planters and local authorities in attempting to keep blacks in line. Army officers urged Negroes to stay on their plantations. Freedmen's Bureau agents frequently assisted in keeping order, too. "My predecessors here worked with a view to please the white citizens, at the expense of, and injustice to, the Freedmen," complained a shocked Bureau assistant superintendent shortly after his arrival in Tuskegee. "They have invariably given permission to inflict punishment for insolence or idleness, and have detailed soldiers to tie up and otherwise punish the laborers who have, in the opinion of the employers, been *refractory*." [Freedmen's Bureau] Commissioner [O. O.] Howard later explained that the Bureau "came to the assistance of the Planters" and succeeded in making the blacks "reliable laborers under the free system." He added that "[t]he good conduct of the millions of freedmen is due to a large extent to our officers of the Army and the Bureau."

A more substantial cause of the demoralization of labor was the mistrust existing between freedman and planter. Where this mistrust was minimal— that is, where planters and freedmen had relatively close ties and where planters readily acknowledged the changed condition of their relations— Negroes continued to work well. More often than not it was the small planter, who worked in the field beside his employees and knew them personally, who managed to remain on good terms with them. But few planters were willing to accept all the implications of the overthrow of slavery. "Thus far," pronounced the state's leading newspaper [*Daily Selma Times*] in October, "we are sorry to say that experience teaches that the negro in a free condition will not work on the old plantations." Another newspaper agreed that freedom had made the blacks "dissatisfied, listless, improvident, and unprofitable drones." Throughout the state, whites refused to believe that Negroes would work without the compulsion of slavery.

Some planters continued to hope that emancipation could either be rescinded or delayed, and "consequently told the negroes they were not free." Others recognized the de jure passing of slavery and concentrated on making the condition of the freedmen as near as possible to that of slaves. Upon his arrival in Montgomery, Conway noted that "the Planters appeared disinclined to offer employment, except with guarantees that would practically reduce the Freedmen again to a state of bondage."

Early contracts between planters and freedmen reflected the disbelief of whites in the possibility of free black labor and their desire to maintain slavery in fact, if not in name. Some planters reached "verbal agreements" with freedmen to continue as they had, without recompense. It was also relatively easy, before the Freedmen's Bureau was firmly established, for planters to lure former slaves into signing contracts that essentially perpetuated their condition. "Today I contracted with Jane and Dick to serve the remainder of the year, such being the federal law," Sarah Espy of the mountain county of Cherokee wrote in her diary in July. "I give them their victuals and clothing, the proceeds of their patches[,] and they are to proceed as heretofore." Similar contracts were made in other regions, and numerous Freedmen's Bureau officials reported upon arrival at their posts that Negroes were working without pay. The practice was summarized in a report to [Assistant Commissioner Wager] Swayne: "We find that the agreements they [the freedmen] have been working under (some of them since last April) are merely a paper drawn up by their later owners," wrote Captain J. W. Cogswell, "in which the negro promises to work for an indefinite time for nothing but his board and clothes, and the white man agrees to do nothing."

When some compensation was provided, as was the case more often than not, it almost always involved a share of the crop. There seems to have been little or no experimentation with wage labor during the first few months after the war. The initial reason for the immediate widespread adoption of sharecropping was simple: the defeated South did not have sufficient currency to pay laborers in cash. Cropping provided a convenient mode of paying freedmen without any money transactions.

Partly for the same reason and partly from tradition, most early contracts specified that food and medical care would be provided by the planter. In addition to being a continuation of the old plantation paternalism, this provision also conformed to the wishes of the Freedmen's Bureau. Shortly after his arrival in Montgomery, Swayne drew up a list of proposed labor regulations. One was that "[p]art of the compensation is required to be in food and medical attendance, lest the improvident leave their families to suffer or the weak are obliged to purchase at unjust rates what they must immediately have." The concern of the Freedmen's Bureau for the welfare of the freedmen, superimposed upon the legacy of slave paternalism and combined with the shortage of currency, insured that early contracts would give Negroes, in addition to their share of the crop, "quarters, fuel, necessary clothes, [and] medical attendance in case of sickness."

Although the size of the shares freedmen received in 1865 varied considerably, it was almost always very small. W. C. Penick agreed to pay his laborers one-quarter of the crop, but such liberality was rare during the summer of 1865. More typical was the contract between Henry Watson and his more than fifty adult blacks, which promised them one-eighth of the crop. In other cases shares varied from one-quarter to one-tenth of the crop.

In addition to appropriating the greater portion of the freedmen's labor, planters were concerned with maintaining control over their lives. "I look upon slavery as gone, gone, gone, beyond the possibility of help," lamented one planter. He added reassuringly, however, that "we have the power to pass stringent police laws to govern the negroes—This is a blessing—For they must be controlled in some way or white people cannot live amongst them." Such an outlook did not necessarily represent a conscious effort to thwart the meaning of freedom, for whites had been conditioned by years of slavery to look upon subservience as the only condition compatible with Negro, or any plantation, labor. Nevertheless, the effect was the same. Early contracts often included provisions regulating the behavior of laborers. A typical one provided that "all orders from the manager are to be promptly and implicitly obeyed under any and all circumstances" and added "[i]t is also agreed that none of the said negroes will under any circumstances leave the plantation without a written permission from the manager." If any of them quit work before the expiration of the contract, he was to forfeit all his wages. Some contracts gave planters authority to whip refractory Negroes.

It is only as a response to such attempts to perpetuate slave conditions that the seeming demoralization of black labor can be understood. Although whites pointed at idle or turbulent Negroes and repeated that they did not comprehend the meaning of freedom, the lack of comprehension was on the part of Alabama's whites. Blacks lost little time in demonstrating their grasp of the essentials of freedom and the tactical flexibility their new condition provided. Just as many felt compelled to leave their old plantations immediately after the war to prevent old relations from being perpetuated, so did they find it necessary to establish at the outset that they would not labor under conditions that made them free in name but slave in fact.

III

In December 1865 events reached something of a crisis as planters continued to strive for a return to the methods of prewar days and blacks continued to resist. Planter-laborer relationships were tense during the summer and fall, but with contracts entered into after the war due to expire on 31 December, the approach of the new year heralded an especially difficult time. Negroes now had the experience of over half a year as freedmen in dealing with planters. They also had the backing of the Freedmen's Bureau, which, if generally ambivalent about the precise position of the freedman in Southern society, refused to sanction his essential re-enslavement. The culmination of the demoralization of labor and the mass migrations of 1865 was the refusal of many blacks to contract for the following year.

One reason Negroes were slow to contract was that many of them expected the plantations of their ex-masters to be divided among them at the start of the year. While this idea proved to be a total misconception, it was neither so ludicrous nor so far-fetched a notion as white Alabamians portrayed it. Southern whites themselves had contributed greatly to the expectation by warning during the war that defeat would result in the confiscation of their lands. Commissioner Howard had originally intended to turn over confiscated and abandoned lands to the freedmen, and it was only when President Johnson directly countermanded this policy in the autumn of 1865 that the Bureau reversed itself and began restoring the lands in its possession to the original owners. As the end of the year approached, Freedmen's Bureau officials carefully explained to Negroes that they were not to be given land and advised them on contract for moderate wages.

White Alabamians responded to the black desire for land by exaggerating the extent to which the freedmen expected confiscation, playing up every minor incident, and predicting ominously that New Year's would bring a black uprising. They complained of Negroes arming themselves, and in at least one area whites organized armed patrols to defend themselves against an imagined impending Negro insurrection. Other observers, however, denied any threat of an uprising, and according to [reformer] Carl Schurz rumors were "spread about impending negro insurrections evidently for no other purpose than to serve as a pretext for annoying police regulations concerning the colored people."

The refusal of the freedmen to contract in December in no way presaged a rebellion, but merely expressed their reluctance to repeat their unhappy experience of the past half-year. Without careful Freedmen's Bureau supervision, the contract system threatened to become little more than an opportunity for whites to take advantage of illiterate and ignorant blacks. As Swayne wrote, with what turned out to be something of an underestimation of the abilities of the newly freed slaves, "[c]ontracts imply bargaining and litigation, and at neither of these is the freedman a match for his Employer." For this reason, the assistant commissioner [Swayne] reported, planters "so vigorously demanded contracts there was danger they would not undertake to plant at all without them."

That the fears of insurrection consisted chiefly of groundless rumors became evident when New Year's day passed without the slightest hint of trouble. To the astonishment and relief of whites, freedmen rushed to contract during the first few days of 1866 and then settled down to work. "The praiseworthy conduct of the negroes has surprised many," declared the Selma *Morning Times* in an editorial that typified the general white response. The demoralizing effects of emancipation about which whites had complained so bitterly vanished in a matter of days. "One thing is obvious," recorded a surprised planter; "the negroes, who are hired are farming and working much better than any one predicted they would work." Other white Alabamians agreed. From Tuskegee, the local Freedmen's Bureau agent boasted that "the Freedmen have commenced work with such a zeal as to merit the praise and approbation of the Planters. Planters say to me [']my negroes have never done so well as they are doing now.[']"

But if planters rejoiced that their laborers were hard at work, the freedmen had won a signal victory that was noticed by the more perceptive whites. "I think the negro hire was very high," complained future Democratic Governor George S. Houston; "[I] never had any idea of paying that much for negroes." He was right. Gone were the days when a typical contract gave the laborers one-eighth of the crop, or merely bed and board. By refusing to contract until the last moment, the freedmen had thrown their prospective employers into a panic and forced a significant alteration in the terms of the ultimate settlement. Although neither so well concerted nor organized, the process had essentially the same effect as a massive general strike.

Aside from the presence of the Freedmen's Bureau, which made blatant cheating by planters more difficult, the prevailing shortage of labor proved an inestimable boon to the freedmen. In 1866, as throughout most of the early postwar period, the pressure was on the planter to find laborers rather than on the Negro to find employment. Freedmen could feel relatively free in refusing to contract on what they regarded as unsatisfactory terms or in leaving employers with whom they were unhappy. Labor stealing, or enticing freedmen to change employers for higher wages, was a persistent complaint among planters. Occasionally, blacks were even able to strike for higher wages, as in the mountain county of Cherokee, "where they bound themselves together, under a penalty of fifty lashes, to be laid on the naked back, not to contract to work for any white man during the present harvest, for less than two dollars per day."

As had been the case in 1865, the terms of working arrangements varied widely among plantations. Both the lower and upper limits of the pay scale, however, were substantially higher than they had been. Half, or perhaps slightly more than half, of the contracts provided for a division of the crop. In such cases, the laborer almost always received a larger share than he had in 1865. Although there are examples of freedmen receiving as little as one-sixth of the crop, the prevailing portion—when, as was usual in 1866, the laborer provided nothing but his own labor—was one-quarter. For the first time, many planters contracted to pay their employees money wages rather than a portion of the crop. A typical small planter recorded that he paid his eight field hands an average of ten dollars per month for men and fifty dollars a year for women, in addition to food. In other cases where Negroes worked for wages, the rate of compensation usually ranged from seven to fifteen dollars per month for men, and somewhat less for women.

IV

The economic disadvantage of sharecropping to the Negro became evident in 1866 as the bright prospects of winter and spring faded in the summer. By August the cotton crop, which once seemed so promising, had been reduced by unseasonal rains to half its usual size, and autumn saw the second straight crop failure. As the extent of the disaster became clear, whites across the state began to decide that free blacks were not working well after all. The *Clarke County Journal,* for example, noted that although freedmen had labored satisfactorily during the winter and spring, now they seemed stubborn and lazy. "What is the matter with the freedmen?" it queried.

The contract system provided innumerable opportunities for friction between planters and freedmen—especially sharecroppers—in time of crisis. True, there were occasional touching instances when planters looked after former slaves. One white wrote to Swayne that an ex-slave of his who had left him after the war "because he would not 'feel free' if he did not" was "about to be imposed upon by an unprincipled man, who is about to employ him for the next year for far less than he is worth. . . . Please write to me," begged the distressed planter in a letter asking the assistant commissioner for advice. "I am willing to put myself to some trouble to protect my former faithful slave." Most planters, however, were primarily interested in receiving the maximum possible labor from the freedmen at minimal cost, even if it involved cheating, violence, and brutality.

The most common complaint of the freedmen was that either after the main labor on the crop was done or when it came time to divide the crop, planters would drive them off the plantations, frequently charging them with some technical violation of contract. Unlike wage earners, who were relatively secure, sharecroppers could be discharged and deprived of any compensation whatsoever. Temporary laborers could then be hired either by the day or week to finish up any remaining work. From Greene County, in the blackbelt, a Freedmen's Bureau agent reported "I find many, many men who employed them [freedmen] are arresting them . . . in a large majority of cases without cause" and sending them to sit in jail until the crop was sold. Although in some instances Bureau officials, or even the courts, mediated between planters and freedmen and were able to secure for the latter some payment, many injustices went unnoticed or unredressed.

The cyclical pattern established in 1865–1866 was repeated with some variations the following year. In December 1866, blacks once again were reluctant to contract. Although many of them now had the additional experience of being cheated out of their share of the crop, the absence of any illusions over the possibility of land confiscation enabled most blacks and planters to come to agreements more quickly and with less bitter feeling on both sides than they had the previous year. By spring, whites were rejoicing over Alabama's good fortune and praising her Negroes for their hard work and reliability. "The freedmen, according to universal testimony, are working better than they did last year," reported the *Daily Selma Messenger* with satisfaction.

There was an almost universal return to sharecropping in 1867, although a very few planters and freedmen continued, despite the shortage of currency, to experiment with wages. Some Freedmen's Bureau officials, who felt that Negroes fared better economically on wages, and some white Alabamians, who supported the system under which blacks were most carefully supervised, continued to advocate wage labor. With very few exceptions, however, planters and freedmen ignored their pleas. Arrangements granting the laborers one-quarter of the crop were most widespread, although in a few instances freedmen contracted to provide their own food and receive half the crop.

Sharecropping triumphed because both planters and freedmen favored the system. To the average planter it continued to be a more feasible labor system than wages, if for no other reason than the shortage of currency. In addition, many whites felt that shares gave blacks an interest in the crop, thus providing them with an incentive to work. Most blacks apparently preferred cropping, despite the economic disadvantages, because it allowed them greater control of their own lives. Because of his interest in the crop, the sharecropper required less supervision. In contrast to the wage laborer, who was a hired hand clearly in a subordinate position to his employer, the cropper was the partner of the landowner in a joint business venture that provided the freedman with opportunities for greater individual discretion, dignity, and self-respect. For this reason, Negroes considered the cropper a notch above the wage laborer in the social scale. "I am not working for wages," declared one freedman to his employer, as he explained why he had a right to leave the plantation at will to attend political meetings, "but am part owner of the crop and as I have all the rights that you or any other man has I shall not suffer them abridged."

V

As in 1866, the cotton crop of 1867 was a poor one. By fall, planters had once again begun to complain about the inefficiencies of freedmen as laborers. "The cause of the cotton crop being so inferior is the inefficiency of labor and the bad season [is] more on account of labor than anything else," lamented George Hagin, the ex-overseer who had rented Henry Watson's plantation. "There has been a few of the old negroes that lived on the place before that have worked very well but the younger ones are worth nothing." A correspondent of the Union Springs *Times* proclaimed free labor a failure.

Once again, planters drove freedmen from their homes without pay. "Negroes are now being dismissed from the plantations[,] there being nothing more for them to do," explained one blackbelt resident. He added calmly that "[t]hey will all be turned loose without homes[,] money or provisions[;] at least no meat." From the northwest corner of the state, 114 Negroes appealed for assistance to Major General John Pope, who in April had assumed command of the Third Military District,* comprising Alabama, Georgia, and Florida. They explained that "unless some person in whom we can place the utmost confidence be appointed to superintend the settling up of our affairs, we do not feel that justice will be done us." In 1867, for the first time, many blacks were also fired for voting Republican or attending political meetings.

Occasionally, through unusual persistence or intelligence, blacks were able to enlist the aid of the Freedmen's Bureau and resist arbitrary discharge. Bernard Houston, a sharecropper on an Athens plantation, told his landlord, "I shall not suffer myself to be turned off[,] and under legal advice and the advice of assistant Commissioner of [the] Freedmans Bureau I shall stay there until the crop is matured[,] gathered and divided according to contract." The planter protested lamely that he objected to the Negro's being "disobedient" and denied that politics had anything to do with the situation, but a month later he complained to Swayne that the freedman was "yet on the place acting in utter and entire disobedience of orders & the necessary discipline of the plantation."

In numerous other cases, freedmen were less fortunate. Freedmen's Bureau agents tried to come to the assistance of persecuted blacks, but there were simply too few agents for the job. Furthermore, since the procedure for handling grievances was not clear, Bureau representatives were not sure how best to dispose of them. Some turned cases over to the civil courts. In general, however, this method proved unsatisfactory. "[B]esides the slow process of the Law, there stands in the way the difficulty of obtaining counsel," explained one Bureau agent. "The Freedmen as a general thing have no mean[s] to pay a fee: consequently they submit to the swindle simply because they cannot purchase justice." The sub-assistant commissioner at Huntsville sent discharged freedmen back to their plantations and told them to stay there. In other locations, officials tried to mediate between laborers and planters. "I notify the parties concerned to appear at this office together, and try either to effect an understanding, or a settlement," explained one Bureau official. He reported that he had "so far been fortunate, to prevent any injustice to be done." But for every such settlement, many other grievances undoubtedly went unheard.

The cumulative effects of three years of substandard crops became increasingly evident during the late autumn and early winter of 1867–1868, a period of considerable tension because of the meeting of the Radical Constitutional Convention in December and the election to ratify the new constitution in February. The problem was no longer that freedmen were reluctant to contract, but rather that planters were unwilling or unable to plant. Their universal reaction to poor crops and low profits was to plan to cut back on

---

*Provisions of the First Reconstruction Act of 1867 divided the former Confederacy—Tennessee excepted—into five military districts, each under a commander responsible for protecting life and property. (Eds.)

planting operations. Unemployment among Negroes threatened to reach serious proportions for the first time since the war. . . .

VI

Hidden behind the daily monotony of agricultural labor, significant changes occurred in the lives of black plantation workers during their first few years of freedom. These changes were evident both in their relations with their employers and in their relations with each other. All of them can, with little inaccuracy and only slight ambiguity, be called moves toward independence. These moves, as much class as racial in nature, represented not only the desire of blacks to be free of white control, but also of ex-slave plantation laborers to be free of planter control.

"Freedom has worked great changes in the negro, bringing out all his inherent savage qualities," proclaimed the Mobile *Daily Register* in 1869. Certainly a growing physical restlessness and self-consciousness among black plantation workers—reinforced by the political emancipation brought about under congressional Reconstruction—were very evident. They were no longer willing to be imposed upon by their former owners. From the end of the war laborers, such as those on the Henry Watson plantation, had revolted against working under their old overseers. But the increasing number of white complaints of Negro "impudence," "insolence," and "insubordination," and the increasing readiness of black laborers to resort to violence and organization when faced with an unpalatable situation, testified to their growing self-assertiveness and confidence. In December 1867, for example, planters in Russell County, who were forced to cut back on planting operations because of poor crops the previous year, complained that their laborers were "seizing and holding property upon some of the places. They are generally armed." A year later, a revolt in the same area had to be put down by military force.

This desire of agricultural laborers for independence, which led them to choose sharecropping over wages even though they usually fared better economically under a wage system, was one of the greatest causes of other changes in modes of life and labor on the plantation. Before the war, field hands on large plantations had usually lived in rows of cabins grouped together. They had worked together in a slave gang, under the authority of an overseer and perhaps a driver. Their lives had been, by and large, collective. After the war, black plantation laborers quickly indicated their preference for a more individual form of life. They objected to working under the control of an overseer. They also objected to the regimented nature of the work gang and the Negro quarters. These had been accepted "in the days of slavery, when laborers were driven by overseers by day, and penned like sheep at night, and not allowed to have any will of their own," reported one Freedmen's Bureau agent. "But now, being *free* to think and act for themselves, they feel their individual responsibility for their conduct, and the importance of maintaining a good character." He noted that fights frequently broke out among Negroes forced to lie among others against their will.

Many planters found it necessary or useful to break up the former slave quarters and allow laborers to have individual huts, scattered across the plantations. The process was far from complete by the end of the 1860s, but the trend was unmistakable. As early as the spring of 1867, an article in the Montgomery *Daily Advertiser* described certain changes that had occurred in the appearance of one plantation community. "You do not see as large gangs together as of old times, but more frequently squads of five or ten in a place, working industriously without a driver," wrote the correspondent. "Several large land owners have broken up their old 'quarters' and have rebuilt the houses at selected points, scattered over the plantation. . . ."

Although most black sharecroppers continued to provide only their labor and receive food and clothing in addition to their usual quarter of the crop, the late 1860s saw the introduction of a new cropping arrangement that would, in a matter of years, be widely adopted. Early in 1868, a Freedmen's Bureau official noted that there "does not seem to be as much uniformity in the tenor of contracts as last year." He wrote that although "some give the freedmen one-fourth of the crop and provide rations as was customary last year . . . others give one third of [the] crop, and require the laborers to furnish their own rations; and some give one half, the laborers bearing an equal share of the expense." The result was to remove the cropper still further from the wage laborer, and accentuate his role as a partner of the planter in a joint business venture.

Such changes in working and living conditions were sometimes fostered by planters themselves. Some, like Henry Watson, found it impossible to adjust to a new situation in which they did not have total control over their labor force. Under such circumstances, it was tempting for them to adopt whatever system would permit the least contact between employer and laborer, even if it resulted in more of the very independence that so troubled them. A correspondent from the blackbelt county of Hale reported to the Mobile *Daily Register* in 1869 that "everything appears experimental. . . . Many planters have turned their stock, teams, and every facility for farming, over to the negroes, and only require an amount of toll for the care of their land, refusing to superintend, direct, or even, in some cases, to suggest as to their management."

By the late 1860s, then, old patterns of agricultural relationships had been irreparably shattered, and the outlines of new ones had emerged. The logical culmination of emancipation for the plantation workers—the acquisition of their own land—remained for most an illusory dream. But within the confines of the plantation system great changes had occurred in the lives of the black laborers. They themselves had helped bring about most of these changes by demonstrating that they were not willing to continue in a position of complete subservience to their former owners. As one white planter lamented succinctly of the freedmen, "[T]hey wish to be free from re-straint." That wish was a potent one in the years immediately following the Civil War.

DOCUMENTS

A Letter
"To My Old Master," c. 1865

TO MY OLD MASTER, COLONEL P.H. ANDERSON,

BIG SPRING, TENNESSEE

Sir: I got your letter, and was glad to find that you had not forgotten Jourdon, and that you wanted me to come back and live with you again, promising to do better for me than anybody else can. I have often felt uneasy about you. I thought the Yankees would have hung you long before this, for harboring Rebs they found at your house. I suppose they never heard about your going to Colonel Martin's to kill the Union soldier that was left by his company in their stable. Although you shot at me twice before I left you, I did not want to hear of your being hurt, and am glad you are still living. It would do me good to go back to the dear old home again, and see Miss Mary and Miss Martha and Allen, Esther, Green, and Lee. Give my love to them all, and tell them I hope we will meet in the better world, if not in this. I would have gone back to see you all when I was working in the Nashville Hospital, but one of the neighbors told me that Henry intended to shoot me if he ever got a chance.

I want to know particularly what the good chance is you propose to give me. I am doing tolerably well here. I get twenty-five dollars a month, with victuals and clothing; have a comfortable home for Mandy—the folks call her Mrs. Anderson—and the children—Milly, Jane, and Grundy—go to school and are learning well. The teacher says Grundy has a head for a preacher. They go to Sunday school, and Mandy and me attend church regularly. We are kindly treated. Sometimes we overhear others saying, "Them colored people were slaves" down in Tennessee. The children feel hurt when they hear such remarks; but I tell them it was no disgrace in Tennessee to belong to Colonel Anderson. Many darkeys would have been proud, as I used to be, to call you master. Now if you will write and say what wages you will give me, I will be better able to decide whether it would be to my advantage to move back again.

SOURCE: L. Maria Child, *The Freedmen's Book* (1865).

As to my freedom, which you say I can have, there is nothing to be gained on that score, as I got my free papers in 1864 from the Provost-Marshal-General of the Department of Nashville. Mandy says she would be afraid to go back without some proof that you were disposed to treat us justly and kindly; and we have concluded to test your sincerity by asking you to send us our wages for the time we served you. This will make us forget and forgive old scores, and rely on your justice and friendship in the future. I served you faithfully for thirty-two years, and Mandy twenty years. At twenty-five dollars a month for me, and two dollars a week for Mandy, our earnings would amount to eleven thousand six hundred and eighty dollars. Add to this the interest for the time our wages have been kept back, and deduct what you paid for our clothing, and three doctor's visits to me, and pulling a tooth for Mandy, and the balance will show what we are in justice entitled to. Please send the money by Adam's Express, in care of V. Winters, Esq., Dayton, Ohio. If you fail to pay us for faithful labors in the past, we can have little faith in your promises in the future. We trust the good Maker has opened your eyes to the wrongs which you and your fathers have done to me and my fathers, in making us toil for you for generations without recompense. Here I draw my wages every Saturday night; but in Tennessee there was never any pay-day for the Negroes any more than for the horses and cows. Surely there will be a day of reckoning for those who defraud the laborer of his hire.

In answering this letter, please state if there would be any safety for my Milly and Jane, who are now grown up, and both good-looking girls. You know how it was with poor Matilda and Catherine. I would rather stay here and starve—and die, if it come to that—than have my girls brought to shame by the violence and wickedness of their young masters. You will also please state if there has been any schools opened for the colored children in your neighborhood. The great desire of my life now is to give my children an education, and have them form virtuous habits.

Say howdy to George Carter, and thank him for taking the pistol from you when you were shooting at me.

FROM YOUR OLD SERVANT,
JOURDON ANDERSON

The Black Code of
St. Landry's Parish, 1865

Whereas it was formerly made the duty of the police jury to make suitable regulations for the police of slaves within the limits of the parish; and whereas slaves have become emancipated by the action of the ruling pow-

SOURCE: U.S. Congress, *Senate Executive Document No. 2* (Washington, D.C., 1865), 93–94.

ers; and whereas it is necessary for public order, as well as for the comfort and correct deportment of said freedmen, that suitable regulations should be established by their government in their changed condition, the following ordinances are adopted, with the approval of the United States military authorities commanding in said parish, viz:

SECTION 1.   *Be it ordained by the police jury of the parish of St. Landry,* That no negro shall be allowed to pass within the limits of said parish without a special permit in writing from his employer. Whoever shall violate this provision shall pay a fine of two dollars and fifty cents, or in default thereof shall be forced to work four days on the public road, or suffer from corporeal punishment as provided hereinafter.

SECTION 2.   *Be it further ordained,* That every negro who shall be found absent from the residence of his employer after 10 o'clock at night, without a written permit from his employer, shall pay a fine of five dollars, or in default thereof, shall be compelled to work five days on the public road, or suffer corporeal punishment as hereinafter provided.

SECTION 3.   *Be it further ordained,* That no negro shall be permitted to rent or keep a house within said parish. Any negro violating this provision shall be immediately ejected and compelled to find an employer; and any person who shall rent, or give the use of any house to any negro, in violation of this section, shall pay a fine of five dollars for each offence.

SECTION 4.   *Be it further ordained,* That every negro is required to be in the regular service of some white person, or former owner, who shall be held responsible for the conduct of said negro. But said employer or former owner may permit said negro to hire his own time by special permission in writing, which permission shall not extend over seven days at any one time. Any negro violating the provisions of this section shall be fined five dollars for each offence, or in default of the payment thereof shall be forced to work five days on the public road, or suffer corporeal punishment as hereinafter provided.

SECTION 5.   *Be it further ordained,* That no public meetings or congregations of negroes shall be allowed within said parish after sunset; but such public meetings and congregations may be held between the hours of sunrise and sunset, by the special permission of writing of the captain of patrol, within whose beat such meetings shall take place. This prohibition, however, is not intended to prevent negroes from attending the usual church services, conducted by white ministers and priests. Every negro violating the provisions of this section shall pay a fine of five dollars, or in default thereof shall be compelled to work five days on the public road, or suffer corporeal punishment as hereinafter provided.

SECTION 6.   *Be it further ordained,* That no negro shall be permitted to preach, exhort, or otherwise declaim to congregations of colored people, without a special permission in writing from the president of the police jury. Any negro violating the provisions of this section shall pay a fine of ten dollars, or in default thereof shall be forced to work ten days on the public road, or suffer corporeal punishment as hereinafter provided.

SECTION 7.   *Be it further ordained,* That no negro who is not in the military service shall be allowed to carry fire-arms, or any kind of weapons, within the parish, without the special written permission of his employers, approved and indorsed by the nearest or most convenient chief of patrol. Any one violating the provisions of this section shall forfeit his weapons and pay a fine of five dollars, or in default of the payment of said fine, shall be forced to work five days on the public road, or suffer corporeal punishment as hereinafter provided.

SECTION 8.   *Be it further ordained,* That no negro shall sell, barter, or exchange any articles of merchandise or traffic within said parish without the special written permission of his employer, specifying the articles of sale, barter or traffic. Any one thus offending shall pay a fine of one dollar for each offence, and suffer the forfeiture of said articles, or in default of the payment of said fine shall work one day on the public road, or suffer corporeal punishment as hereinafter provided.

SECTION 9.   *Be it further ordained,* That any negro found drunk within the said parish shall pay a fine of five dollars, or in default thereof shall work five days on the public road, or suffer corporeal punishment as hereinafter provided.

SECTION 10.   *Be it further ordained,* That all the foregoing provisions shall apply to negroes of both sexes.

SECTION 11.   *Be it further ordained,* That it shall be the duty of every citizen to act as a police officer for the detection of offences and the apprehension of offenders, who shall be immediately handed over to the proper captain or chief of patrol.

SECTION 12.   *Be it further ordained,* That the aforesaid penalties shall be summarily enforced, and that it shall be the duty of the captains and chiefs of patrol to see that the aforesaid ordinances are promptly executed.

SECTION 13.   *Be it further ordained,* That all sums collected from the aforesaid fines shall be immediately handed over to the parish treasurer.

SECTION 14.   *Be it further ordained,* That the corporeal punishment provided for in the foregoing sections shall consist in confining the body of the offender within a barrel placed over his or her shoulders, in the manner practiced in the army, such confinement not to continue longer than twelve hours, and for such time within the aforesaid limit as shall be fixed by the captain or chief of patrol who inflicts the penalty.

SECTION 15.   *Be it further ordained,* That these ordinances shall not interfere with any municipal or military regulations inconsistent with them within the limits of said parish.

SECTION 16.   *Be it further ordained,* That these ordinances shall take effect five days after their publication in the *Opelousas Courier.*

Dedicated Teachers,
Determined Students, 1869

RALEIGH, N.C., FEB 22, 1869

It is surprising to me to see the amount of suffering which many of the people endure for the sake of sending their children to school. Men get very low wages here—from $2.50 to $8 per month usually, while a first-rate hand may get $10, and a peck or two of meal per week for rations—and a great many men cannot get work at all. The women take in sewing and washing, go out by day to scour, etc. There is one woman who supports three children and keeps them at school; she says, "I don't care how hard I has to work, if I can only sen[d] Sallie and the boys to school looking respectable." Many of the girls have but one decent dress; it gets washed and ironed on Saturday, and then is worn until the next Saturday, provided they do not tear it or fall in the mud; when such an accident happens there is an absent mark on the register. . . . One may go into their cabins on cold, windy days, and see daylight between every two boards, or feel the rain dropping through the roof; but a word of complaint is rarely heard. They are anxious to have the children "get on" in their books, and do not seem to feel impatient if they lack comforts themselves. A pile of books is seen in almost every cabin, though there be no furniture except a poor bed, a table and two or three broken chairs.

MISS M. A. PARKER

CHARLOTTESVILLE, VA., OCT. 17, 1866

Mrs. Gibbins (a colored native teacher) is very much liked by the colored people here. Her nature is so noble, that she is not so liable to stimulate petty jealousy among her people as many might under similar circumstances. . . . I think she is doing well in her new sphere of duty, especially in the matter of government. She has a kind of magnetism about her which is a good qualification for a teacher. She is really a fine reader of easy readings, and I should choose her to prepare scholars for me in that line, from among nine-tenths of those engaged in this work, so far as I have known her. She intends to pursue her studies in the evening with my help.

ANNA GARDNER

SOURCE: Edward L. Pierce, "The Freedmen at Port Royal," *Atlantic Monthly* 12 (September 1869): 306–307.

Chapter 2

The Last Frontier

From eastern North Dakota south to the Texas panhandle and west to the Rocky Mountains lay the Great Plains, a region at one time considered so bleak and uninhabitable that travelers referred to it as the "Great American Desert." In time, however, it would prove a source of immense wealth in minerals, grains, and livestock. This last American frontier—the land of the miner, the farmer, and the cowboy—by the late 1800s underwent a dramatic transformation paralleling change in the large cities and smoking factories of the urban, industrial East.

American literature and folklore have immortalized those who settled and tamed the Great Plains—the miners and their wide-open towns; the sod-house farmers; and, above all, the cowboys. But we all too often overlook the racial and ethnic diversity of those who built the West. Moreover, we forget what a critical role technology played in developing this region. The railroad, for example, was among the most important factors propelling the westward movement. In the essay "Linking a Continent and a Nation," Jack Chen highlights the role of Chinese immigrants in building the transcontinental railroad. How does Chen's description compare to popular depictions in western novels, in the movies, and on television?

The story of mining, like that of cattle raising and farming, was one of initial boom and prosperity for some, followed by bust for many. Like the other ventures, mining added to the nations's wealth—$1,242,872,032 in gold and $901,160,660 in silver were unearthed between 1860 and 1890. At the same time, it enriched the nation's folklore. In 1862, before he took the pen name Mark Twain, Samuel Clemens worked as a reporter for the Virginia City (Nevada) Enterprise. *In the first document, taken from his book* Roughing It, *Clemens describes Virginia City, America's premier mining town and home of the world's richest vein of silver, the Comstock Lode.*

Farmers also benefited from technology—steel plows to cut rough sod, windmills to pump water from deep in the ground, and barbed wire to fence off land on the treeless plains. There was also the lure of cheap or free land, thanks to the Homestead Act of 1862. This incentive pulled Americans from the East and immigrants from Europe. Farmers could tolerate the loneliness of rural life, but there were some hardships that they could not overcome. The second document, a memoir of a German woman who farmed in South Dakota in the 1880s, tells of her life there and her eventual decision to give up farming. Why did her family make this decision?

The last document, by Theodore Roosevelt, tells about a typical "cow town," Miles City, Montana. A romantic view of cowboys, it also reveals much about the ethnic diversity of the new Westerners. How does Roosevelt's picture complement the essay by Jack Chen?

ESSAY
·◆·

Linking a Continent
and a Nation

Jack Chen

Without the "Chinamen's" knowledge and respect for explosive powders, ability to work on the side of near vertical cliffs at dizzying heights and survive hardships which white men could not endure, the Central Pacific would never have been completed when it was but much later.

R.W. HOWARD, *The Great Iron Trail*

The Chinese filled swamps, cut into mountains, dug tunnels, built bridges. As one historian notes, "The work was so obviously needed and all groups and areas vied with each other to build a railroad in their area, so that they would have welcomed the devil himself had he built a road. The lack of white

SOURCE: Jack Chen, *The Chinese of America: From the Beginning to the Present.* Copyright © 1980 by Jack Chen. Reprinted by permission of HarperCollins Publishers, Inc.

laborers was too evident to cause even the most ardent anti-
Chinese to resent their employment on such work.
ROBERT E. WYNNE, *Reaction to the Chinese in the
Pacific Northwest and British Columbia*

The expansion of the railroad system in the United States was astonishingly swift. England had pioneered the building of railways and for a time was the acknowledged leader in the field, but from the moment the first locomotive was imported into the United States in 1829 the farsighted saw railways as the obvious solution for transport across the vast spaces of the American continent. By 1850, 9,000 miles of rails had been laid in the eastern states and up to the Mississippi. The California Gold Rush and the opening of the American West made talk about a transcontinental line more urgent. As too often happens, war spurred the realization of this project.

The West was won. California was a rich and influential state, but a wide unsettled belt of desert, plain, and mountains, separated it and Oregon from the rest of the states. As the economic separation of North and South showed, this situation was fraught with danger. It could lead to a political rift. In 1860, it was cheaper and quicker to reach San Francisco from Canton in China—a sixty-day voyage by sea—than from the Missouri River, six months away by wagon train. The urgent need was to link California firmly with the industrialized eastern states and their 30,000 miles of railways. A railway would cut the journey to a week. The threat of civil war loomed larger between North and South over the slavery issue. Abraham Lincoln's Republican administration saw a northern transcontinental railway as a means to outflank the South by drawing the western states closer to the North. In 1862, Congress voted funds to build the 2,500-mile-long railway. It required enormous resourcefulness and determination to get this giant project off the drawing boards. Not much imagination was required to see its necessity, but the actual building presented daunting difficulties. It was calculated that its cost would mount to $100 million, double the federal budget of 1861.

It was Theodore Judah, described by his contemporaries as "Pacific Railroad Crazy," who began to give substance to the dream. An eastern engineer who had come west to build the short Sacramento Valley Railroad, he undertook a preliminary survey and reported that he had found a feasible route crossing the Sierra by way of Dutch Flat. But the mainly small investors who supported his efforts could not carry through the whole immense undertaking. With rumors of civil war between North and South, San Francisco capitalists, mostly Southerners, boycotted the scheme as a northern plot, and pressed for a southern route. Then the "Big Four," Sacramento merchants, took up the challenge: Leland Stanford as president, C. P. Huntington as vice-president, Mark Hopkins as treasurer, and Charles Crocker, in charge of construction, formed the Central Pacific Railway Company. Judah was elbowed out.

The Big Four came as gold seekers in 1849 or soon after but found that there was more money to be made in storekeeping than in scrabbling in the rocks in the mountains. As Republicans, they held the state for the Union against the secessionists. Leland Stanford, the first president of the Central Pacific, was also the first Republican governor of California.

The beginnings were not auspicious. The Union Pacific [UP] was building from Omaha in the East over the plains to the Rockies, but supplies had to come in by water or wagon because the railways had not yet reached Omaha. The Civil War now raged and manpower, materials and funds were hard to get. The Indians were still contesting invasion of their lands. By 1864, however, with the Civil War ending, these problems were solved. The UP hired Civil War veterans, Irish immigrants fleeing famine and even Indian women, and the line began to move westward.

The Central Pacific, building eastward from Sacramento, had broken ground on January 8, 1863, but in 1864, beset by money and labor problems, it had built only thirty-one miles of track. It had an even more intractable manpower problem than the UP. California was sparsely populated, and the gold mines, homesteading, and other lucrative employments offered stiff competition for labor. Brought to the railhead, three out of every five men quit immediately and took off for the better prospects of the new Nevada silver strikes. Even Charles Crocker, boss of construction and raging like a mad bull in the railway camps, could not control them. In the winter of 1864, the company had only 600 men working on the line when it had advertised for 5,000. Up to then, only white labor had been recruited and California white labor was still motivated by the Gold Rush syndrome. They wanted quick wealth, not hard, regimented railway work. After two years only fifty miles of track had been laid.

James Strobridge, superintendent of construction, testified to the 1876 Joint Congressional Committee on Chinese Immigration: "[These] were unsteady men, unreliable. Some would not go to work at all. . . . Some would stay until pay day, get a little money, get drunk and clear out." Something drastic had to be done.

In 1858, fifty Chinese had helped to build the California Central Railroad from Sacramento to Marysville. In 1860, Chinese were working on the San Jose Railway and giving a good account of themselves, so it is surprising that there was so much hesitation about employing them on the Central Pacific's western end of the first transcontinental railway. Faced with a growing crisis of no work done and mounting costs, Crocker suggested hiring Chinese. Strobridge strongly objected: "I will not boss Chinese. I don't think they could build a railroad." Leland Stanford was also reluctant. He had advocated exclusion of the Chinese from California and was embarrassed to reverse himself. Crocker, Huntington, Hopkins, and Stanford, the Big Four of the Central Pacific, were all merchants in hardware, dried goods, and groceries in the little town of Sacramento. Originally, they knew nothing about railroad building, but they were astute and hard-headed businessmen. Crocker was insistent. Wasted time was wasted money. The CP's need for labor was critical. The men they already had were threatening a strike. Finally fifty Chinese were hired for a trial.

Building the Transcontinental Railroad

In February 1865, they marched up in self-formed gangs of twelve to twenty men with their own supplies and cooks for each mess. They ate a meal of rice and dried cuttlefish, washed and slept, and early next morning were ready for work filling dump carts Their discipline and grading—preparing the ground for track laying—delighted Strobridge. Soon fifty more were hired, and finally some 15,000 had been put on the payroll. Crocker was enthusiastic: "They prove nearly equal to white men in the amount of labor they perform, and are much more reliable. No danger of strikes among them. We are training them to all kinds of labor: blasting, driving horses, handling rock as well as pick and shovel." Countering Strobridge's argument that the Chinese were "not masons," Crocker pointed out that the race that built the Great Wall could certainly build a railroad culvert. Up on the Donner Pass today the fine stonework embankments built by the Chinese are serving well after a hundred years.

Charles Nordhoff, an acute observer, reports Stobridge telling him "[The Chinese] learn all parts of the work easily." Nordhoff says he saw them "employed on every kind of work.... They do not drink, fight or strike; they do gamble, if it is not prevented; and it is always said of them that they are very cleanly in their habits. It is the custom, among them, after they have had their suppers every evening, to bathe with the help of small tubs. I doubt if the white laborers do as much." As well he might. Well-run boardinghouses in California in those days proudly advertised that they provided guests with a weekly bath.

Their wages at the start were $28 a month (twenty-six working days), and they furnished all their own food, cooking utensils, and tents. The headman of each gang, or sometimes an American employed as clerk by them, received all the wages and handed them out to the members of the work gang according to what had been earned. "Competent and wonderfully effective because tireless and unremitting in their industry," they worked from sun-up to sundown.

All observers remarked on the frugality of the Chinese. This was not surprising in view of the fact that, with a strong sense of filial duty, they came to America in order to save money and return as soon as possible to their homes and families in China. So they usually dressed poorly, and their dwellings were of the simplest [construction]. However, they ate well: rice and vermicelli (noodles) garnished with meats and vegetables, fish, dried oysters, cuttlefish, bacon and pork, and chicken on holidays, abalone meat, five kinds of dried vegetables, bamboo shoots, seaweed, salted cabbage, and mushrooms, four kinds of dried fruit, and peanut oil and tea. This diet shows a considerable degree of sophistication and balance compared to the beef, beans, potatoes, bread, and butter of the white laborers. Other supplies were purchased from the shop maintained by a Chinese merchant contractor in one of the railway cars that followed them as they carried the railway line forward. Here they could buy pipes, tobacco, bowls, chopsticks, lamps, Chinese-style shoes of cotton with soft cotton soles, and ready-made clothing imported from China.

On Sundays, they rested, did their washing, and gambled. They were prone to argue noisily, but did not become besotted with whiskey and make themselves unfit for work on Monday. Their sobriety was much appreciated by their employers.

Curtis, the engineer in charge, described them as "the best roadbuilders in the world." The once skeptical Strobridge, a smart, pushing Irishman, also now pronounced them "the best in the world." Leland Stanford described them in a report on October 10, 1865, to [President] Andrew Johnson:

> As a class, they are quiet, peaceable, patient, industrious, and economical. More prudent and economical [than white laborers] they are contented with less wages. We find them organized for mutual aid and assistance. Without them, it would be impossible to complete the western portion of this great national enterprise within the time required by the Act of Congress.

Crocker testified before the congressional committee that "if we found that we were in a hurry for a job of work, it was better to put on Chinese at once." All these men had originally resisted the employment of Chinese on the railway.

Four-fifths of the grading labor from Sacramento to Ogden was done by Chinese. In a couple of years more, of 13,500 workers on the payroll 12,000 were Chinese. They were nicknamed "Crocker's Pets."

Appreciating Chinese Skills

The Chinese crews won their reputation the hard way. They outperformed Cornish men brought in at extra wages to cut rock. Crocker testified,

> They would cut more rock in a week than the Cornish miners, and it was hard work, bone labor. [They] were skilled in using the hammer and drill, and they proved themselves equal to the very best Cornish miners in that work. They were very trusty, they were intelligent, and they lived up to their contracts.

Stanford held the Chinese workers in such high esteem that he provided in his will for the permanent employment of a large number on his estates. In the 1930s, some of their descendants were still living and working lands now owned by Stanford University.

The Chinese saved the day for Crocker and his colleagues. The terms of agreement with the government were that the railway companies would be paid from $16,000 to $48,000 for each mile of track laid. But there were only so many miles between the two terminal points of the projected line. The Union Pacific Company, working with 10,000 mainly Irish immigrants and Civil War veterans, had the advantage of building the line through Nebraska over the plains and made steady progress. The Central Pacific, after the first easy twenty-three miles between Newcastle and Colfax, had to conquer the granite mountains and gorges of the Sierra Nevada and Rockies before it could emerge onto the Nevada-Utah plains and make real speed and money. The line had to rise 7,000 feet in 100 miles over daunting terrain. Crocker and the Chinese proved up to the challenge. After reaching Cisco, there was no easy going. The line had to be literally carved out of the Sierra granite, through tunnels and on rock ledges cut on the sides of precipices.

Using techniques from China, they attacked one of the most difficult parts of the work: carrying the line over Cape Horn [promontory], with its sheer granite buttresses and steep shale embankments, 2,000 feet above the American River canyon. There was no foothold on its flanks. The indomitable Chinese, using age-old ways, were lowered from above in rope-held baskets, and there, suspended between earth and sky, they began to chip away with hammer and crowbar to form the narrow ledge that was later laboriously deepened to a shelf wide enough for the railway roadbed, 1,400 feet above the river.

Behind the advancing crews of Chinese builders came the money and supplies to keep the work going. This was an awesome exercise in logistics. The Big Four, unscrupulous, dishonest, and ruthless on a grand scale, were the geniuses of this effort. The marvel of engineering skill being created by Strobridge and his Chinese and Irish workers up in the Sierra was fed by a stream of iron rails, spikes, tools, blasting powder, locomotives, cars, and machinery. These materials arrived after an expensive and hazardous eight-month, 15,000-mile voyage from East Coast ports around Cape Horn to San Francisco, thence by river boat to Sacramento, and so to the railhead by road.

The weather, as well as the terrain, was harsh. The winter of 1865–1866 was one of the severest on record. Snow fell early, and storm after storm blanketed the Sierra Nevada. The ground froze solid. Sixty-foot drifts of snow had to be shoveled away before the graders could even reach the roadbed. Nearly half the work force of 9,000 men were set to clearing snow.

In these conditions, construction crews tackled the most formidable obstacle in their path: building the ten Summit Tunnels on the twenty-mile stretch between Cisco, ninety-two miles from Sacramento and Lake Ridge just west of Cold Stream Valley on the eastern slope of the summit. Work went on at all the tunnels simultaneously. Three shifts of eight hours each worked day and night.

The builders lived an eerie existence. In *The Big Four*, Oscar Lewis writes,

> Tunnels were dug beneath forty-foot drifts and for months, 3,000 workmen lived curious mole-like lives, passing from work to living quarters in dim passages far beneath the snow's surface. . . . [There] was constant danger, for as snows accumulated on the upper ridges, avalanches grew frequent, their approach heralded only by a brief thunderous roar. A second later, a work crew, a bunkhouse, an entire camp would go hurtling at a dizzy speed down miles of frozen canyon. Not until months later were the bodies recovered; sometimes groups were found with shovels or picks still clutched in their frozen hands.

On Christmas Day, 1866, the papers reported that "a gang of Chinamen employed by the railroad were covered up by a snow slide and four or five [note the imprecision] died before they could be exhumed." A whole camp of Chinese railway workers was enveloped during one night and had to be rescued by shovelers the next day.

No one has recorded the names of those who gave their lives in this stupendous undertaking. It is known that the bones of 1,200 men were shipped back to China to be buried in the land of their forefathers, but that was by no means the total score. The engineer John Gills recalled that "at Tunnel No. 10, some 15–20 Chinese [again, note the imprecision] were killed by a slide that winter. The year before, in the winter of 1864–65, two wagon road repairers had been buried and killed by a slide at the same location."

A. P. Partridge, who worked on the line, describes how 3,000 Chinese builders were driven out of the mountains by the early snow. "Most . . . came to Truckee and filled up all the old buildings and sheds. An old barn collapsed and killed four Chinese. A good many were frozen to death." One is astonished at the fortitude, discipline and dedication of the Chinese railroad workers.

Many years later, looking at the Union Pacific section of the line, an old railwayman remarked, "There's an Irishman buried under every tie of that road." Brawling, drink, cholera, and malaria took a heavy toll. The construction crew towns on the Union Pacific part of the track, with their saloons, gambling dens, and bordellos, were nicknamed "hells on wheels." Jack Casement, in charge of construction there, had been a general in the Civil War and prided himself on the discipline of his fighting forces. His work crews worked with military precision, but off the job they let themselves go. One day, after gambling in the streets on payday (instigated by professional gamblers) had gotten too much out of hand, a visitor, finding the street suddenly very quiet, asked him where the gamblers had gone. Casement pointed to a nearby cemetery and replied, "They all died with their boots on." It was still the Wild West.

It is characteristic that only one single case of violent brawling was reported among the Chinese from the time they started work until they completed the job.

The Central Pacific's Chinese became expert at all kinds of work: grading, drilling, masonry, and demolition. Using black powder, they could average 1.18 feet daily through granite so hard that an incautiously placed charge could blow out backward. The Summit Tunnel work force was entirely composed of Chinese, with mainly Irish foremen. Thirty to forty worked on each face, with twelve to fifteen on the heading and the rest on the bottom removing material.

The Donner tunnels, totaling 1,695 feet, had to be bored through solid rock, and 9,000 Chinese worked on them. To speed the work, a new and untried explosive, nitroglycerin, was used. The tunnels were completed in November 1867, after thirteen months. But winter began before the way could be opened and the tracks laid. That winter was worse than the preceding one, but to save time it was necessary to send crews ahead to continue building the line even while the tunnels were being cut. Therefore, 3,000 men were sent with 400 carts and horses to Palisade Canyon, 300 miles in advance of the railhead. "Hay, grain and all supplies for men and horses had to be hauled by teams over the deserts for that great distance," writes Strobridge. "Water for men and animals was hauled at times 40 miles." Trees were felled and the logs laid side by side to form a "corduroy" roadway. On log sleds greased with lard, hundreds of Chinese manhandled three locomotives and forty wagons over the mountains. Strobridge later testified that it "cost nearly three times what it would have cost to have done it in the summertime when it should have been done. But we shortened the time seven years from what Congress expected when the act was passed."

Between 10,000 and 11,000 men were kept working on the line from 1866 to 1869. The Sisson and Wallace Company (in which Crocker's brother was a leading member) and the Dutch merchant Cornelius Koopmanschap of San Francisco procured these men for the line. Through the summer of 1866, Crocker's Pets—6,000 strong—swarmed over the upper canyons of the Sierra, methodically slicing cuttings and pouring rock and debris to make landfills and strengthen the foundations of trestle bridges. Unlike the Caucasian laborers, who drank unboiled stream water, the Chinese slaked their thirst with weak tea and boiled water kept in old whiskey kegs filled by their mess cooks. They kept themselves clean and healthy by daily sponge baths in tubs of hot water prepared by their cooks, and the work went steadily forward.

Crocker has been described as a "hulking, relentless driver of men." But his Chinese crews responded to his leadership and drive and were caught up in the spirit of the epic work on which they were engaged. They cheered and waved their cartwheel hats as the first through train swept down the eastern slopes of the Sierra to the meeting of the lines. They worked with devotion and self-sacrifice to lay that twenty-odd miles of track for the Central Pacific Company in 1866 over the most difficult terrain. The cost of those miles was enormous—$280,000 a mile—but it brought the builders in sight of the easier terrain beyond the Sierra and the Rockies. Here costs of construction by veteran crews were only half the estimated amount of federal pay.

By summer 1868, an army of 14,000 railway builders was passing over the mountains into the great interior plain. Nine-tenths of that work force was Chinese. More than a quarter of all Chinese in the country were building the railway.

When every available Chinese in California had been recruited for the work, the Central Pacific arranged with Chinese labor contractors in San Francisco to get men direct from China and send them up to the railhead. It was evidently some of these newcomers who fell for the Piute Indian's tall tales of snakes in the desert "big enough to swallow a man easily." Thereupon "four or five hundred Chinese took their belongings and struck out to return directly to Sacramento," reports the *Alta California*, "Crocker and Company had spent quite a little money to secure them and they sent men on horseback after them. Most of them came back again kind of quieted down, and after nothing happened and they never saw any of the snakes, they forgot about them." At least one Chinese quit the job for a similar reason. His daughter, married to a professor of Chinese art, told me that her father had worked on the railway but quit because "he was scared of the bears." He later went into domestic service.

By September 1868, the track was completed for 307 miles from Sacramento, and the crews were laying rails across the plain east of the Sierra. Parallel with the track layers went the telegraph installers, stringing their wires on the poles and keeping the planners back at headquarters precisely apprised of where the end of the track was.

The Great Railway Competition

On the plains, the Chinese worked in tandem with all the Indians Crocker could entice to work on the iron rails. They began to hear of the exploits of the Union Pacific's "Irish terriers" building from the east. One day, the Irish laid six miles of track, they were told. The Chinese of the Central Pacific topped this with seven. "No Chinaman is going to beat us," growled the Irish, and the next day, they laid seven and a half miles of track. They swore that they would outperform the competition no matter what it did.

Crocker taunted the Union Pacific that his men could lay ten miles of track a day. Durant, president of the rival line, laid a $10,000 wager that it could not be done. Crocker took no chances. He waited until the day before the last sixteen miles of track had to be laid and brought up all needed supplies for instant use. Then he unleashed his crews. On April 28, 1869, while Union Pacific checkers and newspaper reporters looked on, a combined gang of Chinese and eight picked Irish rail handlers laid ten miles and 1,800 feet more of track in twelve hours. This record was never surpassed until the advent of mechanized track laying. Each Irishman that day walked a total distance of ten miles, and their combined muscle handled sixty tons of rail.

So keen was the competition that when the two lines approached each other, instead of changing direction to link up, their builders careered on and on for 100 miles, building lines that would never meet. Finally, the government prescribed that the linkage point should be Promontory [Point], Utah.

Competition was keen, but there seems to be no truth in the story that the Chinese and Irish in this phase of work were trying to blow each other up with explosives. It is a fact, however, that when the two lines were very near each other, the Union Pacific blasters did not give the Central Pacific men timely warning when setting off a charge, and several Chinese were hurt. Then a Central Pacific charge went off unannounced and several Irishmen found themselves buried in dirt. This forced the foremen to take up the matter and an amicable settlement was arranged. There was no further trouble.

On May 10, 1869, the two lines were officially joined at Promontory [Point], north of Ogden in Utah. A great crowd gathered. A band played. An Irish crew and a Chinese crew were chosen to lay the last two rails side by side. The last tie was made of polished California laurel with a silver plate in its center proclaiming it "The last tie laid on the completion of the Pacific Railroad, May 10, 1869." But when the time came it was nowhere to be found. As consternation mounted, four Chinese approached with it on their shoulders and they laid it beneath the rails. A photographer stepped up and someone shouted to him "Shoot!" The Chinese only knew one meaning for that word. They fled. But order was restored and the famous ceremony began; Stanford drove a golden spike into the last tie with a silver hammer. The news flashed by telegraph to a waiting nation. But no Chinese appears in that famous picture of the toast celebrating the joining of the rails.

Crocker was one of the few who paid tribute to the Chinese that day: "I wish to call to your minds that the early completion of this railroad we have built has been in large measure due to the poor, despised class of laborers called the Chinese, to the fidelity and industry they have shown." No one even mentioned the name of Judah.

The building of the first transcontinental railway stands as a monument to the union of Yankee and Chinese-Irish drive and know-how. This was a formidable combination. They all complemented each other. Together they did in seven years what was expected to take at least fourteen.

In his book on the building of the railway, John Galloway, the noted transportation engineer, described this as "without doubt the greatest engineering feat of the nineteenth century," and that has never been disputed. David D. Colton, then vice-president of the Southern Pacific, was similarly generous in his praise of the Chinese contribution. He was asked, while giving evidence before the 1876 congressional committee, "Could you have constructed that road without Chinese labor?" He replied, "I do not think it could have been constructed so quickly, and with anything like the same amount of certainty as to what we were going to accomplish in the same length of time."

And, in answer to the question, "Do you think the Chinese have been a benefit to the State?" West Evans, a railway contractor, testified, "I do not see how we could do the work we have done, here, without them; at least I have done work that would not have been done if it had not been for the Chinamen, work that could not have been done without them."

It was heroic work. The Central Pacific crews had carried their railway 1,800 miles through the Sierra and Rocky mountains, over sagebrush desert and plain. The Union Pacific built only 689 miles, over much easier terrain. It had 500 miles in which to carry its part of the line to a height of 5,000 feet, with another fifty more miles in which to reach the high passes of the Black Hills. With newly recruited crews, the Central Pacific had to gain an altitude of 7,000 feet from the plain in just over 100 miles and make a climb of 2,000 feet in just 20 miles.

All this monumental work was done before the age of mechanization. It was pick and shovel, hammer and crowbar work, with baskets for earth carried slung from shoulder poles and put on one-horse carts.

For their heroic work, the Chinese workmen began with a wage of $26 a month, providing their own food and shelter. This was gradually raised to $30 to $35 a month. Caucasians were paid the same amount of money, but their food and shelter were provided. Because it cost $0.75 to $1.00 a day to feed a white unskilled worker, each Chinese saved the Central Pacific, at a minimum, two-thirds the price of a white laborer (1865 rates). Chinese worked as masons, dynamiters, and blacksmiths and at other skilled jobs that paid white workers from $3 to $5 a day. So, at a minimum, the company saved about $5 million by hiring Chinese workers.

Did this really "deprive white workers of jobs" as anti-Chinese agitators claimed? Certainly not. In the first place, experience had proved that white workers simply did not want the jobs the Chinese took on the railroad. In fact, the Chinese created jobs for white workers as straw bosses, foremen, railhandlers, teamsters, and supervisors.

The wages paid to the Chinese were, in fact, comparable to those paid unskilled or semiskilled labor in the East (where labor was relatively plentiful), and the Chinese were at first satisfied. Charles Nordhoff estimated that the frugal Chinese could save about $13 a month out of those wages. The *Alta California* estimated their savings at $20 a month and later, perhaps, as wages increased, they could lay aside even more. With a bit of luck, a year and a half to two years of work would enable them to return to China with $400 to buy a bit of land and be well-to-do farmers.

But the Chinese began to learn the American way of life. On one occasion in June 1867, 2,000 tunnelers went on strike, asking for $40 a month, an eight-hour day in the tunnels, and an end to beating by foremen. "Eight hours a day good for white man, all same good for Chinese," said their spokesman in the pidgin English common in the construction camps. But solidarity with the other workers was lacking, and after a week the strike was called off when the Chinese heard that Crocker was recruiting strike-breakers from the eastern states.

When the task was done, most of the Chinese railwaymen were paid off. Some returned to China with their hard-earned savings, and the epic story of building the Iron Horse's pathway across the continent must have regaled many a family gathering there. Some returned with souvenirs of the great work, chips of one of the last ties, which had been dug up and split up among them. Some settled in the little towns that had grown up along the line of the railway. Others took the railway to seek adventure further east and south. Most made their way back to California and took what jobs they could find in that state's growing industries, trades, and other occupations. Many used their traditional and newly acquired skills on the other transcontinental lines and railways that were being swiftly built in the West and Midwest. This was the start of the diaspora of the Chinese immigrants in America.

The Union and Central Pacific tycoons had done well out of the building of the line. Congressional investigation committees later calculated that, of $73 million poured into the Union Pacific coffers, no more than $50 million could be justified as true costs. The Big Four and their associates in the Central Pacific had done even better. They had made at least $63 million and owned most of the CP stock worth around $100 million and 9 million acres of land grants to boot.

Ironically, the great railway soon had disastrous results for the Chinese themselves. It now cost only $40 for an immigrant to cross the continent by rail and a flood of immigrants took advantage of the ease and cheapness of travel on the line the Chinese had helped to build. The labor shortage (and resulting high wages) in California turned into a glut. When the tangled affairs of the Northern Pacific line led to the stock market crash of Black Friday, September 19, 1873, and to financial panic, California experienced its first real economic depression. There was devastating unemployment, and the Chinese were made the scapegoats.

Building Other Lines

The expansion of the railroads was even faster in the following decade. In 1850, the United States had 9,000 miles of track. In 1860, it had 30,000. In 1890, it had over 70,000 miles. Three years later, it had five transcontinental lines.

The first transcontinental railway was soon followed by four more links: (1) the Southern Pacific–Texas and Pacific, completed in 1883 from San Francisco to Texas by way of Yuma, Tucson, and El Paso; (2) the Atcheson, Topeka, and Santa Fe, completed in 1885 from Kansas City to Los Angeles via Santa Fe and Albuquerque; (3) the Northern Pacific completed in 1883 from Duluth, Minnesota, to Portland, Oregon; and (4) the Great Northern (1893). The skill of the Chinese as railroad builders was much sought after, and Chinese worked on all these lines. Some 15,000 worked on the Northern Pacific, laying tracks in Washington, Idaho, and Montana; 250 on the Houston and Texas line; 600 on the Alabama and Chattanooga line; 70 on the New Orleans line. Nearly 500 Chinese were recruited for the Union Pacific even after the lines were joined. Many worked in the Wyoming coal mines and during the summer months doubled as track laborers. They carried the Southern Pacific lines over the burning Mojave Desert. They helped link San Francisco with Portland in 1887.

The Canadian Pacific seized the chance to enlist veteran Chinese railwaymen from the Southern Pacific and Northern Pacific railroads and also brought Chinese workers direct from China. In 1880, some 1,500 were working on that line, increasing to 6,500 two years later. Casualties were heavy on this line. Hundreds lost their lives while working on it.

Chinese railwaymen helped on the Central and Southern Pacific's main line down the San Joaquin Valley in 1870 and 1871. They worked on the hookup to Los Angeles and the loop with seventeen tunnels over the Tehachapi Pass completed in 1876. On this line, 1,000 Chinese worked on the 6,975-foot San Fernando Tunnel, the longest in the West. This rail link between San Francisco and Los Angeles, tapping the rich Central Valley, played a major role in the development of California's agriculture, later its biggest industry. They worked on the line north from Sacramento along the Shasta route to Portland, which was reached in 1887. In 1869, the Virginia and Truckee line employed 450 Chinese, veterans of the Central Pacific, to grade its track. When the Virginia and Truckee's Carson and Colorado branch line was planned from Mound House to Benton, its tough manager Yerington arranged with the unions for the grading to be done by white labor to Dayton and by Chinese from Dayton on south. "If the entire line had to be graded by white labor, I would not think of driving a pick into the ground, but would abandon the undertaking entirely," he said.

Chinese laborers worked on the trans-Panamanian railway, which linked the Pacific and the Atlantic before the Panama Canal was completed. This railway played a major role in speeding up the economic development of the United States, but it was not built without sacrifice: hundreds of the Chinese builders died of fever and other causes during its construction.

This by no means completes the list of contributions of the Chinese railway workers. The transcontinental lines on which they worked "more than any other factor helped make the United States a united nation," writes the

Encyclopedia Britannica ["Railways"]. They played a major role in building the communications network of iron roads that was the transport base of American industrial might in the twentieth century.

Speaking eloquently in favor of the Chinese immigrants, Oswald Garrison Villard said,

> I want to remind you of the things that Chinese labor did in opening up the Western portion of this country. . . . [They] stormed the forest fastnesses, endured cold and heat and the risk of death at hands of hostile Indians to aid in the opening up of our northwestern empire. I have a dispatch from the chief engineer of the Northwestern Pacific telling how Chinese laborers went out into eight feet of snow with the temperature far below zero to carry on the work when no American dared face the conditions.

And these men were from China's sun-drenched south, where it never snows.

In certain circles, there has been a conspiracy of silence about the Chinese railroadmen and what they did. When U.S. Secretary of Transportation John Volpe spoke at the "Golden Spike" centenary, not a single Chinese American was invited, and he made no mention in his speech of the Chinese railroad builders.

DOCUMENTS

Flush Times in Nevada,*
c. 1862

Six months after my entry into journalism that grand "flush times" of Silverland began, and they continued with unabated splendor for three years. All difficulty about filling up the "local department" ceased, and the only trouble now was how to make the lengthened columns hold the world of incidents and happening that came to our literary net every day. Virginia had grown to be the "livest" town, for its age and population, that America had ever produced. The sidewalks swarmed with people—to such an extent, indeed, that it was generally no easy matter to stem the human tide. The streets themselves were just as crowded with quartz-wagons, freight-teams, and other vehicles. The procession was endless. So great was the pack, that

SOURCE: Samuel L. Clemens, *Roughing It* 2 (New York: Harper and Brothers, 1890): 11–13, 16–19.

*The term *flush times* refers to the silver and gold boom in Nevada in the 1860s. (Eds.)

buggies frequently had to wait half an hour for an opportunity to cross the principal street. Joy sat on every countenance, and there was a glad, almost fierce, intensity in every eye, that told of the money-getting schemes that held sway in every heart. Money was as plenty as dust; every individual considered himself wealthy, and a melancholy countenance was nowhere to be seen. There were military companies, fire companies, brass bands, banks, hotels, theaters, "hurdy-gurdy houses,"* wide-open gambling-palaces, political pow-wows, civic processions, street-fights, murders, inquests, riots, a whiskeymill every fifteen steps, a Board of Aldermen, a Mayor, a City Surveyor, a City Engineer, a Chief of the Fire Department, with First, Second, and Third Assistants, a Chief of Police, City Marshal, and a large police force, two Boards of Mining Brokers, a dozen breweries, and a half dozen jails and station-houses in full operation, and some talk of building a church. The "flush times" were in magnificent flower! Large fireproof brick buildings were going up in the principal streets, and the wooden suburbs were spreading out in all directions. Town lots soared up to prices that were amazing.

The great "Comstock lode" stretched its opulent length straight through the town from north to south, and every mine on it was in diligent process of development. One of these mines alone employed six hundred and seventy-five men, and in the matter of elections the adage was, "as the 'Gould & Curry' [mine] goes, so goes the city." Laboring-men's wages were four and six dollars a day, and they worked in three "shifts" or gangs, and the blasting and picking and shoveling went on without ceasing, night and day.

The "city" of Virginia roosted royally midway up the steep side of Mount Davidson, seven thousand two hundred feet above the level of the sea, and in the clear Nevada atmosphere was visible from a distance of fifty miles! It claimed a population of fifteen thousand to eighteen thousand, and all day long half of this little army swarmed the streets like bees and the other half swarmed the drifts and tunnels of the "Comstock," hundreds of feet down in the earth directly under those same streets. . . .

My salary was increased to forty dollars a week. But I seldom drew it. I had plenty of other resources, and what were two broad twenty-dollar gold pieces to a man who had his pockets full of such and a cumbersome abundance of bright half-dollars besides? (Paper money has never come into use on the Pacific coast.) Reporting was lucrative, and every man in the town was lavish with his money and his "feet."** The city and all the great mountainside were riddled with mining-shafts. There were more mines than miners. True, not ten of these mines were yielding rock worth hauling to a mill, but everybody said, "Wait till the shaft gets down where the ledge comes in solid, and then you will see!" So nobody was discouraged. These were

---

Hurdy-gurdy houses is a slang term for dance halls. (Eds.)
**Shares of stock in wildcat mines were measured in feet. (Eds.)

nearly all "wildcat" mines, and wholly worthless, but nobody believed it then. The "Ophir," the "Gould Curry," the "Mexican," and other great mines on the Comstock lode in Virginia and Gold Hill were turning out huge piles of rich rock every day, and every man believed that his little wildcat claim was as good as any on the "main lead" and would infallibly be worth a thousand dollars a foot when he "got down where it came in solid." Poor fellow! he was blessedly blind to the fact that he would never see that day. So the thousand wildcat shafts burrowed deeper and deeper into the earth day by day, and all men were beside themselves with hope and happiness. How they labored, prophesied, exulted! Surely nothing like it was ever seen before since the world began. Every one of these wildcat mines—not mines, but holes in the ground over imaginary mines—was incorporated and had handsome engraved "stock" and the stock was salable, too. It was bought and sold with a feverish avidity on the boards every day. You could go up on the mountainside, scratch around and find a ledge (there was no lack of them), put up a "notice" with a grandiloquent name on it, start a shaft, get your stock printed, and with nothing whatever to prove that your mine was worth a straw, you could put your stock on the market and sell out for hundreds and even thousands of dollars. To make money, and make it fast, was as easy as it was to eat your dinner. Every man owned "feet" in fifty different wildcat mines and considered his fortune made. Think of a city with not one solitary poor man in it! One would suppose that when month after month went by and still not a wildcat mine (by wildcat I mean, in general terms, *any* claim not located on the mother vein, *i.e.*, the "Comstock") yielded a ton of rock worth crushing, the people would begin to wonder if they were not putting too much faith in their prospective riches; but there was not a thought of such a thing. They burrowed away, bought and sold, and were happy.

New claims were taken daily, and it was the friendly custom to run straight to the newspaper offices, give the reporter forty or fifty "feet" and get him to go and examine the mine and publish a notice of it. They did not care a fig what you said about the property so [long as] you said something. Consequently we generally said a word or two to the effect that the "indications" were good, or that the ledge was "six feet wide," or that the rock "resembled the Comstock" (and so it did—but as a general thing the resemblance was not startling enough to knock you down!) . . .

There was *nothing* in the shape of a mining claim that was not salable. We received presents of "feet" every day. If we needed a hundred dollars or so, we sold some; if not we hoarded it away, satisfied that it would ultimately be worth a thousand dollars a foot. I had a trunk about half full of "stock." When a claim made a stir in the market and went up to a high figure, I searched through my pile to see if I had any of its stock—and generally found it.

Homesteading in South Dakota
in the 1880s (1930)

On May 6, 1881, I left my beloved Fatherland and came to America. I still do not know why I left, for I was working for some very fine people with whom I had been for three years. They always said, "Stay here." I would have liked very much to go back once more but that did not come to pass. I was often homesick.

I already knew my husband in the old country. On May 26, 1881, I arrived at my sister's near Bloomington, Illinois. I worked for an English Methodist family. They were very fine people, and I often think of them. They have gone to "The Eternal Home" long ago.

October 20th, 1881, we were married in Bloomington, Illinois, at the parsonage of the Lutheran minister. My husband was working for $20.00 per month and free house rent. We lived in a little log cabin with one room and a small kitchen attached. Those were very beautiful times. We had two cows, hogs and chickens. But my husband was always desirous to have land of his own, and land in Illinois was too high in price for us to buy.

So when reservations were offered in South Dakota in 1883, my husband and his three brothers went to South Dakota and each staked a claim for 160 acres of land. It (South Dakota) has a very beautiful climate but lacks rain. We were there for 12 years. . . .

In 1888 we had the great snowstorm in South Dakota where so many school children lost their lives because the roofs were blown from the schoolhouses. The wind blew from 70 to 80 miles per hour and it was a dreadful storm.

In 1889 we had the great prairie-fire in which we lost everything, by fire, except our house and horses and cows. Everything else was burnt. That almost frightened us into leaving, for our children started to go to school a distance of two miles out in the prairie.

So we traded our land for two horses. There were no good years. We sold our best cows for $15.00, wheat for 35¢, corn for 15¢. We raised two bushels per acre. Those were hard years. But we always had enough to eat to satisfy our hunger.

We had no money, so we hitched our three horses to a moving wagon and started to Missouri, to my husband's brother in Marceline. It took us three weeks and a few days. . . .

SOURCE: Family history of Caroline Reimers, author's possession, 1930

A Montana Cowtown, 1899

A true "cow town" is worth seeing,—such a one as Miles City, for instance, especially at the time of the annual meeting of the great Montana Stock-raisers' Association. Then the whole place is full to overflowing, the importance of the meeting and the fun of the attendant frolics, especially the horse-races, drawing from the surrounding ranch country many hundreds of men of every degree, from the rich stock-owner worth his millions to the ordinary cowboy who works for forty dollars a month. It would be impossible to imagine a more typically American assemblage, for although there are always a certain number of foreigners, usually English, Irish, or German, yet they have become completely Americanized; and on the whole it would be difficult to gather a finer body of men, in spite of their numerous shortcomings. The ranch-owners differ more from each other than do the cowboys; and the former certainly compare very favorably with similar classes of capitalists in the East. Anything more foolish than the demagogic outcry against "cattle kings" it would be difficult to imagine. Indeed, there are very few businesses so absolutely legitimate as stock-raising and so beneficial to the nation at large; and a successful stock-grower must not only be shrewd, thrifty, patient, and enterprising, but he must also possess qualities of personal bravery, hardihood, and self-reliance to a degree not demanded in the least by any mercantile occupation in a community long settled. Stockmen are in the West the pioneers of civilization, and their daring and adventurousness make the after settlement of the region possible. The whole country owes them a great debt. . . .

The bulk of the cowboys themselves are South-westerners; but there are also many from the Eastern and the Northern States, who, if they begin young, do quite as well as the Southerners. The best hands are fairly bred to the work and follow it from their youth up. Nothing can be more foolish than for an Easterner to think he can become a cowboy in a few months' time. Many a young fellow comes out hot with enthusiasm for life on the plains, only to learn that his clumsiness is greater than he could have believed possible; that the cowboy business is like any other and has to be learned by serving a painful apprenticeship; and that this apprenticeship implies the endurance of rough fare, hard living, dirt, exposure of every kind, no little toil, and month after month of the dullest monotony. For cowboy work there is need of special traits and special training, and young Easterners should be sure of themselves before trying it. The struggle for existence is very keen in the far West, and it is no place for men who lack the ruder, coarser virtues and physical qualities, no matter how intellectual or how refined and delicate their sensibilities. Such are more likely to fail

SOURCE: Theodore Roosevelt, *Ranch Life and the Hunting-Trail* (New York: Century Co., 1899), 7, 10–11. Reprinted University Microfilms, Ann Arbor, Michigan, 1966.

there than in older communities. Probably during the past few years more than half of the young Easterners who have come West with a little money to learn the cattle business have failed signally and lost what they had in the beginning. The West, especially the far West, needs men who have been bred on the farm or in the workshop far more than it does clerks or college graduates.

Some of the cowboys are Mexicans, who generally do the actual work well enough, but are not trustworthy; moreover, they are always regarded with extreme disfavor by the Texans in an outfit, among whom the intolerant caste spirit is very strong. Southern-born whites will never work under them, and look down upon all colored or half-caste races. One spring I had with my wagon a Pueblo Indian, an excellent rider and roper, but a drunken, worthless, lazy devil; and in the summer of 1886 there were with us a Sioux half-breed, a quiet, hard-working, faithful fellow, and a mulatto, who was one of the best cow-hands in the whole round-up.

Chapter 3

Indian Schools: "Americanizing" the Native American

The white settlers' movement onto the Great Plains devastated Native American tribes who had roamed the area for centuries. As on previous frontiers farther east, the Indians resisted the encroachment with some initial success, their most notable victory the defeat of General George Custer at the Little Bighorn River in 1876. However, the whites' superior manpower and technology, fueled by their desire to fulfill a "manifest destiny" to develop the entire continent, overcame the Native Americans, and in the end the whites removed virtually all of them to reservations.

During the 1870s and 1880s, even while the last Indian wars raged, the federal government passed legislation and instituted policies designed to solve the "Indian problem" by "Americanizing" them—assimilating them into American society. The federal government encouraged them, sometimes forcefully, to exchange their lands, held by the tribe as a whole, for individual holdings that they were expected to farm. Equally important, the government sought to educate their children away from their traditional cultures and provide them with the skills, knowledge, and attitudes deemed necessary for the new way of life that the dominant white culture dictated.

By 1881 the federal government operated 106 Indian day and boarding schools to accomplish these objectives. Although most of the schools were on or adjacent to reservation land, white educators placed their greatest faith in nonreservation boarding schools far removed from parental and tribal influences. Robert A. Trennert's essay, "Educating Indian Girls at Nonreservation Boarding Schools, 1878–1920," provides a detailed view of this policy in action. What do you think the advocates of Indian education meant by "assimilation"? To what does the author attribute the failure of the government's Indian-school policies during this period?

The first document consists of excerpts from the "Rules for Indian Schools" set forth by the Bureau of Indian Affairs (1890). What attitudes toward their mission and toward Native American youth would these instructions likely engender in the minds of the teachers who read them? In what ways does each of the rules cited contribute to the broad objectives of the government's Indian-education policies? What can you conclude about the immediate and long-term objectives of Indian education?

Although the government expressed its land and educational policies in positive terms, these principles in fact reflected the prevailing belief that the Native American culture was inferior. At the turn of the century, many social scientists had adapted Darwin's biological theories of evolution to explain social development, drawing conclusions totally rejected by their counterparts today. Specifically, they developed a theoretical hierarchy of superior and inferior races that placed northern Europeans at the top and Indians, blacks, and southern and eastern Europeans, among others, at the bottom. The second document, a 1905 report of the Board of Indian Commissioners, typifies the attitudes underlying governmental policies until the 1930s. This report sheds light on the basis for Indian policy and reveals much of the rationale for the immigration-restriction and racial-segregation laws of the era.

Many factors explain why, by the 1920s, Native Americans found themselves mired in poverty at the bottom of the economic ladder: the failure of the federal government's Indian-education policies, the poor land conditions under which they were expected to become independent farmers, and the racism and discrimination meted out by the dominant white culture. During the 1930s, however, conditions began to improve. The Indian Reorganization Act of 1934 called for the establishment of tribal governments and the election of tribal leaders, a decision that exemplified a more enlightened view of Native American culture and reflected the New Deal government's concern for the poor and disadvantaged.

After World War II, Native Americans, like other minority groups, organized to proclaim their cultural identity and to demand full civil rights, economic opportunities, and the preservation of their culture. As a result, new Indian tribal colleges sprang up. As the final document reveals, despite limited financial resources, these institutions have managed to offer Native Americans real hope for a better future. In what significant ways do the new colleges differ from the old Indian boarding schools? What about them elicits such enthusiasm among Native Americans?

43

ESSAY

Educating Indian Girls at
Nonreservation Boarding Schools, 1878–1920

Robert A. Trennert

During the latter part of the nineteenth century the Bureau of Indian Affairs made an intensive effort to assimilate the Indian into American society. One important aspect of the government's acculturation program was Indian education. By means of reservation day schools, reservation boarding schools, and off-reservation industrial schools, the federal government attempted to obliterate the cultural heritage of Indian youths and replace it with the values of Anglo-American society. One of the more notable aspects of this program was the removal of young Indian women from their tribal homes to government schools in an effort to transform them into a government version of the ideal American woman. This program of assimilationist education, despite some accomplishments, generally failed to attain its goals. This study is a review of the education of Indian women at the institutions that best typified the government program—the off-reservation industrial training schools. An understanding of this educational system provides some insight into the impact of the acculturation effort on the native population. Simultaneously, it illustrates some of the prevalent national images regarding both Indians and women.

The concept of educating native women first gained momentum among eighteenth-century New England missionaries who recommended that Indian girls might benefit from formal training in housekeeping. This idea matured to the point that, by the 1840s, the federal government had committed itself to educating Indian girls in the hope that women trained as good housewives would help their mates assimilate. A basic premise of this educational effort rested on the necessary elimination of Indian culture. Although recent scholarship has suggested that the division of labor between the sexes within Indian societies was rather equitable, mid-nineteenth-century Americans accepted a vision of Native American women as slaves toiling endlessly for their selfish, slovenly husbands and fathers in an atmosphere of immorality, degradation, and lust. Any cursory glance at contemporary literature provides striking evidence of this belief. Joel D. Steele, for example, in his 1876 history of the American nation described Indian society in the following terms: "The Indian was a barbarian. . . . Labor he considered degrading, and fit only for women. His squaw, therefore,

SOURCE: Robert A Trennert, "Educating Indian Girls at Nonreservation Boarding Schools, 1878–1920," *Western Historical Quarterly,* 13 (July 1982): 169–90. Copyright by the Western History Association. Reprinted by permission.

built his wigwam, cut his wood, and carried his burdens when he journeyed. While he hunted or fished, she cleared the land ... and dressed skins."

Government officials and humanitarian reformers shared Steele's opinion. Secretary of the Interior Carl Schurz, a noted reformer, stated in 1881 that "the Indian woman has so far been only a beast of burden. The girl, when arrived at maturity, was disposed of like an article of trade. The Indian wife was treated by her husband alternately with animal fondness, and with the cruel brutality of the slave driver." Neither Steele nor Schurz was unique in his day; both expressed the general opinion of American society. From this perspective, if women were to be incorporated into American society, their sexual role and social standing stood in need of change.

The movement to educate Indian girls reflected new trends in women's education. Radical changes in the economic and social life of late nineteenth-century America set up a movement away from the traditional academy education of young women. Economic opportunity created by the industrial revolution combined with the decline of the family as a significant economic unit produced a demand for vocational preparation for women. The new school discipline of "domestic science," a modern homemaking technique, developed as a means to bring stability and scientific management to the American family and provide skills to the increasing number of women entering the work force. In the years following the Civil War, increased emphasis was placed on domestic and vocational education as schools incorporated the new discipline into their curriculum. Similar emphasis appeared in government planning for the education of Indian women as a means of their forced acculturation. However, educators skirted the question of whether native women should be trained for industry or homemaking.

During the 1870s, with the tribes being confined to reservations, the government intensified its efforts to provide education for Indian youth of both sexes. The establishment of the industrial training schools at the end of the decade accelerated the commitment to educate Indian women. These schools got their start in 1878 when Captain Richard Henry Pratt, in charge of a group of Indian prisoners at Fort Marion, Florida, persuaded the government to educate eighteen of the younger male inmates at Hampton Normal Institute, an all-black school in Virginia, run by General Samuel C. Armstrong. Within six months Pratt and Armstrong were pleased enough with the results of their experiment to request more students. Both men strongly believed that girls should be added to the program, and Armstrong even went so far as to stipulate that Hampton would take more Indian students only on condition that half be women. At first Indian Commissioner Ezra A. Hayt rejected the proposal, primarily because he questioned the morality of allowing Indian women to mix with black men, but Armstrong's argument that "without educated women there is no civilization" finally prevailed. Thus, when Pratt journeyed west in the fall of 1878 to recruit more students, he fully expected half to be women.

Pratt was permitted to enlist fifty Indian students on his trip up the Missouri River. Mrs. Pratt went along to aid with the enlistment of girls. Although they found very little problem in recruiting a group of boys, they had numerous difficulties locating girls. At Fort Berthold, for instance, the Indians objected to having their young women taken away from home. Pratt interpreted this objection in terms of his own ethnocentric beliefs, maintaining that Indian tribes made their "squaws" do all the work. "They are too valuable in the capacity of drudge during the years they should be at school to be spared to go," he reported. Ultimately it required the help of local missionaries to secure four female students. Even then there were unexpected problems. As Pratt noted, "One of the girls [age ten] was especially bright and there was a general desire to save her from the degradation of her Indian surroundings. The mother [age twenty-six] said that education and civilization would make her child look upon her as a savage, and that unless she could go with her child and learn too, the child could not come." Pratt included both mother and daughter. Not all the missionaries and government agents, however, shared Pratt's enthusiasm. At Cheyenne River and other agencies a number of officials echoed the sentiments of Commissioner Hayt regarding the morality of admitting girls to a black school, and they succeeded in blocking recruitment. As a result, only nine girls were sent to Hampton.

Although the educational experiences of the first Indian girls to attend Hampton have not been well documented, a few things are evident. The girls were kept under strict supervision and were separated from the boys except during times of classroom instruction. In addition, the girls were kept apart from black pupils. Most of the academic work was focused on learning the English language, and the girls also received instruction in household skills. The small number of girls, of course, made it difficult to implement a general educational plan. Moreover, considerable opposition remained to educating Indian women at Hampton. Many prominent reformers expected confrontations, or even worse, love affairs, between black and red. Others expressed concern that Indian students in an all-black setting would not receive sufficient incentive and demanded they have the benefit of direct contact with white citizens.

Captain Pratt himself wanted to separate the Indians and blacks, and despite the fact that no racial trouble surfaced at Hampton, he pressured the government to create a school solely for Indians. Indian contact with blacks did not fit in with his plans for native education, and he reminded Secretary Schurz that Indians could become useful citizens only "through living among our people." The government consented, and in the summer of 1879 Pratt was authorized to open a school at Carlisle Barracks, Pennsylvania, "provided both boys and girls are educated in said school." Thus, while

Hampton continued to develop its own Indian program, it was soon accompanied by Carlisle and other all-Indian schools.

Under the guidance of General Armstrong at Hampton and Captain Pratt at Carlisle, a program for Indian women developed over a period of several years. Although these men differed on the question of racial mixing, they agreed on what Indian girls should be learning. By 1880, with fifty-seven Indian girls at Carlisle and about twenty at Hampton, the outlines of the program began to emerge. As rapidly as possible the girls were placed in a system that put maximum emphasis on domestic chores. Academic learning clearly played a subordinate role. The girls spent no more than half a day in the classroom and devoted the rest of their time to domestic work. At Carlisle the first arrivals were instructed in "the manufacture and mending of garments, the use of the sewing machine, laundry work, cooking, and the routine of household duties pertaining to their sex."

Discipline went hand in hand with work experience. Both Pratt and Armstrong possessed military backgrounds and insisted that girls be taught strict obedience. General Armstrong believed that obedience was completely foreign to the native mind and that discipline was a corollary to civilization. Girls, he thought, were more unmanageable than boys because of their "inherited spirit of independence." To instill the necessary discipline, the entire school routine was organized in martial fashion, and every facet of student life followed a strict timetable. Students who violated the rules were punished, sometimes by corporal means, but more commonly by ridicule. Although this discipline was perhaps no more severe than that in many non-Indian schools of the day, it contrasted dramatically with tribal educational patterns that often mixed learning with play. Thus, when Armstrong offered assurances that children accepted "the penalty gratefully as part of his [her] education in the good road," it might be viewed with a bit of skepticism.

Another integral part of the program centered on the idea of placing girls among white families to learn by association. The "outing" system, as it was soon called, began almost as quickly as the schools received students. Through this system Pratt expected to take Indian girls directly from their traditional homes and in three years make them acceptable for placement in public schools and private homes. By 1881 both Carlisle and Hampton were placing girls in white homes, most of which were located in rural Pennsylvania or New England. Here the girls were expected to become independent, secure a working knowledge of the English language, and acquire useful domestic skills. Students were usually sent to a family on an individual basis, although in a few cases several young women were placed in the same home. Emily Bowen, an outing program sponsor in Woodstock, Connecticut, reveals something of white motives for participation in the service. Miss Bowen, a former teacher, heard of Pratt's school in 1880 and became convinced that God had called upon her to "lift up the lowly." Hesitating to endure the dangers of the frontier, she volunteered instead to take eight Indian girls into her home to "educate them to return and be a blessing to their people." Bowen proposed to teach the girls "practical things, such as housework, sewing, and all that is necessary to make home comfortable and pleasant." In this manner, she hoped, the girls under her charge would take the "true missionary spirit" with them on their return to their people.

Having set the women's education program in motion, Pratt and his colleagues took time to reflect on just what result they anticipated from the training. In his 1881 report to Commissioner Hiram Price, Pratt charted out his expectations. Essentially he viewed the education of native girls as a supportive factor in the more important work of training boys. To enter American society, the Indian male needed a mate who would encourage his success and prevent any backsliding. "Of what avail is it," Pratt asked, "that the man be hard-working and industrious, providing by his labor, food and clothing for his household, if the wife, unskilled in cookery, unused to the needle, with no habits of order or neatness, makes what might be a cheerful, happy home only a wretched abode of filth and squalor?" Pratt charged Indian women with clinging to "heathen rites and superstitions" and passing them on to their children. They were, in effect, unfit as mothers and wives. Thus, a woman's education was supremely important, not so much for her own benefit as for that of her husband. Pratt did acknowledge that girls were required to learn more than boys. An Indian male needed only to learn a single trade; the woman, on the other hand, "must learn to sew and to cook, to wash and iron, she must learn lessons of neatness, order, and economy, for without a practical knowledge of all these she cannot make a home."

The size of the girls' program increased dramatically during the 1880s. The government was so taken with the apparent success of Carlisle and Hampton that it began to open similar schools in the West. As the industrial schools expanded, however, the women's program became institutionalized, causing a substantial deviation from the original concept. One reason for this change involved economic factors. The Indian schools, which for decades received $167 a year per student, suffered a chronic lack of funds; thus, to remain self-sufficient, they found themselves relying upon student labor whenever possible. Because they already believed in the educational value of manual labor, it was not a large step for school officials to begin relying upon student labor to keep the schools operating. By the mid-1880s, with hundreds of women attending the industrial schools, student labor had assumed a significant role in school operations. Thus, girls, originally expected to receive a useful education, found themselves becoming more important as an economic factor in the survival of the schools.

The girls' work program that developed at Hampton is typical of the increasing reliance on Indian labor. By 1883 the women's training section was divided into such departments as sewing, housekeeping, and laundry, each in the charge of a white matron or a black graduate. The forty-one girls assigned to the sewing department made the school's bedding, wardrobe, and curtains. At Winona Lodge, the dormitory for Indian girls that also supported the housework division, the matron described the work routine as follows: "All of the Indian girls, from eight to twenty-four years old, make their own clothes, wash and iron them, care for their rooms, and a great many of them take care of the teachers' rooms. Besides this they have extra work, such as sweeping, dusting, and scrubbing the corridors, stairs, hall, sewing-room, chapel, and cleaning other parts of the building." In addition, a large group of Indian girls worked in the school laundry doing the institution's wash.

Conditions were even more rigorous at western schools where a lack of labor put additional demands on female students. At Genoa, Nebraska, the superintendent reported that the few girls enrolled in that school were kept busy doing housework. With the exception of the laundry, which was detailed to the boys, girls were responsible for the sewing and repair of garments, including their own clothes, the small boys' wear, underwear for the large boys, and table linen. The kitchen, dining room, and dormitories were also maintained by women students. Similar circumstances prevailed at Albuquerque, where Superintendent P. F. Burke complained of having to use boys for domestic chores. He was much relieved when enough girls enrolled to allow "the making of the beds, sweeping, and cleaning both the boys' and girls' sleeping apartments." Because of inadequate facilities there were no girls enrolled when the Phoenix school opened in 1891; but as soon as a permanent building was constructed, Superintendent Wellington Rich requested twenty girls "to take the places now filled by boys in the several domestic departments of the school." Such uses of student labor were justified as a method of preparing girls for the duties of home life.

Some employees of the Indian Service recognized that assembly line chores alone were not guaranteed to accomplish the goals of the program. Josephine Mayo, the girls' matron at Genoa, reported in 1886 that the work program was too "wholesale" to produce effective housewives. "Making a dozen beds and cleaning a dormitory does not teach them to make a room attractive and homelike," she remarked. Nor did cooking large quantifies of a single item "supply a family with a pleasant and healthy variety of food, nicely cooked." The matron believed that Indian girls needed to be taught in circumstances similar to those they were expected to occupy. She therefore suggested that small cottages be utilized in which girls could be instructed in the care of younger students and perform all the duties of a housewife. Although Mayo expressed a perceptive concern for the inherent problems of the system, her remarks had little impact on federal school officials. In the meantime, schools were expected to run effectively, and women continued to perform much of the required labor.

Not all the girls' programs, of course, were as routine or chore oriented as the ones cited above. Several of the larger institutions made sincere efforts to train young Indian women as efficient householders. Girls were taught to care for children, to set tables, prepare meals, and make domestic repairs. After 1896 Haskell Institute in Kansas provided women with basic commercial skills in stenography, typing, and bookkeeping. Nursing, too, received attention at some schools. A number of teachers, though conventional in their views of Indian women's role, succeeded in relaxing the rigid school atmosphere. Teachers at Hampton, for instance, regularly invited small groups of girls to their rooms for informal discussions. Here girls, freed from the restraints of the classroom, could express their feelings and receive some personal encouragement. Many institutions permitted their girls to have a dress "with at least some imitation of prevailing style" and urged them to take pride in their appearance.

The industrial schools reached their peak between 1890 and 1910. During this period as many as twenty-five nonreservation schools were in operation. The number of Indian women enrolled may have reached three thousand per annum during this period and females composed between 40 and 50 percent of the student body of most schools. The large number of young women can be attributed to several factors: girls were easier to recruit, they presented fewer disciplinary problems and could be more readily placed in the "outing" system, and after 1892 they could be sent to school without parental consent.

Women's education also became more efficient and standardized during the 1890s. This was due in large part to the activities of Thomas J. Morgan, who served as Indian commissioner from 1889 to 1893. Morgan advocated the education of Indian women as an important part of the acculturation process, believing that properly run schools could remove girls from the "degradation" of camp life and place them on a level with "their more favored white sisters." The commissioner hoped to accomplish this feat by completely systematizing the government's educational program. "So far as possible," he urged, "there should be a uniform course of study, similar methods of instruction, the same textbooks, and a carefully organized and well understood system of industrial training." His suggestions received considerable support, and by 1890, when he issued his "Rules for Indian Schools," the standardization of the Indian schools had begun. Morgan, like Pratt before him, fully expected his concept of education to rapidly produce American citizens. The results were not what the commissioner expected. While standardization proved more efficient, it also exacerbated some of the problems of the women's educational program.

Under the direction of Morgan and his successors, the Indian schools of the era became monuments to regimentation from which there was no escape. This development is obvious in the increasing emphasis on military organization. By the mid-nineties most girls were fully incorporated into the soldierly routine. As one superintendent noted, all students were organized into companies on the first day of school. Like the boys, the girls wore uniforms and were led by student officers who followed army drill regulations. Every aspect of student life was regulated. Anna Moore, a Pima girl attending the Phoenix Indian School, remembered life in the girls' battalion as one of marching "to a military tune" and having to drill at five in the morning. Most school officials were united in their praise of military organization. Regimentation served to develop a work ethic; it broke the students' sense of "Indian time" and ordered their life. The merits of military organization, drill, and routine in connection with discipline were explained by one official who stated that "it teaches patriotism, obedience, courage, courtesy, promptness, and constancy."

Domestic science continued to dominate the women's program. Academic preparation for women never received much emphasis by industrial school administrators despite Morgan's promise that "literary" training would occupy half the students' time. . . . One reason for the lack of emphasis on academics was that by 1900 many school administrators had come to feel that Indians were incapable of learning more. One school superintendent did not consider his "literary" graduates capable of accomplishing much in white society, while another educator described the natives as a "child race."

The extent to which every feature of the girls' program was directed toward the making of proper middle-class housewives can be seen in the numerous directives handed down by the government. By the early twentieth century every detail of school life was regulated. In 1904 Superintendent of Indian Schools Estelle Reel issued a three-page circular on the proper method of making a bed. Much of this training bore little relationship to the reservation environment to which students would return. A few programs were entirely divorced from reality. The cooking course at Sherman Institute in California, for instance, taught girls to prepare formal meals including the serving of raw oysters, shrimp cocktails, and croquettes. In another instance, Hampton teachers devoted some of their energies to discussing attractive flower arrangements and the proper selection of decorative pictures.

Another popular program was the "industrial" cottage. These originated in 1883 at Hampton when the school enrolled several married Indian couples to serve as examples for the students. The couples were quartered in small frame houses while learning to maintain attractive and happy homes. Although the married students did not long remain at Hampton, school officials began to use the cottages as model homes where squads of Indian girls might practice living in white-style homes. By 1900 similar cottages were in use at western schools. The industrial cottage at Phoenix, for example, operated a "well-regulated household" run by nine girls under a matron's supervision. The "family" (with no males present) cleaned and decorated the cottage, did the regular routine of cooking, washing, and sewing, and tended to the poultry and livestock in an effort "to train them to the practical and social enjoyment of the higher life of a real home."

The outing system also continued to be an integral part of the girls' program. As time went on, however, and the system was adopted at western locations, the original purposes of the outings faded. Initially designed as a vehicle for acculturation, the program at many locations became a means of providing servants to white householders. At Phoenix, for example, female pupils formed a pool of cheap labor available to perform domestic services for local families. From the opening of the school in 1891, demands for student labor always exceeded the pool's capacity. One superintendent estimated that he could easily put two hundred girls to work. Moreover, not all employers were interested in the welfare of the student. As the Phoenix superintendent stated in 1894, "The hiring of Indian youth is not looked upon by the people of this valley from a philanthropic standpoint. It is simply a matter of business." In theory, school authorities could return pupils to school at any time it appeared they were not receiving educational benefits; but as one newspaper reported, "What a howl would go up from residents of this valley if the superintendent would exercise this authority."

Even social and religious activities served an educational purpose. When Mrs. Merial Dorchester, wife of the superintendent of Indian schools, made a tour of western school facilities in the early 1890s, she recommended that school girls organize chapters of the King's Daughters, a Christian service organization. Several institutions implemented the program. At these locations girls were organized by age into "circles" to spend spare time producing handcrafted goods for charity. School officials supported such activity because the necessity of raising their own funds to pay dues instilled in the girls a spirit of Christian industry. The manufacture of goods for charity also enhanced their sense of service to others. Said one school superintendent, the organization is "effective in furnishing a spur to individual effort and makes the school routine more bearable by breaking the monotony of it." Although maintaining a nonsectarian stance, the schools encouraged all types of religious activity as an effective method of teaching Christian values and removing the girls from the home influence.

An important factor in understanding the women's program at the industrial schools is the reaction of the girls themselves. This presents some problems, however, since most school girls left no record of their experiences. Moreover, many of the observations that have survived were published in closely controlled school magazines that omitted any unfavorable remarks. Only a few reliable reminiscences have been produced, and even these are not very informative. Despite such limitations, however, several points are evident. The reaction of Indian girls to their education varied greatly. Some came willingly and with the approval of their parents. Once enrolled in school, many of these individuals took a keen interest in their education, accepted discipline as good for them, and worked hard to learn the ways of white society. An undetermined number may have come to school to escape intolerable conditions at home. Some evidence suggests that schools offered safe havens from overbearing parents who threatened to harm their children. For other girls the decision to attend a nonreservation school was made at considerable emotional expense, requiring a break with conservative parents, relatives, and tribesmen. In a few cases young women even lost their opportunity to marry men of their own tribe as they became dedicated to an outside lifestyle.

Many girls disliked school and longed to return home. The reasons are not hard to find. The hard work, discipline, and punishment were often oppressive. One Hopi girl recalled having to get down on her knees each Saturday and scrub the floor of the huge dining hall. "A patch of floor was scrubbed, then rinsed and wiped, and another section was attacked. The work was slow and hard on the knees," she remembered. Pima schoolgirl [Anna] Moore experienced similar conditions working in the dining hall at Phoenix: "My little helpers and I hadn't even reached our teen-aged years yet, and this work seemed so hard! If we were not finished when the 8:00 a.m. whistle sounded, the dining room matron would go around strapping us while we were still on our hands and knees. . . . We just dreaded the sore bottoms." In a number of instances, teachers and matrons added to the trauma by their dictatorial and unsympathetic attitudes. A few girls ran away from school. Those who were caught received humiliating punishment. Runaway girls might be put to work in the school yard cutting grass with scissors or doing some other meaningless drudgery. In a few cases recalcitrant young ladies had their hair cut off. Such experiences left many girls bitter and anxious to return to the old way of life.

The experiences of Indian girls when they returned home after years of schooling illustrate some of the problems in evaluating the success of the government program. For many years school officials reported great success for returned students. Accounts in articles and official documents maintained that numbers of girls had returned home, married, and established good homes. The Indian Bureau itself made occasional surveys purporting to show that returned students were doing well, keeping neat homes, and speaking English. These accounts contained a certain amount of truth. Some graduates adapted their education to the reservation environment and succeeded quite well. Many of these success stories were well publicized. There is considerable evidence to suggest, however, that the reports were overly optimistic and that most returning girls encountered problems.

A disturbingly large number of girls returned to traditional life upon returning home. The reasons are rather obvious. As early as 1882, the principal of Hampton's Indian Division reported that "there is absolutely no position of dignity to which an Indian girl after three years' training can look forward to with any reasonable confidence." Although conditions improved somewhat as time went on, work opportunities remained minimal. Girls were usually trained in only one specialty. As the superintendent of the Albuquerque school reported, girls usually returned home with no relevant skills. Some spent their entire school stay working in a laundry or sewing room, and though they became expert in one field, they had nothing to help them on the reservation. As the Meriam Report* later noted, some Indian girls spent so much time in school laundries that the institutions were in violation of state child labor laws. In another instance, one teacher noted how girls were taught to cook on gas ranges, while back on the reservation they had only campfires.

Moreover, the girls' educational achievements were not always appreciated at home. Elizabeth White tells the story of returning to her Hopi home an accomplished cook only to find that her family shunned the cakes and pies she made in place of traditional food, called her "as foolish as a white woman," and treated her as an outcast. As she later lamented, her school-taught domestic skills were inappropriate for the Hopis. Girls who refused to wear traditional dress at home were treated in like manner. Under these circumstances, many chose to cast off their learning, to marry, and return to traditional living. Those young women who dedicated themselves to living in the white man's style often found that reservations were intolerable, and unable to live in the manner to which they had become accustomed, they preferred to return to the cities. Once there the former students tended to become maids, although an undetermined number ended up as prostitutes and dance hall girls.

Employment opportunities for educated Indian women also pointed up some of the difficulties with the industrial schools. In fairness, it must be admitted that trained women probably had more opportunities than their male counterparts. Most of those who chose to work could do so; however, all positions were at the most menial level. If a girl elected to live within the white community, her employment choices were severely limited. About the only job available was that of domestic service, a carryover from the outing system. In this regard, the Indian schools did operate as employment agencies, finding jobs for their former students with local families. Despite the fact that some Indian women may have later come to feel that their work, despite its demeaning nature, provided some benefits for use in later life, many of their jobs proved unbearably hard. After being verbally abused, one former student wrote that "I never had any Lady say things like that to me." Another reported on her job, "I had been working so hard ever since I came here cleaning house and lots of ironing. I just got through ironing now I'm very tired my feet get so tired standing all morning." Unfortunately, few respectable jobs beyond domestic labor were available. Oc-

*The 1928 Meriam Report was an intense study of the conditions of American Indians and the operations of the Bureau of Indian Affairs, conducted by the Institute for Government Research under the auspices of the Department of the Interior. (Eds.)

casionally girls were trained as nurses or secretaries only to discover that they could find no work in Anglo society.

The largest employer of Indian girls proved to be the Indian Bureau. Many former students were able to secure positions at Indian agencies and schools; in fact, had it not been for the employment of former students by the paternalistic Indian service, few would have found any use for their training. The nature of the government positions available to Indian girls is revealing. Almost all jobs were menial in nature; only a few Indian girls were able to become teachers, and none worked as administrators. They were, rather, hired as laundresses, cooks, seamstresses, nurses' helpers, and assistant matrons. Often these employees received little more than room, board, and government rations, and even those who managed to be hired as teachers and nurses received less pay than their white counterparts. . . . Indian girls could find work, but only in the artificial environment of Indian agencies and schools located at remote western points and protected by a paternalistic government. Here they continued to perform tasks of domestic nature without promise of advancement. Nor were they assimilated into the dominant society as had been the original intent of their education.

School administrators were reluctant to admit the failings of the system. As early as the 1880s some criticism began to surface, but for the most part it was lost in the enthusiasm for training in a nonreservation environment. After 1900, however, critics became more vocal and persistent, arguing that the Indian community did not approve of this type of education, that most students gained little, and that employment opportunities were limited at best. More important, this type of education contributed little to the acculturation effort. As one opponent wrote, "To educate the Indian out of his [or her] home surroundings is to fill him with false ideas and to endow him with habits which are destructive to his peace of mind and usefulness to his community when the educational work is completed." Commissioner Leupp (1905–1909) was even more vocal. He generally accepted the increasingly prevalent theory that Indians were childlike in nature and incapable of assimilating into white society on an equal basis. Leupp suggested that the system failed to produce self-reliant Indians and, instead of giving Indian children a useful education, protected them in an artificial environment. Other school officials echoed the same sentiments. In this particular respect it was suggested that boarding school students were provided with all the comforts of civilization at no cost and thus failed to develop the proper attitude toward work. Upon returning to the reservations, therefore, they did not exert themselves and lapsed into traditionalism.

Despite increasing criticism, the women's educational program at the nonreservation schools operated without much change until after 1920. Girls were still taught skills of doubtful value, were hired out as maids through the outing system, did most of the domestic labor at the schools, and returned to the reservation either to assume traditional life or accept some menial government job. By the late twenties, however, the movement to reform Indian education began to have some impact. Relying upon such studies as the 1928 Meriam Report, reformers began to demand a complete change in the Indian educational system. Among their suggestions were that industrial boarding schools be phased out and the emphasis on work training be reduced. Critics like [future Commissioner of Indian Affairs] John Collier argued that the policy of removing girls from their homes to educate them for a life among whites had failed. Instead, girls were discouraged from returning to the reservation and had received little to prepare them for a home life. Collier's arguments eventually won out, especially after he became Indian commissioner in 1933. Thus ended this particular attempt to convert Native American women into middle-class American housewives. . . .

DOCUMENTS

Rules for Indian Schools, 1890

General Rules

39. The Sabbath must be properly observed. There shall be a Sabbath school or some other suitable service every Sunday, which pupils shall be required to attend. The superintendent may require employés to attend and participate in all the above exercises; but any employé declining as a matter of conscience shall be excused from attending and participating in any or all religious exercises. . . .

41. All instruction must be in the English language. Pupils must be compelled to converse with each other in English, and should be properly rebuked or punished for persistent violation of this rule. Every effort should be made to encourage them to abandon their tribal language. To facilitate this work it is essential that all school employés be able to speak English fluently, and that they speak English exclusively to the pupils, and also to each other in the presence of pupils.

42. Instruction in music must be given at all schools. Singing should be a part of the exercises of each school session, and wherever practicable instruction in instrumental music should be given.

43. Except in cases of emergency, pupils shall not be removed from school either by their parents or others, nor shall they be transferred from a Government to a private school without special authority from the Indian Office.

SOURCE: U.S. Bureau of Indian Affairs, "Rules for Indian Schools;" *Annual Report of the Commissioner of Indian Affairs, 1890* (Washington, D C, 1890), cxivi, cl–clii.

44. The school buildings should be furnished throughout with plain, inexpensive, but substantial furniture. Dormitories or lavatories should be so supplied with necessary toilet articles, such as soap, towels, mirrors, combs, hair, shoe, nail, and tooth brushes, and wisp brooms, as to enable the pupils to form exact habits of personal neatness.

45. Good and healthful provisions must be supplied in abundance; and they must be well cooked and properly placed on the table. A regular bill of fare for each day of the week should be prepared and followed. Meals must be served regularly and neatly. Pains should be taken not only to have the food healthful and the table attractive, but to have the bill of fare varied. The school farm and dairy should furnish an ample supply of vegetables, fruits, milk, butter, cottage cheese, curds, eggs, and poultry. Coffee and tea should be furnished sparingly; milk is preferable to either, and children can be taught to use it. Pupils must be required to attend meals promptly after proper attention to toilet, and at least one employé must be in the dining room during each meal to supervise the table manners of the pupils and to see that all leave the table at the same time and in good order. . . .

47. So far as practicable, a uniform style of clothing for the school should be adopted. Two plain, substantial suits, with extra pair of trousers for each boy, and three neat, well-made dresses for each girl, if kept mended, ought to suffice for week-day wear for one year. For Sunday wear each pupil should be furnished a better suit. The pupils should also be supplied with underwear adapted to the climate, with night clothes, and with handkerchiefs, and, if the climate requires it, with overcoats and cloaks and with overshoes.

48. The buildings, outhouses, fences, and walks should at all times be kept in thorough repair. Where practicable, the grounds should be ornamented with trees, grass, and flowers.

49. There should be a flag staff at every school, and the American flag should be hoisted, in suitable weather, in the morning and lowered at sunset daily.

50. Special hours should be allotted for recreation. Provision should be made for outdoor sports, and the pupils should be encouraged in daily healthful exercise under the eye of a school employé; simple games should also be devised for indoor amusement. They should be taught the sports and games enjoyed by white youth, such as baseball, hopscotch, croquet, marbles, bean bags, dominoes, checkers, logomachy, and other word and letter games, and the use of dissected maps, etc. The girls should be instructed in simple fancy work, knitting, netting, crocheting, different kinds of embroidery, etc.

51. Separate play grounds, as well as sitting rooms, must be assigned the boys and the girls. In play and in work, as far as possible, and in all places except the school room and at meals, they must be kept entirely apart. It should be so arranged, however, that at stated times, under suitable

supervision, they may enjoy each other's society; and such occasions should be used to teach them to show each other due respect and consideration, to behave without restraint, but without familiarity, and to acquire habits of politeness, refinement, and self-possession. . . .

53. Corporal punishment must be resorted to only in cases of grave violations of rules, and in no instances shall any person inflict it except under the direction of the superintendent to whom all serious questions of discipline must be referred.* Employés may correct pupils for slight misdemeanors only.

54. Any pupil twelve years of age or over, guilty of persistently using profane or obscene language; of lewd conduct; stubborn insubordination; lying; fighting; wanton destruction of property; theft; or similar misbehavior, may be punished by the superintendent either by inflicting corporal punishment or imprisonment in the guardhouse; but in no case shall any unusual or cruel or degrading punishment be permitted. . . .

Industrial Work

56. A regular and efficient system of industrial training must be a part of the work of each school. At least half of the time of each boy and girl should be devoted thereto—the work to be of such character that they may be able to apply the knowledge and experience gained, in the locality where they may be expected to reside after leaving school. In pushing forward the school-room training of these boys and girls, teachers, and especially superintendents, must not lose sight of the great necessity for fitting their charges for the every-day life of their after years.

57. A farm and garden, if practicable an orchard also, must be connected with each school, and especial attention must be given to instruction in farming, gardening, dairying, and fruit growing.

58. Every school should have horses, cattle, swine, and poultry, and when practicable, sheep and bees, which the pupils should be taught to care for properly. The boys should look after the stock and milk the cows, and the girls should see to the poultry and the milk.

59. The farm, garden, stock, dairy, kitchen, and shops should be so managed as to make the school as nearly self-sustaining as practicable, not only because Government resources should be as wisely and carefully utilized as private resources would be, but also because thrift and economy are among

---

*In some of the more advanced schools it will be practicable and advisable to have material offenses arbitrated by a school court composed of the advanced students, with school employés added to such court in very aggravated cases. After due investigation, the amount of guilt should be determined and the quantity of punishment fixed by the court, but the approval of the superintendent shall be necessary before the punishment is inflicted, and the superintendent may modify or remit but may not increase the sentence.

the most valuable lessons which can be taught Indians. Waste in any department must not be tolerated.

60. The blacksmith, wheelwright, carpenter, shoemaker, and harness maker trades, being of the most general application, should be taught to a few pupils at every school. Where such mechanics are not provided for[,] the school pupils should, so far as practicable, receive instruction from the agency mechanics.

61. The girls must be systematically trained in every branch of housekeeping and in dairy work; be taught to cut, make, and mend garments for both men and women; and also be taught to nurse and care for the sick. They must be regularly detailed to assist the cook in preparing the food and the laundress in washing and ironing.

62. Special effort must be made to instruct Indian youth in the use and care of tools and implements. They must learn to keep them in order, protect them properly, and use them carefully.

A Government Official Describes Indian Race and Culture, 1905

We believe that the strength of our American life is due in no small part to the fact that various and different race elements have entered into the making of the American the citizen of the United States in the twentieth century. No one racial stock is exclusively in control in our land. The typical modern American is a fine "composite," with race elements drawn from many sources. We do not believe that the Government of the United States in dealing with its Indian wards would act righteously or wisely if it were to attempt to crush out from those who are of Indian descent all the racial traits which differentiate the North American Indian from the other race stocks of the world. Certain conceptions of physical courage, a certain heroic stoicism in enduring physical pain, an inherited tendency to respect one's self, even if that tendency shows itself at times in unwarrantable conceit, are race traits which have value, if the people who have them become civilized and subject themselves to the laws of social morality and to the obligation of industrial efficiency, which are essential if any race stock or any group of families is to hold its own in the modern civilized world.

But the facts seem to us to be that good results are to be hoped for not by keeping the North American Indians peculiar in dress or in customs. We think that the wisest friends of the Indian recognize with great delight and value highly the art impulse in certain Indian tribes, which has shown itself

SOURCE: U.S. Department of Interior, "Board of Indian Commissioners' Reports," in *Annual Reports* (June 30, 1905), H. Doc. 20: 59th Cong., 1st sess., 17–18.

in Indian music, in Indian art forms—such as the birchbark canoe, in Indian basketry, and more rarely in Indian pottery. But we firmly believe that the way to preserve the best of what is distinctively characteristic in the North American Indians is to civilize and educate them, that they may be fit for the life of the twentieth century under our American system of self-government. Because we value the elements for good which may come into our American life through the stock of North American Indians, we wish to see children of Indian descent educated in the industrial and practical arts and trained to habits of personal cleanliness, social purity, and industrious family life. We do not believe that it is right to keep the Indians out of civilization in order that certain picturesque aspects of savagery and barbarism may continue to be within reach of the traveler and the curious, or even of the scientific observer. In the objectionable "Indian dances" which are breaking out afresh at many points we see not a desirable maintenance of racial traits, but a distinct reversion toward barbarism and superstition. We believe that while the effort should never be made to "make a white man out of an Indian," in the sense of seeking to do violence to respect to parents or a proper or intelligent regard for what is fine in the traits and the history of one's ancestors, it is still most desirable that all the Indians on our territory should come as speedily as possible to the white man's habits of home-making, industry, cleanliness, social purity, and family integrity.

Precisely as all intelligent American patriots have seen danger to our national life in the attempt, wherever it has been made, to perpetuate in the United States large groups of foreign-born immigrants who try to keep their children from learning English and seek to perpetuate upon our territory (at the cost of true Americanism for their children) what was characteristic in the life of their own people on other continents and in past generations, precisely as in such cases we feel that the hope of our American system lies in the public schools and such educational institutions as shall maintain standards of public living that inevitably bring the children of foreign-born immigrants into the great body of English-speaking, home-loving, industrious, and pure-minded Americans—precisely so does it seem to us that all the efforts of the Government, and far more of distinctive missionary effort on the part of the Christian people of this country than has ever yet been used with this end in view, should be steadily employed in the effort to make out of the Indian children of this country intelligent, English-speaking, industrious, law-abiding Americans. We believe that the breaking up of tribal funds as rapidly as practicable will help toward this end. Even if many of the Indians do for a time misuse money while they are learning how to use it properly, even if some of them squander it utterly, we believe that there is hope for the Indians in the future only as by education, faith in work, and obedience to Christian principles of morality and clean living, their children shall come to have the social standards and the social habits of our better American life throughout the land.

Our task is to hasten the slow work of race evolution. Inevitably, but often grimly and harshly by the outworking of natural forces, the national life of the stronger and more highly civilized race stock dominates in time the life of the less civilized, when races like the Anglo-Saxon and the Indian are brought into close contact. In our work for the Indians we want to discern clearly those influences and habits of life which are of the greatest advantage in leading races upward into Christian civilization; and these influences and habits we wish to make as strongly influential as possible, and as speedily as possible influential upon the life of all these American tribes. It is not unreasonable to hope that through governmental agencies and through the altruistic missionary spirit of one of the foremost Christian races and governments of the world much can be done to hasten that process of civilization which natural law, left to itself, works out too slowly and at too great a loss to the less-favored race. We want to make the conditions for our less-favored brethren of the red race so favorable that the social forces which have developed themselves slowly and at great expense of time and life in our American race and our American system of government shall be made to help in the uplifting of the Indians and to shorten that interval of time which of necessity must elapse between savagery and Christian civilization.

Cause for Hope: The Establishment of Tribal Colleges, 1994

ROSEBUD RESERVATION, S.D.—There are no ivy walls or fraternity houses on the campus of Sinte Gleska University. It is a small, horseshoe-shaped jumble of aging mobile homes, a log building and squat Government housing. In the parking lot sit weathered pickups and rusting old cars.

But the college is the jewel of the Rosebud reservation, a dry, shadowless stretch in western South Dakota where the clouds are stingy with rainfall and relentless winds rattle the flimsy walls of tar-paper shacks and house trailers.

Some 750 students are enrolled in this college, where Irene Garrett, who grew up in a shack without running water or electricity in the reservation town of Mission, teaches the writings of Linda Hogan, an Osage; Lisa Cook-Lynn, a Lower Brule Sioux; and Simon Ortiz, a Hopi.

"This is one of the most wonderful revolutions in Indian Country, the right to educate on our own terms," said Dr. David Gipp of the American Indian Higher Education Committee.

The first tribal college opened on the Navajo reservation in Arizona in 1968. Today there are 26 such colleges, with more than 16,000 Indian students. While the institutions started as community colleges granting associate degrees, three of them, including Sinte Gleska (SIN-teh GLES-ka), offer four-year bachelor's programs and have recently expanded to offer master's degrees.

Perhaps the colleges' greatest success has been a transformation in the way Indians view school. For generations, Indians have been suspicious of formal education, a legacy that dates to the Government boarding schools, where native languages were forbidden and teachers denigrated tribal culture.

"We're about restoring culture," said Cheryl Crazybull, the vice president of Sinte Gleska, where the Lakota language is a required subject.

As a child, Ms. Garrett never saw an Indian teacher. "I remember one teacher demanding that I look her in the eye," she said. "She didn't know that we consider that a sign of disrespect."

After high school, Ms. Garrett won a scholarship to attend college in Albany, where she encountered only one other Indian, an Oneida from upstate New York, and quit in 1971 after two years.

She came home, took a job with a Federal agency and gave up on college. But the next year, Sinte Gleska opened. Ms. Garrett, a single mother, enrolled.

Today she tells her students, many of whom are single parents, "If you don't have day care, bring your kids to class."

And when the students are busy reading in class, or writing essays, the teacher plays with the children.

Chapter 4

Woman's Sphere: Woman's Work

During the final decades of the nineteenth century, America's urban growth and expanding industrial economy opened innumerable jobs in the private and public sectors. For many white men with ambition, intelligence, and education, the choice of careers was broad and the chance of success promising. For immigrants, for blacks, for poor youth off the farm, and for women, however, opportunities expanded in a much more limited way. The barriers of ethnicity, race, gender, and inadequate schooling were formidable.

Margery W. Davies's essay "Office Work After the Civil War" recounts the feminization of clerical work during these decades. She illustrates the relationship between the increasing numbers of women in the office work force and significant developments in American society: the rise of urban industrialism, the decline of the family farm, the impact of technology on the home and workplace, and the "drastic changes in the scale and shape of business enterprise." At the same time, she illuminates how, despite expanding employment opportunities, the popular perception of a separate woman's sphere continued to restrict women to particular occupations. What does Davies identify as the most significant factors in transforming clerical work from a male-dominated to a female-dominated occupation? What made this kind of work attractive to women?

The popular belief in the notion of "women's work" required some justification for admitting females to certain jobs. Teaching, as Davies notes, preceded office work as the first "literacy-required" occupation deemed suitable to a woman's nature. In the first document, Horace Mann, Secretary of the Massachusetts Board of Education and famous crusader for public schooling, applauds the entry of women as teachers in the primary grades, a position for which he believed they were particularly fit. Though this Annual Report was written in 1844, it expressed attitudes toward women that would remain common throughout the rest of the century. Note the reference to woman's special qualities with which "the Author of nature preadapted her." By the Civil War, the schoolmistress had almost completely replaced the schoolmaster in the nation's public elementary schools, a development that highlights the persuasiveness of Mann's argument. Of course, differences in salaries might also have exerted influence as communities hired teachers: in 1861, the average salary for male teachers in rural districts was $6.30 per week; for women, it was $4.05. In urban districts, men earned $18.00 per week; women, only $6.91.

Women attempting to enter prestigious, traditionally male occupations often met with considerable resistance and drew on huge stores of courage in their perseverance. The second document is a 1916 newspaper account of the recollections of Dr. Anna Manning Comfort, who graduated in the first class of the New York Medical College and Hospital for Women in 1865. How did the perception of a separate place for women within the medical profession shift between 1865 and 1916?

Although popular beliefs about women's natural capacities supported their entry into teaching, clerical jobs, nursing, factory work, librarianship, social work, and even medicine, they were also used to exclude women from positions of leadership in those fields, to deny them the right to vote, and to bar their entry into other professions. In 1872 the United States Supreme Court upheld a decision of the Illinois courts denying Myra Bradwell a license to practice law on the grounds of her sex. The third document presents Supreme Court Justice Bradley's majority opinion in support of the Court's decision. Notice that his argument rested heavily on traditional perceptions of women's natures.

The Court's decision in Bradwell v. Illinois *set back women's rights, yet the era saw victories as well. That same year (1872), the Illinois legislature removed all restrictions to women's entry into the professions. Similar actions were taken in other states. In 1869 Arabella Mansfield of Iowa had become the first woman licensed to practice law. By 1891 the nation boasted two hundred licensed women lawyers. (Of course, the figure represented less than 1 percent of all the nation's at-*

torneys.) The struggle has continued well into our own century. How would you describe popular beliefs today concerning separate spheres for men and women in the home, in politics, and in the world of work?

ESSAY

————— •◆• —————

Office Work After the Civil War

Margery W. Davies

The last third of the nineteenth century witnessed drastic changes in the scale and shape of business enterprise. The small and highly competitive firms that had dominated production in the antebellum United States gave way to giant corporations integrated vertically and horizontally in the merger movement that swept through industry during the 1890s. In the steel, oil, tobacco, food, and meat-packing sectors, to name just a few, such corporations enjoyed virtual monopolies.

As is now well known, profound changes in production techniques accompanied the rise of the trusts. But innovation was not restricted to the shop floor. It also reached upwards into the office, for the increase in the volume of business, coupled with the development of regional, national, and international markets, led to a proliferation of correspondence and inspired the need for more accurate record keeping. As the amount and geographic range of a firm's activities grew, it became more difficult for that firm to conduct the bulk of its transactions in person. While face-to-face business contacts by no means disappeared, a businessman might choose to pay a bill, order merchandise, or confirm an appointment in writing rather than in person, particularly when the transaction took place between cities. Even after the invention of the telephone, many businesses preferred to keep a written record of transactions rather than having to rely on memory.

As a firm's operations expanded and became more complex, accurate records of its transactions became more important. A small entrepreneurial butcher did not need very complex records. He might keep a list of which customers owed him money and how much, and of how many pounds of beef and how many pounds of pork he could expect each week from various meat-slaughterers, but he would not need much more. A large meat-packing firm, however, required more complex records: how many head of cattle were fattening in pens in Omaha or Kansas City, and how many were being driven across the plains from points farther west; how much the workers in the slaughterhouses were being paid; how many refrigerated cars were on their way to the eastern cities, and how many on their way back. These records had to be accurate and up-to-date, for the managers needed detailed information at their fingertips in order to make plans for the future. Furthermore, . . . firms required elaborate records to guard against fraud both by their own employees and by the companies with which they did business.

Among the outstanding features of the reorganization of the office was the division of businesses into departments. This became necessary as firms grew so large and complex that it was no longer possible for one capitalist, or even a small group, to make all the decisions. The ultimate control of a firm's capital and direction still rested with the owner or owners, but the more mundane operations were decentralized into various functionally defined departments. The Pennsylvania Railroad management, for example, one of the first to introduce this method of organization, instituted separate offices for accounting and for the supervision of roadbeds and moving stock. It also worked out a more elaborate structure of relations between the major departments and their ancillary units.

These organizational innovations were accompanied by the subdivision of clerical labor. Before the Civil War there had been four basic clerical jobs in the office: copyist, bookkeeper, messenger or office boy, and clerk. This relatively simple range of occupations was expanded and elaborated following the war, with the division of labor most pronounced in the largest offices. File clerks, shipping clerks, billing clerks and other "semiskilled" workers began to appear. The exact pattern that the division of labor followed in a particular office depended, of course, on the nature of the business at hand. An insurance company might have many billing or file clerks, but no shipping clerks whatsoever; a mail-order house would use an army of shipping and file clerks, but no billing clerks since orders were paid in advance.

Not surprisingly, the most popular change resulted from the introduction of the typewriter. Once it was adopted, stenographers and typists quite rapidly replaced copyists. A stenographer's job consisted of taking dictation, usually from a firm's manager or owner, although occasionally also from a higher-level clerical worker, and then transcribing the notes into a letter, report, or whatever. For a while, it was considered rude or disrespectful for a firm to type its correspondence, and some dictation was at first transcribed in a fine longhand. Before long, however, typewriting became the accepted mode of business correspondence, and handwritten letters yielded to typewritten ones. The stenographer was in effect a direct replacement for a copyist, since in general stenography encompassed transcription as well as dictation. The integration of these tasks came about not only because many different systems of shorthand were in use, but also because stenographers tended to add individual quirks or shortcuts to the system being used. Hence the stenographer might be the only one who could read his or her notes. At first glance it would seem that the shift from copyist to stenographer involved no further division of labor. But the fact that typists were being hired as well as stenographers suggests even greater specialization. Take the example of a manufacturer with outstanding debts from thirty customers. He might decide to send each of them a dunning letter couched in the strongest language instead of an invoice with "Third and Final Notice" stamped on it in red ink. He might dictate this letter to a stenographer, who would transcribe it in longhand and pass it on, along with the names and addresses of the overdue debtors, to two or three typists, who would produce as many copies of the letter as necessary. The result was that what had once been done by one kind of clerk, a copyist, was now done by two, a stenographer and a typist. In this example, the typists execute the bulk of the task at hand, and the manufacturer congratulates himself on the efficiency of his system and on the money saved by using a stenographer only where necessary and by using typists whenever possible.

This increasing division of labor constituted a basic change in the organization of office work. In antebellum offices clerical workers were responsible for a wide range of tasks and in some cases their work bore the aspects of a craft. But the division and redivision of clerical tasks meant that an individual clerical worker performed only a small number of tasks in a larger range of operations. This reorganization of work was uneven. It first appeared immediately before the Civil War (the Erie Railroad) and was clearly taking hold by the 1870s. Thus the post–Civil War expansion and consolidation of capitalism drastically rearranged the office by partitioning firms into departments and dividing up clerical work into specialized tasks. Another factor which did much to alter the appearance of clerical work, and which had some influence on the changing nature of that work, was technological innovation, with the typewriter being far and away the most important of the new office machines. . . .

One of the ways women entered clerical work was by mastering the typewriter and then finding a job as a typist. When Mark Twain bought his first typewriter in early 1875, the salesman had a "type girl" on hand to demonstrate the machine to prospective customers. And in late 1875 this ad for the Remington typewriter appeared in the *Nation*:

CHRISTMAS PRESENT
for a boy or girl

And the benevolent can, by the gift of a "Type-Writer" to a poor, deserving young woman, put her at once in the way of earning a good living as a copyist or corresponding clerk.

No invention has opened for women so broad and easy an avenue to profitable and suitable employment as the "Type-Writer," and it merits the careful consideration of all thoughtful and charitable persons interested in the subject of work for woman.

Mere girls are now earning from \$10 to \$20 per week with the "Type-Writer," and we can at once secure good situations for one hundred expert writers on it in court-rooms in this city.

The public is cordially invited to call and inspect the working of the machine, and obtain all information at our showrooms.

But in 1875 and for a few years thereafter, the typewriter was still thought of as a frill by most businessmen. It was not until the 1880s that typewriters were manufactured and sold in large numbers.

In the 1880s, also, the employment of women in offices began to climb sharply. . . . This coincidence has led some analysts to conclude that the invention of the typewriter was basically responsible for the employment of women in offices in the United States. For example, a pamphlet put out by the Women's Bureau of the United States Department of Labor asserts that "not only . . . has the typewriter revolutionized modern business methods but it has *created* an occupation calling for more women than have been employed as a result of any other invention." Bruce Bliven, the author of a history of the typewriter, recounts the story of how the New York YWCA started training young women typists in 1881. Far from succumbing to mental and physical breakdowns under the strain of their new occupation, as some observers had warned, these women quickly found jobs. The YWCA was soon deluged with many more requests for typists than it could fill. Bliven concludes that "the revolution came rather quietly, on high-buttoned shoes, accompanied not by gunfire or bombs bursting in air, but by a considerable amount of rather obnoxious snickering."

Just as it would be a mistake to say that the typewriter was responsible for the growth of offices after the Civil War, so would it be erroneous to credit it with the employment of women in those offices. . . . [F]emale employment was increasing rapidly throughout the clerical occupations, and not just among stenographers and typists.

Although the typewriter was not responsible for the employment of women as clerical workers, its existence probably facilitated or eased the entrance of women into offices. It was such a new machine that it had not been "sex-typed" as masculine. Thus women who worked as typists did not face the argument that a typewriter was a machine fit only for men. In fact, it was not too long afterwards that women were claimed to be more manually dexterous and tolerant of routine than men and therefore more suited, by virtue of their very natures, to operate typewriters.

Changes in the structure of capitalism in the United States brought women into offices. The expansion and consolidation of capitalist firms after the Civil War caused a rapid increase in the amount of correspondence and record keeping required by those firms. This in turn resulted in the growth of offices and an immediate increase in the need for clerical workers. That, in short, explains the demand. Where was the supply to come from?

The basic skill required of clerical workers was literacy. The supply therefore had to come from those segments of the population that had some education, and at this time[,] women, as well as men, had advanced schooling. In fact, . . . the number of women high school graduates exceeded that of men during the last decades of the nineteenth century.

And women's labor was cheaper than men's. Patriarchal social relations devalued the labor of women compared to that of men from similar backgrounds. The reasons for this are legion. First of all, there was the widespread belief that women were simply, and by the very nature of things, inferior to men. In addition, women were often thought to be working for "pin money" with which to make frivolous purchases. Since they were not thought to be supporting themselves or their families, there was nothing the matter with paying them low wages. Then there was the argument that women were not serious members of the labor force: they would be returning to an exclusively domestic life either as soon as they married or, at the very latest, as soon as they bore children. Such transient workers did not deserve the higher wage with which an employer might try to attract and keep a more steadfast male worker. Finally, women's depressed wages did drive them back into the home, where they again became available to fill a subordinate position within the domestic division of labor. Whether or not this worked to the ultimate benefit of men, it certainly provided them with short-term benefits.

On the face of it, the cheapness of labor ought to explain why employers preferred women over men. But women's labor in the United States has always come cheaper than men's, so that it is not immediately obvious why employers did not always show preference for females. There must be a further reason why employers started to favor women for certain clerical positions.

The supply of literate male labor was simply not large enough to fill the great demand for office workers. The expansion of capitalist firms created not only a much larger need for clerical workers, but also an increased demand for managerial personnel. As is clear from the discussion of the proliferation of hierarchical structures within late nineteenth-century firms, the managerial corps necessitated by this new system of finely delegated authority expanded mightily. An educated man, faced with the choice among positions within the office hierarchy, was unlikely to choose to be a typist instead of a manager, who was higher-paid and invested with a fair degree of authority and power. The expansion of capitalist firms, coupled with the growth of cities at the end of the nineteenth century, also led to a rise in the number of jobs ancillary to business operations. Lawyers are an excellent example: in 1870 there were 40,736 lawyers in the United States, all but five of whom were men. By 1900 there were almost three times as many lawyers, 114,640, over 99 percent of whom were men. There had been one lawyer for every 307 people employed in all occupations in the United

States in 1870; by 1900 there was one lawyer for every 254 such persons. Thus a man who had enough education and literacy skills (the ability to spell reasonably well, to write [in] a legible hand, to do basic arithmetic accurately) to obtain a job as a clerical worker was also probably educated enough to at least aspire to, and in many cases to attain, a managerial or professional position. As a consequence, the supply of men available for clerical work was considerably diminished.

Furthermore, fewer boys than girls were graduating from high school in the United States. . . . If high school and college graduations are considered together, more men than women were receiving secondary school diplomas or better during the years 1870 and 1880. But in 1890 and 1900, the number of women receiving high school diplomas or better had outstripped the number of men. Despite the fact that consistently far more men than women graduated from college, the number of women finishing high school grew to so outweigh the number of men that the surplus of male over female college graduates was cancelled out. In addition, the men who were reaching those high educational levels were likely to be supplying the demand for managers and professionals. Thus the demand for managers and professionals and the fact that more women than men were reaching relatively high levels of formal education combine to explain why it was that the ever-increasing demand for clerical workers was met by women.

Other factors, though secondary, also influenced feminization. First of all, the employment of women as clerks in the United States Treasury Department during the Civil War established a precedent that may have eased the entrance of women into offices ten and fifteen years later. The employment of female clerks in the Treasury Department showed that it was possible for women to work in offices. Women had gotten a toe in the office door. As a result, when structural changes in capitalism produced a dramatic rise in the demand for clerical workers, it was slightly easier for women to push the door wide open.

A second factor that facilitated—as opposed to caused—the employment of women was the invention and production of the typewriter. Women were employed in increasing numbers throughout the entire gamut of clerical occupations, and not just as typists. The process that underlay the employment of women in offices was similar to that which underlay the successful manufacture of a typewriter in the first place—the expansion and consolidation of capitalist firms. But the fact that the typewriter was sex-neutral, without historical ties to workers of either sex, meant that female typists did not have to meet the argument that they were operating a man's machine.

Finally, the reorganization of the division of labor within the office may have abetted its feminization. It is possible that if offices had simply expanded without being reorganized, women would have had a more difficult time entering clerical work. The reorganization of many offices often resulted in a redivision of clerical labor and in the creation of new jobs, from stenographers and typists to file clerks, billing clerks, and the like. Since many of these jobs, or at least their labels, had not existed before the growth of the office, they were not defined as men's jobs. Women who took such positions did not face the argument that they were taking over men's work.

Nonetheless, the roots of the feminization of clerical work lay in political-economic conditions that were independent of the job itself. Changes in the structure of capitalism caused a rapid increase in the demand for clerical workers, a demand that was met in part by an available supply of literate women. Furthermore, it seems that many employers were only too glad to employ female labor in place of more costly male labor. The feminization of clerical work was not intrinsic to the job itself, despite ideological justifications that arose after the fact. By its very nature, clerical work was neither men's work nor women's work.

Clerical jobs were available to women, but, for feminization to occur, women had to be available to take the jobs. A variety of factors produced a supply of women to fill the demand. The economic decline of small, family-owned farms and businesses frequently forced daughters into the labor force. Clerical work was generally seen as more desirable than industrial work, and this spurred women of working-class origins to seek clerical jobs. Productive work in the home was on the decline, making the labor of both working-class and non-working-class women available for jobs outside the domestic sphere. And clerical work was one of the few options for literate women seeking jobs that required literate workers. . . .

Although the decline of the small, independent farmer as a class had hardly begun in earnest, by the end of the nineteenth century the large cities of the East were already beginning to feel the effects. The new homesteads of the West absorbed only some of the eastern farmers forced off their land. Others who found they could no longer make ends meet were already moving into the cities in the waning years of the nineteenth century, although it was not until the twentieth that displaced small farmers really began to swell the urban labor force. The ranks of clerical workers included people of small-farm origins from the outset.

The situation of small-business proprietors differed significantly from that of farmers. From 1870 to 1930 they not only held their own numerically and as a proportion of the labor force but, in fact, grew. Although the class as a whole maintained itself through the years, . . . individual members of the classic petite bourgeoisie did not always manage to make ends meet, much less prosper. Thousands of fledgling businesses were started by hopeful entrepreneurs; almost as many failed.

These small entrepreneurs lived in constant dread of failure and imposed long hours on themselves and their families in order to fend off financial disaster. "But the average life of these old middle-class, especially urban, units in the twentieth century is short; the coincidence of family unit and work-situation among the old middle class is a pre-industrial fact. So even as the centralization of property contracts their 'independence,' it liberates the children of the old middle class's smaller entrepreneurs."

Some of those children were "liberated" to become clerical workers. The endemic financial insecurity of many small businessmen often meant not only that their children were reluctant to follow them in an unstable occupation, but also, in many cases, that the children were forced to support themselves. Thus the classic petite bourgeoisie contributed to the pool of people available for work in offices. . . .

For many daughters of working-class families, however, membership in the labor force was nothing new. The vast majority of working-class families were unable to afford the luxury of keeping out of the labor force an unmarried daughter whose labor was not essential to the maintenance of the home. Single working-class women were expected to enter the labor force as a matter of course. In fact, a writer in 1929 considered it a sign of the improved condition of the working class that its children were staying in school longer and longer, rather than entering the labor force out of economic necessity:

> The rising standard of living of manual workers has made it possible for more of them to provide their children with the high school education necessary to clerical positions, and the popular belief in education as the open sesame to opportunity has been an incentive to increased high school attendance. This increase in the high school population—the rate of which, within the last thirty years, has been about twenty times the rate of the increase in the population— has thrown upon the vocational market thousands of girls with a high school education, a large proportion of whom aspire to clerical positions.

The main reason working-class girls "aspired" to clerical work was that it paid better than most jobs open to women. In 1883, at the very beginning of the influx of large numbers of women into clerical work, female office workers in Boston were relatively well off compared to women in other working-class occupations. Copyists in personal service earned an average weekly wage of $6.78, bookkeepers earned $6.55, cashiers earned $7.43, and clerks (it is not clear from the available information whether "clerks" refers to clerks in offices or stores, or both) earned $5.28. Although a highly skilled craft-worker in manufacturing, such as a button-hole-maker for men's shirts, could earn as much as $10.00, most women working in manufacturing did not make over $5.00, and some made considerably less. These wages do not take into account the shorter hours women in offices enjoyed, a factor that would make their average hourly wage even better when compared to that of other working-class women. In 1910 a study of the incomes and expenditures of 450 Boston working women found that clerical work was second only to professional occupations in annual net income.

In addition to better wages, clerical work brought higher status than many other "female" occupations, such as factory work, domestic service, and clerking in stores. The argument has been made that this higher status was a result of a cleaner work environment, shorter hours, such benefits as vacation and sick leave, and the notion that clerical work could lead to promotions of some importance in the business world. Whether or not such analyses are correct, the fact that clerical work enjoyed higher status does not seem to be in question. . . . [A]t least some working-class women saw clerical work not only as more prestigious, but even as a means of rising out of the working class itself. . . .

In *The Long Day: The Story of a New York Working Girl*, Dorothy Richardson also saw clerical work as a means of escaping the drudgery of working-class jobs. Her heroine started out in jobs that were typical of most turn-of-the-century working women: making artificial flowers or paper boxes and working first as a sales clerk and then as a demonstrator of a new brand of tea or coffee in a department store. Determined to better her position, she took a night-school course in stenography and studied English grammar and composition on her own. After having attained a typing speed of one hundred words a minute, she sought her first clerical job. It "paid me only six dollars a week, but it was an excellent training-school, and in it I learned self confidence, perfect accuracy, and rapidity. Although this position paid me two dollars less than what I had been earning brewing tea and coffee and handing it over the counter, and notwithstanding the fact that I knew of places where I could go and earn ten dollars a week, I chose to remain where I was." Armed with clerical experience, she then moved on to a fifteen-dollar-a-week stenographic position at a publishing house. It was at this point in her life that Richardson's heroine started writing and selling articles. Richardson's account shows not only that she considered clerical work to be a cut above other kinds of working-class jobs, but also that she believed that one could use office work as a means of moving from a purely working-class job to a higher position with some autonomy.

The number of women available to work in offices was also augmented by the decline of productive work in the home. For farm families, there was ample work both in the field and in the home to keep the various family members busy. In addition to all of the chores that accompanied farming itself, there was a lot of work that served to keep the family self-sufficient and relatively independent of the market. Even after rural Americans no longer performed such tasks as weaving cloth or making candles, which had been part of the normal household's work in the seventeenth and eighteenth centuries, much still remained. Vegetables and fruits were preserved, butter and cheese were made, some furniture was constructed from scratch, and almost everyone's clothes were handmade. In addition, the absence of running water, central heating, and electricity meant that water had to be carried from a well or pump, wood chopped to supply cooking and heating needs, and kerosene lamps filled and kept in good running order. There was plenty of work to keep parents and children occupied most of the time.

But with the move from country to city that was well under way by the end of the nineteenth century, productive work done in the home began to decrease. The same growth of industrialism that drew a labor force to the cities resulted in the mass production of consumer goods. Items that had been produced in the home were now available in stores. Canned goods, bakery bread, and readymade clothing gained gradual acceptance in more and more urban homes, despite the fact that a kitchen garden plot was a common feature of many urban dwellings into the twentieth century. Even more important changes, perhaps, were running water and indoor plumbing, central heating, and electrical wiring, all of which became standard features of more and more urban homes, beginning with those of the well-to-do.

The decrease of productive work in the home had its most dramatic effect on women. "Woman's place is in the home" made economic sense when there was plenty of work to be done. But as domestic work diminished, women who remained there began to lose their productive function in society. In fact, as [historian] Gerda Lerner has pointed out, one of the long-term developments of the nineteenth century was the elevation of this nonproductive function of women to a symbol of high status and wealth. The "lady" was living testament to her husband's or father's ability to earn money and to a relatively high place in the class structure.

A woman's ability to enjoy nonproductive leisure was determined, of course, by her family's economic position. Booth Tarkington's Alice Adams and her parents were anxious that she should enjoy just as much leisure and luxury as the town's bourgeois daughters.* A good example of the way Alice liked to spend her time is this account of her activities on the morning of a high-class dance given by one of the girls in town.

> "Where are you going?" [asked her mother.]
> "Oh, I've got lots to do. I thought I'd run out to Mildred's to see what she's going to wear tonight, and then I want to go down and buy a yard of chiffon and some narrow ribbon to make new bows for my slippers,—you'll have to give me some money."

Alice would have preferred to spend her time on such frivolous errands, but her family's financial straits sent her into the labor market, her hopes of rising into the bourgeoisie dashed. The relatively small amount of productive work done in the Adams home permitted the grown daughter to spend most of her time in leisure activities, at least for a while. And when Alice en-

---

*Booth Tarkington's novel *Alice Adams* was published in 1921. (Eds.)

tered the labor force, she was able to do so because her labor was not needed in the home.

During the period from 1870 to 1930, the number of occupations open to women was relatively limited. In general, women found employment in factory work of various kinds, in the smaller manufacturing concerns that employed sweated labor, behind the counter in retail stores, in domestic service, in nursing, in clerical work, in teaching, and to a very small degree in some of the higher-level professions. Manufacturing and other factory work, as well as domestic service, did not require literacy. And in positions where neither bills nor orders were written out, neither did retail selling. A literate woman who used her education in her work was restricted to a narrow range of occupational choices. Among these options, the better-paid were clerical work, teaching, and the various professions.

The teaching and professional positions that were open to women absorbed a small proportion of the female labor force. . . . In fact, teaching was the only occupation requiring literacy that in any way rivaled clerical work as an employer of women after the Civil War. . . . [T]eaching employed more women than did the clerical occupations until 1900, after which the number of female clerical workers rose so dramatically that teaching fell far behind. [Scholar] Elizabeth Baker argues that women may have preferred clerical work to teaching because of the severe restrictions placed on the personal and social life of teachers. Women teachers were not allowed to smoke, to drink, or, in some instances, to "keep company" with men. Those who married were often asked to leave their jobs. And sometimes "the new view of science and religion which they were bringing to the classroom from their college and university experience was opposed. Conditions such as these prompted many young girls to take up stenography instead of teaching when they graduated from high school; and it is not surprising that more than 100,000—a sixth of the teachers—were reported to have left the profession every year."

There is also some evidence that teachers were paid less than clerical workers. In 1912 the superintendent of schools in Council Bluffs, Iowa, argued that the student who completed the high school's business course was in a better economic position than the one who chose the classical course: "If a graduate of the classical course in the . . . high school had decided to teach in the public schools of the same city, under the most favorable circumstances possible[,] she could not have commenced teaching until one year after graduation. Her salary for the third year after graduation could not have been more than fifty dollars per month for nine months, or $450 per year. The average pupil (female) who graduated from the business department of the high school would have received for the same year an annual salary of slightly over $660. A male graduate of the same year would have received an annual salary of slightly over $840. You may judge for yourself of the economic efficiency from the standpoint of salary."

That women's low level of employment in the professions was due in part to outright discrimination is made clear by a study of women in government service published in 1920. It indicates that the federal government primarily hired women as clerical workers and goes on to demonstrate that the civil service examinations themselves (a prerequisite to government employment) discriminated against women and shunted them into clerical positions. . . .

Some of the very institutions where literacy skills were taught and polished led directly to clerical work. Both private commercial schools and the commercial track of public high schools trained girls and young women for clerical work. Commercial schools, where skills such as arithmetic, penmanship, and bookkeeping were taught, had been established in the United States by the 1840s and 1850s. Their doors were open to both men and women. Men were urged to obtain an education that would give them a solid start in their climb to success in the business world. Women were encouraged to apply their brains to pursuits other than gracing the domestic circle, or, in the case of working-class women, to aspire to jobs that would liberate them from the drudgery of the factory or sweatshop. In the latter half of the nineteenth century, such institutions were very successful. By 1890 there were over 80,000 students enrolled in commercial schools (by comparison enrollment in grades nine to twelve of public and private high schools totaled 298,000). Women made up only 4 percent of the 6,460 students enrolled in commercial schools in 1871, but they accounted for 32 percent of the 96,135 enrolled in 1894–95.

By the twentieth century, private business schools were being supplanted by other institutions. University business schools were offering training to aspiring capitalists and managers, while public high schools were initiating commercial education departments to teach clerical skills. By 1915 enrollment in the commercial courses of public high schools outstripped that in private commercial schools. In these high school courses girls predominated. In 1902–3 they already made up 54 percent of the total; in 1930 this had increased to 67 percent. It has been argued that public commercial education furthered the feminization of clerical work. Not only did the commercial courses provide clerical training for girls, but school guidance materials often funneled girls into commercial courses and advised them to plan for clerical jobs. . . .

For some women, participation in the labor force afforded psychological benefits such as increased independence and self-reliance. This, however, should not distract attention from the central fact of working-class life: most women worked because they had to.

DOCUMENTS

"Is Not Woman Destined to Conduct the Rising Generation?" 1844

One of the most extraordinary changes which have taken place in our schools, during the last seven years, consists in the great proportionate increase in the number of female teachers employed.

In 1837, the number of male teachers in all our public schools, including
summer and winter terms, was, ... 2370
Of females. 3591
In the school year 1843–4, it was,–males 2529
Females 4581
Increase in the number of male teachers 159
Increase in the number of female teachers 990
During the same time, the number of schools, in the State, has
increased only 418

This change in public sentiment, in regard to the employment of female teachers, I believe to be in accordance with the dictates of the soundest philosophy. Is not woman destined to conduct the rising generation, of both sexes, at least through all the primary stages of education? Has not the Author of nature preadapted her, by constitution, and faculty, and temperament, for this noble work? What station of beneficent labor can she aspire to, more honorable, or more congenial to every pure and generous impulse? In the great system of society, what other part can she act, so intimately connected with the refinement and purification of the race? How otherwise can she so well vindicate her right to an exalted station in the scale of being; and cause that shameful sentence of degradation by which she has so long been dishonored, to be repealed? Four-fifths of all the women who have ever lived, have been the slaves of man—the menials in his household, the drudges in his field, the instruments of his pleasure, or, at best, the gilded toys of his leisure days in court or palace. She has been outlawed from honorable service, and almost incapacitated, by her servile condition, for the highest aspirations after usefulness and renown. But a noble revenge awaits her. By a manifestation of the superiority of moral power, she can triumph over that physical power which has hitherto subjected her to bondage. She can bless those by whom she has

SOURCE: Horace Mann, "Eighth Annual Report of the Secretary of the Board of Education (1844)," In Life and Words of Horace Mann, vol. 3, ed. Mary Mann (Boston, 1891), 426–29.

been wronged. By refining the tastes and sentiments of man, she can change the objects of his ambition; and, with changed objects of ambition, the fields of honorable exertion can be divided between the sexes. By inspiring nobler desires for nobler objects, she can break down the ascendency of those selfish motives that have sought their gratification in her submission and inferiority. All this she can do, more rapidly, and more effectually than it can ever be done in any other way, unless through miracles, by training the young to juster notions of honor and duty, and to a higher appreciation of the true dignity and destiny of the race.

The more extensive employment of females for educating the young, will be the addition of a new and mighty power to the forces of civilization. It is a power, also, which, heretofore, to a very great extent, has been unappropriated; which has been allowed, in the administration of the affairs of men, to run to waste. Hence it will be an addition to one of the grandest spheres of human usefulness, without any subtraction from other departments—a gain without a loss. For all females—the great majority—who are destined, in the course of Providence, to sustain maternal relations, no occupation or apprenticeship can be so serviceable; but, in this connection, it is not unworthy of notice, that, according to the census of Massachusetts, there are almost eight thousand more females than males belonging to the State.

But if a female is to assume the performance of a teacher's duties, she must be endowed with high qualifications. If devoid of mental superiority, then she inevitably falls back into that barbarian relation, where physical strength measures itself against physical strength. In that contest, she can never hope to succeed; or, if she succeeds, it will be only as an Amazon, and not as a personification of moral power. Opportunities, therefore, should be everywhere opened for the fit qualification of female teachers; and all females possessing in an eminent degree, the appropriate natural endowments, should be encouraged to qualify themselves for this sacred work. Those who have worthily improved such opportunities, should be rewarded with social distinction and generous emoluments. Society cannot do less than this, on its own account, for those who are improving its condition; though for the actors themselves, in this beneficent work, the highest rewards must forever remain where God and nature have irrevocably placed them—in the consciousness of well-doing.

Could public opinion, on this one subject, be rectified, and brought into harmony with the great law of Christian duty and love, there are thousands of females amongst us, who now spend lives of frivolity, of unbroken wearisomeness and worthlessness, who would rejoice to exchange their days of painful idleness for such ennobling occupations; and who, in addition to the immediate rewards of well-doing, would see, in the distant prospect, the consolations of a life well spent, instead of the pangs of remorse for a frivolous and wasted existence.

Only Heroic Women Were
Doctors Then (1865), 1916

Changes in the position of women in the world in the last fifty years were emphasized by Dr. Anna Manning Comfort, graduate of the New York Medical College and Hospital for Women in its first class in 1865, at a luncheon in her honor, given by the Faculty and Trustees of the college at Delmonico's yesterday. Dr. Comfort was graduated at the age of 20, and she is only in the early seventies, alert and well preserved, though she has had a vigorous career, has been married, and is the mother of three children.

"Students of today have no idea of conditions as they were when I studied medicine," said Dr. Comfort. "It is difficult to realize the changes that have taken place. I attended the first meeting when this institution was proposed, and was graduated from the first class. We had to go to Bellevue Hospital for our practical work, and the indignities we were made to suffer are beyond belief. There were 500 young men students taking post-graduate courses, and we were jeered at and catcalled, and the 'old war horses,' the doctors, joined the younger men.

"We were considered aggressive. They said women did not have the same brains as men and were not trustworthy. All the work at the hospital was made as repulsively unpleasant for us as possible. There were originally six in the class, but all but two were unable to put up with the treatment to which we were subjected and dropped out. I trembled whenever I went to the hospital and I said once that I could not bear it. Finally the women went to the authorities, who said that if we were not respectfully treated they would take the charter from the hospital!

"As a physician there was nothing that I could do that satisfied people. If I wore square-toed shoes and swung my arms they said I was mannish, and if I carried a parasol and wore a ribbon in my hair they said I was too feminine. If I smiled they said I had too much levity, and if I sighed they said I had no sand.

"They tore down my sign when I began to practice, the drug stores did not like to fill my prescriptions, and the older doctors would not consult with me. But that little band of women made it possible for the other women who have come later into the field to do their work. When my first patients came and saw me they said I was too young, and they asked in horrified tones if I had studied dissecting just like the men. They were shocked at that, but they were more shocked when my bills were sent in to find that I charged as much as a man.

"I believe in women entering professions," said Dr. Comfort, "but I also believe in motherhood. For the normal woman it is no more of a tax to have

SOURCE: "Only Heroic Women Were Doctors Then," *The New York Times,* 9 April 1916.

a profession as well as family life than it is for a man to carry on the multi-tudinous duties he has outside the family. I had three sons of my own and two adopted ones, and I am as proud of my motherhood as of my medical career. I gave as much of my personality to my children in an hour as some mothers do in ten. My children honored me and have been worth while in the world."

There were many expressions of esteem for Dr. Comfort and she was overcome when it was announced that money had been raised for an Anna Manning Comfort scholarship in the hospital.

Letters of regret were read from John Burroughs and Colonel Theodore Roosevelt among others.

"I believe in women in the medical profession, and in politics, and in all worthy pursuits," said John Burroughs.

"I am amazed to learn that this is the only institution in this State, and one of two in the United States, exclusively for the woman medical student," said Colonel Roosevelt. "There should be others and women of refinement would be drawn into the profession who will not study medicine in a co-educational college, and more women doctors are needed."

Dr. Walter G. Crump, who spoke of the need for medical colleges exclusively for women, said:

"We learn from the [1910] Flexner report that there is an overproduction of doctors, but nine out of ten of the women doctors practice. There are demands continually for women physicians which cannot be filled. They are needed in many places where women and girls are to be under a physician's care."

Dr. Mary A. Brinkman, who was one of the early graduates of the college, spoke. She said she could corroborate many of the things told by Dr. Comfort. . . .

Women's Separate Sphere, 1872

The claim of the plaintiff, who is a married woman, to be admitted to practice as an attorney and counsellor-at-law, is based upon the supposed right of every person, man or woman, to engage in any lawful employment for a livelihood. The Supreme Court of Illinois denied the application on the ground that, by the common law, which is the basis of the laws of Illinois, only men were admitted to the bar, and the legislature had not made any change in this respect, but had simply provided that no person should be admitted to practice as attorney or counsellor without having previously obtained a license for that purpose from two justices of the Supreme Court,

SOURCE: Justice Bradley's majority opinion in *Bradwell* v. *Illinois* (December 1872).

and that no person should receive a license without first obtaining a certificate from the court of some county of his good moral character. In other respects it was left to the discretion of the court to establish the rules by which admission to the profession should be determined. The court, however, regarded itself as bound by at least two limitations. One was that it should establish such terms of admission as would promote the proper administration of justice, and the other that it should not admit any persons, or class of persons, not intended by the legislature to be admitted, even though not expressly excluded by statute. In view of this latter limitation the court felt compelled to deny the application of females to be admitted as members of the bar. Being contrary to the rules of the common law and the usages of Westminster Hall* from time immemorial, it could not be supposed that the legislature had intended to adopt any different rule.

The claim that, under the fourteenth amendment of the Constitution, which declares that no State shall make or enforce any law which shall abridge the privileges and immunities of citizens of the United States, the statute law of Illinois, or the common law prevailing in that State, can no longer be set up as a barrier against the right of females to pursue any lawful employment for a livelihood (the practice of law included), assumes that it is one of the privileges and immunities of women as citizens to engage in any and every profession, occupation, or employment in civil life.

It certainly cannot be affirmed, as an historical fact, that this has ever been established as one of the fundamental privileges and immunities of the sex. On the contrary, the civil law, as well as nature herself, has always recognized a wide difference in the respective spheres and destinies of man and woman. Man is, or should be, woman's protector and defender. The natural and proper timidity and delicacy which belongs to the female sex evidently unfits it for many of the occupations of civil life. The constitution of the family organization, which is founded in the divine ordinance, as well as in the nature of things, indicates the domestic sphere as that which properly belongs to the domain and functions of womanhood. The harmony, not to say identity, of interests and views which belong, or should belong, to the family institution is repugnant to the idea of a woman adopting a distinct and independent career from that of her husband. So firmly fixed was this sentiment in the founders of the common law that it became a maxim of that system of jurisprudence that a woman had no legal existence separate from her husband, who was regarded as her head and representative in the social state; and, notwithstanding some recent modifications of this civil status, many of the special rules of law flowing from and dependent upon this cardinal principle still exist in full force in most States. One of these is, that a married woman is incapable, without her husband's con-

---

*Westminster Hall was the ancient seat of English law, established in the twelfth century. (Eds.)

sent, of making contracts which shall be binding on her or him. This very incapacity was one circumstance which the Supreme Court of Illinois deemed important in rendering a married woman incompetent fully to perform the duties and trusts that belong to the office of an attorney and counsellor.

It is true that many women are unmarried and not affected by any of the duties, complications, and incapacities arising out of the married state, but these are exceptions to the general rule. The paramount destiny and mission of woman are to fulfil the noble and benign offices of wife and mother. This is the law of the Creator. And the rules of civil society must be adapted to the general constitution of things, and cannot be based upon exceptional cases.

The humane movements of modern society, which have for their object the multiplication of avenues for woman's advancement, and of occupations adapted to her condition and sex, have my heartiest concurrence. But I am not prepared to say that it is one of her fundamental rights and privileges to be admitted into every office and position, including those which require highly special qualifications and demanding special responsibilities. In the nature of things it is not every citizen of every age, sex, and condition that is qualified for every calling and position. It is the prerogative of the legislator to prescribe regulations founded on nature, reason, and experience for the due admission of qualified persons to professions and callings demanding special skill and confidence. This fairly belongs to the police power of the State; and, in my opinion, in view of the peculiar characteristics, destiny, and mission of woman, it is within the province of the legislature to ordain what offices, positions, and callings shall be filled and discharged by men, and shall receive the benefit of those energies and responsibilities, and that decision and firmness which are presumed to predominate in the sterner sex.

For these reasons I think that the laws of Illinois now complained of are not obnoxious to the charge of abridging any of the privileges and immunities of citizens of the United States.

Chapter 5

Life and Labor in Industrial America

By the close of the nineteenth century, the benefits of industrialization had grown apparent. The United States had become a wealthy and powerful nation, a leader among the countries of the world. But it paid a price for this growth in terms of human suffering, a price that was only beginning to be realized. Working conditions were often abysmal; immigrant families engaged in cigar manufacturing, for example, both lived and labored in overcrowded, foul-smelling tenements. Factories and mines were designed with minimal concern for worker health and safety. Workers toiled long days at bare-subsistence wages, with virtually no compensation benefits or legal safeguards.

Bonnie Mitelman's article "Rose Schneiderman and the Triangle Fire" describes one of the most horrible examples of the consequences of such conditions. Although it focuses primarily on the tragedy of an industrial fire, the article also offers insights into working conditions in the garment industry, the attitudes of management toward their employees and workers toward their unions, and the circumstances that finally spurred public support and government action for workplace reform.

The first two documents illustrate that the hazards of the workplace were by no means restricted to the Greenwich Village garment district, but also included the tenement workshops of New York City and the coal mines of Pennsylvania. What attitude is reflected in the miner's statement, "We are American citizens and we don't go to hospitals and poorhouses"?

If working conditions were so bad here, why did so many immigrants come to America from Europe? We might find one answer in the third document, the story of Rocco Corresca, a poor Italian immigrant. What does his description of his first days in the United States indicate about the hardships experienced by the new-comers? In the end, what was the consequence of Rocco's success in America?

ESSAY

—————— •◆• ——————

Rose Schneiderman and the Triangle Fire

Bonnie Mitelman

On Saturday afternoon, March 25, 1911, in New York City's Greenwich Village, a small fire broke out in the Triangle Waist Company, just as the 500 shirtwaist employees were quitting for the day. People rushed about, trying to get out, but they found exits blocked and windows to the fire escape rusted shut. They panicked.

As the fire spread and more and more were trapped, some began to jump, their hair and clothing afire, from the eighth and ninth floor windows. Nets that firemen held for them tore apart at the impact of the falling bodies. By the time it was over, 146 workers had died, most of them young Jewish women.

A United Press reporter, William Shepherd, witnessed the tragedy and reported, "I looked upon the heap of dead bodies and I remembered these girls were the shirtwaist makers. I remembered their great strike of last year in which these same girls had demanded more sanitary conditions and more safety precautions in the shops. These dead bodies were the answer."

The horror of that fire touched the entire Lower East Side ghetto community, and there was a profuse outpouring of sympathy. But it was Rose Schneiderman, an immigrant worker with a spirit of social justice and a powerful way with words, who is largely credited with translating the ghetto's emotional reaction into meaningful, widespread action. Six weeks following the tragedy, and after years of solid groundwork, with one brilliant, well-timed speech, she was able to inspire the support of wealthy uptown New Yorkers and to swing public opinion to the side of the labor

SOURCE: Bonnie Mitelman, "Rose Schneiderman and the Triangle Fire," *American History Illustrated* 16 (July 1981): 38–47. Reprinted through courtesy of Cowles Magazines, publisher of *American History Illustrated.*

movement, enabling concerned civic, religious, and labor leaders to mobilize their efforts for desperately needed safety and industrial reforms.

The Triangle fire, and the deaths of so many helpless workers, seemed to trigger in Rose Schneiderman an intense realization that there was absolutely nothing or no one to help working women except a strong union movement. With fierce determination, and the dedication, influence, and funding of many other people as well, she battled to regulate hours, wages, and safety standards and to abolish the sweatshop system. In so doing, she brought dignity and human rights to all workers.

The dramatic "uprising of the 20,000" of 1909–10, in which thousands of immigrant girls and women in the shirtwaist industry had endured three long winter months of a general strike to protest deplorable working conditions, had produced some immediate gains for working women. There had been agreements for shorter working hours, increased wages, and even safety reforms, but there had not been formal recognition of their union. At Triangle, for example, the girls had gained a 52 hour week, a 12–15 percent wage increase, and promises to end the grueling subcontracting system. But they had not gained the only instrument on which they could depend for lasting change: a viable trade union. This was to have disastrous results, for in spite of the few gains that they seemed to have made, the workers won no rights or bargaining power at all. In fact, "The company dealt only with its contractors. It felt no responsibility for the girls."

There were groups as well as individuals who realized the workers' impotence, but their attempts to change the situation accomplished little despite long years of hard work. The Women's Trade Union League [WTUL] and the International Ladies' Garment Workers' Union, through the efforts of Mary Dreier, Helen Marot, Leonora O'Reilly, Pauline Newman, and Rose Schneiderman, had struggled unsuccessfully for improved conditions: the futility that the union organizers were feeling in late 1910 is reflected in the WTUL minutes of December 5 of that year.

A scant eight months after their historic waistmakers' strike, and three months before the deadly Triangle fire, a Mrs. Malkiel (no doubt Theresa Serber Malkiel, who wrote the legendary account of the strike, *The Diary of a Shirtwaist Striker: A Story of the Shirtwaist Makers' Strike in New York)* is reported to have come before the League to urge action after a devastating fire in Newark, New Jersey, killed twenty-five working women. Mrs. Malkiel attributed their loss to the greed and negligence of the owners and the proper authorities. The WTUL subsequently demanded an investigation of all factory buildings and it elected an investigation committee from the League to cooperate with similar committees from other organizations.

The files of the WTUL contain complaint after complaint about unsafe factory conditions; many were filled out by workers afraid to sign their names for fear of being fired had their employers seen the forms. They describe factories with locked doors, no fire escapes, and barred windows. *The*

New York Times carried an article which reported that fourteen factories were found to have no fire escapes, twenty-three that had locked doors, and seventy-eight that had obstructed fire escapes. In all, according to the article, 99 percent of the factories investigated in New York were found to have serious fire hazards.

Yet no action was taken.

It was the Triangle fire that emphasized, spectacularly and tragically, the deplorable safety and sanitary conditions of the garment workers. The tragedy focused attention upon the ghastly factories in which most immigrants worked; there was no longer any question about what the strikers had meant when they talked about safety and sanitary reform, and about social and economic justice.

The grief and frustration of the shirtwaist strikers were expressed by one of them, Rose Safran, after the fire: "If the union had won we would have been safe. Two of our demands were for adequate fire escapes and for open doors from the factories to the street. But the bosses defeated us and we didn't get the open doors or the better fire escapes. So our friends are dead."

The families of the fire victims were heartbroken and hysterical, the ghetto's *Jewish Daily Forward* was understandably melodramatic, and the immigrant community was completely enraged. Their Jewish heritage had taught them an emphasis on individual human life and worth; their shared background in the *shtetl* [Jewish village in Eastern Europe] and common experiences in the ghetto had given them a sense of fellowship. They were, in a sense, a family—and some of the most helpless among them had died needlessly.

The senseless deaths of so many young Jewish women sparked within these Eastern Europeans a new determination and dedication. The fire had made reform absolutely essential. Workers' rights were no longer just socialist jargon: They were a matter of life and death.

The Triangle Waist Company was located on the three floors of the Asch Building, a 10-story, 135-foot-high structure at the corner of Greene Street and Washington Place in Greenwich Village. One of the largest shirtwaist manufacturers, Triangle employed up to 900 people at times, but on the day of the fire, only about 500 were working.

Leon Stein's brilliant and fascinating account of the fire, entitled simply *The Triangle Fire*, develops and documents the way in which the physical facilities, company procedures, and human behavior interacted to cause this great tragedy. Much of what occurred was ironic, some was cruel, some stupid, some pathetic. It is a dramatic portrayal of the eternal confrontation of the "haves" and the "have-nots," told in large part by those who survived.

Fire broke out at the Triangle Company at approximately 4:45 P.M. (because time clocks were reportedly set back to stretch the day, and because other records give differing times of the first fire alarm, it is uncertain exactly what time the fire started), just after pay envelopes had been distributed and employees were leaving their work posts. It was a small fire at first, and there was a calm, controlled effort to extinguish it. But the fire began to spread, jumping from one pile of debris to another, engulfing the combustible shirtwaist fabric. It became obvious that the fire could not be snuffed out, and workers tried to reach the elevators or stairway. Those who reached the one open stairway raced down eight flights of stairs to safety; those who managed to climb onto the available passenger elevators also got out. But not everyone could reach the available exits. Some tried to open the door to a stairway and found it locked. Others were trapped between long working tables or behind the hordes of people trying to get into the elevators or out through the one open door.

Under the work tables, rags were burning; the wooden floors, trim, and window frames were also afire. Frantically, workers fought their way to the elevators, to the fire escape, and to the windows—to any place that might lead to safety.

Fire whistles and bells sounded as the fire department raced to the building. But equipment proved inadequate, as the fire ladders reached only to the seventh floor. And by the time the firemen connected their hoses to douse the flames, the crowded eighth floor was completely ablaze.

For those who reached the windows, there seemed to be a chance for safety. The *New York World* describes people balancing on window sills, nine stories up, with flames scorching them from behind, until firemen arrived: "The nets were spread below with all promptness. Citizens were commandeered into service, as the firemen necessarily gave their attention to the one engine and hose of the force that first arrived. The catapult force that the bodies gathered in the long plunges made the nets utterly without avail. Screaming girls and men, as they fell, tore the nets from the grasp of the holders, and the bodies struck the sidewalks and lay just as they fell. Some of the bodies ripped big holes through the life nets."

One reporter who witnessed the fire remembered how,

> A young man helped a girl to the window sill on the ninth floor. Then he held her out deliberately, away from the building, and let her drop. He held out a second girl the same way and let her drop. He held out a third girl who did not resist. They were all as unresisting as if he were helping them into a street car instead of into eternity. He saw that a terrible death awaited them in the flames and his was only a terrible chivalry. He brought around another girl to the window. I saw her put her arms around him and kiss him. Then he held her into space—and dropped her. Quick as a flash, he was on the window sill himself. His coat fluttered upwards—the air filled his trouser legs as he came down. I could see he wore tan shoes.

Those who had rushed to the fire escape found the window openings rusted shut. Several precious minutes were lost in releasing them. The fire escape itself ended at the second floor, in an airshaft between the Asch Building and the building next door. But too frantic to notice where it ended, workers climbed onto the fire escape, one after another until, in one terrifying moment, it collapsed from the weight, pitching the workers to their death.

Those who had made their way to the elevators found crowds pushing to get into the cars. When it became obvious that the elevators could no longer run, workers jumped down the elevator shaft, landing on the top of the cars, or grabbing for cables to ease their descent. Several died, but incredibly, some did manage to save themselves in this way. One man was found, hours after the fire, beneath an elevator car in the basement of the building, nearly drowned by the rapidly rising water from the firemen's hoses.

Several people, among them Triangle's two owners, raced to the roof, and from there were led to safety. Others never had that chance. "When Fire Chief Croker could make his way into the [top] three floors," states one account of the fire, "he found sights that utterly staggered him. . . . He saw as the smoke drifted away bodies burned to bare bones. There were skeletons bending over sewing machines."

The day after the fire, *The New York Times* announced that "the building was fireproof. It shows hardly any signs of the disaster that overtook it. The walls are as good as ever, as are the floors: nothing is worse for the fire except the furniture and 141 [*sic*] of the 600 men and girls that were employed in its upper three stories."

The building *was* fireproof. But there had never been a fire drill in the factory, even though the management had been warned about the possible hazard of fire on the top three floors. Owners Max Blanck and Isaac Harris had chosen to ignore these warnings in spite of the fact that many of their employees were immigrants who could barely speak English, which would surely mean panic in the event of a crisis.

The New York Times also noted that Leonora O'Reilly of the League had reported Max Blanck's visit to the WTUL during the shirtwaist strike, and his plea that the girls return to work. He claimed a business reputation to maintain and told the Union leaders he would make the necessary improvements right away. Because he was the largest manufacturer in the business, the League reported, they trusted him and let the girls return.

But the improvements were never made. And there was nothing that anybody could or would do about it. Factory doors continued to open in instead of out, in violation of fire regulations. The doors remained bolted during working hours, apparently to prevent workers from getting past the inspectors with stolen merchandise. Triangle had only two staircases where there should have been three, and those two were very narrow. Despite the fact that the building was deemed fireproof, it had wooden window frames, floors, and trim. There was no sprinkler system. It was not legally required.

These were the same kinds of conditions which existed in factories throughout the garment industry; they had been cited repeatedly in the complaints filed with the WTUL. They were not unusual nor restricted to Triangle; in fact, Triangle was not as bad as many other factories.

But it was at Triangle that the fire took place.

The *Jewish Daily Forward* mourned the dead with sorrowful stories, and its headlines talked of "funerals instead of weddings" for the dead young girls. The entire Jewish immigrant community was affected, for it seemed there was scarcely a person who was not in some way touched by the fire. Nearly everyone had either been employed at Triangle themselves, or had a friend or relative who had worked there at some time or another. Most worked in factories with similar conditions, and so everyone identified with the victims and their families.

Many of the dead, burned beyond recognition, remained unidentified for days, as searching family members returned again and again to wait in long lines to look for their loved ones. Many survivors were unable to identify their mothers, sisters, or wives; the confusion of handling so many victims and so many survivors who did not understand what was happening to them and to their dead led to even more anguish for the community. Some of the victims were identified by the names on the pay envelopes handed to them at quitting time and stuffed deeply into pockets or stockings just before the fire. But many bodies remained unclaimed for days, with bewildered and bereaved survivors wandering among them, trying to find some identifying mark.

Charges of first- and second-degree manslaughter were brought against the two men who owned Triangle, and Leon Stein's book artfully depicts the subtle psychological and sociological implications of the powerful against the oppressed, and of the Westernized, German-Jewish immigrants against those still living their old-world, Eastern European heritage. Ultimately, Triangle owners Blanck and Harris were acquitted of the charges against them, and in due time they collected their rather sizable insurance.

The shirtwaist, popularized by Gibson girls, had come to represent the new-found freedom of females in America. After the fire, it symbolized death. The reaction of the grief-stricken Lower East Side was articulated by socialist lawyer Morris Hillquit:

The girls who went on strike last year were trying to readjust the conditions under which they were obliged to work. I wonder if there is not some connection between the fire and that strike. I wonder if the magistrates who sent to jail the girls who did picket duty in front of the Triangle shop realized last Sunday that some of the responsibility may be theirs. Had the strike been successful, these girls might have been alive today and the citizenry of New York would have less of a burden upon its conscience.

For the first time in the history of New York's garment industry there were indications that the public was beginning to accept responsibility for the exploitation of the immigrants. For the first time, the establishment seemed to understand that these were human beings asking for their rights, not merely troublemaking anarchists.

The day after the Triangle fire a protest meeting was held at the Women's Trade Union League, with representatives from twenty leading labor and civic organizations. They formed "a relief committee to cooperate with the Red Cross in its work among the families of the victims, and another committee . . . to broaden the investigation and research on fire hazards in New York factories which was already being carried on by the League."

The minutes of the League recount the deep indignation that members felt at the indifference of a public which had ignored their pleas for safety after the Newark fire. In an attempt to translate their anger into constructive action, the League drew up a list of forceful resolutions that included a plan to gather delegates from all of the city's unions to make a concerted effort to force safety changes in factories. In addition, the League called upon all workers to inspect factories and then report any violations to the proper city authorities and to the WTUL. They called upon the city to immediately appoint organized workers as unofficial inspectors. They resolved to submit the following fire regulations suggestions: compulsory fire drills, fireproof exits, unlocked doors, fire alarms, automatic sprinklers, and regular inspections. The League called upon the legislature to create the Bureau of Fire Protection and finally, the League underscored the absolute need for all workers to organize themselves at once into trade unions so that they would never again be powerless.

The League also voted to participate in the funeral procession for the unidentified dead of the Triangle fire.

The city held a funeral for the dead who were unclaimed. "More than 120,000 of us were in the funeral procession that miserable rainy April day," remembered Rose Schneiderman. "From ten in the morning until four in the afternoon we of the Women's Trade Union League marched in the procession with other trade-union men and women, all of us filled with anguish and regret that we had never been able to organize the Triangle workers."

Schneiderman, along with many others, was absolutely determined that this kind of tragedy would never happen again. With single-minded dedication, they devoted themselves to unionizing the workers. The searing example of the Triangle fire provided them with the impetus they needed to gain public support for their efforts.

They dramatized and emphasized and capitalized on the scandalous working conditions of the immigrants. From all segments of the community came cries for labor reform. Stephen S. Wise, the prestigious reform rabbi, called for the formation of a citizens' committee. Jacob H. Schiff, Bishop David H. Greer, Governor John A. Dix, Anne Morgan (of *the* Morgans) and other leading civic and religious leaders collaborated in a mass meeting at the Metropolitan Opera House on May 2 to protest factory conditions and to show support for the workers.

Several people spoke at that meeting on May 2, and many in the audience began to grow restless and antagonistic. Finally, 29-year-old Rose Schneiderman stepped up to the podium.

In a whisper barely audible, she began to address the crowd.

I would be a traitor to these poor burned bodies, if I came here to talk good fellowship. We have tried you good people of the public and we have found you wanting. The old Inquisition had its rack and its thumbscrews and its instruments of torture with iron teeth. We know what these things are today: the iron teeth are our necessities, the thumbscrews the high-powered and swift machinery close to which we must work, and the rack is here in the fire-proof structures that will destroy us the minute they catch on fire.

This is not the first time girls have burned alive in the city. Every week I must learn of the untimely death of one of my sister workers. Every year thousands of us are maimed. The life of men and women is so cheap and property is so sacred. There are so many of us for one job it matters little if 140-odd are burned to death.

We have tried you, citizens; we are trying you now, and you have a couple of dollars for the sorrowing mothers and daughters and sisters by way of a charity gift. But every time the workers come out in the only way they know to protest against conditions which are unbearable, the strong hand of the law is allowed to press down heavily upon us.

Public officials have only words of warning to us—warning that we must be intensely orderly and must be intensely peaceable, and they have the workhouse just back of all their warnings. The strong hand of the law beats us back when we rise into the conditions that make life bearable.

I can't talk fellowship to you who are gathered here. Too much blood has been spilled. I know from my experience it is up to the working people to save themselves. The only way they can save themselves is by a strong working-class movement.

Her speech has become a classic. It is more than just an emotional picture of persecution; it reflects the pervasive sadness and profound understanding that comes from knowing, finally, the cruel realities of life, the perspective of history, and the nature of human beings.

The devastation of that fire and the futility of the seemingly successful strike that had preceded it seemed to impart an undeniable truth to Rose Schneiderman: They could not fail again. The events of 1911 seemed to have made her, and many others, more keenly aware than they had ever been that the workers' fight for reform was absolutely essential. If they did not do it, it would not be done.

In a sense, the fire touched off in Schneiderman an awareness of her own responsibility in the battle for industrial reform. This fiery socialist worker had been transformed into a highly effective labor leader.

The influential speech she gave did help swing public opinion to the side of the trade unions, and the fire itself had made the workers more aware of the crucial need to unionize. Widespread support for labor reform and unionization emerged. Pressure from individuals, such as Rose Schneiderman, as well as from groups like the Women's Trade Union League and the International Ladies' Garment Workers' Union, helped form the New York State Factory Investigating Commission, the New York Citizens' Committee on Safety, and other regulatory and investigatory bodies. The League and Local 25 (the Shirtwaist Makers' Union of the ILGWU) were especially instrumental in attaining a new Industrial Code for New York State, which became "the most outstanding instrument for safeguarding the lives, health, and welfare of the millions of wage earners in New York State and . . . in the nation at large."

It took years for these changes to occur, and labor reform did not rise majestically, Phoenix-like, from the ashes of the Triangle fire. But that fire, and Rose Schneiderman's whispered plea for a strong working-class movement, had indeed become the loud clear call for action.

DOCUMENTS

Tenement Cigarmakers, c. 1890

Take a row of houses in East Tenth Street. . . . They contained thirty-five families of cigarmakers, with probably not half a dozen persons in the whole lot of them, outside of the children, who could speak a word of English, though many had been in the country half a lifetime. This room with two windows giving on the street, and a rear attachment without windows, called a bedroom by courtesy, is rented at $12.25 a month. In the front room[,] man and wife work at the bench from six in the morning till nine at night. They make a team, stripping the tobacco leaves together; then he

SOURCE: Jacob Riis, *How the Other Half Lives* (New York: Scribner's, 1903), 103–108.

makes the filler, and she rolls the wrapper on and finishes the cigar. For a thousand they receive $3.75, and can turn out together three thousand cigars a week. The point has been reached where the rebellion comes in, and the workers in these tenements are just now on a strike, demanding $5.00 and $5.50 for their work. The manufacturer having refused, they are expecting hourly to be served with notice to quit their homes, and the going of a stranger among them excites their resentment, until his errand is explained. While we are in the house, the ultimatum of the "boss" is received. He will give $3.75 a thousand, not another cent. Our host is a man of seeming intelligence, yet he has been nine years in New York and knows neither English nor German. Three bright little children play about the floor.

His neighbor on the same floor has been here fifteen years, but shakes his head when asked if he can speak English. He answers in a few broken syllables when addressed in German. With $11.75 rent to pay for like accommodation, he has the advantage of his oldest boy's work besides his wife's at the bench. Three properly make a team, and these three can turn out four thousand cigars a week, at $3.75. This Bohemian has a large family; there are four children, too small to work, to be cared for.... [T]his Bohemian's butcher's bill for the week, with meat at twelve cents a pound ... is from two dollars and a half to three dollars.... Here is a suite of three rooms, two dark, three flights up. The ceiling is partly down in one of the rooms. "It is three months since we asked the landlord to fix it," says the oldest son, a very intelligent lad who has learned English in the evening school. His father has not had that advantage, and has sat at his bench, deaf and dumb to the world about him except his own, for six years. He has improved his time and become an expert at his trade. Father, mother, and son together, a full team, make from fifteen to sixteen dollars a week....

Probably more than half of all the Bohemians in this city are cigarmakers, and it is the herding of these in great numbers in the so-called tenement factories, where the cheapest grade of work is done at the lowest wages, that constitutes at once their greatest hardship and the chief grudge of other workmen against them....

Men, women and children work together seven days in the week in these cheerless tenements to make a living for the family, from the break of day till far into the night. Often the wife is the original cigarmaker from the old home, the husband having adopted her trade here as a matter of necessity, because, knowing no word of English, he could get no other work. As they state the cause of the bitter hostility of the trades unions, she was the primary bone of contention in the day of the early Bohemian immigration. The unions refused to admit the women, and, as the support of the family depended upon her to a large extent, such terms as were offered had to be accepted. The manufacturer has ever since industriously fanned the antagonism between the unions and his hands, for his own advantage. The victory rests with him, since the Court of Appeals decided that the law, passed a few years ago, to prohibit cigarmaking in tenements was unconstitutional, and thus put an end to the struggle. While it lasted, all sorts of frightful stories were told of the shocking conditions under which people lived and worked in these tenements, from a sanitary point of view especially, and a general impression survives to this day that they are particularly desperate. The Board of Health, after a careful canvass, did not find them so then. I am satisfied from personal inspection, at a much later day, guided in a number of instances by the union cigarmakers themselves to the tenements which they considered the worst, that the accounts were greatly exaggerated. Doubtless the people are poor, in many cases very poor; but they are not uncleanly, rather the reverse; they live much better than the clothing-makers in the Tenth Ward, . . .

"Our Daily Life Is Not a Pleasant One," 1902

I am thirty-five years old, married, the father of four children, and have lived in the coal region all my life. Twenty-three of these years have been spent working in and around the mines. My father was a miner. He died ten years ago from "miners' asthma [black lung disease]."

Three of my brothers are miners; none of us had any opportunities to acquire an education. We were sent to school (such a school as there was in those days) until we were about twelve years of age, and then we were put into the screen room of a breaker to pick slate. From there we went inside the mines as driver boys. As we grew stronger we were taken on as laborers, where we served until able to call ourselves miners. We were given work in the breasts and gangways. There were five of us boys. One lies in the cemetery—fifty tons of top rock dropped on him. He was killed three weeks after he got his job as a miner—a month before he was to be married.

In the fifteen years I have worked as a miner I have earned the average rate of wages any of us coal heavers get. To-day I am little better off than when I started to do for myself. I have $100 on hand; I am not in debt; I hope to be able to weather the strike without going hungry.

I am only one of the hundreds you see on the street every day. The muscles on my arms are no harder, the callous on my palms no deeper than my neighbor's whose entire life has been spent in the coal region. By years I am only thirty-five. But look at the marks on my body; look at the lines of worriment on my forehead; see the gray hairs on my head and in my mustache; take my general appearance, and you'll think I'm ten years older.

SOURCE: *Independent* 54 (June 12, 1902): 1407–1410.

You need not wonder why. Day in and day out, from Monday morning to Saturday evening, between the rising and the setting of the sun, I am in the underground workings of the coal mines. From the seams water trickles into the ditches along the gangways; if not water, it is the gas which hurls us to eternity and the props and timbers to a chaos.

Our daily life is not a pleasant one. When we put on our oil soaked suit in the morning we can't guess all the dangers which threaten our lives. We walk sometimes miles to the place—to the main way or traveling way, or to the mouth of the shaft on top of the slope. And then we enter the darkened chambers of the mines. On our right and on our left we see the logs that keep up the top and support the sides which may crush us into shapeless masses, as they have done to many of our comrades.

We get old quickly. Powder, smoke, after-damp, bad air—all combine to bring furrows to our faces and asthma to our lungs.

I did not strike because I wanted to; I struck because I had to. A miner— the same as any other workman—must earn fair living wages, or he can't live. And it is not how much you get that counts. It is how much what you get will buy. I have gone through it all, and I think my case is a good sample.

I was married in 1890, when I was 23 years old—quite a bit above the age when we miner boys get into double harness [married]. The woman I married is like myself. She was born beneath the shadow of a dirt bank; her chances for school weren't any better than mine; but she did have to learn how to keep house on a certain amount of money. After we paid the preacher for tying the knot we had just $185 in cash, good health and the good wishes of many friends to start us off.

Our cash was exhausted in buying furniture for housekeeping. In 1890 work was not so plentiful, and by the time our first baby came there was room for much doubt as to how we would pull out. Low wages, and not much over half time in those years, made us hustle. In 1890–91, from June to May, I earned $368.72. That represented eleven months' work, or an average of $33.52 per month. Our rent was $10 per month; store not less than $20. And then I had my oil suits and gum boots to pay for. The result was that after the first year and a half of our married life we were in debt. Not much, of course, and not as much as many of my neighbors, men of larger families, and some who made less money, or in whose case there had been sickness or accident or death. These are all things which a miner must provide for.

I have had fairly good work since I was married. I made the average of what we contract miners are paid; but, as I said before, I am not much better off than when I started.

In 1896 my wife was sick eleven weeks. The doctor came to my house almost every day. He charged me $20 for his services. There was medicine to buy. I paid the drug store $18 in that time. Her mother nursed her, and we kept a girl in the kitchen at $1.50 a week, which cost me $15 for ten weeks, besides the additional living expenses.

In 1897, just a year afterward, I had a severer trial. And mind, in those years, we were only working about half time. But in the fall of that year one of my brothers struck a gas feeder. There was a terrible explosion. He was hurled downward in the breast and covered with the rush of coal and rock. I was working only three breasts away from him and for a moment was unable to realize what had occurred. Myself and a hundred others were soon at work, however, and in a short while we found him, horribly burned over his whole body, his laborer dead alongside of him.

He was my brother. He was single and had been boarding. He had no home of his own. I didn't want him taken to the hospital, so I directed the driver of the ambulance to take him to my house. Besides being burned, his right arm and left leg were broken, and he was hurt internally. The doctors—there were two at the house when we got there—said he would die. But he didn't. He is living and a miner today. But he lay in bed just fourteen weeks, and was unable to work for seven weeks after he got out of bed. He had no money when he was hurt except the amount represented by his pay. All of the expenses for doctors, medicine, extra help and his living were borne by me, except $25, which another brother gave me. The last one had none to give. Poor work, low wages and a sickly woman for a wife had kept him scratching for his own family.

It is nonsense to say I was not compelled to keep him, that I could have sent him to a hospital or the almshouse. We are American citizens and we don't go to hospitals and poorhouses. . . .

An Italian Bootblack's Story, 1902

We came to Brooklyn to a wooden house in Adams Street that was full of Italians from Naples. [A man named] Bartolo had a room on the third floor and there were fifteen men in the room, all boarding with Bartolo. He did the cooking on a stove in the middle of the room and there were beds all around the sides, one bed above another. It was very hot in the room, but we were soon asleep, for we were very tired.

The next morning, early, Bartolo told us to go out and pick rags and get bottles. He gave us bags and hooks and showed us the ash barrels. On the streets where the fine houses are the people are very careless and put out good things, like mattresses and umbrellas, clothes, hats and boots. We brought all these to Bartolo and he made them new again and sold them on the sidewalk; but mostly we brought rags and bones. The rags we had to wash in the backyard and then we hung them to dry on lines under the ceil-

SOURCE: *Independent* 54 (December 4, 1902): 2865–2867.

ing in our room. The bones we kept under the beds till Bartolo could find a man to buy them.

Most of the men in our room worked at digging the sewer. Bartolo got them the work and they paid him about one quarter of their wages. Then he charged them for board and he bought the clothes for them, too. So they got little money after all.

Bartolo was always saying that the rent of the room was so high that he could not make anything, but he was really making plenty. He was what they call a padrone* and is now a very rich man. The men that were living with him had just come to the country and could not speak English. They had all been sent by the young man we met in Italy. Bartolo told us all that we must work for him and that if we did not the police would come and put us in prison.

He gave us very little money, and our clothes were some of those that were found on the street. Still we had enough to eat and we had meat quite often, which we never had in Italy. Bartolo got it from the butcher—the meat that he could not sell to other people—but it was quite good meat. Bartolo cooked it in the pan while we all sat on our beds in the evening. Then he cut it into small bits and passed the pan around, saying:

"See what I do for you and yet you are not glad. I am too kind a man, that is why I am so poor."

We were with Bartolo nearly a year, but some of our countrymen who had been in the place a long time said that Bartolo had no right to us and we could get work for a dollar and a half a day, which, when you make it *lire* (reckoned in the Italian currency) is very much. So we went away one day to Newark and got work on the street. Bartolo came after us and made a great noise, but the boss said that if he did not go away soon the police would have him. Then he went, saying that there was no justice in this country.

We paid a man five dollars each for getting us the work and we were with that boss for six months. He was Irish, but a good man and he gave us our money every Saturday night. We lived much better than with Bartolo, and when the work was done we each had nearly $200 saved. Plenty of the men spoke English and they taught us, and we taught them to read and write. That was at night, for we had a lamp in our room, and there were only five other men who lived in that room with us.

We got up at half-past five o'clock every morning and made coffee on the stove and had a breakfast of bread and cheese, onions, garlic and red herrings. We went to work at seven o'clock and in the middle of the day we had soup and bread in a place where we got it for two cents a plate. In the evenings we had a good dinner with meat of some kind and potatoes. We got from the butcher the meat that other people would not buy because they

---

*Padrone is a labor boss who secured employment for immigrants. (Eds.)

said it was old, but they don't know what is good. We paid four or five cents a pound for it and it was the best, tho I have heard of people paying sixteen cents a pound.

When the Newark boss told us that there was no more work Francisco and I talked about what we would do and we went back to Brooklyn to a saloon near Hamilton Ferry, where we got a job cleaning it out and slept in a little room upstairs. There was a bootblack named Michael on the corner and when I had time I helped him and learned the business. Francisco cooked the lunch in the saloon and he, too, worked for the bootblack and we were soon able to make the best polish.

Then we thought we would go into business and we got a basement on Hamilton Avenue, near the Ferry, and put four chairs in it. We paid $75 for the chairs and all the other things. We had tables and looking glasses there and curtains. We took the papers that have the pictures in and made the place high toned. Outside we had a big sign that said:

THE BEST SHINE FOR TEN CENTS

Men that did not want to pay ten cents could get a good shine for five cents, but it was not an oil shine. We had two boys helping us and paid each of them fifty cents a day. The rent of the place was $20 a month, so the expenses were very great, but we made money from the beginning. We slept in the basement, but got our meals in the saloon till we could put a stove in our place, and then Francisco cooked for us all. That would not do, tho, because some of our customers said that they did not like to smell garlic and onions and red herrings. I thought that was strange, but we had to do what the customers said. So we got the woman who lived upstairs to give us our meals and paid her $1.50 a week each. She gave the boys soup in the middle of the day—five cents for two plates. . . .

We had said that when we saved $1,000 each we would go back to Italy and buy a farm, but now that the time is coming we are so busy and making so much money that we think we will stay. We have opened another parlor near South Ferry, in New York. We have to pay $30 a month rent, but the business is very good. The boys in the place charge sixty cents a day because there is so much work.

Chapter 6

The Triumph of Racism

NORTH CAROLINIANS TAKE NOTICE.

NEGROES WHO CANNOT READ OR WRITE CANNOT VOTE. WHITES WHO CANNOT READ OR WRITE CAN VOTE. BY ORDER OF THE RED SHIRT BRYANITES.

A TRIUMPH FOR WHITE SUPREMACY.

In the decades following the Civil War, while the northern and western states turned to industrialization with the aid of immigrant laborers, the South remained largely agricultural. Some white Southerners, like Henry Grady of the Atlanta Constitution, urged the former Confederate states to follow the example of the rest of the nation and build cities, factories, and railroads. Indeed, the South did experience a modicum of industrial and urban growth before World War I. But the region still lagged behind the rapid pace of change elsewhere in the United States.

In another way, too, the white South continued to look to the past. Once Congress admitted the ex-Confederate states back into the union and federal troops had withdrawn from the South, white Southerners were free to pursue a system of race relations more to their taste than that imposed by Radical Republicans during the Reconstruction era (1865–1876). This system stipulated that blacks be segregated in most areas of public life, be denied the right to vote, and generally be limited to working as landless farmers.

In his essay on the Supreme Court's Plessy v. Ferguson decision (1896), Keith Weldon Medley points out that among the southern states, postwar Louisiana *offered the brightest hope for easing racial inequality. African Americans partici-pated in politics and benefited from the integration of many public facilities for a number of years after the removal of federal troops. But soon the rising tide of white racism destroyed their dreams; as in other states around the turn of the century, Louisiana ultimately established a rigid system of white supremacy.*

It was one thing for white legislators to enact measures to disfranchise and seg-regate African Americans; it was another for these laws to receive the sanction of the United States Supreme Court. After all, the Fourteenth and Fifteenth Amend-ments to the Constitution seem to preclude such legislation. Medley's essay centers on the case of Homer Plessy's challenge to Louisiana's separate coach law. How did the Supreme Court manage to conclude that segregation did not violate the Four-teenth Amendment, which supposedly guarantees equal protection of the law? What implications did the Plessy decision hold for racial segregation in other areas of southern life?

Segregation was only one of the injustices suffered by African Americans in the age of Jim Crow. From the 1880s until World War I, there were approximately 100 lynchings yearly, mostly of blacks and mostly in the South. Not all mob executions were lynchings; some blacks were burned to death—this witnessed by hundreds of spectators who were known to fight over bones to take home as souvenirs. Only a small number of these acts of violence involved allegations of black men raping white women. In most cases, the mere accusation of rape was sufficient to trigger the gathering of a mob. The first document presents Senator Benjamin Tillman's defense of such acts of terror in an address on the floor of the United States Con-gress. On what grounds did he argue that lynching was justified?

Faced with the triumph of racism at the turn of the century, blacks protested through organizations such as the National Association for the Advancement of Colored People (NAACP). In the second document, W.E.B. Du Bois, a founder of the NAACP, issues a call for equality. In view of the conditions portrayed in the essay and Senator Tillman's racial outbursts, do you think that there was any real possibility for the realization of Du Bois's program in the first decade of the twenti-eth century?

While black leaders and intellectuals debated future programs and strategies, many Southern blacks took matters into their own hands and headed north. The third document is a letter from a black Mississippi mechanic to the Chicago De-fender, an influential black newspaper. The letter reflects the determination of African Americans to find a better life in the North, the reluctance of Southern whites to let them leave, and the key role that the Defender played in encouraging northward migration.

ESSAY

The Birth of "Separate but Equal"

Keith Weldon Medley

"On Tuesday evening, a Negro named [Homer] Plessy was arrested by Private Detective Cain on the East Louisiana train and locked up for violating Section 2 of Act 111 of 1890, relative to separate coaches. . . . He waived examination yesterday before Recorder Monlin and was sent before the criminal court under $500 bond."

This modest announcement appeared in the New Orleans *Daily Picayune* on June 9, 1892. Little noticed at the time, it recorded a moment of tragic significance for the people of America. For it marked not only the end of an era that had begun with Reconstruction, but the start of a half-century in which the rights and hopes of black people in the South, briefly raised up by Reconstruction, were all but extinguished.

In time it would make famous the names of a New Orleans shoemaker and a judge from Massachusetts, as the joint label on the landmark Supreme Court decision *Plessy* v. *Ferguson*. The issue was apparently resolved by the Court in 1896. But the running racial and judicial struggle involved did not have its most dramatic climax until a half-century later, with the decision known as *Brown* v. *Board of Education*.

Confrontation over a place in a public conveyance suggests a parallel with Rosa Parks. But her refusal to give up her bus seat to a white passenger in Montgomery, Alabama, was partly triggered by happenstance. Plessy's action on that warm New Orleans afternoon a century ago was an act of civil disobedience carefully planned and orchestrated by a group of black Republicans, lawyers and journalists known in the French-speaking areas of New Orleans as the Comité des Citoyens.

The story of their case and of their calculated yet desperate judicial fight is rooted not merely in the history of what happened in the South after the Civil War, but in the texture of life in New Orleans itself. Even before the Civil War, New Orleans had been a rich, cosmopolitan trading port and a place where people of color had accomplished a great deal.

Originally French, then Spanish, then French again before being bought by Thomas Jefferson in 1803 (along with what would become half of the United States), it was a city with a remarkable mix of colors and cultures, as well as a penchant for violence and vice. On the eve of the war in 1860, the

SOURCE: "The Sad Story of how 'Separate but Equal' was Born," by Keith Weldon Medley, from *Smithsonian* (February 1994) 104–117. Copyright © by Keith Weldon Medley. Reprinted by permission of the author.

population was pushing 170,000, including 25,000 Irish and 20,000 German immigrants, and 15,000 African-American slaves about to be freed. But New Orleans also had a greater concentration of free people of color than any other city in the Deep South, some 10,000 people who had gained their freedom well before the Civil War began.

Homer Plessy was born free in March 1862, only a month before Yankee gunboats overran the city's Mississippi River defenses, taking control of the port while the war lasted. Like Plessy's family, many black New Orleanians were French-speaking and Roman Catholic. Some had come from Haiti to escape the bloody revolution at the beginning of the 19th century, when Haitians won their independence from France. Some had fought in 1815 with Andrew Jackson against the British in the Battle of New Orleans. The majority were working class, but many were landowners, businessmen, skilled artisans.

Full Inheritances and Paternal Surnames

Though interracial marriage had been officially banned and streetcars segregated, the city had fewer social restrictions about intermingling between whites and blacks than other areas in the South. Many de facto marriages between the races lasted a lifetime; the children produced often received full inheritances and paternal surnames. Some were sent to Europe for their education. Some became rich and prominent citizens.

So hopes ran high on June 11, 1864, as thousands joyfully gathered in Congo Square, the site of weekend slave gatherings, to celebrate a great event: on May 9 of that year, Louisiana had approved an emancipation ordinance. Ratification of the 13th Amendment to the Constitution would come in 1865, followed by the 14th in 1868, which said that if you were born in the United States you were a citizen, and that no state could deprive you of your rights, liberty or property without due process of law. By 1870 the 15th Amendment made clear that no citizen could be deprived of the right to vote on the basis of race, color or previous condition of servitude.

In 1867 New Orleans removed the black stars previously used to designate the city's segregated streetcars. That was the year of the Reconstruction Act, passed by still-powerful Radical Republicans in Washington, which sent U.S. armies of occupation into the South and gave military commanders in five areas there the right to protect life and property with federal force. They set up a procedure to register voters and see that lately freed slaves were allowed to vote, held elections, established black schools, and created machinery whereby Southern states were to ratify the 14th Amendment. In New Orleans and all over the South, Army commanders had the power to appoint and dismiss local officials.

By 1869 when Homer Plessy was 7, New Orleans began experimenting with integrated public schools—the only Southern city to do so. Blacks served with whites on juries and public boards. New Orleans had an integrated police department with a color-blind municipal pay scale. Thanks to Reconstruction, too, Plessy grew to manhood while blacks, who made up most of the Republican Party in the South, voted enthusiastically in large numbers and served in high office. Between the years 1868 and 1896, racial intermarriage was made legal, and Louisiana elected 32 black state senators and 95 state representatives. It had the only black governor in U.S. history before the late 1980s. (In the same period the South as a whole voted 600 black state representatives into office and sent 16 black congressmen to Washington.)

Apparently Plessy left no papers. City records, however, tell a good deal about him and about the racially mixed, middle-class faubourg, or suburb, where he lived. He began making shoes in 1879, married Louise Bordenave in 1888 and attended Mass at St. Augustine's Catholic Church on St. Claude Street. The church had been established by whites and free people of color before the war; services were conducted in French and Latin. The newlyweds could afford to rent a house near the corner of Ursulines Street on North Claiborne Avenue in the Faubourg Tremé.

Outside the Plessys' bedroom window was Congregation Hall, home of Saturday night "grand dancing festivals" where, for 15 cents, New Orleanians swayed to the sounds of Professor Moret's String Band. By the 1890s, Tremé had become an integrated enclave of several races, numbering among its residents many musicians and artists, who tended to be radical and egalitarian. There were also a number of dramatic clubs and benevolent religious societies that would contribute heavily to the Comité des Citoyens, among them the Société des Francs Amis (Homer Plessy became its vice president), which provided medical and funeral expenses for dues-paying members.

Following the Civil War, the full-scale occupation of the South as a defeated nation, along with Reconstruction programs, cost the American taxpayers considerable money, not including the pay and maintenance of the 6,000-odd federal soldiers. Yet for years the Republican Party, dominated by former abolitionists, maintained the political power and the will necessary to try remaking the former Confederate States.

There was no swift and easy way, however, for four million ex-slaves, just freed and without education, to be integrated into a racist, bitterly defeated and economically collapsing South. Race hatred, intimidation and riots flared. The Ku Klux Klan spread pamphlets and terror, which eventually included the murder of influential Reconstruction figures both black and white. It also embarked on the systematic intimidation of newly enfranchised black voters. The power of the Republican Party in Southern states, overwhelmingly based on those same black voters, began to wane, and Southern Democrats started to take back the South. The power of Republicans in Washington, especially after the Recession of 1873, was vulnerable to Democrats who could claim that Reconstruction cost money and had no hope of success.

In the North there had been optimistic expectations for economic recovery in a free-labor South and for the immediate effects of black suffrage. "We need no vast expenditures. We need no standing army," Senator Richard Yates, a Radical Republican, had once declared. "The ballot will finish the Negro question." By the early 1870s that was clearly not so, and just as clear was the fact that many states in the North and West, which as late as 1868 did not permit black suffrage or integration, would not long concern themselves with the rights of blacks in the South. After the ratification of the 15th Amendment, an Illinois newspaper expressed a prevalent Northern view: "The Negro is now a voter and a citizen. Let him hereafter take his chances in the battle of life."

The specific political event that brought an end to Reconstruction and the withdrawal of occupation troops from the South was the Presidential election of 1876. Republicans had dominated national politics since Lincoln. But in 1876 neither Republican Rutherford B. Hayes nor Democrat Samuel J. Tilden got enough undisputed electoral votes to win. A deal was made, known as the Hayes-Tilden Compromise. Hayes would become President by being ceded the electoral votes of a number of Southern states in return for recalling the armies of occupation (they departed in 1877) and yielding to Democrats the control of the last three Southern states—including Louisiana—still run by the Republican Party. For their part, Southern Democratic leaders in those states agreed to maintain civil rights policies.

Among them was Louisiana's Democratic gubernatorial candidate Francis T. Nicholls, an ex-Confederate general who lost an arm and a leg in the Civil War. Nicholls swore to uphold "equal rights and common interests" and to "obliterate the color line in politics." For a while he kept his word. But without the Reconstruction programs and the bayonets of the armies to support them, lately freed blacks were at a hopeless disadvantage. All over the South, the advances made in the 1870s began to be undone. The pace accelerated in 1883 when the Supreme Court, which was also changing its makeup, declared the civil rights enforcement act of 1875 unconstitutional. This meant that the federal government, lacking the means and will, pretty well got out of the business of making sure that the new civil rights laws were applied in the South.

The erosion of civil rights went more slowly in New Orleans than elsewhere. But the city began reestablishing segregated schools, and in 1890 Nicholls approved the Louisiana Legislature's passage of the Separate Car Act.

The act decreed "equal but separate accommodations for the white and colored races" on Louisiana railway cars. Under its terms any railway company that did not provide separate coaches for blacks and whites could be fined $500. Except for "nurses attending children of the other race," individual whites and blacks would be forbidden to ride together, or risk a $25 fine or 20 days in jail. It was the passage of this bill that finally launched Homer

Plessy into history. The fight involved a black newspaper, *The Crusader*, the six remaining black state senators and ultimately the Comité des Citoyens, which coalesced around *The Crusader*.

At the State Capitol, Senator Henry Demas thundered at his fellow legislators: "Like the Jews, we have been driven from our houses and firesides, from our churches and schoolhouses . . . and from the elevated avenues of livelihood, and now, in order to reach the lowest depth of infamy . . . you are willing to forget that you are men and vote for the passage of this bill." But the Separate Car Act passed the Louisiana Senate by a vote of 23 to 6.

The Crusader was a formidable enemy. A weekly founded in 1889 by attorney Louis Martinet to combat the increasingly virulent racism of other New Orleans papers, it called itself "spicy, progressive, liberal, stalwart, fearless," and stood for "A Free Vote and Fair Count, Free Schools, Fair Wages, Justice and Equal Rights." It cost a nickel and carried classified ads for everything from pianos, sails, cotton scales and first communion wreaths to ointments that claimed to "relax"—straighten—the hair. *The Crusader's* star contributor was Rodolphe Desdunes. The son of a Cuban mother and a Haitian father, Desdunes worked as a customs agent by day and, with smoking pen, scribbled polemical columns by night. Hundreds of his articles, still preserved in the archives of Xavier University in New Orleans, offer a window into the desperate fight to keep civil rights from slipping away.

"Colored people have largely patronized the railroads heretofore," Desdunes wrote on July 19, 1890. "They can withdraw the patronage from these corporations and travel only by necessity." He proposed a boycott not unlike the one launched in Montgomery, Alabama, 70 years later.

The 1890s were not a good time to exercise civil disobedience in the American South, or to get on the wrong side of a mob, whether you were black or not. The year 1892 alone produced 226 mob murders, mostly of black men, the highest number in the recorded history of lynchings. In New Orleans, on March 14, 1891, a newspaper editor and a prominent attorney led a crowd of several thousand to Parish Prison. Angry over the acquittal of Italian immigrants accused of the killing of police chief David Hennessy, they broke in, hunted down a group of 11 Italians, shot them, then hanged some from streetlamps and shot them again. Mournfully reflecting on the mood in New Orleans, a black woman told a reporter: "Thank God it wasn't a nigger who killed the Chief."

To combat what became known as the "Jim Crow car law," *The Crusader* and the Comité des Citoyens acquired a small but influential membership. It involved C. C. Antoine, a former officer in the Union Army, who had served four years (1873–77) as Louisiana's lieutenant governor, and wealthy philanthropist Aristide Mary, who had financed lawsuits against other resegregated establishments.

The Comité also included sail manufacturer Arthur Estèves, who became its president. To fight the Jim Crow car law, it was prepared to solicit funds not only from benevolent, social and religious societies in town but from former abolitionists in such faraway cities as Washington, D.C., Chicago and San Francisco. About $3,000 was quickly raised to launch two test cases: one to challenge legal segregation of trains on interstate routes and one to challenge segregation on conveyances within the state. The aim: to "seek redemption" from the Supreme Court of the United States. "We find this the only means left us," a Comité statement concluded. "We must have recourse to it, or sink into a state of helpless inferiority."

It was a forlorn hope, but not as forlorn as it would become in the slow process of going through the legal system. For one thing, on the face of it, if you gave any thought to the intent of the men who wrote the 14th Amendment, the Separate Car Act seemed a clear violation of the constitutional rights of the black citizens of Louisiana. But public opinion in the North had changed rapidly, and so, in the years after 1877, had the makeup of the Supreme Court, which lost its reasonable mix of justices sympathetic to the subject of civil rights.

Some railroad companies initially had been against the bill. It was going to cost money to build and run extra cars—for the bill implied that if a half empty "white" car was waiting, and even if only one black passenger showed up, he or she would have to have a whole separate-but-equal vehicle made available. In a city that had for so long seen so much racial mixing, railway conductors would now have to decide who was white and who was black—a touchy business, especially since some wives and husbands would not be allowed to ride together.

One of the reasons that Homer Plessy was picked for the job was that he had fair skin. Had it been left to chance, he probably could have ridden the train in the "whites only" section unnoticed. But by prearrangement between the Comité and the East Louisiana Railroad, everything was ready for him when he came.

On June 7, 1892, Plessy strolled to the Press Street depot, which included a restaurant and a combination waiting room and ticket office (both still open to him), bought a first-class ticket and, ignoring the new "Colored Only" sign, sat down in the coach reserved for whites. It was to depart at 4:15 P.M., cross a bridge spanning Lake Pontchartrain and pass through Abita Springs for a two-hour run to Covington.

Hardly had the train started moving when conductor J. J. Dowling approached Plessy. "Are you a colored man?" he asked. "Yes," answered Plessy. "Then you will have to retire to the colored car," said Dowling. Plessy stated that he had paid for his ticket and intended to ride to Covington. Dowling signaled the engineer to stop. A private detective, Captain Chris Cain, hired by the Comité, came aboard and warned Plessy: "If you are colored you should go into the car set apart for your race. The law is plain and must be obeyed."

When Plessy again refused, he was taken a half-mile down to Elysian Fields Avenue for booking at the Fifth Precinct Station. Members of the Comité met him, and a judge released him on temporary bail. The next day a story in a New Orleans daily described Plessy as a "snuff-colored descendant of Ham." After a hearing, Comité member Paul Bonseigneur plunked down a $500 bond (raised by putting his own house in hock) to guarantee Plessy's appearance for trial. Plessy was 30 years old. The future of constitutional rights for blacks in America would ride on his day in court.

Enter John Howard Ferguson, 54, the judge whose name would forever be linked to Plessy's in American history. The lawyer son of a shipowner on the island of Martha's Vineyard, Massachusetts, Ferguson had come South after hearing of opportunities there from returning Civil War soldiers. He was what Southerners called a carpetbagger—meaning anybody who came South after the fighting to administer the remade South or to look for profit in the South's adversity. He married the daughter of a prominent local attorney, a Louisiana Unionist noted for his condemnations of slavery, and began practicing law. Ferguson served in Governor Nicholls' 1876 Legislature. Eventually he campaigned for Murphy Foster, the man who replaced Nicholls as governor and engineered passage of the Separate Car Act. Ferguson was made a judge and assigned the Plessy case a month after Plessy's arrest.

But only a short time after becoming a judge, in another Comité-generated case, he ruled that the Separate Car Act was unconstitutional on trains that traveled through several states—because of the federal government's predominant interest in interstate commerce. The Comité celebrated the decision, and Louis Martinet chortled in print: "Jim Crow is dead as a doornail."

He was wrong. At Plessy's arraignment, *Homer Adolph Plessy* v. *The State of Louisiana,* one of Plessy's lawyers, James Walker, argued that neither the state nor any railroad conductor representing it had the right to deny Plessy's liberty on the basis of race, since Plessy was a citizen, and the 14th Amendment clearly said that "no state shall make or enforce any law which shall abridge the privileges or immunities of any citizen of the United States." Judge Ferguson did not agree. The state, he claimed, had a legal right to regulate railroad companies operating solely within the state. Plessy had not been deprived of his liberty. "He was simply deprived of the liberty of doing as he pleased, and of violating a penal statute with impunity."

A swift appeal was presented to the State Supreme Court, which instantly agreed with Ferguson's decision. The 14th Amendment guaranteed black individuals "equality" but did not guarantee "identity or community" with white society. The glum Comité now could look only northward to the Supreme Court of the United States in Washington. As time passed, Plessy's prospects grew worse.

In the decade leading up to 1896, when the case at last was argued before the Court, seven Justices had been replaced—mostly by men who shared the increasingly prevalent belief that Reconstruction had largely failed and that blacks must fend for themselves. The only holdovers from Reconstruction times were John Marshall Harlan of Kentucky, a Hayes appointee, and the aging Stephen J. Field, who had been appointed in 1863 by Lincoln.

Attorney Albion Tourgée, who eventually argued the case for the Comité, estimated that only one Justice would firmly lean to Plessy's side, three would be uncertain and five, frankly opposed. In a letter to Louis Martinet he added a foreboding postscript: "It is of the utmost importance that we should not have a decision *against* us as the court has *never* reversed itself on a constitutional question."

Tourgée was not the only one to notice the changing temper of the Supreme Court. In 1894 Louisiana again placed racial restrictions on marriage and prohibited citizens of opposite races from using the same railroad depot waiting rooms.

The Comité's chances dwindled as the climate of opinion changed, even among people of color. Voices in some quarters argued that resisting white supremacy always evoked harsher responses, and that the struggle for decent conditions was what mattered most, not integration. In 1895 Booker T. Washington, head of Tuskegee Institute, publicly called for accommodation with segregation. Washington argued that in the face of white hatred, integration simply stirred up opposition. The main thing was to concentrate on making segregated schools work, on learning trades and on getting ahead in life.

But the Comité had pledged to see the case to the end. By late fall 1895 everything was in place. Albion Tourgée, with lawyers S. F. Phillips and F. D. McKenny, had filed final papers for the October 1895 term in *Homer A. Plessy* v. *J. H. Ferguson*. Tourgée went before the Supreme Court in April 1896. State arguments were made by Louisiana's Attorney General M. J. Cunningham and lawyers Lionel Adams and Alexander Porter Morse.

On May 18 the Court issued a ruling. With only one dissent it granted states the right to forcibly segregate people of different races. Writing for the majority, Justice Henry Billings Brown, appointed by Benjamin Harrison, dismissed Plessy's 14th Amendment claims and, as precedent, pointed to the existence of separate schools in the District of Columbia and the long-standing bans on interracial marriage. The only test of such segregation, he said, would be whether or not the regulations were reasonable. The Court also stated that "legislation is powerless to eradicate racial instincts or to abolish distinctions based upon physical differences." As for determining who was black or white, that was left to the discretion of each state.

The lone dissenter was Justice John Marshall Harlan. "The destinies of two races in this country," Harlan wrote, "are indissolubly linked together, and the interests of both require that the common government of all shall not permit the seeds of race hate to be planted under the sanction of law. . . . The thin disguise of 'equal' accommodations for passengers in railroad coaches will not mislead anyone, nor atone for the wrong this day done."

The decision was remanded to the Supreme Court of Louisiana on September 28, 1896. The Comité issued a final statement: "In passing laws which discriminate between its citizens," it declared, "the State was wrong. . . . Notwithstanding this decision . . . we, as freemen, still believe that we were right, and our cause is sacred."

On January 11, 1897, Homer Plessy returned to court for sentencing. By then, times had changed dramatically. The Comité had disbanded; *The Crusader* had ceased publication. All over the South, white supremacists were firmly in control of the Legislatures. Judge Ferguson had stepped down in 1896, and Judge Joshua Baker was presiding. Plessy changed his plea to guilty, paid a $25 fine and walked out into the brave new world of a segregated Louisiana.

Those in the black community who thought racial separation would bring peace were in for a rude awakening. Emboldened by the Supreme Court's Plessy decision, in February 1898 Louisiana called a constitutional convention in New Orleans to lay down a blueprint for white supremacy. Endorsed by Governor Foster, the delegates made it illegal to run an integrated school, allocated state money as a "pension fund" for the relatives of Confederate soldiers, declared the Louisiana Democratic Party a "whites only" organization and used various devices, such as the "grandfather clause," to keep blacks and immigrants from voting. "Our mission was to establish the supremacy of the white race," the chairman of the judiciary committee bluntly declared. In the four years from 1896 to 1900, more than 120,000 black voters were removed from the rolls, their numbers dropping from 45 percent to 4 percent of eligible voters. By 1900 Louisiana did not have a single black representative in its Legislature. There would be none until 1967.

While legislation made things "separate," the "equal" treatment of the Supreme Court ruling seldom materialized. The greatest disaster would come in education. The South spent very little money on black schools. In New Orleans, the city school board did not open a public high school for blacks until 1917. Even then, black teachers were paid less than their white counterparts, and their pupils received second-hand books and supplies.

One by one the civil rights gains of Reconstruction vanished. So too did the principals in the *Plessy* v. *Ferguson* case. Judge Ferguson died in 1915 at age 77. In a front-page story, the *Times-Picayune* lauded him as one who "allied himself with the Democratic reform element" and "took part in the struggle for white supremacy." He was buried in the Lafayette Cemetery on Washington Avenue. In August 1925, some 50,000 white-robed members of the Ku Klux Klan marched in Washington, D.C.

Homer Plessy had died a few months earlier that year. His obituary in the *Times-Picayune* was simple: "PLESSY—on Sunday, March 1, 1925, at 5:10 A.M., Homer A. Plessy, 63 years, beloved husband of Louise Bordenave." On the front page of the same paper was the headline "Supreme Court Puts Approval on Segregation," referring to a Louisiana Supreme Court ruling that upheld a segregated housing ordinance in New Orleans. Plessy lies with his mother's family in St. Louis Cemetery No. 1, a 200-year-old integrated Catholic graveyard in the Tremé area. Fifteen years after his death there were only 886 registered black voters in the state of Louisiana.

Nearly 15 more years would pass before NAACP attorney Thurgood Marshall obtained a rehearing of Plessy's cause in another landmark case, *Brown* v. *Board of Education.* In that instance, the Court overturned the 1896 ruling and declared "separate but equal" to be unconstitutional. That time, Homer Plessy won.

DOCUMENTS

A United States Senator Defends Lynching, 1907

Mr. President, the Senator from Wisconsin speaks of "lynching bees." As far as lynching for rape is concerned, the word is a misnomer. When stern and sad-faced white men put to death a creature in human form who has deflowered a white woman, there is nothing of the "bee" about it. There is more of the feeling of participating as mourner at a funeral. They have avenged the greatest wrong, the blackest crime in all the category of crimes, and they have done it, not so much as an act of retribution in behalf of the victim as a duty and as a warning as to what any man may expect who shall repeat the offense. They are looking to the protection of their own loved ones. . . . .

Now let me suppose a case. Let us take any Senator on this floor—I will not particularize—take him from some great and well-ordered State in the North, where there are possibly twenty thousand negroes, as there are in Wisconsin, with over two million whites. Let us carry this Senator to the backwoods in South Carolina, put him on a farm miles from a town or railroad, and environed with negroes. We will suppose he has a fair young

Source: *The Congressional Record,* Senate, 59th Cong., 2nd sess., 1907. Document from Bibliobase®, edited by Michael Bellesiles. Copyright © Houghton Mifflin Company. Reprinted by permission.

daughter just budding into womanhood: and recollect this, the white women of the South are in a state of siege; the greatest care is exercised that they shall at all times where it is possible not be left alone or unprotected, but that can not always and in every instance be the case. That Senator's daughter undertakes to visit a neighbor or is left home alone for a brief while. Some lurking demon who has watched for the opportunity seizes her: she is choked or beaten into insensibility and ravished, her body prostituted, her purity destroyed, her chastity taken from her, and a memory branded on her brain as with a red-hot iron to haunt her night and day as long as she lives. Moore has drawn us the picture in most graphic language:

> One fatal remembrance, one sorrow that throws
> Its bleak shade alike o'er our joys and our woes,
> To which life nothing darker or brighter can bring,
> For which joy hath no balm and affliction no sting.

In other words, a death in life. This young girl thus blighted and brutalized drags herself to her father and tells him what has happened. Is there a man here with red blood in his veins who doubts what impulses the father would feel? Is it any wonder that the whole countryside rises as one man and with set, stern faces seek the brute who has wrought this infamy? Brute, did I say? Why, Mr. President, this crime is a slander on the brutes. No beast of the field forces his female. He waits invitation. It has been left for something in the shape of a man to do this terrible thing. And shall such a creature, because he has the semblance of a man, appeal to the law? Shall men coldbloodedly stand up and demand for him the right to have a fair trial and be punished in the regular course of justice? So far as I am concerned he has put himself outside the pale of the law, human and divine. He has sinned against the Holy Ghost. He has invaded the holy of holies. He has struck civilization a blow, the most deadly and cruel that the imagination can conceive. It is idle to reason about it; it is idle to preach about it. Our brains reel under the staggering blow and hot blood surges to the heart. Civilization peels off us, any and all of us who are men, and we revert to the original savage type whose impulses under any and all such circumstances has always been to "kill! kill! kill!"

I do not know what the Senator from Wisconsin would do under these circumstances; neither do I care. I have three daughters, but, so help me God, I had rather find either one of them killed by a tiger or a bear and gather up her bones and bury them, conscious that she had died in the purity of her maidenhood, than have her crawl to me and tell me the horrid story that she had been robbed of the jewel of her womanhood by a black fiend.

A Call for Equality, 1905

. . . We believe that [Negro] American citizens should protest emphatically and continually against the curtailment of their political rights. We believe in manhood suffrage: we believe that no man is so good, intelligent or wealthy as to be entrusted wholly with the welfare of his neighbor.

We believe also in protest against the curtailment of our civil rights. All American citizens have the right to equal treatment in places of public entertainment according to their behavior and deserts.

We especially complain against the denial of equal opportunities to us in economic life; in the rural districts of the south this amounts to peonage and virtual slavery; all over the south it tends to crush labor and small business enterprises; and everywhere American prejudice, helped often by iniquitous laws is making it more difficult for Negro-Americans to earn a decent living.

Common school education should be free to all American children and compulsory. High school training should be adequately provided for all, and college training should be the monopoly of no class or race in any section of our common country. We believe that in defense of its own institutions, the United States should aid common school education, particularly in the south, and we especially recommend concerted agitation to this end. We urge an increase in public high school facilities in the south, where the Negro-Americans are almost wholly without such provisions. We favor well-equipped trade and technical schools for the training of artisans, and the need of adequate and liberal endowment for a few institutions of higher education must be patent to sincere well-wishers of the race.

We demand upright judges in courts, juries selected without discrimination on account of color and the same measure of punishment, and the same efforts at reformation for black as for white offenders. We need orphanages and farm schools for dependent children, juvenile reformatories for delinquents, and the abolition of the dehumanizing convict-lease system. . . .

We hold up for public execration the conduct of two opposite classes of men; the practice among employers of importing ignorant Negro-American laborers in emergencies, and then affording them neither protection nor permanent employment; and the practice of labor unions of proscribing and boycotting and oppressing thousands of their fellow-toilers, simply because they are black. These methods have accentuated and will accentuate the war of labor and capital, and they are disgraceful to both sides. . . .

We regret that this nation has never seen fit adequately to reward the black soldiers who in its five wars, have defended their country with their

SOURCE: W. E. B. Du Bois, *Cleveland Gazette*, July 22, 1905.

blood, and yet have been systematically denied the promotions which their abilities deserve. And we regard as unjust, the exclusion of black boys from the military and navy training schools. . . .

The Negro race in America, stolen, ravished and degraded, struggling up through difficulties and oppression, needs sympathy and receives criticism; needs help and is given hindrance, needs protection and is given mob violence, needs justice and is given charity, needs leadership and is given cowardice and apology, needs bread and is given a stone. This nation will never stand justified before God until these things are changed.

Especially are we surprised and astonished at the recent attitude of the church of Christ—on the increase of a desire to bow to racial prejudice, to narrow the bounds of human brotherhood, and to segregate black men in some outer sanctuary. This is wrong, unchristian and disgraceful to twentieth century civilization. . . .

And while we are demanding, and ought to demand, and will continue to demand the rights enumerated above, God forbid that we should ever forget to urge corresponding duties upon our people.

> The duty to vote.
> The duty to respect the rights of others.
> The duty to work.
> The duty to obey the laws.
> The duty to be clean and orderly.
> The duty to send our children to school,
> The duty to respect ourselves, even as we respect others. . . .

"I Want to Come North," 1917

GRANVILLE, MISSISSIPPI, MAY 16, 1917

Dear Sir [editor of the *Defender*]: This letter is a letter of information of which you will find stamp envelop for reply. I want to come north some time soon but I do not want to leve here looking for a job where I would be in dorse all winter. Now the work I am doing here is running a guage edger in a saw mill. I know all about the grading of lumber. I have been working in lumber about 25 or 27 years. My wedges here is $3.00 a day 11 hours a day. I want to come North where I can educate my 3 little children also my wife. Now if you cannot fit me up at what I am doing down here I can learn anything any one els can. also there is a great deal of good women cooks here would leave any time all they want is to know where to go and some

SOURCE: Emmett J. Scott, "Letters of Negro Migrants of 1916–1918," *Journal of Negro History*, 4 (July 1919): 435.

way to go. please write me at once just how I can get my people where they can get something for their work. There are women here cookeing for $1.50 and $2.00 a week. I would like to live in Chicago or Ohio or Philadelphia. Tell Mr. Abbott [owner of the *Defender*] that our pepel are tole that they can not get anything to do up there and they are being snatched off the trains here in Greenville and a rested but in spite of all this, they are leaving every day and every night 100 or more is expecting to leave this week. Let me here from you at once.

Chapter 7

America Goes to War

25026

In April 1917, after months of debate and disagreement on whether to join the war in Europe, the United States declared war on Germany. Unlike the major European powers embroiled in the conflict since 1914, America's participation in the war was brief—only about a year and a half. Nevertheless, the war exerted a tremendous impact on Americans, soldiers, and civilians alike. For the first time, Americans went off to fight on European soil, and they felt certain that their participation would play a crucial role in defeating the Germans and their allies.

The United States had to mobilize its economy in order to support its allies and build an army to fight in Europe. After some confusion, the nation's industrial and agricultural might was effectively organized and financed. The building of an army also required great effort. The immense problems encountered in creating a fighting force capable of assisting our allies on the battlefields are vividly described in an essay by Meirion and Susie Harries. Based on your reading of this piece, what appear to have been the most difficult challenges facing the civilian and military leaders in their efforts to create this force? How effectively, in your opinion, did they meet the challenges? Finally, what does the essay indicate were the most serious *obstacles a new recruit had to overcome in making the transition from civilian to military life?*

Throughout the war, the federal government used propaganda to convince the public that the cause was noble, a clash between the forces of good and evil. Victory required the absolute loyalty and support of all citizens; any hint of questionable patriotism prompted great concern. For German Americans particularly, the patriotic near-hysteria of these times proved a terrible burden. In restaurants sauerkraut was renamed "liberty cabbage," and hamburger emerged as "liberty steak." Cincinnati's German Street was renamed English Street, and Pittsburgh banned the playing of Ludwig van Beethoven's music. German Americans were harassed and threatened with physical harm if they failed to demonstrate their commitment to the American war effort. The pressure on German Americans to declare their loyalty is vividly reflected in the first document, a statement by a German American distributed by the Committee on Public Information, an agency created by the federal government to generate public support for the war. How did the author's assessment of the war enable him to embrace the American cause without cutting his emotional ties to his native land?

Although a large segment of the population opposed entry into the war right up until 1917, support for the war effort flourished once the United States joined the conflict. Nevertheless, not all Americans supported the war; those who did not and refused to serve in the armed forces on the grounds of religion or conscience suffered condemnation. The second document reveals the experiences and convictions of Mennonites, who, despite their profound religious objections to the war, were drafted into the army. What relationship, if any, can you discern between the patriotic fervor of wartime society and intensified intolerance?

As the essay reveals, conscientious objectors were not the only ones to suffer prejudice during the war. The final document is a directive issued by a French liaison office to French officers at the insistence of the American army. What does it reveal about white America's attitudes toward black troops and African Americans generally?

ESSAY
·◆·

Building a National Army

Meirion and Susie Harries

In the early fall of 1917, watchers by the rail tracks would have seen a remarkable display of young Americans riding to their appointed camps and cantonments, an unrehearsed pageant of America's ethnic diversity: Chock-

SOURCE: *The Last Days of Innocence: America at War, 1917–1918* by Meirion and Susie Harries. Copyright 1997 by Meirion and Susie Harries, 127–141. Reprinted by permission of Random House, Inc.

taws and Cochin Chinese, "Hebrews" (the Army's classification) from everywhere in the Diaspora, Greeks, Italians, English, Irish, Scots, Slavs, Swedes, Germans, Austrians, Albanians, Poles, Armenians, Syrians, Finns, Hispanics, and Japanese. (In Hawaii, the National Guard gained its first Japanese company.) Blacks went on separate trains.

To this army of Babel came men of all shapes and sizes: lanky recruits of Scots blood from the mountains of North Carolina, short and stocky Mediterraneans from the Northeast, where recent immigration had been heaviest. The minimum size was five feet, one inch and 128 pounds; any smaller, and the man would have been unable to carry the regulation army pack (though occasionally lighter men were accepted if they had special skills). The maximum was six feet, six inches; any taller, and the man was likely to have poor circulation. The weight limits were 190 pounds for infantry, engineers, and artillery and 165 pounds for the cavalry.

The average recruit measured five feet, seven and a half inches and weighed 141½ pounds, a meaningless statistic in this miscellany of manhood—except at the unit level, where the average was crucial in determining the sizes of uniforms to be supplied and quantity of rations allocated. Divisions with a high proportion of immigrants from eastern Europe received a smaller average ration and smaller uniforms than midwestern divisions formed of strapping Scandinavians and Germans. Few were racially as mixed as New York's 77th Division, whose theme song ran: "The Jews and the Wops,/The Dutch and the Irish cops,/They're all in the Army now" and which boasted forty-two different languages or dialects spoken in its ranks.

During the war, some 400,000 first-generation immigrants were drafted, including some who were alien enemies and ineligible. This influx was too much for Major General George Bell of the 33rd Division, whose contingent of around 15,000 National Guard volunteers had been fleshed out with conscripts. He complained to the Adjutant General that "the local boards in Illinois had very evidently spared men of the draft age of American birth or stock at the expense of those of foreign birth or patronage."

Many who had known only the ghettos of the East Coast cities could not speak English or understand commands. Bombarded with unintelligible instructions and forced to eat such unfamiliar substances as boiled potatoes and stewed apricots, they created serious morale problems in their units. Recent German or Austrian immigrants had the additional anxiety, so military intelligence reported, of having been warned that "if it were known in their home countries that they were in the American army, their families would be hunted out and killed." This rumor was recognized as one of many deliberate propaganda attempts to disrupt recruitment and ruin morale in the camps. Army authorities believed the Lutheran Church Board to be one of Germany's instruments, noting "its efforts to place its pastors in as many camps, forts and other military establishments as possible."

The plight of these first-generation immigrants was compounded by prejudice. Anti-Semitism inevitably surfaced. One night, six weeks after his induction from the Bronx, Private Otto Gottschalk found himself dragged from his tent, stripped, and thrown into a ditch of black muck. He was forced to drink the filthy water and was then badly beaten.

In the early days of the draft, a high proportion of "unsuitable" immigrants appears to have been sent straight back to the ghetto. Later, attempts were made to fit them for service. Where there were enough of them, immigrants were branded together into "development battalions" under officers of their own. At one point, Camp Gordon, in Georgia, had two Slav companies and two Italian and one Russian-Jewish battalion. They quickly became well disciplined and proficient in drill, and when asked how many of them were ready and willing to go abroad immediately, 92 percent stepped forward.

This jumble of colors, cultures, and languages, European, Asian, and Latin, mercilessly underlined the isolation of the black Americans who formed a large section of the intake—larger, perhaps, than was just. No blacks were appointed to the draft boards, and local boards often used their powers to conscript a far higher proportion of blacks than whites relative to population. In part, this was to compensate for the higher number of whites enlisting voluntarily. (Blacks, after all, had very few units to volunteer for.) But draft boards also had a tendency to use selective service as a means of "cleaning up" the neighborhood. A General Staff report noted, "The physical condition of a large part of the colored draft is very poor. Many must be entirely eliminated and a large proportion of those left are not fit for combat duty. The Surgeon General reports that 50% are infected with venereal disease." There was no organized conspiracy to fill the Army with the poorest and "least socially desirable" blacks, but, judging from the results, that is often what happened.

Whatever damage the draft boards had inflicted by their "selection" techniques the Army compounded by its treatment of its black draftees. Few received more than six weeks' training, and their living conditions were often appalling. In October 1917, black stevedore and labor battalions were formed at Camp Hill, Virginia. Six thousand men arrived at the camp to find "no barracks, no mess halls, no clothing, no sanitary arrangements of any kind." In the coldest winter in Virginia for twenty-five years, those who could find room packed themselves into small, dirty tents pitched on the bare earth, while the less fortunate were obliged to stand in front of fires all night. Those who inevitably fell sick were taken to the crowded large tent that served as a hospital, where they lay on the frozen ground with neither cots nor thick blankets.

Camp Hill was an extreme case, but a War Department inspector criticized the white officers of all these black noncombatant units for their indifference to their men. The NCOs, he continued, had often been promoted to their positions "because of previous knowledge of negroes, usually gotten on plantations, public works, turpentine farms and the like." At Camp Hill, an NCO was often selected from the ranks "because he is a 'husky' and will beat and abuse the men. Two such sergeants are in the guard house now for killing other soldiers under their command." The seeds of hatred, ineffi-ciency, and even mutiny were being sown.

The inevitable consequence was low morale and indifference among black labor units when they got to Europe. "We have experienced consider-able difficulty in getting the proper amount of work out of the negro steve-dores at the various ports," W. W. Atterbury, Pershing's Director General of Transportation, was later to complain. "Fining them and putting them in the guard-house is very little punishment for them and to be dishonorably discharged and sent home is just what they desire." From Liverpool, one of England's major ports, the commanding officer of a detachment of steve-dores reported that police and local citizens had begged for them to be with-drawn. "They are without exception the most worthless aggregation of humanity that was ever collected in one unit."

As for the black combat troops, who had originally been intended to share facilities with white troops, they were eventually consigned to segre-gated units; worse, they were at no point allowed to assemble and train as complete divisions in the United States. While white divisions could seek to develop esprit and identity from the beginning of their training, the frag-mented black divisions barely knew what their senior officers looked like, so infrequently could these officers visit the various units scattered among the cantonments in which the National Army was training.

Arriving at the railheads, the new recruits were marshaled into columns by newly commissioned lieutenants trying to summon up the principles of command. The officers at least had the advantage of being in uniform; the recruits were still in civilian clothes, many wearing their best suits as if they were going to a wedding and clutching a few belongings or the remains of the food they had been given for the journey by the send-off committees in their hometowns.

After a brisk march, they got their first sight of the camp or cantonment that was to be home for months to come: "a far-spreading city of wooden buildings," one remembered, "whose flat roofs extended one after another in exact order like the biscuits in a baker's pan." (He was describing one of the sixteen hutted cantonments built for the National Army; members of the National Guard, who were used to living in tents, were housed in sixteen canvas cities farther south.)

If the recruits still cherished any spark of chivalry or romance about their induction, the medical orderlies waiting inside the gates soon intro-duced a note of gritty realism. Inspections for vermin and venereal disease and a vicious schedule of inoculations against smallpox, typhoid, and other contagious diseases left the new arrivals with barely the strength to crawl to their barracks.

And what they found there was rarely inspiriting. The basic design of the company barracks was sound. Each was to be a two-storied wooden building, the second floor a vast dormitory lined with iron cots, the first floor equipped with kitchen, storerooms, mess hall, and captain's office. Unfortunately, few of the buildings were ready. The delay in deciding on the precise size and structure of the infantry division had entailed constant alterations to the cantonment blueprint. Infirmary buildings, for example, were planned at a time when the Table of Organization prescribed thirty-three men for the medical detachment of an infantry regiment. This number was increased to forty-eight, and the building was too small before it was ever used.

The quality of the work that had been done left much to be desired. Far to the south, near a Houston still in shock after the summer massacre,* the officers and men of the Illinois National Guard—now designated the 33rd Division—found Camp Logan "in a decidedly unfinished state." The hospital had been built without heating or running water—the construction quartermaster had put in two faucets on his own initiative—and the engineers pronounced the storehouses to be so faulty that it was only a matter of time before they collapsed. At Camp MacArthur, Texas, the builders laid water mains made of wood that had been lying around for months, and when the water was turned on, typhoid ran through the camp.

All these camps were huge, and the numbers rose as the war progressed. Camp Dix, near Trenton, New Jersey, was built for 38,000 men but at one point housed 54,500. The sanitation demands of such concentrations of human life were immense, yet little thought had been given to them. Camp Sherman, Ohio, produced without effort 982,500 pounds of garbage a month and its horses 120 tons of manure a day. The men of Camp Custer, Michigan, filled 1,200 garbage cans a day. None of the camps had waterproof surfaces where the trash cans could be kept, so the earth around the cans became a morass of mashed and rotting waste, magnificent breeding grounds for flies—but nothing compared to the lakes of sewage that loitered in the vicinity of most camps.

At Camp Lee, Virginia, home to the 80th Division, a single creek carried the daily consignment of effluent into a marsh nearby, where it settled. The division's engineers decided to clear the marsh by dredging a channel, but in damming the creek to permit dredging to begin, they created, in the words of a visiting entomologist, a "semi-solid mass of sewage 600 feet long and alive with fly larvae." The comfort levels of latrines matched their sani-

---

*Several black soldiers were killed in a race riot in 1917. (Eds.)

tary standards; the seats in most had a square hole—an easier shape to cut than an oval.

Among the new arrivals at the camps and cantonments were the conscientious objectors. The Selective Service Act had forced the draft boards to induct them for combatant or noncombatant duty, depending on the nature of their objection, but several months passed before the War Department laid down a policy as to their treatment.

Newton Baker's* intention was that the government's attitude to those who had "personal scruples" about the war should be reasonably liberal, especially in the case of those whose objections were religious: Mennonites (who had come from Russia specifically to avoid war), Quakers, Dukhobors, Seventy-Day Adventists, Plymouth Brethren, Christadelphians, and so on. He specifically ordered that Mennonites and the members of certain other sects should not be compelled to wear uniforms, as their raiment was a tenet of their faith. It was his express wish that conscientious objectors should be segregated from serving soldiers, given noncombatant duty if they had been deemed eligible for it, and treated with "tact and consideration."

The military authorities had far less sympathy. Going "soft on slackers," they felt, was unfair to ordinary conscripts. Many objectors, now that they had been inducted, flatly refused to perform even noncombatant duties, since these still served the purpose of the war, and declined to obey army discipline, wear uniforms, march, drill, or even, in extreme cases, keep clean. Most of the division commanders, like Leonard Wood at Camp Funston, Kansas, felt it their duty to convert them to the ways of war. The pressure they applied took various forms—verbal abuse, humiliation, courts-martial and exaggerated legal penalties, beating, and, in extreme cases, what amounted to torture.

Hutterites, whose faith forbade them to cut their hair, had their beards shaved off by force. Dukhobors were forced into military dress or tormented if they refused. One who was ducked under a faucet on a freezing day subsequently died of pneumonia; his widow, upon receiving his body for burial, was appalled to find it in full uniform, a desecration of his faith.

The most brutal treatment was generally reserved for those whose scruples were ideological rather than religious—and this included not only socialists and others with political objections to the war but those whose objections were made in the name of humanity rather than that of any recognized creed. A great many were eventually "persuaded" to accept military discipline or noncombatant duties, but almost four thousand held out.

Sheldon W. Smith refused to sign the Army's clothing slip. "They put a pen in my hand and held it there to make a mark. . . . Next I was stripped in

*Newton Baker was Secretary of War from 1916 to 1921. (Eds.)

a violent manner and taken inside and dressed [in uniform] amidst arm twisting, thumping etc." Then he was taken to the bathhouse, where he was stripped again, held under the shower, and scrubbed with a broom. His captors whipped him with their belts, put a rope around his neck, and lashed it to a pipe, hauling on it until he could not breathe and all the while shouting at him to give in. "The bathing was continued until I was chilled and shook all over; part of the time they had me on my back with face under a faucet and held my mouth open. They got a little flag ordering me to kiss it and kneel down to it."

When the severity of the treatment being handed out in some camps was brought to Baker's attention at the end of 1917, he was horrified and ordered that, from the start of 1918, all "personal scruples," including nonreligious ones, should be classed as objections of conscience and his previous strictures observed. Baker would ultimately review all courtmartial sentences, disapproving a tenth of them altogether and mitigating a further 185 out of a total of 540. None of the seventeen death sentences was carried out.

But in the interim neither he nor the President would intervene any more closely to protect individual rights. The force of public opinion—from the press, the parents of serving soldiers, even the clergy—was against the objectors, and it was a factor neither Wilson nor Baker was prepared to ignore.

Far more worrisome to the Army than either immigrants or conscientious objectors were the draft boards' peculiar ideas as to what constituted physical suitability for service on the Western Front. Of the conscripts inducted during the war, an estimated 196,000 had venereal disease on arrival at camp. Of the 22,000 men examined at Camp Lewis, Washington, 5,000 had thyroid enlargement. Orthopedic problems, particularly foot defects, were commonplace; in one camp, 18 percent of the men had foot trouble, which drill soon revealed. The dentists at Camp Lee examined 38,963 draftees and found 10,596 suffering from infected root canals.

Problems varied with the conscripts' ethnic stock. According to Army Medical Department statistics, French Canadians had the poorest overall health in general: a high incidence of stunted growth, tuberculosis, and nervous and mental defects. Germans and Austrians were prone to alcoholism, varicose veins, and flat feet. "Sections of the black belt of the South," medical officers reported, showed higher-than-average arthritis, manic-depressive psychoses, and heart valve disease, lower-than-average obesity.

From an intake of 6,600 at one camp—and these were men who had passed through the mill of the draft boards—1,600 were immediately discharged as unfit and/or "unsuited, worthless, non-English-speaking, illiterate and venereally diseased." Where there was some hope of remedying the defects, the men were assigned to holding units. Camp Devens, Massachusetts, for example, had a battalion including 134 venereal, 151 neuropsychiatric, 368 cardiovascular, and 1,271 orthopedic cases.

Whatever their vital statistics or their moral standards, the raw levies all had one thing in common; they were in the camps and cantonments to be trained individually in the skills of the soldier and collectively, with their officers, molded into efficient units ready for war. The War Department's strategy had no frills. Besides instructors sent over from Europe by the English and French, they produced company-grade officers—captains and lieutenants—to train the men and then depended on the regular army (and, to a lesser extent, National Guard) officers—majors, colonels, and above—to weld the companies into battalions, regiments, and brigades. The objective was a division that was militarily efficient, a responsive organism of great power.

Many of the professional officers had theoretical knowledge of how to handle large units, but none had any practical experience of anything resembling a 28,000-man division; nevertheless, they rose to their task. The newly commissioned company-grade officers, in the Army for less than half a year, were even further at sea, each finding himself suddenly responsible for the welfare, discipline, and instruction of 250 men, with no protective shield of seasoned drill sergeants to cow the insubordinate.

Black company-grade officers of the 92nd Division struggled to create cohesion and maintain morale. Not only was the division never assembled in one place, but hanging over it was General Ballou's warning that "white men made the Division, and they can break it just as easily if it becomes a trouble-maker." The officers hardly advanced their own cause. "The vast majority of colored officers," remembered the regimental surgeon of the 349th Field Artillery, "held themselves distinctly aloof from the colored enlisted men . . . [who] used to nickname their colored officers 'Monkey Chasers.'"

At first, not surprisingly, the key figures in the National Army cantonments were the eight hundred or so British and French instructors. They were all veterans, often with wound stripes on their sleeves, and they brought the callousness of the front with them. "We made an attack one day," one told his pupils.

> As our first wave carried the enemy trench, they heard shouts from a dugout: "Kamerad!" The Germans surrendered. The first wave rushed on, leaving it to the second wave to take the prisoners. As soon as the first wave had passed, the Germans emerged from their dugout with a hidden machine gun and broke it out on the backs of the men who had been white enough not to give them the cold steel. So now, men, when we hear "Kamerad" coming from the depths of a dugout in a captured trench we call down: "How many?" If the answer comes back "Six," we decide that one hand grenade ought to be enough to take care of six and toss it in.

It was impossible in these home camps for either men or units to be made fully ready for combat. Communications being what they were, the knowledge and experience accumulating daily in France was simply not crossing the Atlantic. After six months of war, the General Staff in Washington recognized that it was receiving information that was at best three weeks old. In France, Pershing created an elaborate system of schools to provide instruction for every branch and level of the service: staff officers, unit commanders, candidates for commissions, specialists from every staff and supply department, artillerymen, intelligence officers, pilots. Ideally, all the incomers should have achieved a basic level of competence before crossing to France, but the AEF* schools were equipped to improve on the training of any unit in any branch, with the benefit of having more immediate knowledge of field conditions.

At Langres, forty miles south of Chaumont, Pershing established the critically important Staff College, which, in a frenetic three-month course, attempted to turn out war managers. In addition, his Training Branch developed a three-month training cycle for divisions in France, covering small-unit training, staff work, and combined arms practice and ending with a period in the trenches brigaded with Allied units.

Infantry training was only one of the specializations that together created the complex mechanisms of a division. A man's occupation in civilian life would often dictate his role in the Army: typists were assigned to headquarters staff, garment workers to the quartermaster, construction workers to engineer battalions, pharmacists to medical units, cooks to the kitchens, backwoodsmen to sniper units. In theory, motorized transportation units should have been especially hard to staff. There were usually men who knew how to handle horses, but in 1917 truck and tractor drivers were few and far between. Nevertheless, the appeal of driving was irresistible and men often lied about their experience with motor vehicles in order to get behind the wheel.

Native Americans made some of the U.S. Army's most awe-inspiring soldiers. Though Americanization was accelerating, and as many Indians were lawyers, doctors, and engineers by 1914 as were employed in hunting, trapping, or guiding, many still brought skills that adapted remarkably well to conditions on the Western Front. Possibly because of Chief of Staff Hugh Scott's deep interest in their culture, they were not discriminated against, provided there was "no colored admixture." In all, 6,509 were inducted and the same number volunteered, a total of almost 30 percent of all adult Indian males. The percentages varied from tribe to tribe: roughly 40 percent of the Oklahoma Osage and Quapaw served, while less than 1 percent of the Navajo did so. In the federal Indian schools where Americanization had free rein, almost 100 percent of males enlisted, many lying about their age. "I felt no American could or should be better than the first American," explained one Siletz volunteer.

*American Expeditionary Force (Eds.)

In 1917–1918, young Indian males were still in touch with traditional hunting and fighting skills. In the cantonments, they provided an object lesson to the urban conscripts in techniques of concealment and stealth by slipping across "no-man's-land" to snatch a "German" from the trenches opposite. Their languages were regarded as excellent substitutes for code, though a new vocabulary had to be evolved to deal with the terminology of modern war: machine guns became "little guns shoot fast" and battalions were indicated by "one, two and three grains of corn."

Zane Grey,* touring Wild West shows, and other more authentic by-products of a culture so recently vibrant had all imprinted the Germans with stereotypical images of "Red Indians." They were terrified of the specter of the "red man" and drafted extra snipers into sectors where Indians were spotted, "specially to pick off these dangerous men." Recognizing an opportunity for psychological warfare, the War Department gave serious thought to "attempting a limited number of night raids with men camouflaged as Indians in full regalia."

In the early days of sorting and allocating men, the Army relied a good deal on personal impressions and the direct question "What can you do?" But this was the second decade of the twentieth century, when the psychologist had begun to make an impression, and when Pershing complained that "too many mental incompetents were being shipped abroad," it seemed time to try newer methods. Psychologist Robert M. Yerkes was able to persuade the War Department "to adopt a scientific basis for assessing the quality of the new recruits."

During the war, 3 million soldiers were given intelligence tests—one test for the literate, another for those considered illiterate. (The literacy test itself provided perhaps the biggest shock: throughout the Army, 24.9 percent of men could neither read the paper nor write a letter home—in English, at least—and this was the criterion employed.) Men who were rated "feebleminded" because they scored so low on the intelligence test were immediately discharged from the Army without review by a disability board—until the authorities realized that many college graduates were using this as an ingenious escape route from the Army.

By today's standards, the tests were obviously flawed, geared remorselessly to the middle-class native English speaker with questions on literature, tennis, and the like. Even so, a grading of "A" to "E" offered a simple, convenient reference tool to personnel officers struggling to allocate thousands of new recruits in a hurry. Once the men with relevant experience had been assigned, each company would receive a mixture of grades. Men who had scored lower than "C" would not be permitted to apply for commissions.

---

*A well-known author of the American West (Eds.)

Life in the Army offered the clearest demonstration that the grip of the federal government was closing ever more tightly around the individual. It was a protective as well as coercive clasp. In the late 1890s, William Gibbs McAdoo (then a dealer in railway bonds) had helped the "penniless and starving" wives and families of servicemen in the Spanish-American War. Now, as Secretary of the Treasury, he urged that "the basis of the family's support . . . should be an allotment of a fixed proportion of the soldier's pay." Enlisted married men were obliged to make over half their $33 monthly pay to their families, which the government then supplemented.

The allotment could not fully compensate for the induction of a husband or son. Draft boards seem to have applied the "genuine dependency" exemption very narrowly, and across the country division headquarters were inundated with applications for the release of enlisted men or for more money in lieu. Desperate letters told of starving children, sick and bedridden relatives. In their bemused incoherence and their combination of greed and optimism with genuine hardship, these were a constant source of amusement to headquarters staff, who circulated a list of the choicest pleas. "My boy has been put in charge of a spittoon. Will I get more money now?" "I didn't know my husband had a middle name, and if he did, I do not think it was 'None.'" "You ask for my allotment number: I have four boys and two girls." "I am writing to ask you why I have not received my elopement." "I have not received my husband's pay and will be forced to lead an immortal life." "Please return my marriage certificate. Baby has not eaten in three days."

Material support was only one aspect of the government's paternalism. McAdoo and Cabinet colleagues such as Daniels, Baker, and Wilson made the soldier's moral welfare in camp their concern as well. Baker, a reformer by inclination, remembered the public outrage in 1916 at the plague of brothels spreading along the Mexican border with the soldiers. He knew people were afraid of the effects of these huge new concentrations of troops, and he threw his weight behind a morality campaign; by the end of 1917, some 110 red-light districts near camps had been closed. At the level of private enterprise, the concerned citizens of the National Allied Relief Committee raised funds to bus vulnerable American servicemen through "the London danger zone" and save them "from the distressing and terrible dangers of the streets."

For help in finding something to take the place of the customary army pleasures, Baker turned to a friend, Raymond Fosdick, a thirty-three-year-old moralist and social reformer and the brother of the well-known clergyman Harry Emerson Fosdick. Baker asked him to provide the men with "wholesome recreation and enjoyment." This he was to achieve by coordinating the various voluntary organizations operating in the camps—bodies such as the YMCA, the Jewish Welfare Board, and the Knights of Columbus, up to thirty-six of them in some camps. Under Fosdick's Committee on

Training Camp Activities, the men came to enjoy community songs, Liberty Theaters (occasionally graced by the singing of the President's daughter Margaret), YMCA huts (blacks usually excluded) where they could read magazines and write letters, Hostess Houses (separately provided for blacks) where they could meet female visitors in civilized surroundings, athletics, football and baseball, and educational programs aimed particularly at illiterates and the foreign-born. A small pamphlet published by the YMCA in 1917 offered the man about to go overseas a remarkable selection of handy French expressions: "I should like very much to see the periscope of a submarine"; "I have pawned my watch"; "A piece of shell hit me in the arm"; "Do not stick your head above the trench"; "Here I am, here I stay."

The young American male in those days was deemed by the War Department to be remarkably ignorant about sex; Fosdick's committee set out to put him straight. He was taught the facts of life and the risks of low life. "A German bullet is cleaner than a whore," announced one poster, showing a surprising lack of tact. "You wouldn't use another man's toothbrush. Why use his whore?" The potentially horrific results of normal intercourse seem so to have traumatized the youths of America that some of the young men moved swiftly from a state of ignorance to a widespread preference for alternatives, or so the Paris prostitutes claimed.

The motive of the military authorities for combating vice was military efficiency, not spiritual improvement. Where Fosdick's civilians concentrated on deterrence and moral suasion, the Army blandly provided prophylaxis at any hour of the day and night, somewhat undermining the credibility of the righteous. Contracting a venereal disease was a punishable offense, but this was because it was careless and unnecessary and detracted from the soldier's usefulness, not because it was wicked.

Neither military personnel nor civilians were entirely successful in combating venereal disease. At some camps the scale of the problem verged on the unmanageable. So many conscripts on leave from the camps in Kansas and Missouri headed for the prostitutes on Kansas City's Twelfth Avenue that it had been nicknamed "Woodrow Wilson Avenue—a piece at any price." Local authorities often refused to cooperate in the campaign against the local red-light district, which might be a useful factor of a community's economy. Seattle had to be declared off limits, New Orleans failed to see the point of the campaign, and Galveston, Texas, remained an open city. Where prostitutes were pushed out, they often took up residence in the black districts of town, beyond the reach of the authorities' interest, and into the vacuum stepped the amateurs, hero-worshiping girls, some as young as twelve, who were determined to give themselves to the uniform.

In France, Pershing was very much more draconian, certainly more so than the natives. The French provided licensed brothels for their troops, and in 1918 Premier Georges Clemenceau offered similar services to the AEF. When Baker saw the letter, he exclaimed to Fosdick, "For God's sake,

Raymond, don't show this to the President or he'll stop the war." Pershing personally inspected the VD returns every day. He declared red-light districts off limits and had them patrolled; MPs were then found to have the highest incidence of VD in the AEF. Men returning to camp drunk were automatically assumed to be infected and were treated, by force if necessary.

The Army also fought a constant, if losing, battle at home against the temptations of alcohol. In the "dry" states, soldiers helped bootleggers make a killing; in "wet" ones, the authorities created "dry" zones around the camps, but the regulations proved nearly impossible to enforce. Men found lemon or ginger "extracts" with a 9 percent alcohol content perfectly satisfactory. The punishment for selling liquor to men in uniform was a year's imprisonment, so the soldiers took off their tunics or paid the proprietor in advance, whereupon the barman "treated" them to drinks.

In Pershing's domain, beyond the reach of the moral crusaders, military efficiency was again the only criterion. Spirits were forbidden, but the men were allowed to buy beer and wine, and "Major Van Rooge" and "Captain Van Blank" became constant companions. Pershing did curb the intake by supporting the move to retain half the pay even of men without dependants. The soldiers' spending power worried him because of the impact it was having on the morale of French and British soldiers, who were paid far less. "$10 a month," he remarked, "is more spending money than a man in the trenches ought to have."

Drugs, which were widely used in society, duly made their appearance in the Army. Military intelligence gave warning of the sale to troops in southern cantonments of "the Chihuahua or Marihuana weed. This is a plant smoked by Mexicans of the lower classes; its use produces insanity and homicidal mania." The death-dealing weed proved popular, and by the summer of 1918 it had spread as far as Seattle. At Camp Devens, Special Agent Kelleher surprised a narcotics dealer in barracks at six one evening "with a complete outfit of hypodermic syringes, a spoon for heating the concoction, and quite a lot of morphine." Waiting in line were three conscripts with their sleeves rolled up.

DOCUMENTS

German-American Loyalty, 1917

My emotions tell me one thing at this awful time, but my reason tells me another. As a German by birth it is a horrible calamity that I may have to fight Germans. That is natural, is it not? But as an American by preference, I can see no other course open. . . .

For 25 years Germany has shown dislike for the United States—the Samoan affair, the Hongkong contretemps, the Manila Bay incident, the unguarded words of the Kaiser himself, and, lastly, the Haitian controversy in 1914. . . . And it has not been from mere commercial or diplomatic friction. It is because their ideals of government are absolutely opposite. One or the other must go down. It is for us to say now which it shall be.

Because of my birth and feelings beyond my control I have no particular love for the French and less for the British. But by a strange irony of fate I see those nations giving their blood for principles which I hold dear, against the wrong principles of people I individually love. It is a very unhappy paradox, but one I can not escape. I do not want to see the allies triumph over the land of my birth. But I very much want to see the triumph of the ideas they fight for.

It sickens my soul to think of this Nation going forth to help destroy people many of whom are bound to me by ties of blood and friendship. But it must be so. It is like a dreadful surgical operation. The militaristic, undemocratic demon which rules Germany must be cast out. It is for us to do it—now. I have tried to tell myself that it is not our affair, that we should have contented ourselves with measures of defense and armed neutrality. But I know that is not so. The mailed fist has been shaken under our nose before. If Prussianism triumphs in this war the fist will continue to shake. We shall be in real peril, and those ideas for which so much of the world's best blood has been spilled through the centuries will be in danger of extinction. It seems to me common sense that we begin our defense by immediate attack when the demon is occupied and when we can command assistance.

There is much talk of what people like me will do, and fear of the hyphen. No such thing exists. The German-American is as staunch as the American of adoption of any other land and perhaps more so. Let us make war upon Germany, not from revenge, not to uphold hairsplitting quibbles of international law, but let us make war with our whole heart and with all

SOURCE: C. Kotzenabe, "German-American Loyalty," in Committee on Public Information, War Information Series, *American Loyalty* (Washington, D.C.: Government Printing Office, 1917), 5–6.

our strength, because Germany worships one god and we another and because the lion and the lamb can not lie down together. One or the other must perish.

Let us make war upon the Germany of the Junkerthum,* the Germany of frightfulness, the Germany of arrogance and selfishness, and let us swear not to make peace until the Imperial German Government is the sovereign German people.

Letters from Mennonite Draftees, 1918

DEAR BROTHER————:

I went to Camp Cody, N. Mex., June 25, 1918. At first I drilled without a rifle, but later was asked to take one, explaining that the President's orders concerning the C. O.'s [conscientious objectors] required it, and I would get into noncombatant service in due time. I accepted it, and in two weeks was transferred to the infantry where, of course, I was asked again to take the rifle, and I saw that I had been deceived. I refused and explained why. Several nights after this, while I was in bed, some privates threw water into my bed, put a rope around my neck and jerked me out on the floor.

The next day two sergeants came to my tent and took me out, tied a gun on my shoulder and marched me down the street, one on each side of me, kicking me all the way. I was asked again whether I would take the rifle and drill. I refused and was taken to the bath-house, put under the shower bath where they turned on the water, alternating hot and cold, until I was so numb that I could scarcely rise. Just then one of the higher officers came in and asked what they were about. They explained that they were giving me a bath. The officer told me to dress and go to my tent, that he wanted to interview me himself. He asked if I would take a rifle and drill. I told him that I could not. He ordered my sergeant to put me on company street work until they got my transfer, and in three weeks I was given noncombatant service.

VERY TRULY YOURS,————

DEAR BROTHER:

I came home Wednesday evening, Feb. 5. To get home, receive a hearty welcome and many expressions of joy for the effort made to maintain the faith, was alone worth the hardships which we endured.

SOURCE: J. S. Hartzler, *Mennonites in the World War or Nonresistance Under Test* (Scottdale, Pa.: Mennonite Publishing House, 1922), 124–127.
Junkerthum refers to the Prussian military aristocracy. (Eds.)

I had been gone a few days more than ten months, of which I spent twenty-four days in our company, ten days in detention camp, seventy-eight days in the guard-house, one night in the Kansas City Police "lock-up," one hundred ninety-seven days in the disciplinary barracks (Fort Leavenworth, Kans.) and two days on the way home. . . .

I do not approve of such practices as the world was engaged in, and will give them neither moral nor material support though it may mean imprisonment or even death for not doing so. If the army would never kill a man, I can not see how a person could become a part of it, giving moral and material support to its maintenance and still retain a Christian character. The standards it upholds and the injustices it practices are unbelievable to a man who never saw them. . . . The only part that I can have in the army is suffering its punishments. Its purposes and those of Christianity are as different as night and day. The aims of the army are coercion, terrorism, carnal force; the ideals of Christianity are love, meekness, gentleness, obedience to the will of God, etc. When these ideals are maintained to the best of our ability, by God's grace He will provide care and protection in ways not imagined by man.

As to noncombatant service: all branches of service have one purpose; viz., to make the whole system a stronger organization of terrorism, destruction, and death. While I would not have been directly killing any one, I would have been doing a man's part in helping another do the act, and lending encouragement to the same. To support a thing and refuse to do the thing supported is either ignorance or cowardice. To refuse to go to the trenches and still give individual assistance to another doing so, is either an improper knowledge of the issues at stake or downright fear to face the bullets. I have a greater conscientious objection against noncombatant than against combatant service. I feel that the principle is the same, and that both are equally wrong. I would feel guilty toward the other man to accept service where the danger was not so great. . . .

To an observer it may have seemed ridiculous to refuse to even plant flowers at the base hospital. In the first place, that was the duty of the working gang under the quartermaster's department. Technically I would not have been doing military duty for I had not "signed up"; virtually I would have been rendering service because I was at work. . . . The farther one went with the military officers the farther they demanded him to go. I felt that the farther I went the less reason I could give for stopping, so I concluded that the best place to stop was in the beginning. It was on the charge of refusing to plant flowers that I received my court-martial sentence of ten years of hard labor in the disciplinary barracks at Fort Leavenworth, Kans.

FRATERNALLY YOURS,———

Racism and the Army, 1918

French Military Mission

STATIONED WITH THE AMERICAN ARMY

AUGUST 7, 1918

Secret Information Concerning Black American Troops

1. It is important for French officers who have been called upon to exercise command over black American troops, or to live in close contact with them, to have an exact idea of the position occupied by Negroes in the United States. The information set forth in the following communication ought to be given to these officers and it is to their interest to have these matters known and widely disseminated. It will devolve likewise on the French Military Authorities, through the medium of the Civil Authorities, to give information on this subject to the French population residing in the cantonments occupied by American colored troops.

2. The American attitude upon the Negro question may seem a matter for discussion to many French minds. But we French are not in our province if we undertake to discuss what some call "prejudice." American opinion is unanimous on the "color question" and does not admit of any discussion.

The increasing number of Negroes in the United States (about 15,000,000) would create for the white race in the Republic a menace of degeneracy were it not that an impassable gulf has been made between them.

As this danger does not exist for the French race, the French public has become accustomed to treating the Negro with familiarity and indulgence.

This indulgence and this familiarity are matters of grievous concern to the Americans. They consider them an affront to their national policy. They are afraid that contact with the French will inspire in black Americans aspirations which to them [the whites] appear intolerable. It is of the utmost importance that every effort be made to avoid profoundly estranging American opinion.

Although a citizen of the United States, the black man is regarded by the white American as an inferior being with whom relations of business or service only are possible. The black is constantly being censured for his want of intelligence and discretion, his lack of civic and professional conscience and for his tendency toward undue familiarity.

The vices of the Negro are a constant menace to the American who has to repress them sternly. For instance, the black American troops in France have, by themselves, given rise to as many complaints for attempted rape as

SOURCE: W. E. B. DuBois, ed., "Documents of the War." *The Crisis* 28 (May 1919): 16–18. Document from Bibliobase®, edited by Michael Bellesiles. Copyright © by Houghton Mifflin Company. Reprinted by permission.

all the rest of the army. And yet the [black American] soldiers sent us have been the choicest with respect to physique and morals, for the number disqualified at the time of mobilization was enormous.

Conclusion

1. We must prevent the rise of any pronounced degree of intimacy between French officers and black officers. We may be courteous and amiable with these last, but we cannot deal with them on the same plane as with the white American officers without deeply wounding the latter. We must not eat with them, must not shake hands or seek to talk or meet with them outside of the requirements of military service.

2. We must not commend too highly the black American troops, particularly in the presence of [white] Americans. It is all right to recognize their good qualities and their services, but only in moderate terms, strictly in keeping with the truth.

3. Make a point of keeping the native cantonment population from "spoiling" the Negroes. [White] Americans become greatly incensed at any public expression of intimacy between white women with black men. They have recently uttered violent protests against a picture in the "Vie Parisienne" entitled "The Child of the Desert" which shows a [white] woman in a "cabinet particulier" with a Negro. Familiarity on the part of white women with black men is furthermore a source of profound regret to our experienced colonials who see in it an over-weening menace to the prestige of the white race.

Military authority cannot intervene directly in this question, but it can through the civil authorities exercise some influence on the population.

PART I

Suggestions for Further Reading

On Southern black Americans after the Civil War, consult two works by Eric Foner: *Nothing but Freedom: Emancipation and Its Legacy* (1983) and his impressive *Reconstruction: America's Unfinished Revolution, 1863–1967* (1988). See also John Hope Franklin, *Reconstruction After the Civil War* (1961); Leon Litwack, *Been in the Storm So Long: The Aftermath of Slavery* (1979); and Howard Rabinowitz, *Race Relations in the Urban South, 1865–1890* (1980). On black poverty, see Jay R. Mandle, *The Roots of Black Poverty* (1978). C. Vann Woodward, *The Strange Career of Jim Crow* (1966), remains an important work. See also Edward Ayers, *The Promise of the New South: Life After Reconstruction* (1992), and Jacqueline Jones, *The Disposed: America's Underclass from the Civil War to the Present* (1992). Neil McMillen, *Dark Journey: Black Mississippi in the Age of Jim Crow* (1989) is especially good. Very comprehensive is Leon F. Litwack, *Trouble in Mind: Black Southerners in the Age of Jim Crow* (1998).

For settlement of the frontier, general works are Donald Worster, *Under Western Skies: Nature and History in the American West* (1992); Richard White "It's Your Misfortune and None of My Own": A History of the American West (1991); and Richard Bartell, *The New Country: Social History of the American Frontier, 1776–1890* (1974). An older book of value is Everett Dick, *Sod House Frontier: 1854–1890* (1937). See also W. Eugene Hollon, *The Great American Desert* (1966), and Joe B. Frantz and Julian E. Choate, Jr., *The American Cowboy: The Myth and the Reality* (1955). A comprehensive view of the West is presented in Rodman Paul, *The Far West and the Great Plains in Transition, 1859–1900* (1988), while a more controversial view is found in Patricia Nelson Limerick, *The Legacy of Conquest: The Unbroken Past of the American West* (1987).

On American Indians, consult Francis Paul Prucha, *The Great White Father: The United States Government and the American Indians* (1984); Angie Debo, *A History of the Indians of the United States* (1970); and Vine Deloria, Jr., *Custer Died for Your Sins: An Indian Manifesto* (1969). On reform and assimilation, see Robert W. Mardock, *Reformers and the American Indians* (1971), and Frederick E. Hoxie, *A Final Promise: The Campaign to Assimilate the Indians, 1880–1920* (1984). On the New Deal and the Indians, see Philip Kenneth, *John Collier's Crusade for Indian Reform, 1920–1954* (1977). On education, see Margaret Szasz, *Education and the American Indian: The Road to Self-Determination, 1928–1973* (1974). Rex Smith, *Moon of the Popping Trees: The Tragedy at Wounded Knee and the End of the Indian Wars* (1975), is a good book on cultural conflict. On boarding schools, see Clyde Ellis, *To Change Them Forever: Indian Education at the Rainy Mountain Boarding School, 1893–1920* (1996), and David Wallace Adams, *Education for Extinction: American Indians and the Boarding School Experience, 1875–1928* (1995).

For women after the Civil War, there are a number of useful works. General books are Peter Filene, *Him/Her Self: Sex Roles in Modern America* (1975), and Sheila M. Rothman, *Woman's Proper Place: A History of Changing Ideals and Practices, 1870 to the Present* (1978). On women and education, see Barbara Solomon, *In the Company of Educated Women* (1985). On women and reform, see Theda Skocpol, *Protecting Soldiers and Mothers: The Political Origins of Social Policy in the United States* (1992). On women and work, consult David Katzman, *Seven Days a Week: Women and Domestic Service in Industrializing America* (1978); Leslie Tentler, *Wage-Earning Women: Industrial Work and Family in the United States, 1900–1930* (1979); Dee Garrison, *Apostles of Culture: The Public Libraries and American Society, 1876–1920* (1979); Barbara Harris, *Beyond Her Sphere: Women and the Professions in American History* (1978); and Nancy Dye, *As Equals and Sisters: The Labor Movement and the Women's Trade Union League of New York* (1980). On changing attitudes and practices about birth control, see Linda Gordon, *Woman's Body, Woman's Right: A Social History of Birth Control in America* (1979), and James Reed, *From Private Vice to Public Virtue: The Birth Control Movement and American Society Since 1830* (1977). On feminism, the standard work is Eleanor Flexner, *Century of Struggle: The Women's Rights Movement in the United States* (1959). Also helpful are William O'Neill, *Everyone Was Brave: A History of Feminism in America* (1971), and William Leach, *True Love and Perfect Union: The Feminist Reform of Sex and Society* (1980). For feminism in the early twentieth century, Nancy Cott, *The Grounding of Modern Feminism* (1987), is also stimulating.

On immigration, Stephan Thernstrom (ed.), *The Harvard Encyclopedia of American Ethnic Groups* (1980), is outstanding. Two general works are Leonard Dinnerstein and David Reimers, *Ethnic Americans: A History of Immigration and Assimilation* (1999), and John Bodnar, *The Transplanted: A History of Immigrants in Urban America* (1985). John Higham, *Strangers in the Land: Patterns of Nativism, 1860–1925* (1955), is an especially good study of nativism. On the Italians, see Virginia Yans-McLaughlin, *Family and Community: Italian Immigrants in Buffalo, 1880–1930* (1977), and Humbert Nelli, *Italians in Chicago, 1880–1930: A Study in Ethnic Mobility* (1970). On Jews, see Moses Rischin, *The Promised City: New York's Jews, 1870–1914* (1962), and Irving Howe, *World of Our Fathers: The Journey of the East European Jews to America and the Life They Found and Made* (1976). Useful comparative studies are Thomas Kessner, *The Golden Door: Italian and Jewish Mobility in New York City, 1880–1915* (1977), and John Bodnar et al., *Lives of Their Own: Blacks, Italians and Poles in Pittsburgh, 1900–1960* (1982). On New York City, consult Nathan Glazer and Daniel Patrick Moynihan, *Beyond the Melting Pot: The Negroes, Puerto Ricans, Jews, Italians and Irish of New York City* (1963). See also Frederick M. Binder and David M. Reimers, *All the Nations Under Heaven: An Ethnic and Racial History of New York City* (1995). For immigration restriction, John Higham, *Strangers in the Land: Patterns of American Nativism, 1860–1925* (1968) is the standard work.

For Jewish women, see Sydney Stahl Weinberg, *The World of Our Mothers: The Lives of Jewish Immigrant Women* (1988). Jewish women also are covered in Susan Glenn, *Daughters of the Shtetl* (1989), while Kathy Peis, *Cheap Amusements: Leisure in Turn-of-the-Century New York* (1985), explores the lives of working-class immigrant women in New York City. For Irish women see Hasia Diner, *Erin's Daughters in America: Irish Immigrant Women in the Nineteenth Century* (1983). For Chinese women, see Judy Yung, *Unbound Feet: A Social History of Chinese Women in San Francisco* (1995). See also Sucheng Chan, *Asian Americans: An Interpretive History* (1991).

For industrialization and American workers, see Herbert Gutman, *Work, Culture and Society in Industrializing America* (1976); Stephan Thernstrom, *The Other Bostonians* (1973); and Melvyn Dubofsky, *Industrialism and the American Worker, 1865–1920* (1975). David Brody, *Steelworkers in America: The Non-Union Era* (1976), is an excellent book. On workers in the Southern cotton mills, see Jacqueline Dowd Hall et al., *Like a Family: The Making of a Southern Cotton Mill World* (1987).

For the migration of blacks to the North, Forette Henri, *Black Migration: Movement North, 1900–1920* (1976), provides a general overview. For particular cities, see Gilbert Osofsky, *Harlem: The Making of a Ghetto, 1890–1930* (1968); David Katzman, *Before the Ghetto: Black Detroit in the Nineteenth Century* (1973); Allan Spear, *Black Chicago: The Making of a Ghetto, 1890–1920* (1967); Thomas Lee Philpott, *The Slum and the Ghetto: Neighborhood Deterioration and Middle Class Reform, Chicago, 1880–1930* (1976). Two excellent studies of white racism are George Frederickson, *The Black Image in the White Mind: The Debate on Afro-American Character and Destiny, 1817–1914* (1971), and Joel Williamson, *The Crucible of Race* (1984). An outstanding study of black culture is Lawrence Levine, *Black Culture and Black Consciousness: Afro-American Folk Thought from Slavery to Freedom* (1977). For a new view of the migration north, see James R. Grossman, *Land of Hope: Chicago, Black Southerners and the Great Migration* (1989).

On World War I, Frederick Luebke, *Bonds of Loyalty: German Americans and World War I* (1974), is informative. For the home front, see David Kennedy, *Over Here: The First World War and American Society* (1980). On women during the war, see Maurie W. Greenwald, *Women, War and Work: The Impact of World War I on Women Workers in the United States* (1980). For military aspects of the war, the standard treatment is Edward Coffman, *The War to End All Wars: The American Military Experience in World War I* (1968). On the economy see Ronald Schofer, *America in the Great War* (1991).

Part II

*Modern American Society
1920–Present*

Chapter 8

Intolerance: A Bitter Legacy of Social Change

At the turn of the century, few issues sparked so much debate and concern as the large-scale immigration to the United States from southern and eastern Europe. To many native-born Americans, whose roots lay in northern and western Europe, these millions of newcomers came to symbolize the disappearance of an older, simpler American society. Native-born Americans feared that the new immigrants would not adapt to established ways and values, and that they would lower the standard of living by taking jobs from American citizens and by working for low wages. During World War I, several prominent leaders also expressed apprehension about the potential for divided loyalties on the part of immigrants. Such leaders as Theodore Roosevelt believed that immigrants, especially German Americans, might retain allegiance to Germany, the nation's wartime enemy. Roosevelt wanted absolute patriotism—what he called "100 percent Americanism."

Fear and dread of foreigners intensified in the postwar years, with eastern European Jews and Roman Catholics being blamed for many of the nation's social problems. As one result of this mood, the Ku Klux Klan revived. This post–Civil

War vigilante group had first directed its hatred toward blacks, and later toward immigrants, whom it feared and despised. Within a few years of its reemergence in the early 1920s, the Klan spread its message of bigotry not only in the South, where it originated, but throughout the rest of the country as well. The Klan's growth and influence was imposing but brief. David Chalmers's essay "The Hooded Knights Revive Rule by Terror in the Twenties" examines the revival and eventual decline of the Klan during that decade. According to the essay, what attractions did the Klan hold for the thousands who joined it?

The first document comes from a 1926 article, "The Klan's Fight for American-ism," by Klan leader Hiram Evans. Notice how Evans's message combines bigotry and an alleged adherence to traditional American values. How does the document help to explain the Klan's appeal in sections of the country as different from each other in racial and ethnic makeup as Oregon, Georgia, and Massachusetts?

Although Evans's rantings seem outrageous to modern sensibilities, many people during this period, even in the highest levels of government, echoed the Klan philosophy. Evidence of this is found in the second document, an excerpt from congressional testimony in 1921 concerning U.S. immigration policy. Although those testifying do not refer to any specific countries of origin in their condemnation of immigrants, federal legislation passed in 1924 (the National Origins Act) makes it clear that legislators believed immigrants from some countries to be less desirable than those from others. The new approach, generally referred to as the "national-origins system," gave preference to immigrants from northern and western Europe; it severely limited immigration from the rest of the continent, and virtually barred Asians.

In 1952 Congress passed the McCarran-Walter Act, which was also based on the national-origins system. The final document reveals how the Senate subcommittee introducing the bill continued to defend this prejudicial system; both the Senate and the House demonstrated their concurrence through passage of the Act. In 1965 Congress finally replaced this law with a nondiscriminatory one.

ESSAY

The Hooded Knights Revive Rule by Terror in the Twenties

David Chalmers

D. W. Griffith's 1915 melodrama, *The Birth of a Nation*, was a blockbuster of a motion picture, and it helped revive the Ku Klux Klan. The Kentucky-born Griffith created his pioneering film from a novel written by a North Carolin-

SOURCE: David Chalmers, "The Hooded Knights Revive Rule by Terror in the Twenties," *American History Illustrated* 14 (February 1980): 28–37. Reprinted through courtesy of Cowles Magazines, publisher of *American History Illustrated*.

ian named Thomas Dixon. Dixon's life was built on eloquence and passion. A fellow-student and friend of Woodrow Wilson at Johns Hopkins graduate school, Dixon had been a legislator, Baptist preacher, lecturer, novelist, playwright, and actor, always reaching out to a larger audience. Griffith gave him his biggest one.

Dixon's 1905 book, *The Clansman: An Historical Romance of the Ku Klux Klan,* was one of three that he wrote on the Invisible Empire which his uncle had helped lead in the Carolina piedmont. The story revolved around two star-crossed families, the Camerons and the Stonemans, one from the South and the other from the North. Their sons and daughters fell in love, but the War Between the States separated them and Reconstruction brought them disaster. Congressman Stoneman, copied from life after Radical Republican leader Thaddeus Stephens, was presented as a crippled, hate-filled villain, urged on by his mulatto mistress to degrade the captured South. With the murder of "The Great Soul," Abraham Lincoln, there was nothing to stop him. Black tyranny ruled the South, black corruption stained its legislative halls, and brutish black lust stalked its womanhood. However, at this darkest moment, the hooded knights of the Ku Klux Klan, led by young Ben Cameron, Civil War hero and beloved of Stoneman's daughter, rode forth to save the South and its downtrodden people.

D. W. Griffith took Dixon's story and made it into the movies' first colossal spectacular. In place of the usual fifteen-minute flicker, Griffith created a three-hour epic, dramatically restaging the war's battles, Sherman's March to the Sea, and Lincoln's assassination at Ford's Theater. Congressman Stoneman comes to the Southern town of Piedmont to oversee his schemes for melding the races. Cameron's "Little Sister," as he called her, and her mother, Mrs. Lenoir, leap from a cliff to their deaths after ravishment by a black renegade soldier. Cameron is arrested and sentenced to death for murder; Stoneman's son, in love with Cameron's sister, takes his place. Just in time, the Klan arrives to save the living, avenge the fallen, and reunite the lovers.

Breaking the former static role of the camera, using angles, movement, and changing focus, expanding irises, reaching in and out of close-ups, juxtaposing, and paralleling, Griffith created his masterpiece. As the bugle call rang out and the Klan rode to the rescue, theater orchestras pounded out themes from Wagner and "The Hall of the Mountain King." Audiences rose cheering in the South, and crowds demonstrated in protest in the North. The picture was seen by President Woodrow Wilson, members of Congress and the Supreme Court, and millions of spectators at $2 apiece, while William J. Simmons, a fraternal organizer, colonel in the Woodmen of the World, and failed Methodist minister, dreamed of a revival of the Klan itself.

"Colonel" Simmons's plan for the Klan was revealed in the words of the advertisement which he inserted in the December 7, 1915, Atlanta *Journal.* The "Knights of the Ku Klux Klan" was "A High Class Order for Men of Intelligence and Character." It was to be "The World's Greatest *Secret*, Social, Patriotic, Fraternal, Beneficiary Order." In other words, it was to be a lodge, a fraternity. The fact that it was to exclude all who were not white, native-born, or Protestant did not make it substantially different from other such organizations and most college fraternities. It was the chance factor of its Southern origin that provided the dynamic element—the name and legend of the Ku Klux Klan. In *The Birth of a Nation*, whose Atlanta advertisement shared the page with Simmons's hand-drawn announcement of the Klan, Thomas Dixon and D. W. Griffith had engraved an image of flowing robes and mystic, masked, night-riding, patriotic violence on the national imagination. While most fraternities guarded their lodge hall secrets against outsiders and aliens, the vigilante heritage of the Klan took it out into the cow-pastures and city streets to protect its version of American values.

Simmons's initial plans had been less extravagant. His specialty was lodge ritual. He had hoped for a mildly successful organization in the Southeast to which he could sell memberships, regalia, and insurance. World War I enabled the Klan to do a little public marching and patriotic snooping. After the war the Klan, with a small membership in Georgia and Alabama, emerged into a time of opportunity. The heightened emotions and restlessness that were not immediately stilled by an end to the fighting, the manly camaraderie of the war and the habit of violence, people going home and not going home, black men who had served in the Army or who had left the farms for the cities and Northern factories—all were unsettling elements.

There were race riots in Chicago, Omaha, and Knoxville, in Duluth, Springfield, and Tulsa, in Texas, Arkansas, Kansas, and Florida. Large numbers of immigrants were arriving from the Southern and Eastern European dwelling places of the Roman Catholic, Jew, Slav, and Bolshevik. Life in the cities was confusing; the war to end war had turned sour, and the attempt to make society better by prohibition was either being flouted or downright corrupted. As with the original Ku Klux Klan, the unsettled times and the mysterious name (now potent with the legacy of its vigilante role during Reconstruction) undoubtedly shaped the direction the Klan would take for years to come.

Simmons engaged a pair of fund raisers, Edward Young Clarke and Mrs. Elizabeth Tyler, who were the Southern Publicity Association, to handle recruitment. Simmons was to receive $2 of the $10 initiation fee paid by each new member. The rest was to go to Clarke, Tyler, and their salesmen. The results were phenomenal. The Klan made good copy and the press rushed to spread reports of its doings. Within a year membership was nationwide and soared to almost 100,000.

The basic Southern emphasis on patriotism and white supremacy was expanded into the protection of basic morality and 100 percent Americanism. The American way of life and moral values were to be guarded not only against the Negroes, but from Roman Catholics, Jews, and Orientals, from aliens and immigrants, from bootleggers and road houses, from crime and corrupt politicians, from marital infidelity and sexual immorality, and from scoffers and unbelievers. Salesmen, or "kleagles," were selected from the Masonic and other lodges, touring lecturers from the evangelical ministry, and the country was divided and subdivided into sales districts. Local groups brought the Klan into town to combat bootlegging or corrupt city government, and Atlanta's usual advice to new chapters was to "clean up the town." Crosses burned on nearby hillsides, sheeted horsemen paraded down Main Street on Saturday night and the next morning marched down church aisles to make donations while choirs sang "The Old Rugged Cross" or "Onward Christian Soldiers."

Georgia . . . was the cradle for the reborn Klan. Colonel Simmons's blazing cross on Stone Mountain had been its first annunciation and Peachtree Street in Atlanta brought the robed faithful to its Imperial Palace. For fifty years Georgians would march in its parades and elect its candidates, as well as fight against its violence and intolerance. Nathan Bedford Forest Klan No. 1 was the Imperial Empire's mother lodge, and in 1920 when Simmons triumphantly attended the annual reunion of the United Confederate Veterans in Houston, its Exalted Cyclops Nathan Bedford Forrest III rode beside him.

The Klan spread through the cities and small towns of Georgia. The mighty Robert E. Lee No. 1 of Birmingham was the heart of its strength in Alabama and Sam Houston No. 1 led the way in Texas, although probably outstripped in size and violence by Dallas's No. 66 and Beaumont's No. 7. Klan organizers did well in northern Louisiana and throughout Arkansas, but the Imperial Empire's earliest bastion of terror was in Texas and Oklahoma. Klan salesmen jumped across the continent to California, selling patriotism, fraternity, and moral enforcement. They spread out from Los Angeles, and moved northward across the border to power in Oregon, offering anti-Catholicism to the descendants of the New England and Midwestern Puritans. Its legions grew in Missouri and Kansas, and its salesmen worked their way up the Mississippi Valley, across the Great Plains, and into the mountain states. In 1924 Colorado became even a greater success story than Oregon, as the Klan helped elect the mayor of Denver, the governor, and both senators.

But in no realm did Klan political power become greater than in Indiana. Its ambitious Grand Dragon D. C. Stephenson built his organization on a bloc by bloc basis throughout the state, carrying in tow the governor and both senators, negotiating for the purchase of Valparaiso University, and working his own way toward the White House. The Klan's fraternal appeal to what its Ohio Grand Dragon described as "the submerged majority of Protestants" swelled the tide of its membership in Cincinnati, Columbus, Toledo, Akron, and the steel centers of the Mahoning Valley. The Klan did well in the small towns and industrial cities of central Michigan and among the anti-Catholic socialists of Wisconsin. It signed up its thousands in Chicago and the suburbs, battling against an anti-Klan city administration. In "Bloody Herrin" County down in fundamentalist southern Illinois, where the mountain people from Kentucky and Tennessee shared their country uneasily with French and Italian immigrant coal miners, labor conflict turned into a murderous Klan and anti-Klan war that brought in the National Guard some eight times in four years.

Nor was the East immune from the recruitments of the Invisible Empire. Torn from its past as an instrument by which the post–Civil War Reconstruction was undone, the Klan, which was mainly Democratic in the South, was Republican in the North. In both sections it represented the old moral values against the newcomers and social change. There was the same concern about foreigners, the Roman Catholic "threat" to the public schools, and the enforcement of prohibition. Klan marchers brought in by chartered trains "to give the micks something to think about" were attacked by mobs in the western Pennsylvania mill towns of Carnegie, Lilly, and Scottdale, but in the Philadelphia suburbs and down in Lancaster County, once the Klan got organized, it stayed organized.

While New York City was generally enemy territory, Klan weddings, christenings, church visits, volunteer fire departments, parades, rallies, county fair days, and local political victories marked the Klan as a leading organization in Long Island's Suffolk and Nassau counties. Upstate, Klan domain stretched from its Binghamton headquarters to Buffalo. It entered New Jersey from New York and Pennsylvania and despite denunciation at church conferences, it found a home among Methodist prohibitionists and along the seacoast from Atlantic City to Cape May. Portions of the Klan-infiltrated National Guard were disarmed in Rhode Island. Boston's Mayor [James] Michael Curley cracked down on Klan meetings with the same sternness he had shown to the birth control crusader Margaret Sanger (despite American Civil Liberties Union protest in both cases), and Klansmen and Irishmen fought on summer nights in central Massachusetts. On the other side of the ethnic line, the prominent Boston blue-blood author Lothrop Stoddard found no conflict between his Americanism and that of the Klan, which also helped elect *Mayflower* descendant William Owen Brewster governor of Maine.

Simmons's talents lay in the area of lodge ritual and florid oratory, and many of his rising territorial leaders felt that he was not fully capitalizing on the Klan's potential. Led by the Dallas dentist Hiram Wesley Evans, whom Simmons had brought to Atlanta to help run things at the Imperial Palace, they staged a coup on the eve of the first national Klonvokation in 1922. When Simmons realized that he had been pushed upstairs out of control of the Klan, he was furious. Evens only laughed and replied, "Let's get the money, colonel."

There has never been a reliable tally of the number who belonged to the Klan. Between its veil of secrecy and its public boastings, the estimates run from two to four million members. During its peak years in the early twenties, members were streaming in and out in such numbers that the Klan itself probably never knew its own size. The consensus of historians is that Indiana took the lead with perhaps several hundred thousand Klansmen, Klanswomen, Tri-K's, and Junior Klansmen, with Texas, Oklahoma, Illinois, Ohio, and Pennslyvania probably close to 100,000 each. At one time or another in the 1920s, perhaps at least one out of every ten white, native-born, Protestant adult males belonged to the Invisible Empire. While sheer size did not necessarily mean political domination or long life for a Klan realm, in communities all across the country its strength gave a sense of power and immunity from the law. The mayor of Enid, Oklahoma, explained to the American Civil Liberties Union that since the Klan had 1,500 members and he had ten policemen, there was no point in investigating a reported Klan flogging.

A part of the fraternal excitement of the Klan was violence, a heritage from its Reconstruction days and not out of keeping with the Klan's vigilante role as a fighter against crime and immorality. The Klan was secret, masked, decentralized, and righteous, often operating with community approval and police participation. Although some Northern realms such as Ohio and Pennsylvania had their "Night Riders" and "Triple S" ("Super-Secret-Society") squads, the Southwest particularly liked "a little rough stuff." In the early twenties there were regular whippings and tar-and-feather parties in the meadows along Dallas's Trinity River bottoms. The Mer Rouge murders* brought a portion of Louisiana close to civil war, and Governor Jack Walton got himself impeached when he called out the National Guard and imposed martial law on much of Klan-ridden Oklahoma. Texas and Oklahoma led the way, but Klan floggers were also active in Georgia, Alabama, Florida, North Carolina, and Kern County, California, with scattered incidents elsewhere. In those areas where the Klan dominated, however, it was the fellow white, native-born Anglo-Saxon, Protestant rather than the Negro, Roman Catholic, Jew, or alien who was on the receiving end—which may be a commentary on the extent of the alien danger against which the Klan warned.

What drew its scores of thousands to the Klan? Later generations have looked upon the hooded knights as sour, defensive, bigoted, and something of a joke. To their contemporaries, they were serious business. Famed juvenile court judge, Ben Lindsey, who fought the Klan in Denver, commented,

---

*On August 24, 1922, in Mer Rouge, Louisiana, two white critics of the Ku Klux Klan were brutally tortured and then hanged by Klan members. (Eds.)

"They paid ten dollars to hate somebody and they were determined to get their money's worth." Julian Harris, son of the creator of the Uncle Remus tales, won a Pulitzer Prize for the anti-Klan campaign of his Columbus, Georgia, *Enquirer-Sun.* Taking the popular booster slogan "It's Great To Be a Georgian," he asked, "Is it great to be a citizen of a state whose governor is a member of and subservient to that vicious masked gang?" New Jersey Methodist Bishop E. H. Hughes found it necessary to remind his fellow ministers that "It is not Anglo-Saxon blood but the blood of Jesus Christ that has made us what we are."

However, to the Klansmen, their purpose was a positive expression of good fellowship and what America was all about. The Klan was a reform movement, even as prohibition was. It was a means to protect society, to keep things good "the way they had been," to get rid of criminals and corrupt politicians, dangerous radicals and those who scoffed at or violated church and home, bought illegal alcohol, or threatened racial purity and the Anglo-Saxon heritage of America.

People prefer simple explanations and scapegoats. Presidents Warren Harding and Calvin Coolidge, the Congress, and the Supreme Court hardly seemed dangerous forces for change. The Klansman found a symbol that he enjoyed blaming: the outsider-alien, personified in the Roman Catholic Church and personalized in the Roman Pope. Ex-priests and "escaped" nuns were popular on the Klan lecture circuit where stories of papal intrigue, convent sin, guns hidden in church basements, and the menace of the Knights of Columbus were staples. From Maine to California, the Klan girded its emotional loins against the Roman menace. While no Episcopal, Methodist, or Baptist convention approved of the Klan and many church leaders denounced it, the Klan appeared to be taking a noisy leadership in protecting community morality. In short, it was doing what the churches talked about: the Klan spoke their language, made donations, and filled their benches. So it was very difficult for many ministers and parishioners to turn it down.

In addition to fraternalism, nativism, and the protection of basic moral Americanism, the Invisible Empire offered fellowship, excitement, and a sense of power—and advantage. The ritual and life of the Klan were those of the lodge, and the Ku Klux Klan was the fastest growing fraternity of the 1920s, far outdistancing the newly formed American Legion. Through the early years, Klansmen gathered at monster initiations, cross burnings and rallies, at Klan Day at the state fair in Dallas or the inauguration of Grand Dragon D. C. Stephenson at Kokomo. From the lodge halls of Birmingham's Robert E. Lee No. 1 to Phoenix's Kamelback Klan No. 6, from Shreveport and Grand Island, Portland, New Haven, Beaumont, Bangor, Billings, Binghamton, and Bakersfield, Klansmen felt that they were part of a full-throated, rising, powerful force in the nation.

Of course there was always the possibility of more than the psychological advantage of being in on it. Merchants put "TWK" (Trade With a Klansman) and "SYMWA" (Spend Your Money With Americans) stickers in their shop windows. Rising young politicians such as lawyer Hugo Black in Alabama joined, and county judge hopeful Harry Truman of Independence, Missouri, went through the first steps before he withdrew. With its soaring membership, the Klan seemed to have the votes.

Earle Mayfield in Texas was its first genuine U.S. Senator, and in Arkansas the Klan had its own primary first to decide which brother to support in the regular Democratic party one. Success whetted the appetites of the imperial potentates in Atlanta, and other eager hopefuls, from Maine to California. Altogether, the Klan substantially helped elect both senators from Colorado, Indiana, Oklahoma, and Alabama, and one each from Iowa, Oregon, Texas, Georgia, Tennessee, and Kentucky, as well as governors in Maine, Kansas, California, Wisconsin, Colorado, Indiana, Ohio, Tennessee, Alabama, Georgia, and Oregon. While some only accepted Klan support, at least five of the senators and four of the governors were Klan members.

In 1924, the Klan played a major role in presidential politics. The two candidates battling it out at the Democratic Convention Madison Square Garden were the "wet," Catholic, New York governor, Al Smith, and the Georgia-born senator from California, William Gibbs McAdoo. McAdoo was not a bigot, but he had important support from Klan regions. The Platform Committee presented a plank opposing racial or religious discrimination, but the Smith supporters, and others, wanted the Klan denounced by name. As the Convention fought over the three crucial syllables, the supporters in the galleries chanted "Ku, Ku, McAdoo!" and "Booze! Booze! Booze!" at each other. The party's elder statesman and three times nominee, William Jennings Bryan, was hissed and booed when he asked for party unity and compassion, not condemnation, for those who belonged to the Klan. By an embittered 542 3/20 to 541 3/20 vote, the angry, shouting delegates failed to name the Klan. It was the climax of the Convention. Afterward it took nine days and 103 ballots to eventually send out John W. Davis as the compromise candidate to lose the election to Calvin Coolidge, who kept silent about it all.

In many communities, as the mayor of Enid, Oklahoma, had told the American Civil Liberties Union, the Klan held unchallenged power. That power, however, was unimaginative and soon squandered. The Klan was conservative, not revolutionary, and had little program other than to enjoy the spoils of office. Its members were a mixed bag of town and city blue- and white-collar workers, shopkeepers, and professional men. Although a potent force in politics, the Klan probably knew as little about economics as Warren G. Harding. Where it became involved, the Klan was pro-business and manipulated. Its leaders were friends to the electrical utilities in Oregon, and to the oil companies in Texas. In Kansas its top attorney also represented the anti-labor Associated Industries, and the Klan opposed street car regulation in Denver, public power ownership in Minneapolis, and the United Mine Workers in Kentucky. In the zones of emergence of the Northern cities, instead of organizing exclusionist neighborhood improvement associations, Klansmen spent their time at parades, church socials, fried chicken dinners, and lectures by Klan clergymen from Atlanta. The Klan's prime concern was fellowship and morality, not economics and urban dynamics.

On the national scene, the Klan supported immigration restriction, Federal aid to public education (as a counter to parochial schools), and non-participation in such "foreign" organizations as the League of Nations and the World Court. In state legislatures, Klansmen concentrated on protecting the flag, the Bible, racial purity, and the little red schoolhouse. This meant patriotic observances and readings from the King James Bible in the schools, and the exclusion of Roman Catholic teachers, or at least their wearing of religious garb. In Oregon the Klan combined with other fraternal lodges to pass a compulsory public school law, which the U.S. Supreme Court soon overruled.

But politics helped to undo the Klan's imperium. Leadership from Atlanta and in the state realms was remarkably inept. Conflict over which Klan candidate was going to be endorsed in Texas, Arkansas, and Oregon left bitter feelings. A jump to the Republican party did help produce a Klan senator from Oklahoma and a shift the other way elected a Democratic governor in Oregon, but the internal costs were high. State realms did not like being dictated to from Atlanta, and local Klansmen were no happier with the divisive, manipulative politics and authoritarian candidate-picking of their own Grand Dragons, who, in turn, had been imposed on the membership. Generally, the Klan was not successful in replacing other political associations and loyalties, and the men Klansmen elected, as well as those who told the Klansmen whom to elect, turned out to be of equally poor quality.

Although the Klan numbers and power often grew impressively, there was almost always someone to fight it, an editor such as Julian Harris or the Emporia, Kansas, *Gazette's* William Allen White to expose it, or a district attorney such as future Texas Governor Dan Moody, Denver's Philip Van Cise, or Alabama Attorney General Charles McCall to investigate and indict it. The New York *World;* Memphis *Commercial Appeal;* Columbus, Georgia, *Enquirer-Sun;* Montgomery, Alabama, *Advertiser;* and Indianapolis *Times* received Pulitzer Prizes for their anti-Klan campaigns.

Initially, all press coverage helped spread the Klan, and violence gave the Klan a "hell-of-a-fellow" sense of power. By the mid-1920s, almost everything the Klan did or that was reported about it revealed its ineptitude, immorality, corruption, and community destructiveness. When Indiana Grand Dragon D. C. Stephenson, the most powerful leader of the Northern Klan, went to prison for a sex murder, the Klan's reputation was further badly damaged. The more the Klan's linen was hung out in public, the dirtier it appeared for all to see, and the Invisible Empire was almost continually in court to settle internal disputes. Colonel Simmons and "Doc" Evans fought over who would be Imperial Wizard; Grand Dragons struggled against Imperial headquarters, and local klaverns against their state realms. The leadership on most levels ruled dictatorially and was out for the money. This struggle for the spoils and the exploitation of the membership wrecked the Klan in practically every state where it existed. By the latter half of the 1920s, membership was melting away. In 1926, when the Klan staged its second national parade down Pennsylvania Avenue in Washington, D.C., only half as many Klansmen and women came, and they marched in columns of four instead of sixteen and twenty abreast as they had done the year before.

During its years of glory, the Klan produced no statesmanlike leaders or social programs, but rather violence, local turmoil, and scandal. By the latter 1920s the country had settled down—even if the Klan had not—to enjoy Republican prosperity. The dangers of Rome or Russia seemed more distant and less real. The Klan's role in the American fraternal world had been irreparably damaged by its mismanagement and extremism. The self-confidence of the great early days had become a sour defensiveness laboring under a damaged reputation, which contrasted badly with a more dominant American optimism.

Even in 1928 when the Democrats picked the Irish Catholic Al Smith as [their] presidential candidate, Klan leaders could not produce a revival. With the crash and Great Depression of the 1930s, the Klan ranks thinned to even fewer thousands. Shrunken to the Southeastern United States, the Klan sometimes had friends in power and engaged in occasional night riding and anti-union violence. It denounced the New Deal as communistic, but offered no alternatives.

At the end of the 1930s, Imperial Wizard Hiram Evans sold the Klan's Peachtree Street Palace to the Roman Catholic Church and the Klan itself to a veterinarian, Jimmy Colescott, from Terre Haute in the once potent realm of Indiana. A joint meeting with the German-American bund, in New Jersey, drew bad publicity. World War II, gas rationing, and a lien from the Internal Revenue Service for back taxes temporarily put the Imperial Empire out of business.

It was brought back to life after the end of the greater war in Europe, and maintains a fragmented existence mainly in the Southeast today, unmasked by state and local laws and watched by the F.B.I. It failed as a resistance movement during the civil rights days of the 1950s and 1960s in the South. Despite the annual compulsion of the press, wire services, and television to rediscover the Klan and announce its "revival," the Klan endures but has not regained any of the unity, numbers, or influence it once had in the 1920s. It was still capable of violence, but at the end of the 1970s, the most serious Klan watcher, the Anti-Defamation League, computed the strength of the various contending Klans at no more than 10,000.

DOCUMENTS

The Klan's Fight for Americanism, 1926

The real indictment against the Roman Church is that it is, fundamentally and irredeemably, in its leadership, in politics, in thought, and largely in membership, actually and actively alien, un-American and usually anti-American. The old stock Americans, with the exception of the few such of Catholic faith—who are in a class by themselves, standing tragically torn between their faith and their racial and national patriotism—see in the Roman Church today the chief leader of alienism, and the most dangerous alien power with a foothold inside our boundaries. It is this and nothing else that has revived hostility to Catholicism. By no stretch of the imagination can it fairly be called religious prejudice, though, now that the hostility has become active, it does derive some strength from the religious schism.

We Americans see many evidences of Catholic alienism. We believe that its official position and its dogma, its theocratic autocracy and its claim to full authority in temporal as well as spiritual matters, all make it impossible for it as a church, or for its members if they obey it, to cooperate in a free democracy in which Church and State have been separated. It is true that in this country the Roman Church speaks very softly on these points, so that many Catholics do not know them. It is also true that the Roman priests preach Americanism, subject to their own conception of Americanism, of course. But the Roman Church itself makes a point of the divine and unalterable character of its dogma, it has never seen fit to abandon officially any of these un-American attitudes, and it still teaches them in other countries. Until it does renounce them, we cannot believe anything except that they all remain in force, ready to be called into action whenever feasible, and temporarily hushed up only for expediency.

The hierarchical government of the Roman Church is equally at odds with Americanism. The Pope and the whole hierarchy have been for centuries almost wholly Italian. It is nonsense to suppose that a man, by enter-

SOURCE: Reprinted from Hiram Evans, "Klan's Fight for Americanism," *North American Review* 123 (March–May 1926): 33–63, by permission of the University of Northern Iowa.

ing a church, loses his race or national loyalties. The Roman Church today, therefore, is just what its name says—Roman; and it is impossible for its hierarchy or the policies they dictate to be in real sympathy with Americanism. Worse, the Italians have proven to be one of the least assimilable of people. The autocratic nature of the Catholic Church organization, and its suppression of free conscience or free decision, need not be discussed; they are unquestioned. Thus it is fundamental to the Roman Church to demand a supreme loyalty, overshadowing national or race loyalty, to a power that is inevitably alien, and which at the best must inevitably inculcate ideals un-American if not actively anti-American. . . .

The facts are that almost everywhere, and especially in the great industrial centers where the Catholics are strongest, they vote almost as a unit, under control of leaders of their own faith, always in support of the interests of the Catholic Church and of Catholic candidates without regard to other interests, and always also in support of alienism whenever there is an issue raised. They vote, in short, not as American citizens, but as aliens and Catholics! They form the biggest, strongest, most cohesive of all the alien *blocs.* On many occasions they form alliances with other alien *blocs* against American interests, as with the Jews in New York today, and with others in the case of the recent opposition to immigrant restriction. . . .

There are three of these great racial instincts, vital elements in both the historic and the present attempts to build an America which shall fulfill the aspirations and justify the heroism of the men who made the nation. These are the instincts of loyalty to the white race, to the traditions of America, and to the spirit of Protestantism, which has been an essential part of Americanism ever since the days of Roanoke and Plymouth Rock. They are condensed into the Klan slogan: "Native, white, Protestant supremacy."

First in the Klansman's mind is patriotism—America for Americans. He believes religiously that a betrayal of Americanism or the American race is treason to the most sacred of trusts, a trust from his fathers and a trust from God. He believes, too, that Americanism can only be achieved if the pioneer stock is kept pure. . . .

Americanism, to the Klansman, is a thing of the spirit, a purpose and a point of view, that can only come through instinctive racial understanding. It has, to be sure, certain defined principles, but he does not believe that many aliens understand those principles, even when they use our words in talking about them. Democracy is one, fairdealing, impartial justice, equal opportunity, religious liberty, independence, self-reliance, courage, endurance, acceptance of individual responsibility as well as individual rewards for effort, willingness to sacrifice for the good of his family, his nation and his race before anything else but God, dependence on enlightened conscience for guidance, the right to unhampered development— these are fundamental. But within the bounds they fix there must be the utmost freedom, tolerance, liberalism. In short, the Klansman believes in the greatest possible diversity and individualism within the limits of the American spirit. But he believes also that few aliens can understand that spirit, that fewer try to, and that there must be resistance, intolerance even, toward anything that threatens it, or the fundamental national unity based upon it.

The second word in the Klansman's trilogy is "white." The white race must be supreme, not only in America but in the world. This is equally undebatable, except on the ground that the races might live together, each with full regard for the rights and interests of others, and that those rights and interests would never conflict. Such an idea, of course, is absurd; the colored races today, such as Japan, are clamoring not for equality but for their supremacy. The whole history of the world, on its broader lines, has been one of race conflicts, wars, subjugation or extinction. This is not pretty, and certainly disagrees with the maudlin theories of cosmopolitanism, but it is truth. The world has been so made that each race must fight for its life, must conquer, accept slavery or die. The Klansman believes that the whites will not become slaves, and he does not intend to die before his time.

Moreover, the future of progress and civilization depends on the continued supremacy of the white race. The forward movement of the world for centuries has come entirely from it. Other races each had its chance and either failed or stuck fast, while white civilization shows no sign of having reached its limit. Until the whites falter, or some colored civilization has a miracle of awakening, there is not a single colored stock that can claim even equality with the white; much less supremacy.

The third of the Klan principles is that Protestantism must be supreme; that Rome shall not rule America. The Klansman believes this is not merely because he is a Protestant, nor even because the Colonies that are now our nation were settled for the purpose of wresting America from the control of Rome and establishing a land of free conscience. He believes it also because Protestantism is an essential part of Americanism; without it America could never have been created and without it she cannot go forward. Roman rule would kill it.

Congress Debates Immigration Restriction, 1921

HOUSE OF REPRESENTATIVES

Mr. [Lucian Walton] PARISH [D.-Tex.]. We should stop immigration entirely until such a time as we can amend our immigration laws and so write them that hereafter no one shall be admitted except he be in full sympathy

SOURCE: *Congressional Record,* April 20, 1921, 450, December 10, 1921, 177.

with our Constitution and laws, willing to declare himself obedient to our flag, and willing to release himself from any obligations he may owe to the flag of the country from which he came.

It is time that we act now, because within a few short years the damage will have been done. The endless tide of immigration will have filled our country with a foreign and unsympathetic element. Those who are out of sympathy with our Constitution and the spirit of our Government will be here in large numbers, and the true spirit of Americanism left us by our fathers will gradually become poisoned by this uncertain element.

The time once was when we welcomed to our shores the oppressed and downtrodden people from all the world, but they came to us because of oppression at home and with the sincere purpose of making true and loyal American citizens, and in truth and in fact they did adapt themselves to our ways of thinking and contributed in a substantial sense to the progress and development that our civilization has made. But that time has passed now; new and strange conditions have arisen in the countries over there; new and strange doctrines are being taught. The Governments of the Orient are being overturned and destroyed, and anarchy and bolshevism are threatening the very foundation of many of them, and no one can foretell what the future will bring to many of those countries of the Old World now struggling with these problems.

Our country is a self-sustaining country. It has taught the principles of real democracy to all the nations of the earth; its flag has been the synonym of progress, prosperity, and the preservation of the rights of the individual, and there can be nothing so dangerous as for us to allow the undesirable foreign element to poison our civilization and thereby threaten the safety of the institutions that our forefathers have established for us.

Now is the time to throw about this country the most stringent immigration laws and keep from our shores forever those who are not in sympathy with the American ideals. It is the time now for us to act and act quickly, because every month's delay increases the difficulty in which we find ourselves and renders the problems of government more difficult of solution. We must protect ourselves from the poisonous influences that are threatening the very foundation of the Governments of Europe; we must see to it that those who come here are loyal and true to our Nation and impress upon them that it means something to have the privileges of American citizenship. We must hold this country true to the American thought and the American ideals. . . .

Mr. [James V.] McClintic [D.-Okla.]. Some time ago it was my privilege to visit Ellis Island, not as a member of the committee but as a private citizen interested in obtaining information relative to the situation which exists at that place. I stood at the end of a hall with three physicians, and I saw them examine each immigrant as they came down the line, rolling back the upper eyelid in order to gain some information as to the individual's physical condition. I saw them place the chalk marks on their clothing which indicated that they were in a diseased condition, so that they could be separated when they reached the place where they were to undergo certain examinations. Afterwards I went to a large assembly hall where immigrants came before the examiners to take the literacy test, and the one fact that impressed me more than anything else was that practically every single immigrant examined that day had less than $50 to his credit. . . .

Practically all of them were weak, small of stature, poorly clad, emaciated, and in a condition which showed that the environment surrounding them in their European homes was indeed very bad.

It is for this reason that I say the class of immigrants coming to the shores of the United States at this time are not the kind of people we want as citizens in this country. It is a well-known fact that the majority of immigrants coming to this country at the present time are going into the large industrial centers instead of the agricultural centers of the United States, and when it is taken into consideration that the large centers are already crowded to the extent that there was hardly sufficient living quarters to take care of the people, it can be readily seen that this class of people, instead of becoming of service to the communities where they go, they will become charges to be taken care of by charitable institutions. The week I visited Ellis Island I was told that 25,000 immigrants had been unloaded at that port. From their personal appearance they seemed to be the offcasts of the countries from which they came. . . .

National-Origins Formula Reaffirmed, 1951

The subcommittee [on immigration and naturalization] is cognizant of the facts existing at the time of the adoption of the national-origins formula and the bitter charges of discrimination hurled at the incorporation of the principle in our immigration laws. The formula is still subjected to such charges but they seem to have lost some of their force over the intervening period of years. Experience has demonstrated that the national-origins formula has been more of a numerically restrictive measure than a means of automatically selecting immigrants from the various nationalities in desired proportions.

Without giving credence to any theory of Nordic superiority, the subcommittee believes that the adoption of the national-origins formula was a rational and logical method of numerically restricting immigration in such a manner as to best preserve the sociological and cultural balance in the pop-

SOURCE: U.S. Congress, Senate Committee on the Judiciary, *U.S. Immigration and Naturalization*, S. Rept. 1515, 82d Cong., 1st sess., 1951, 455.

ulation of the United States. There is no doubt that it favored the peoples of the countries of northern and western Europe over those of southern and eastern Europe, but the subcommittee holds that the peoples who had made the greatest contribution to the development of this country were fully justified in determining that the country was no longer a field for further colonization, and henceforth, further immigration would not only be restricted but directed to admit immigrants considered to be more readily assimilable because of the similarity of their cultural background to those of the principal components of our population. . . .

Chapter 9

Morals and Manners in the 1920s

Following World War I, many Americans eagerly embraced what President Warren G. Harding called "a return to normalcy." The term conveyed a nostalgic vision of an America dotted with small towns and farms, with men and women pursuing traditional roles, oblivious to events in other parts of the world. But the clock could not be turned back. Indeed, this image of the "good old days" was not an accurate view of the nation even before the war. The sweeping urban-industrial revolution of post–Civil War America had stretched the social fabric and would continue to do so.

The 1920 census provided dramatic evidence of the changes, revealing that for the first time a majority of Americans lived in urban areas. More Americans than ever before, including many women, now worked in factories and offices and saw their style of living affected by the automobile, the movies, a vast array of new consumer goods, and better housing. For much of the younger generation, the good days were not to be found in some distant past; they were to be enjoyed right now.

The essay by John D'Emilio and Estelle Friedman centers on the sexual revolution of the 1920s, particularly among American youth. How extensive were the post–World War I changes that the authors describe? How do D'Emilio and Friedman account for the revolution in sexual mores during the 1920s?

No one, as D'Emilio and Friedman indicate, was more prominently identified with the new morality than Margaret Sanger. In the first document, she strongly advocates family planning. What reasons does she give for families to control their size and the spacing of children? Does her argument have a contemporary quality in light of today's debates on abortion?

Many Americans were shocked by the ideas put forth by Sanger and alarmed by many of the societal changes that marked the decade. Some offered plans for countering these developments. In the second document, Senator Henry Myers of Montana singles out for criticism the movies (and the messages that they conveyed), to which millions—especially the young—flocked weekly. Could the movies have wielded as much influence as the senator claimed? What do you think his proposal of censorship would have accomplished?

Criticism of the social climate in the United States did not originate in the 1920s; neither did attempts at reform. Nonetheless, in 1920 reformers had great hopes for a new age about to dawn. In that year the century-old battle against the consumption of alcoholic beverages appeared to have been won with the passage of the Eighteenth (Prohibition) Amendment to the Constitution. However, the third document—an excerpt from a statement issued in 1931 by a government commission established to investigate the effectiveness of the amendment and its accompanying legislation—provides findings to the contrary. Can you give any examples of illegal behavior widely practiced today? What are the difficulties in outlawing an activity that a large segment of the public deems acceptable?

ESSAY
•◆•

The Sexual Revolution

John D'Emilio and Estelle Friedman

In the winter of 1924, the sociologists Robert and Helen Lynd arrived in Muncie, Indiana, to embark upon an intensive investigation of life in a small American city. The study that resulted, *Middletown*, became an American classic. Casting their net widely, the Lynds examined work, home, youth, leisure, religious beliefs, and civic institutions in an effort to draw a complex picture of life in the modern age. In the process, *Middletown* had much to say about the social context that was shaping sexuality in the 1920s and that would continue to affect American mores.

In order to emphasize the rapidly changing nature of social life in an industrial era, the Lynds offered 1890 as a counterpoint to the 1920s.

SOURCE: John D'Emilio and Estelle Friedman, *Intimate Matters: A History of Sexuality in America*, 239–242, 256–265. Copyright © 1988 by John D'Emilio and Estelle Friedman. Reprinted by permission of HarperCollins Publishers, Inc.

Reflecting the small-town values that still survived at the turn of the century in parts of the country, males and females moved in different spheres; daughters remained at home with their mothers, and adolescent boys entered the public world of work which their fathers inhabited. Young men and women rarely mingled without the careful chaperonage of adults. Socializing continued to take place in public settings that brought families and community residents together. Once a couple had embarked upon a serious courtship, they gained the permission to be alone together, but most often in the family parlor or on the front porch, not far from parental supervision. A heavy taboo hung over sexual relations outside of marriage. Sex was an intensely private matter that came into public view only occasionally, when Muncie's small red-light district overstepped its boundaries, angering the citizenry.

Even as the Lynds described it, contemporary readers would have recognized this as the portrait of a world irrevocably lost. Indeed, the youth of Muncie, for whom change had been most dramatic, would not even have remembered what that earlier world was like. Instead, by the 1920s, adolescents moved in a youth-centered world, based in the high schools that most now attended. School had become, according to the Lynds, "a place from which they go home to eat and sleep." Males and females met in classes, at after-school activities and evening socials. Cars provided privacy, and marked the end of the "gentleman caller" who sat in the parlor. A majority of the students went out with friends four or more evenings a week. Youth patronized movies together, drove to nearby towns for weekend dances, and parked in lovers' lanes on the way home. Almost half of Muncie's male high school students, and a third of its female students, had participated in the recent vogue of the "petting" party; girls who did not were decidedly less popular. After graduation, boys and girls alike left home to work. Increasing economic independence led to less parental supervision over premarital behavior, at the same time that work allowed the young to continue to meet away from home.

This new autonomy and mobility of youth came at a time when Muncie society, through many of the items and activities of a consumer economy, was focused more and more on sexuality. The newspaper advice columns of Dorothy Dix and other syndicated writers instructed female readers in how to catch a man, the thrill and magic of love, and the nature of modern marriage at the same time that relationships were being redefined in romantic, erotic terms. Popular songs of the decade, such as "It Had to Be You," taught that love was a mysterious experience that occurred in a flash when the "chemistry" was right. Sex adventure magazines had become big sellers with stories titled "The Primitive Lover" ("She wanted a caveman husband") and "Indolent Kisses." Muncie's nine movie theaters, open daily and offering twenty-two programs a week, filled their houses by offering such fare as *Married Flirts*, *Rouged Lips*, and *Alimony*. One popular film of the decade, *Flaming*

Youth, attracted audiences by promising images of "neckers, petters, white kisses, red kisses, pleasure-mad daughters, sensation-craving mothers."

The world that the Lynds described, of autonomous youth coming of age in a social environment where erotic images beckoned, has remained fixed in the popular view of the 1920s as a time of new sexual freedoms. Frederick Lewis Allen, in his best-selling account of the decade, *Only Yesterday,* looked at the cultural landscape and detected a "revolution in manners and morals." Images from the 1920s abound to sustain his assessment— flappers and jazz babies; rumble seats and raccoon coats; F. Scott Fitzgerald novels and speakeasies; petting parties and Hollywood sex symbols. And, in fact, despite the evidence of change in sexual mores in the years before World War I, the 1920s do stand out as a time when something in the sexual landscape decisively altered and new patterns clearly emerged. The decade was recognizably modern in a way that previous ones were not. The values, attitudes, and activities of the pre-Depression years unmistakably point to the future rather than the past.

One reason, perhaps, why the twenties have loomed so large as a critical turning point is that patterns of behavior and sexual norms formerly associated with other groups in the population had, by then, spread to the white middle class. The more lavish cabaret appropriated the music and dancing of black and white working-class youth. Movie palaces replaced storefront theaters, and Hollywood directors churned out feature-length films that attracted youths and adults of every class. Bohemian radicals relinquished their proprietorship over the work of modern sexual theorists such as Ellis and Freud, whose ideas received wide currency. Purity crusaders lost the momentum of the prewar years and found themselves rapidly left behind by a culture that scoffed at the sexual prudery of its ancestors. Although each of these developments had roots in the prewar era, not until the 1920s did they experience a full flowering.

The sexual issues that preoccupied the 1920s—the freedom of middle-class youth, the continuing agitation over birth control, debates about the future of marriage, the commercial manipulation of the erotic—suggest the direction in which American values were heading. Sexual expression was moving beyond the confines of marriage, not as the deviant behavior of prostitutes and their customers, but as the normative behavior of many Americans. The heterosocial world in which youth matured encouraged the trend, and the growing availability of contraceptives removed some of the danger attached to nonmarital heterosexuality. New ideas about the essential healthfulness of sexual expression reshaped marriage, too, as couples approached conjugal life with the expectation that erotic enjoyment, and not simply spiritual union, was an integral part of a successful marital relationship. To be sure, resistance to these modern norms surfaced. Some supporters of a new "companionate" marriage advocated it as a way of containing the excesses of youthful libido, while the new visibility of the erotic in popular culture antagonized some and spawned opposition. But, in general, American society was moving by the 1920s toward a view of erotic expression that can be defined as sexual liberalism—an overlapping set of beliefs that detached sexual activity from the instrumental goal of procreation, affirmed heterosexual pleasure as a value in itself, defined sexual satisfaction as a critical component of personal happiness and successful marriage, and weakened the connections between sexual expression and marriage by providing youth with room for some experimentation as preparation for adult status.

At times during the succeeding generation, the crises that punctuated mid-twentieth-century American life seemed to obscure this trend. Under the pressure of the Depression of the 1930s, for instance, the consumerism and commercialized amusements that gave play to sexual adventure temporarily withered. Sobriety and gloom replaced the buoyant exuberance of the previous decade. Dating became a simpler affair, while the anxieties of unemployment and hard times created sexual tensions in many marriages. Birth control became less an issue of freedom for women, and more a method of regulating the poor. After World War II, the impulse to conform and settle down after years of depression, war, and cold war encouraged a rush to early marriage and saw the birth rate zoom upward. Sexual experimentation appeared lost in a maze on suburban housing developments as a new generation took on family responsibilities and raised more children than their parents had. The erotic seemed to disappear under a wave of innocent domesticity, captured in television shows like *Father Knows Best* or the Hollywood comedies of Rock Hudson and Doris Day. A resurgent purity impulse attacked symbols of sexual permissiveness such as pornography and imposed penalties on those who deviated too sharply from family values.

Despite these appearances, however, the forces that fed sexual liberalism developed apace. The availability and accessibility of reliable contraceptives highlighted the divorce of sexual activity from the procreative consequences that inhibited erotic enthusiasm. Sexual imagery gradually became an integral feature of the public realm, legitimate and aboveground. A youth culture that encouraged heterosexual expressiveness became ubiquitous. Couples looked to marriage as a source of continuing erotic pleasures. By the mid-1960s, sexual liberalism had become the dominant ethic, as powerful in its way as was the civilized morality of the late nineteenth century. . . .

Birth control offers perhaps the most dramatic example of the change that occurred in American sexual mores during the middle of the twentieth century. At the start of the 1920s, it still bore the mark of radicalism, and the birth control movement appeared to many as a threat to moral order. The federal Comstock law, with its prohibition on the importation, mailing, and interstate shipment of contraceptive information and devices, remained in effect, and almost half of the states, including most of the populous ones of the Northeast and Midwest, had their own anti-contraceptive statutes. To agitate for birth control placed one outside the law. By the late 1960s, however, virtually all legal impediments to access had collapsed, and the federal government was actively promoting it. Advances in technology and shifts in values made reliable contraceptives an integral feature of married life as well as widely available to the unmarried.

For most of the 1920s and 1930s Margaret Sanger remained the key figure in the birth control movement and the individual most responsible for the changes that occurred. Though her leadership and visibility provided continuity with the pre–World War I agitation, the politics of the movement was undergoing an important shift. Government repression of radicalism and the decline of organized feminism after suffrage altered the context in which the fight for birth control was occurring. Sanger adapted to the new circumstances by detaching the question of contraception from larger social issues and movements. Throughout the twenties and thirties, she campaigned solely to make contraception freely available to women.

Even with a narrowed focus, however, Sanger remained a militant fighter, willing to use any means necessary to achieve her goals. She continued to risk arrest, believing as she did that "agitation through violation of the law was the key to the public." She also propagandized widely, through the pages of her journal (the *Birth Control Review*), through the books that she authored, and through her extensive speaking tours and public conferences. With the backing of her organization, the American Birth Control League, Sanger lobbied for legislative change and embarked once again on a venture in clinical services when she established the Clinical Research Bureau in 1923.

Sanger's lobbying efforts and the clinic that she supported point to an important way in which her strategy was evolving. In New York State in the 1920s, she campaigned for a "doctors only" bill, designed to allow physicians to provide contraceptives, but restricting that right to licensed practitioners. The Clinical Research Bureau, though it provided female clients with contraceptive devices, existed mainly to gather data that would persuade a science-conscious profession that safe, reliable methods of fertility control were available. Both initiatives aimed at enlisting the medical profession as allies in her cause, since its hostility to contraception constituted a major obstacle to success. In the process, however, the politics of birth control tilted in a more conservative direction. From a key issue in the struggle for female emancipation, contraception was gradually becoming a matter of professional health care. . . .

As one might expect, the contraceptive revolution moved hand in hand with changes in both sexual behavior and attitudes. Historians of twentieth-century mores have tended to underplay this shift, by emphasizing instead the stability of one important index of sexual behavior, the female premarital coital rate. For women coming of age in the 1920s, the incidence of premarital intercourse jumped sharply, to roughly fifty percent of the cohort, and thereafter remained relatively constant until the late 1960s. Yet hidden behind the stability of these figures lay a whole world of sexual change. Activity that provoked guilt in the 1920s had become integrated by the 1960s into a new code of sexual ethics that made it morally acceptable. What was daring and nonconformist in the earlier period appeared commonplace a generation later. And, as attitudes and ideals altered, so too did aspects of sexual activity. Dating, necking, and petting among peers became part and parcel of the experience of American youth, providing an initiatory stage, uncommon for their elders, leading to the coital experience of adulthood and marriage. To marriage itself, couples brought new expectations of pleasure, satisfaction, and mutual enjoyment, encouraged by a more explicit advice literature that emphasized the sexual component of conjugal life. The integration of contraception into middle-class married life also meant that the reproductive requirement for marital intimacy had receded far into the background. Though experience might not always live up to these new standards, men and women in the mid-twentieth century were approaching marriage with heightened anticipation of physical pleasure.

Evidence abounds of shifts in both standards and patterns of behavior among American youth in the decades after World War I. During the 1920s, white college youth captured the lion's share of attention of contemporaries seeking to chart the society's changing values. Although less than thirteen percent of the eighteen- to twenty-one-year-old population were enrolled in colleges at the end of the 1920s, the numbers had more than tripled since 1890. For the first time, a distinctive subculture took shape among the middle-class young, with values and activities that set them apart from their parents' generation.

Sexual innovation played a key role in this new world of youth. Particularly in coeducational institutions, heterosocial mixing became the norm. Young men and women mixed casually in classes, extracurricular activities, and social spaces, with a great deal of freedom from adult supervision. Dating in pairs, unlike the informal group socializing of the nineteenth century, permitted sexual liberties that formerly were sanctioned only for couples who were courting. College youth flaunted their new freedoms. As one male editor of a campus paper provocatively expressed it, "there are only two kinds of co-eds, those who have been kissed, and those who are sorry they haven't been kissed." Magazines debated the implications of "petting parties," an increasingly common feature of college life. One study of college youth during the 1920s found that ninety-two percent of coeds had engaged in petting, and that those "rejecting all sex play feel that they are on the defensive."

What a relatively small percentage of middle-class youth were experiencing in college, much larger numbers tasted in high school. By the 1920s, high school had become a mass experience, with almost three-quarters of the young enrolled. Here, too, adolescent boys and girls encountered one another daily, with casual interaction throughout the day that often continued into evening social activities. One observer of youthful mores estimated that a large majority of high school youth engaged in hugging and kissing and that a significant minority "do not restrict themselves to that, but go further, and indulge in other sex liberties which, by all the conventions, are outrageously improper." Automobiles allowed young people still living at home greater freedom of movement than ever before. Groups of teenagers might drive to the next town for a Saturday-night dance; on weeknights, too, it became easier to escape parental supervision. So quickly and widely did cars become an essential part of this heterosocial world of youth that one commentator labeled the auto "a house of prostitution on wheels." Assessing these changes, Ben Lindsey, a Colorado juvenile court judge who had dealt with the young for a generation, considered them to be reflective of a historic transformation in American life. "Not only is this revolt from the old standards of conduct taking place," he wrote, "but it is unlike any revolt that has ever taken place before. Youth has always been rebellious. . . . But this is different. It has the whole weight and momentum of a new scientific and economic order behind it."

Although the innovations in sexual behavior among middle-class youth were real, they nonetheless operated within certain peer-defined limits. Young men took liberties with women of their own class that their parents would have considered improper, but the sexual freedom of the 1920s was hardly a promiscuous one. The kissing and petting that occurred among couples who dated casually did not often progress beyond that. Surveys of sexual behavior among white middle-class women revealed that the generation coming of age in the 1920s had a significantly higher incidence of premarital intercourse than women born in the preceding decades. But the evidence also suggests that, for the most part, young women generally restricted coitus to a single partner, the man they expected to marry. "Going all the way" was permissible, but only in the context of love and commitment. For men, the changes in female sexual behavior had important implications. Beginning in the 1920s, the frequency of recourse to prostitution began to decline. As Lindsey noted, "with the breaking up of those districts, [boys] turned to girls of their own class, a thing they had seldom done in the past."

As young people adopted the novel practice of dating, they shaped, learned, and refashioned its rules. Newspaper advice columns in the years after World War I printed letters from confused youth who wondered whether a good-night kiss was an appropriate ending for an evening date, and who searched for words to define the feelings aroused by the dating relationship. By the 1930s, the elaboration of this teenage ritual had produced words other than "love" to describe the emotions, and had differentiated "courting" and "keeping company" from the more casual, and common, practices of "going out" and "going steady." When the Lynds returned to Muncie in the 1930s, one young man reported to them that "the fellows regard necking as a taken-for-granted part of a date. We fellows used occasionally to get slapped for doing things, but the girls don't do that much any more. . . . Our high school students of both sexes . . . know everything and do everything—openly." Although he likely exaggerated in his claims about "everything," numerous surveys of American youth confirm the widening boundaries of permissible sexual activity. The rapid acceptance of this peer-directed system of dating, as well as the quick demise of its predecessor, can be inferred from changes in that reliable arbiter of social behavior, Emily Post's *Etiquette*. A chapter which, in the 1923 edition, was titled "Chaperons and Other Conventions" became "The Vanishing Chaperon and Other New Conventions" four years later; the passing of another decade brought the wistful heading "The Vanished Chaperon and Other Lost Conventions." One study of high school students in St. Louis on the eve of World War II found dating to be ubiquitous, with most couples returning home after one in the morning. Freed from parental supervision for long hours, boys and girls alike exhibited "a fairly general acceptance of the naturalness" of kisses and light petting as part of a date. Indeed, St. Louis's high school students proved far more tolerant about sexual matters than about other kinds of behavior such as smoking and drinking.

The system of dating, at least as it evolved between the two world wars, did not extend to all youth. Its adoption depended upon surplus income for clothes and entertainment, access to automobiles outside major cities, school attendance to enforce peer-based norms, and sufficient population density to sustain a range of commercialized amusements. Its contours thus mark it as a ritual of white middle-class youth in the cities and suburbs.

Among poor blacks in the rural South, for instance, older patterns of sociability persisted as young people experienced both traditional freedoms and constraints. With few sanctions against premarital intercourse, "sex play," according to one observer, "becomes matter-of-fact behavior for youth." As one young girl explained it, "I ain't never thought of there being anything wrong about it." Denied access because of segregation, poverty, and rural isolation from most of the places where formal dating took place, young rural blacks met at church, harvest festivals, picnics, and while working in the fields, much as they had in the past. Yet, an awareness of the world beyond the small rural community also generated a "longing for pleasures like those of the city." One young man expressed his discontent by telling an interviewer, "there ain't no decent place to take a girl. . . . If you ain't got a car, you just ain't nowhere." Meanwhile, black parents of moderate wealth and status, in an effort to differentiate themselves from the rural masses and to provide education and mobility for the next generation, socialized their children into strict moral codes. In his study of youth in the Black Belt before World War II, Charles Johnson found that among the elite, even young men accepted rigid standards of chastity. Parents kept close rein on their daughters, as the testimony of one North Carolina girl made clear: "Yes, I have a boy friend. He calls on me and takes me to socials. Sometimes mama lets me go to movies with him in the afternoon, but if he goes with me at night papa and mama go too."

For white youth as well, rural and small-town residence affected patterns of sexual interaction. In rural communities many young people lacked mobility. "I had no car," explained one youth who bemoaned his inability to date. "We lived 20 miles from town and to get to town I had to ride with my father or some other adult." Then, too, in smaller communities adults were able to watch the behavior of the young more closely. "I'll tell you, it's really tough getting it in a small town," one young man complained. "Everyone has their eyes on you and especially on the girl. You can hardly get away with anything." A young man who moved to the city when he was seventeen noted the difference it made. He had never felt much sexual desire during his years in the country, he commented, but city life with its abundant opportunities suddenly seemed to generate "much more interest in it."

Although urban working-class youth did not share in the sexual culture of the middle class, this by no means implied a sentence of chastity. In some cases it could translate into freedom from the constraints of peer-enforced norms. In cities and towns, white and black youth who dropped out of high school or who did not immediately marry after graduation found themselves earning wages, yet without the expense of maintaining a household. Removed from the web of daily gossip that shaped the behavior of high school and college students, they were more likely to move beyond petting in their sexual relationships. Dance halls, bowling alleys, skating rinks, and, after prohibition, bars provided settings for young men and women to meet; automobiles, bought with hard-earned wages, offered privacy. One high school dropout embarked upon her first sexual affair with a dance-hall partner. "I made up my mind at the dance Oscar could have it," she recalled. "Oh, it was wonderful. That night, I thought, 'I don't care if I have a baby.'" Several more relationships ensued before she married in her late teens. The thriving business in condoms that Malcolm X operated at a Boston dance hall suggests the ease with which sexual favors could be exchanged among working-class youth in the city. So, too, does evidence of prenuptial conceptions and illegitimacy among the poor and the working class. In one Illinois town, over half of the girls who did not graduate from high school gave birth within eight months of their wedding. And almost a quarter of the births in the lowest social class of whites occurred outside of marriage.

By accelerating the shift to city living, and by providing youth with more economic autonomy and freedom from adult supervision, World War II brought unprecedented opportunities for premarital experience. The war released millions of youth from the social environments that inhibited erotic expression, and threw them into circumstances that opened up new sexual possibilities. Millions of young men left home to join the military, while many young women migrated in search of employment. The demands of wartime drew teenagers into the paid labor force while weakening the influence that family and community held over their behavior.

Ample testimony from the war years confirms the sexual expressiveness of youth. For many young women, men in uniform held erotic appeal. "When I was 16," one college student recalled,

> I let a sailor pick me up and go all the way with me. I had intercourse with him partly because he had a strong personal appeal for me, but mainly because I had a feeling of high adventure and because I wanted to please a member of the armed forces.

Another, rebuffed by a sailor boyfriend who felt she was too young, went on to have affairs with fifteen others by war's end. Civilian men, too, partook of the sexual freedom of the war years. One teenager described his life then as "a real sex paradise. The plant and the town were just full of working girls who were on the make. Where I was, a male war worker became the center of loose morality. It was a sex paradise." A high school student lost his virginity with a woman of thirty whose husband was overseas. "We weren't in love," he recalled, "although we were very fond of each other. The times were conducive for this sort of thing. Otherwise, nothing would ever have happened between us."

The response of moral reformers points to the changes that had occurred since the previous generation. Whereas those of the First World War focused on the dangers of prostitution, by the 1940s it was the behavior of "amateur girls"—popularly known as khaki-wackies, victory girls, and good-time Charlottes—that concerned moralists. "The old time prostitute in a house or formal prostitute on the street is sinking into second place," wrote one venereal-disease expert. "The new type is the young girl in her late teens and early twenties, the young woman in every field of life who is determined to have one fling or better." Efforts to scare GIs into continence by emphasizing the danger of disease had little impact on men who, according to one officer, "think as little of a gonorrheal infection as they do of the ordinary common cold." Or, as another phrased it, "the sex act cannot be made unpopular." Local law-enforcement officials worked overtime to contain the sexual behavior of young women, yet their efforts only seemed to confirm the perception that prostitution was not the issue. Arrests for selling sexual favors rose less than twenty percent during the war years, but charges of disorderly conduct increased almost two hundred percent, and those for other morals offenses, such as promiscuous behavior or patronizing bars too frequently, increased nearly as much. . . .

DOCUMENTS

Happiness in Marriage, 1926

We must recognize that the whole position of womanhood has changed today. Not so many years ago it was assumed to be a just and natural state of affairs that marriage was considered as nothing but a preliminary to motherhood. A girl passed from the guardianship of her father or nearest male relative to that of her husband. She had no will, no wishes of her own. Hers not to question why, but merely to fulfill duties imposed upon her by the man into whose care she was given.

Marriage was synonymous with maternity. But the pain, the suffering, the wrecked lives of women and children that such a system caused, show us that it did not work successfully. Like all other professions, motherhood must serve its period of apprenticeship.

Today women are on the whole much more individual. They possess as strong likes and dislikes as men. They live more and more on the plane of social equality with men. They are better companions. We should be glad that there is more enjoyable companionship and real friendship between men and women.

This very fact, it is true, complicates the marriage relation, and at the same time ennobles it. Marriage no longer means the slavish subservience of the woman to the will of the man. It means, instead, the union of two strong and highly individualized natures. Their first problem is to find out just what the terms of this partnership are to be. Understanding full and complete cannot come all at once, in one revealing flash. It takes time to arrive at a full and sympathetic understanding of each other, and mutually to arrange lives to increase this understanding. Out of the mutual adjustments, harmony must grow and discords gradually disappear.

These results cannot be obtained if the problem of parenthood is thrust upon the young husband and wife before they are spiritually and economically prepared to meet it. For naturally the coming of the first baby means that all other problems must be thrust aside. That baby is a great fact, a reality that must be met. Preparations must be made for its coming. The layette must be prepared. The doctor must be consulted. The health of the wife may

SOURCE: Margaret Sanger, *Happiness in Marriage* (Blue Ribbon Books, New York, 1926), 83–97.

need consideration. The young mother will probably prefer to go to the hospital. All of these preparations are small compared to the regime after the coming of the infant.

Now there is a proper moment for every human activity, a proper season for every step in self-development. The period for cementing the bond of love is no exception to this great truth. For only by the full and glorious living through these years of early marriage are the foundations of an enduring and happy married life rendered possible. By this period the woman attains a spiritual freedom. Her womanhood has a chance to bloom. She wins a mastery over her destiny; she acquires self-reliance, poise, strength, a youthful maturity. She abolishes fear. Incidentally, few of us realize, since the world keeps no record of this fact, how many human beings are conceived in fear and even in repugnance by young mothers who are the victims of undesired maternity. Nor has science yet determined the possibilities of a generation conceived and born of conscious desire.

In the wife who has lived through a happy marriage, for whom the bonds of passionate love have been fully cemented, maternal desire is intensified and matured. Motherhood becomes for such a woman not a penalty or a punishment, but the road by which she travels onward toward completely rounded self-development. Motherhood thus helps her toward the unfolding and realization of her higher nature.

Her children are not mere accidents, the outcome of chance. When motherhood is a mere accident, as so often it is in the early years of careless or reckless marriages, a constant fear of pregnancy may poison the days and nights of the young mother. Her marriage is thus converted into a tragedy. Motherhood becomes for her a horror instead of a joyfully fulfilled function.

Millions of marriages have been blighted, not because of any lack of love between the young husband and wife, but because children have come too soon. Often these brides become mothers before they have reached even physical maturity, before they have completed the period of adolescence. This period in our race is as a rule complete around the age of twenty-three. Motherhood is possible after the first menstruation. But what is physically possible is very often from every other point of view inadvisable. A young woman should be fully matured from every point of view—physically, mentally and psychically—before maternity is thrust upon her. . . .

The problem of premature parenthood is intensified and aggravated when a second infant follows too rapidly the advent of the first, and inevitably husband and wife are made the slaves of this undreamed of situation, bravely trying to stave off poverty, whipped to desperation by the heavy hand of chance and involuntary parenthood. How can they then recapture their early love? It is not surprising that more often they do not even trouble themselves to conceal the contempt which is the bitter fruit of that young and romantic passion. . . .

Instead of being a self-determined and self-directing love, everything is henceforward determined by the sweet tyranny of the child. I have known of several young mothers, despite a great love for the child, to rebel against this intolerable situation. Vaguely feeling that this new maternity has rendered them unattractive to their husbands, slaves to a deadly routine of bottles, baths and washing, they have revolted. I know of innumerable marriages which have been wrecked by premature parenthood.

Love has ever been blighted by the coming of children before the real foundations of marriage have been established. Quite aside from the injustice done to the child who has been brought accidentally into the world, this lamentable fact sinks into insignificance when compared to the injustice inflicted by chance upon the young couple, and the irreparable blow to their love occasioned by premature or involuntary parenthood.

For these reasons, in order that harmonious and happy marriage may be established as the foundation for happy homes and the advent of healthy and desired children, premature parenthood must be avoided. Birth Control is the instrument by which this universal problem may be solved.

Moving Pictures Evoke Concern, 1922

Moving pictures, their educational influence for good or for bad, their growing importance as a factor in our civilization, the announced determination of those controlling the industry boldly to enter politics, and the desirability of regulation by law through censorship constitute a subject of acknowledged importance to the American people. . . .

The motion picture is a great invention, and it has become a powerful factor for good or bad in our civilization. It has great educational power for good or bad. It may educate young people in the ways of good citizenship or in ways of dissoluteness, extravagance, wickedness, and crime. It furnishes recreation, diversion, and amusement at a cheap price to many millions of our people—largely the young. It is the only form of amusement within the means of millions. It possesses great potential possibilities for good. It may furnish not only amusement but education of a high order.

Through motion pictures the young and the old may see depicted every good motive, laudable ambition, commendable characteristic, ennobling trait of humanity. They may be taught that honesty is the best policy; that virtue and worth are rewarded; that industry leads to success. Those who live in the country or in small interior towns, and who never visit large cities, may see pictured the skyscrapers, the crowded streets, the rush and jam of metropolitan cities. Those who live in the interior, and never see the

SOURCE: A speech by Senator Henry Myers, *Congressional Record*, June 29, 1922, 9655–9657.

seacoast, may see on the screen the great docks and wharves of seaports and see the loading and unloading of giant ocean steamers. Those who live in crowded cities, and never see the country or get a glimpse of country life, may have depicted to them all the beauties of rural life and scenery. All may see scenes of the luxuriant Tropics, the grandeur of Alpine Mountains, polar conditions, life in the Orient. The cities, palaces, cathedrals, ports, rural life, daily routine, scenic attractions, mode of living of every country on the globe, may be brought to our doors and eyes for a small price. The industry may be made an education to the young.

However, from all accounts, the business has been conducted, generally speaking, upon a low plane and in a decidedly sordid manner. Those who own and control the industry seem to have been of the opinion that the sensual, the sordid, the prurient, the phases of fast life, the ways of extravagance, the risqué, the paths of shady life, drew the greatest attendance and coined for them the most money, and apparently they have been out to get the coin, no matter what the effect upon the public, young or old; and when thoughtful people have suggested or advocated official censorship, in the interest of good citizenship and wholesome morals, the owners of the industry have resented it and, in effect, declared that it was nobody's business other than theirs and concerned nobody other than them what kind of shows they produced; that if people did not like their shows they could stay away from them; that it was their business, and they would conduct it as they might please. At least they have vigorously fought all attempts at censorship and resented them. . . .

I have no doubt young criminals got their ideas of the romance of crime from moving pictures. I believe moving pictures are dong as much harm today as saloons did in the days of the open saloon—especially to the young. They are running day and night, Sunday and every other day, the year round, and in most jurisdictions without any regulation by censorship. I would not abolish them. They can be made a great force for good. I would close them on Sunday and regulate them week days by judicious censorship. Already some dozen or more States have censorship laws, with the right of appeal to the courts, and the movement is on in many other States.

When we look to the source of the moving pictures, the material for them, the personnel of those who pose for them, we need not wonder that many of the pictures are pernicious.

The pictures are largely furnished by such characters as Fatty Arbuckle, of unsavory fame, notorious for his scandalous debauchery and drunken orgies, one of which, attended by many "stars," resulted in the death of Virginia Rappe, a star artist; William Desmond Taylor, deceased, murdered for some mysterious cause; one Valentino, now figuring as the star character in rape and divorce sensations. Many others of like character might be mentioned.

At Hollywood, Calif., is a colony of these people, where debauchery, riotous living, drunkenness, ribaldry, dissipation, free love, seem to be conspicuous. Many of these "stars," it is reported, were formerly bartenders, butcher boys, sopers, swampers, variety actors and actresses, who may have earned $10 or $20 a week, and some of whom are now paid, it is said, salaries of something like $5,000 a month or more, and they do not know what to do with their wealth, extracted from poor people, in large part, in 25 or 50 cent admission fees, except to spend it in riotous living, dissipation, and "high rolling."

These are some of the characters from whom the young people of today are deriving a large part of their education, views of life, and character-forming habits. From these sources our young people gain much of their views of life, inspiration, and education. Rather a poor source is it not? Looks like there is some need for censorship, does it not? There could be some improvement, could there not? . . .

Prohibition Nonobserved, 1931

There is a mass of information before us as to a general prevalence of drinking in homes, in clubs, and in hotels; of drinking parties given and attended by persons of high standing and respectability; of drinking by tourists at winter and summer resorts; and of drinking in connection with public dinners and at conventions. In the nature of the case it is not easy to get at the exact facts in such a connection, and conditions differ somewhat in different parts of the country and even to some extent from year to year. This is true likewise with respect to drinking by women and drinking by youth, as to which also there is a great mass of evidence. In weighing this evidence much allowance must be made for the effect of new standards and independence and individual self-assertion, changed ideas as to conduct generally, and the greater emphasis on freedom and the quest for excitement since the war. As to drinking among youth, the evidence is conflicting. Votes in colleges show an attitude of hostility to or contempt for the law on the part of those who are not unlikely to be leaders in the next generation. It is safe to say that a significant change has taken place in the social attitude toward drinking. This may be seen in the views and conduct of social leaders, business and professional men in the average community. It may be seen in the tolerance of conduct at social gatherings which would not have been possible a generation ago. It is reflected in a different way of regarding drunken

SOURCE: U.S. Congress, House, U.S. National Commission on Law Enforcement, *Enforcement of the Prohibition Laws of the United States,* H. Doc. 722, 71st Cong., 3d sess., 1931, 21.

youth, in a change in the class of excessive drinkers, and in the increased use of distilled liquor in places and connections where formerly it was banned. It is evident that, taking the country as a whole, people of wealth, business men and professional men, and their families, and, perhaps, the higher paid workingmen and their families, are drinking in large numbers in quite frank disregard of the declared policy of the National Prohibition Act. . . .

Chapter 10

The Depression Years

The crusades against changing morals and manners during the 1920s seem trivial when compared to the challenges of the Great Depression of the 1930s. Although the United States had suffered economic declines before, the Great Depression was the worst ever: nearly a quarter of the work force was unemployed by 1933, banks failed, the stock market crashed, businesses declared bankruptcy, and families lost their homes and farms.

In the essay "The Texas Hill Country Before the New Deal," Robert Caro describes life in Lyndon Johnson's Texas Hill Country congressional district in the years before the New Deal brought electricity to that land. He notes just how difficult it was for farmers to make a living in those lean years. How were the lives of Texas farm families transformed by the New Deal's rural electrification program?

Like Hill Country Texans, urban families also faced hard times. When relief funds ran out, families survived as best they could. The first document consists of excerpts from the testimony of Jacob Billikopf, executive director of the Federation of Jewish Charities in Philadelphia, before a Senate subcommittee studying the issue.

*What light does the document shed on the reasons why millions of Americans re-
sponded so positively to President Franklin Roosevelt's message of hope and to his
New Deal programs of relief and public employment?*

*Today we think of California as a land of sunshine and wealth. Indeed, during
and after World War II millions of Americans, as well as many immigrants, set out
for California in pursuit of the good life. Still, the second document points out that
many of those heading for the Golden State during the depression years were Okies—
farmers from Texas, Oklahoma, and elsewhere on the southern plains who migrated to
California, driven from their homes by poverty and great clouds of dust. John Stein-
beck's novel* The Grapes of Wrath *brought the plight of these dust bowl refugees to
the attention of the public, as did the writings of political activist Carey McWilliams.
The second document, a statement by McWilliams before a Congressional committee,
describes the conditions facing the Okies in California. That the Okies continued to
flock to and remain in California reveals the desperate situation from which they fled.
Why did they choose California as the place to rebuild their lives?*

*The final document tells about the miseries of black families—especially
women—in Depression-era New York City. How does the reading support claims
that African Americans were the poorest and most disadvantaged Americans during the 1930s? What does the document suggest about racism?*

*The New Deal programs, particularly those directed toward relief and reform,
helped businesses, farmers, and workers survive the worst ravages of the 1930s, but
economic woes persisted until the boom of World War II finally vanquished the
Great Depression.*

ESSAY
——— •◆• ———

The Texas Hill Country
Before the New Deal

Robert A. Caro

Obtaining the financing and the authorization for the four dams being built
along the Lower Colorado had been difficult. Now Lyndon Johnson undertook a task more difficult still. By ensuring completion of the dams, he had
ensured the creation of electric power, which would be generated by the fall
of water through dam penstocks. Now he was going to try to get the power
to the people. He was going to try to bring electricity to the Hill Country.

Electricity had, of course, been an integral part of life in urban and
much of small-town America for a generation and more, lighting its streets,

SOURCE: Robert A. Caro, *The Years of Lyndon Johnson: The Path to Power* (New York: Knopf,
1982), 502–514. Copyright © 1982 by Robert A. Caro. Reprinted by permission of Alfred A.
Knopf, Inc.

powering the machinery of its factories, running its streetcars and trolleys, its elevated trains and subways, moving elevators and escalators in its stores, and cooling the stores with electric fans. Devices such as electric irons and toasters (which were in widespread use by 1900), refrigerators (which were widely sold beginning in 1912), and vacuum cleaners, dish-washers, hot plates, waffle irons, electric stoves and automatic washing machines for clothes had freed women from much of the drudgery of housework. In the evenings, thanks to electricity, there were the movies, and by 1922, forests of radio antennae had sprouted on tenement roofs. By 1937, when Lyndon Johnson went to Congress, electricity was so integral a part of life that it was hard to remember what life had been like without it.

It was not a part of life in the Hill Country. In Lyndon Johnson's congressional district, the sole source of power had been Texas Power & Light, a subsidiary of the New York–based utility holding giant, Electric Bond & Share. TP&L had, in 1927, agreed to "electrify" a handful of Hill Country towns (Johnson City was one), but not with power from its central generating station at Marble Falls; according to the TP&L, which put the cost of building electric lines at $3,000 per mile, the limited use such small communities would make of electric power would never justify the investment required to build lines across the wide spaces of the Edwards Plateau. The TP&L "power plant" in each of these towns was, therefore, no more than a single thirty-horsepower diesel engine; it generated only enough voltage for ten-watt bulbs, which were constantly dimming and flickering—and which could not be used at all if an electric appliance (even an electric iron) was also in use. Since the "power plant" operated only between "dark to midnight," a refrigerator was useless. To most of the residents in these towns, such problems were academic: so high were TP&L's rates that few families hooked up to its lines. And in any case, the diesel engine was constantly breaking down under the strain placed on it. On the rare occasions on which a movie was shown, there was as much suspense in the audience over whether the electricity would hold out to the end of the film as there was in the film itself. Recalls Lucille O'Donnell of Burnet: "I'd be watching *The Perils of Pauline* and I'd just be about to see whether or not the train was going to run over her and the lights would go out." And the residents of these towns were the only inhabitants of the Hill Country with any electricity at all. TP&L refused even to consider building lines to the area's tens of thousands of individual farms and ranches.

As a result, although the electric milking machine had been invented almost two decades before, the Hill Country farmer had to milk his cows by hand—arising at three-thirty or four o'clock in the morning to do so, because milking was a time-consuming chore (more than two hours for twenty cows) and it had to be finished by daylight: every hour of daylight was needed for work in the fields. Milking was done by the dim light of kerosene lanterns; although Sears, Roebuck was boasting in 1937 that a new, deluxe kerosene lamp provided as much illumination as a forty-watt electric bulb, the lamps in use in the Hill Country furnished—at most—twenty-five watts of light. Or it was done in the dark. And there was a constant danger of fire with kerosene lamps, and even a spark could burn down a hay-filled barn, and destroy a farmer's last chance of holding on to his place, so many farmers were afraid to use a lantern in the barn. "Winter mornings," recalls one, "it would be so dark ... you'd think you were in a box with the lid shut." Because without electricity there could be no refrigerator, the milk was kept on ice. The ice was expensive and farmers had to lug it from town at enormous cost in time. Though they kept it underground—covered with sawdust—it still, as farmer Chester Franklin of Wimberley puts it, "melted away so quick." And often even the ice didn't help. Farmers would have to take the milk out of their pit and place it by the roadside to be picked up by the trucks from Austin dairies, but often—on those unpaved Hill Country roads on which flat tires were a constant occurrence—the trucks would be late, and the milk would sit outside in the Hill Country heat. Even if it was not actually spoiled, the dairy would refuse to accept it if its temperature was above fifty degrees Fahrenheit—and when the truck driver pulled his thermometer out of the milk, a farmer, seeing the red line above fifty, would know that his hours of work in the barn in the dark had been for nothing.

Because there was no electricity, moreover, a Hill Country farmer could not use an electric pump. He was forced not only to milk but to water his cows by hand, a chore that, in dry weather, meant hauling up endless buckets from a deep well. Because he could not use an electric auger, he had to feed his livestock by hand, pitchforking heavy loads of hay up into the loft of his barn and then stomping on it to soften it enough so the cows could eat it. He had to prepare the feed by hand: because he could not use an electric grinder, he would get the corn kernels for his mules and horses by sticking ears of corn—hundreds of ears of corn—one by one into a corn sheller and cranking it for hours. Because he could not use electric motors, he had to unload cotton seed by hand, and then shovel it into the barn by hand; to saw wood by hand, by swinging an axe or riding one end of a ripsaw. Because there was never enough daylight for all the jobs that had to be done, the farmer usually finished after sunset, ending the day as he had begun it, stumbling around the barn milking the cows in the dark, as farmers had done centuries before.

But the hardness of the farmer's life paled beside the hardness of his wife's.

Without electricity, even boiling water was work.

Anything which required the use of water was work. Windmills (which could, acting like a pump, bring water out of a well into a storage tank) were very rare in the Hill Country; their cost—almost $400 in 1937—was out of the reach of most families in that cash-poor region, and the few that had been built proved of little use in a region where winds were always uncertain and, during a drought, non-existent, for days, or weeks, on end. And without electricity to work a pump, there was only one way to obtain water: by hand.

The source of water could be either a stream or a well. If the source was a stream, water had to be carried from it to the house, and since, in a country subject to constant flooding, houses were built well away from the streams, it had to be carried a long way. If the source was a well, it had to be lifted to the surface—a bucket at a time. It had to be lifted quite a long way: while the average depth of a well was about fifty feet in the valleys of the Hill Country, in the hills it was a hundred feet or more.

And so much water was needed! A federal study of nearly half a million farm families even then being conducted would show that, on the average, a person living on a farm used 40 gallons of water every day. Since the average farm family was five persons, the family used 200 gallons, or four-fifths of a ton, of water each day—73,000 gallons, or almost 300 tons, in a year. The study showed that, on the average, the well was located 253 feet from the house—and that to pump by hand and carry to the house 73,000 gallons of water a year would require someone to put in during that year 63 eight-hour days, and walk 1,750 miles.

A farmer would do as much of this pumping and hauling as possible himself, and try to have his sons do as much of the rest as possible (it was Lyndon Johnson's adamant refusal to help his mother with the pumping and hauling that touched off the most bitter of the flareups with his father during his youth). As soon as a Hill Country youth got big enough to carry the water buckets (which held about four gallons, or thirty-two pounds, of water apiece), he was assigned the job of filling his mother's wash pots before he left for school or the field. Curtis Cox still recalls today that from the age of nine or ten, he would, every morning throughout the rest of his boyhood, make about seven trips between his house and the well, which were about 300 feet apart, on each of these trips carrying two large buckets, or more than sixty pounds, of water. "I felt tired," he says, "It was a lot of water." But the water the children carried would be used up long before noon, and the children would be away—at school or in the fields—and most of the hauling of water was, therefore, done by women. "I would," recalls Curtis' mother, Mary Cox, "have to get it, too—more than once a day, more than twice; oh, I don't know how many times. I needed water to wash my floors, water to wash my clothes, water to cook. . . . It was hard work. I was always packing [carrying] water." Carrying it—after she had wrestled off the heavy wooden lid which kept the rats and squirrels out of the well; after she had cranked the bucket up to the surface (and cranking—lifting thirty pounds fifty feet or more—was very hard for most women even with a pulley; most would pull the rope hand over hand, as if they were climbing it, to get their body weight into the effort; they couldn't do it with their arms alone). Some Hill Country women make wry jokes about getting water. Says Mrs. Brian Smith of Blanco: "Yes, we had running water. I always said we had running water because I grabbed those two buckets up and ran the two hundred yards to the house with them." But the joking fades away as the memories sharpen. An interviewer from the city is struck by the fact that Hill Country women of the older generation are noticeably stooped, much more so than city women of the same age. Without his asking for an explanation, it is given to him. More than once, and more than twice, a stooped and bent Hill Country farm wife says, "You see how round-shouldered I am? Well, that's from hauling the water." And, she will often add, "I was round-shouldered like this well before my time, when I was still a young woman. My back got bent from hauling the water, and it got bent when I was still young."

The Hill Country farm wife had to haul water, and she had to haul wood.

Because there was no electricity, Hill Country stoves were wood stoves. The spread of the cedar brakes had given the area a plentiful supply of wood, but cedar seared bone-dry by the Hill Country sun burned so fast that the stoves seemed to devour it. A farmer would try to keep a supply of wood in the house, or, if he had sons old enough, would assign the task to them. (Lyndon Johnson's refusal to chop wood for his mother was another source of the tension between him and Sam). They would cut down the trees, and chop them into four-foot lengths that could be stacked in cords. When wood was needed in the house, they would cut it into shorter lengths and split the pieces so they could fit into the stoves. But as with the water, these chores often fell to the women.

The necessity of hauling the wood was not, however, the principal reason so many farm wives hated their wood stoves. In part, they hated these stoves because they were so hard to "start up." The damper that opened into the firebox created only a small draft even on a breezy day, and on a windless day, there was no draft—because there was no electricity, of course, there was no fan to move the air in the kitchen—and a fire would flicker out time after time. "With an electric stove, you just turn on a switch and you have heat," says Lucille O'Donnell, but with a wood stove, a woman might have to stuff kindling and wood into the firebox over and over again. And even after the fire was lit, the stove "didn't heat up in a minute, you know," Lucille O'Donnell says—it might in fact take an hour. In part, farm wives hated wood stoves because they were so dirty, because the smoke from the wood blackened walls and ceilings, and ashes were always escaping through the grating, and the ash box had to be emptied twice a day—a dirty job and dirtier if, while the ashes were being carried outside, a gust of wind scattered them around inside the house. They hated the stoves because they could not be left unattended. Without devices to regulate the heat and keep the temperature steady, when the stove was being used for baking or some other cooking in which an even temperature was important, a woman would have to keep a constant watch on the fire, thrusting logs—or corncobs, which ignited quickly—into the firebox every time the heat slackened.

Most of all, they hated them because they were so hot.

When the big iron stove was lit, logs blazing in its firebox, flames licking at the gratings that held the pots, the whole huge mass of metal so hot that it was almost glowing, the air in the kitchen shimmered with the heat pouring out of it. In the Winter the heat was welcome, and in Spring and Fall it was bearable, but in the Hill Country, Summer would often last five months. Some time in June the temperature might climb to near ninety degrees, and would stay there, day after day, week after week, through the end of September. Day after day, week after week, the sky would be mostly empty, without a cloud as a shield from the blazing sun that beat down on the Hill Country, and on the sheet-iron or corrugated tin roofs of the box-like kitchens in the little dog-run homes that dotted its hills and valleys. No matter how hot the day, the stove had to be lit much of the time, because it had to be lit not only for meals but for baking; Hill Country wives, unable to afford store-bought bread, baked their own, an all-day task. (As Mrs. O'Donnell points out, "We didn't have refrigerators, you know, and without refrigerators, you just about have to start every meal from scratch.") In the Hill Country, moreover, Summer was harvest time, when a farm wife would have to cook not just for her family but for a harvesting crew—twenty or thirty men, who, working from sun to sun, expected three meals a day.

Harvest time, and canning time.

In the Hill Country, canning was required for a family's very survival. Too poor to buy food, most Hill Country families lived through the Winter largely on the vegetables and fruit picked in the Summer and preserved in jars.

Since—because there was no electricity—there were no refrigerators in the Hill Country, vegetables or fruit had to be canned the very day they came ripe. And, from June through September, something was coming ripe almost every day, it seemed; on a single peach tree, the fruit on different branches would come ripe on different days. In a single orchard, the peaches might be reaching ripeness over a span as long as two weeks; "You'd be in the kitchen with the peaches for two weeks," Hill Country wives recall. And after the peaches, the strawberries would begin coming ripe, and then the gooseberries, and then the blueberries. The tomatoes would become ripe before the okra, the okra before the zucchini, the zucchini before the corn. So the canning would go on with only brief intervals—all Summer.

Canning required constant attendance on the stove. Since boiling water was essential, the fire in the stove had to be kept roaring hot, so logs had to be continually put into the firebox. At least twice during a day's canning, moreover—probably three or four times—a woman would have to empty the ash container, which meant wrestling the heavy, unwieldy device out from under the firebox. And when the housewife wasn't bending down to the flames, she was standing over them. In canning fruit, for example, first sugar was dropped into the huge iron canning pot, and watched carefully and stirred constantly, so that it would not become lumpy, until it was completely dissolved. Then the fruit—perhaps peaches, which would have been peeled earlier—was put in the pot, and boiled until it turned into a soft and mushy jam that would be packed into jars (which would have been boiling—to sterilize them—in another pot) and sealed with wax. Boiling the peaches would take more than an hour, and during that time they had to be stirred constantly so that they would not stick to the pot. And when one load of peaches was finished, another load would be put in, and another. Canning was an all-day job. So when a woman was canning, she would have to spend all day in a little room with a tin or sheet-iron roof on which a blazing sun was beating down without mercy, standing in front of the iron stove and the wood fire within it. And every time the heat in that stove died down even a bit, she would have to make it hotter again.

"You'd have to can in the Summer when it was hot," says Kitty Clyde Ross Leonard, who had been Johnson's first girlfriend. "You'd have to cook for hours. Oh, that was a terrible thing. You wore as little as you could. I wore loose clothing so that it wouldn't stick to me. But the perspiration would just pour down my face. I remember the perspiration pouring down my mother's face, and when I grew up and had my own family, it poured down mine. That stove was so hot. But you had to stir, especially when you were making jelly. So you had to stand over that stove." Says Bernice Snodgrass of Wimberley: "You got so hot that you couldn't stay in the house. You ran out and sat under the trees. I couldn't stand it to stay in the house. Terrible. Really terrible. But you couldn't stay out of the house long. You had to stir. You had to watch the fire. So you had to go back into the house."

And there was no respite. If a bunch of peaches came ripe a certain day, that was the day they had to be canned—no matter how the housewife might feel that day. Because in the fierce Hill Country heat, fruit and vegetables spoiled very quickly. And once the canning process was begun, it could not stop. "If you peeled six dozen peaches, and then, later that day, you felt sick, you couldn't stop," says Gay Harris. "Because you can't can something if it's rotten. The job has to be done the same day, no matter what." Sick or not, in the Hill Country, when it was time to can, a woman canned, standing hour after hour, trapped between a blazing sun and a blazing wood fire. "We had no choice, you see," Mrs. Harris says.

Every week, every week all year long—every week without fail—there was washday.

The wash was done outside. A huge vat of boiling water would be suspended over a larger, roaring fire and near it three large "Number Three" zinc washtubs and a dishpan would be placed on a bench.

The clothes would be scrubbed in the first of the zinc tubs, scrubbed on a washboard by a woman bending over the tub. The soap, since she couldn't afford store-bought soap, was soap she made from lye, soap that was not very effective, and the water was hard. Getting farm dirt out of clothes required hard scrubbing.

Then the farm wife would wring out each piece of clothing to remove from it as much as possible of the dirty water, and put it in the big vat of boiling water. Since the scrubbing would not have removed all of the dirt, she would try to get the rest out by "punching" the clothes in the vat—standing over the boiling water and using a wooden paddle or, more often, a broomstick, to stir the clothes and swish them through the water and press them against the bottom or sides, moving the broom handle up and down and around as hard as she could for ten or fifteen minutes in a human imitation of the agitator of an automatic—electric—washing machine.

The next step was to transfer the clothes from the boiling water to the second of the three zinc washtubs: the "rinse tub." The clothes were lifted out of the big vat on the end of the broomstick, and held up on the end of the stick for a few minutes while the dirty water dripped out.

When the clothes were in the rinse tub, the woman bent over the tub and rinsed them, by swishing each individual item through the water. Then she wrung out the clothes, to get as much of the dirty water out as possible, and placed the clothes in the third tub, which contained bluing, and swished them around in *it*—this time to get the bluing all through the garment and make it white—and then repeated the same movements in the dishpan which was filled with starch.

At this point, one load of wash would be done. A week's wash took at least four loads: one of sheets, one of shirts and other white clothing, one of colored clothes and one of dish towels. But for the typical, large, Hill Country farm family, two loads of each of these categories would be required, so the procedure would have to be repeated eight times.

For each load, moreover, the water in each of the three washtubs would have to be changed. A washtub held about eight gallons. Since the water had to be warm, the woman would fill each tub half with boiling water from the big pot and half with cold water. She did the filling with a bucket which held three or four gallons—twenty-five or thirty pounds. For the first load or two of wash, the water would have been provided by her husband or her sons. But after this water had been used up, part of washday was walking—over and over—that long walk to the spring or well, hauling up the water, hand over laborious hand, and carrying those heavy buckets back. Another part of washday was also a physical effort: the "punching" of the clothes in the big vat. "You had to do it as hard as you could—swish those clothes around and around and around. They never seemed to get clean. And those clothes were heavy in the water, and it was hot outside, and you'd be standing over that boiling water and that big fire—you felt like you were being roasted alive." Lifting the clothes out of the vat was an effort, too. A dripping mass of soggy clothes was heavy, and it felt heavier when it had to be lifted out of that vat and held up for minutes at a time so that the dirty water could drip out, and then swung over to the rinsing tub. Soon, if her children weren't around to hear her, a woman would be grunting with the effort. Even the wringing was, after a few hours, an effort. "I mean, wringing clothes might not seem hard," Mrs. Harris says. "But you have to wring every piece so many times—you wring it after you take it out of the scrub tub, and you wring it after you take it out of the rinse tub, and after you take it out of the bluing. Your arms got tired." And her hands—from scrubbing with lye soap and wringing—were raw and swollen. Of course, there was also the bending—hours of bending—over the rub boards. "By the time you got done washing, your back was broke," Ava Cox says. "I'll tell you—of the things of my life that I will never forget, I will never forget how much my back hurt on washdays." Hauling the water, scrubbing, punching, rinsing: a Hill Country farm wife did this for hours on end—while a city wife did it by pressing the button on her electric washing machine.

Washday was Monday. Tuesday was for ironing.

Says Mary Cox, in words echoed by all elderly Hill Country farm wives: "Washing was hard work, but ironing was the worst. Nothing could be as hard as ironing."

The Department of Agriculture finds that "Young women today are not aware of the origin of the world 'iron,' as they press clothes with lightweight appliances of aluminum or hollow stainless steel." In the Hill Country, in the 1930s an iron was *iron*—a six- or seven-pound wedge of iron. The irons used in the Hill Country had to be heated on the wood stove, and they would retain their heat for only a few minutes—a man's shirt generally required two irons; a farm wife would own three or four of them, so that several could be heating while one was working. An iron with a wooden handle cost two dollars more than one without the handle, so Hill Country wives did their weekly loads of ironing—huge loads because, as Mary Cox puts it, "in those days you were expected to starch and iron almost everything"—with irons without handles. They would either transfer a separate wooden handle from one iron to another, or they would protect their hands with a thick pot holder.

Since burning wood generates soot, the irons became dirty as they sat heating on the stove. Or, if any moisture was left on an iron from the sprinkled clothes on which it had just been used, even the thinnest smoke from the stove created a muddy film on the bottom. The irons had to be cleaned frequently, therefore, by scrubbing them with a rag that had been dipped in salt, and if the soot was too thick, they had to be sanded and scraped. And no matter how carefully you checked the bottom of the irons, and sanded and scraped them, there would often remain some little spot of soot—as you would discover when you rubbed it over a clean white shirt or dress. Then you had to wash that item of clothing over again.

Nevertheless, the irons would burn a woman's hand. The wooden handle or the potholder would slip, and she would have searing metal against her flesh; by noon, she might have blister atop blister—on hands that had to handle the rag that had been dipped in salt. Ironing always took a full day—often it went on into Tuesday evening—and a full day of lifting and carrying six- or seven-pound loads was hard on even these hardy Hill Country women. "It would hurt so bad between the shoulders," Elsie Beck remembers. But again the worst aspect of ironing was the heat. On ironing day, a fire would have to be blazing in the wood stove all day, filling the kitchen, hour after hour, with heat and smoke. Ironing had to be done not only in the Winter but in the Summer—when the temperature outside the kitchen might be ninety or ninety-five or one hundred, and inside the kitchen would be considerably higher, and because there was no electricity, there was no fan to so much as stir the air. In a speech in Congress some years later, Representative John E. Rankin described the "drudgery" a typical farm wife endured, "burning up in a hot kitchen and bowing down over the washtub or boiling the clothes over a flaming fire in the summer heat." He himself remembered, he said, "seeing his mother lean over that hot iron hour after hour until it seemed she was tired enough to drop." Rankin was from Mississippi, but his description would have been familiar to the mothers of the Edwards Plateau. The women of the Hill Country never called the instruments they used every Tuesday "irons," they called them "sad irons."

Washing, ironing—those were chores that were performed every week. Then, of course, there were special occasions—harvest time and threshing time, when a woman had to cook not just for her family but for a crew of twenty or thirty men; the shearing, when, because there was no electricity and her husband had to work the shears, she had to crank the shearing machine, pedaling as if she were pumping a bicycle up a steep hill, pedaling, with only brief pauses, hour after hour; "He was always yelling 'Faster, faster,' Mrs. Walter Yett of Blanco recalls. "I could hardly get up the next morning, I was so tired after that." Washing, ironing, cooking, canning, shearing, helping with the plowing and the picking and the sowing, and, every day, carrying the water and the wood, and because there was no electricity, having to do everything by hand by the same methods that had been employed by her mother and grandmother and great-great-great-grandmother before her—"They wear these farm women out pretty fast," wrote one observer. In the Hill Country, as many outside observers noted, the one almost universal characteristic of the women was that they were worn out before their time, that they were old beyond their years, old at forty, old at thirty-five, bent and stooped and tired.

A Hill Country farm wife had to do her chores even if she was ill—no matter how ill. Because Hill Country women were too poor to afford proper medical care, they often suffered perineal tears in childbirth. During the 1930s, the federal government sent physicians to examine a sampling of Hill Country women. The doctors found that, out of 275 women, 158 had perineal tears. Many of them, the team of gynecologists reported, were third-degree tears, "tears so bad that it is difficult to see how they stand on their feet." But they *were* standing on their feet, and doing all the chores that Hill Country wives had always done—hauling the water, hauling the wood, canning, washing, ironing, helping with the shearing, the plowing and the picking.

Because there was no electricity.

The lack of electricity meant that the days of the people of the Hill Country were filled with drudgery; at night they were denied the entertainment—movies, radio—that would have made the drudgery more bearable. The radio could, moreover, have ended the area's isolation. The feeling of the Hill Country youngsters of the 1920s—Lyndon Johnson's generation— that "we were completely cut off out here," that "we were back in the woods, compared to the rest of the world," that "everything had already happened before we found out about it," was the feeling of the 1930s generation as well. Because there was no electricity, the only radios in the Hill Country were the occasional crystal sets with earphones and poor reception. Amos 'n' Andy, Lum 'n' Abner, Ma Perkins—theirs were voices familiar to most of America; it was a rare inhabitant of the Edwards Plateau who had heard them even once. "What we missed most was the fireside chats," says Mary Cox. "I mean, we loved Franklin D. Roosevelt in this country, and we kept reading about these wonderful fireside chats. But we never got to hear them."

Even reading was hard.

Evening was often the only time in which Hill country farm couples could read ("There was no other time," says Lucille O'Donnell. "There was never a minute to read during the day, it seemed"), but the only light for reading came from kerosene lamps. In movies about the Old West, these lamps appear so homey that it is difficult for a city dweller to appreciate how much—and why—some farm dwellers disliked them so passionately.

Lighting the kerosene lamp was a frustrating job. "You had to adjust the wick just right," says Curtis Cox of Bryan. "If you turned it too high, it would flame up and start to smoke. The chimney—that's the glass part— would get all black, and your eyes would start to smart." Keeping it lit was even more frustrating. It burned straight across for only a moment, and then would either flare up or die down to an inadequate level. Even when the wick was trimmed just right, a kerosene lamp provided only limited illumination. The approximately twenty-five watts of light provided by most such lamps was adequate for children doing their homework—although surveys would later find that the educational level of rural children improved markedly immediately upon the introduction of electricity—but their parents, whose eyes were not so strong, had more difficulty. Mary Cox says that she couldn't read with their lamp for more than a short period: "I always loved to read," she recalls. "But I couldn't enjoy it on the farm. It was hard on the eyes, a strain on the eyes. I had to force myself to read at night." Lucille O'Donnell came to Burnet from Virginia, where she had liked to read in bed; she couldn't do that on her farm, she says, because she couldn't afford the kerosene. When she did read at night, she couldn't read in bed. Her husband, Tom, "would be asleep," she recalls, "and I would put the lamp beside him on the bed, and sit on that little stool and read in the most awkward position." Pointing to deep vertical lines between her eyebrows, more than one Hill Country farm wife says: "So many of us have these lines from squinting to read."

The circle of light cast by a kerosene lamp was small, and there were seldom enough lamps in the home of an impoverished farm family. If a family had so many children that they completely surrounded the one good lamp while studying, their mother could not do her sewing until they were finished. And outside the small circles of light, the rooms of a farmhouse were dark. "The house looked scary," says Mary Cox. "If I was alone at night, it was awfully lonely." And, of course, there were no lamps in the outhouse. Many a Hill country farm wife echoes the words of Betty MacDonald: "I had a horrible choice of either sitting in the dark and not knowing what was crawling on me or bringing a lantern and attracting moths, mosquitoes, nighthawks and bats."

No radio; no movies; limited reading—little diversion between the hard day just past and the hard day just ahead. "Living was just drudgery then," says Carroll Smith of Blanco. "Living—just *living*—was a problem. No lights. No plumbing. Nothing. Just living on the edge of starvation. That was farm life for us. God, city people think there was something fine about it. If they only knew. . . ."

So many conveniences taken for granted in American cities were unknown on the Edwards Plateau: not just vacuum cleaners and washing machines but, for example, bathrooms, since, as a practical matter, indoor plumbing is unfeasible without running water, which requires an electric pump. In the Summer, bathing could be done in the creek (when the creek wasn't dry); in the Winter, it entailed lugging in water and heating it on the stove (which entailed lugging in wood) before pouring it into a Number Three washtub. Because bathing was so hard, "you bathed about once a week," Bernice Snodgrass says. Children went barefoot, so "we'd make them wash their feet [at the pump outside] you know. We [adults] would wash our face and hands and ears in washpans but we didn't take a bath but once a week." There were few toilets, and most Hill Country outhouses were the most primitive sort. Many had no pit dug under them. "It would just drop on the ground," Guthrie Taylor recalls. "No, it wouldn't be cleared away"; every so often the flimsy little shelter would just be moved to another spot. Since toilet paper was too expensive, pages from a Sears, Roebuck catalogue, or corncobs, were used. And some families did not have outhouses. When the Snodgrasses moved to Mount Gaynor from Austin, Bernice Snodgrass says, "We were the only people in the neighborhood that had one. You know what everybody else did? They went out behind the barn, or behind a tree, or something." Frederick Law Olmsted had found the same situation—houses at which there was "no other water-closet than the back of a bush or the broad prairies"—on his journey through the Hill Country in 1857. He had been shocked then, because the America he knew had advanced beyond such primitive conditions. Now it was 1937; four more generations had been living in the Hill Country—with no significant advance in the conditions of their life. Many of the people of Lyndon Johnson's congressional district were still living in the same type of dwelling in which the area's people had been living in 1857: in rude "dog-run" shelters one board thick, through which the wind howled in the winter. They were still squatting behind a bush to defecate. Because of their poverty, they were still utterly bereft not only of tractors and feed grinders, but of modern medical assistance—and were farming by methods centuries out of date.

Although they understood that, as Louise Casparis says, "we were behind the rest of the world," natives of the Hill Country did not realize how *far* behind the rest of the world.

How could they be expected to realize? Without many books to read—or, in general, newspapers, either, except for those pathetic four-page local weeklies; without radio to listen to, with only an occasional movie to watch—how was news of advances in the rest of the world to reach them? Since many of them never saw that world for themselves—an astonishing high proportion of Hill Country residents would never visit even Austin or San Antonio—the Hill Country's awareness of the outside world was dim. The life of Hill Country natives was, moreover, the same life that their mothers and fathers—and grandmothers and grandfathers—had lived; how were they to know, except in general, vague terms, that there was another kind of life? When they heard about the wonders of electricity, they thought electricity was the electricity they saw in Johnson City, the dim, flickering lights hardly better than lamplight; the wonders they imagined were the electric iron and the radio, little more; "I remember when someone started telling me about these washing machines," recalls Ava Cox. "A machine that *washed?* I couldn't picture that *at all!*" Even the concept of the toilet was difficult for them to accept completely; when Errol Snodgrass, newly arrived in Mount Gaynor, began not only to build an outhouse but to dig a pit underneath it, a neighbor asked him: "What do you want that pit for?" And when he explained, Bernice Snodgrass recalls, the reaction of the neighborhood was, "They're so highfalutin that they have to have a toilet.' They thought an outhouse with a pit under it—they thought that was what people meant when they spoke about a toilet!" Natives of the Hill Country couldn't understand why families that had moved away from the Hill Country never returned. It is not, therefore, by lifelong residents of the Hill Country that the contrast between life there and in the outside world is most clearly enunciated, but by newcomers: from families which, due to economic necessity, moved to the Hill Country in the 1930s.

The Depression had cost Brian and Mary Sue Smith their home and their once-profitable automobile-repair shop in Portland, Texas, a town near Corpus Christi. In 1937, they moved with their three children to the Hill Country—to a fifty-three-acre farm near Blanco—because "that was the only place where land was cheap enough so we could buy a farm."

Portland had electricity—had had it for years. "You never even thought about electricity," Mrs. Smith says. "I just accepted it. I mean, if I thought about it, I suppose I would have thought, 'Doesn't *everyone* have electricity?'"

Now she found out that not everyone did.

The Smiths had brought their radio, a big black Atwater Kent with an amplifying horn on top, to their new home, but it could not be played. "You know, it was very lonely on that farm," Mrs. Smith says. "The quiet was nice sometimes. But sometimes it was so quiet it hurt you." They had brought their washing machine, but that could not work, either. Mrs. Smith loved to read, but "The light was hard on your eyes. My eyes just weren't good enough to read at night." In Portland, she had crocheted at night, but she found the light was too dim for her to do that at night. And, of course, there was no time to do it during the day; what time wasn't consumed by her household chores was taken up husking, shelling and grinding corn by hand for feed for the 150 hens whose eggs she was selling; by cranking the sheep-shearing machine. Soon after she arrived on the farm, her husband became very ill, and for more than a year she had to care for the livestock too, and to plow behind a pair of mules—although she had never plowed before. "Up before daylight. Build the fire in the wood range. Put on the biscuits. Go out and milk the cows. Breakfast. Work was all there was. It was a bare existence."

Getting the water, from a well some 200 yards from the house, was the chore that bothered her most. "The children had had running water in Portland, of course, and they acted like they still had it," she says. When she started meeting other Hill Country women, she noticed that many of them were round-shouldered, and they told her it was from carrying heavy buckets of water. She didn't want to be round-shouldered. But there seemed no solution. "Carry and carry. Back and forth. Sometimes I would get awfully discouraged. When I first moved there [to the Hill Country], I felt like a pioneer lady, like one of the women who had come here in covered wagons. I said, if they could do it, I could, too. But it was very hard. After you spent all morning lugging those big buckets back and forth, you felt more like an ox or a mule than a human being. Portland was just a little town. It was no great metropolis. But moving from Portland into the Hill Country was like moving from the twentieth century back into the Middle Ages."

DOCUMENTS

The Great Depression in Philadelphia, 1933

Relief stopped in Philadelphia on June 25 [1932]. For months previously 52,000 destitute families had been receiving modest grocery orders and a little milk.

The average allowance to a family at that time was about $4.35 per week, no provision being made for fuel, clothing, rent or any of the minimum accessories that go to make up the family budget.

Their rent was unpaid, their credit and their borrowing power exhausted. Most of them were absolutely dependent for existence on the food orders supplied through State funds administered by the Committee for Unemployment Relief. Then there were no more funds, and relief—except for a little milk for half-sick children, and a little Red Cross flour—was suddenly discontinued. And Philadelphia asked itself what was happening to these 52,000 families. There were no reports of people starving in the streets, and yet from what possible source were 52,000 families getting enough food to live on?

It was a fair question and the Community Council under the direction of Mr. Ewan Clague, a competent economist and in charge of its Research Bureau, set out to find the answer by a special study of 400 families who had been without relief for a period varying from 10 to 25 days. The families were not picked out as the worst cases, but as stated before were fairly typical of the 52,000.

SOURCE: Jacob Billikopf, testimony from U.S. Congress, Senate Subcommittee of the Committee on Manufacturers, Hearings, *Federal Aid for Unemployment Relief,* 72d Cong., 2d sess., 1933, 8–11.

According to Mr. Clague, and I am quoting him quite liberally, the count of the 400 families showed a total of 2,464 persons. The great majority ranged from five to eight persons per family.

In their effort to discover how these 2,464 human beings were keeping themselves alive the investigators inquired into the customary sources of family maintenance, earnings, savings, regular help from relatives, credit and, last but not least, the neighbors.

Some current income in the form of wages was reported by 128 families, though the amounts were generally small and irregular, two or three dollars a week perhaps, earned on odd jobs, by selling knickknacks on the street or by youngsters delivering papers or working nights. For the whole 128 the average wage income was $4.16 a week and 272 families of the 400 had no earnings whatsoever.

Savings were an even more slender resource. Only 54 families reported savings and most of these were nothing more than small industrial insurance policies with little or no cash surrender value, technically an asset, actually an item of expense. This does not mean that these families had not had savings—take for instance, the Baker family—father, mother, and four children. They had had $1,000 in a building and loan association which failed. They had had more than $2,000 in a savings bank, but the last cent had been withdrawn in January, 1931. They had had three insurance policies, which had been surrendered one by one. Both the father and the oldest son were tubercular, the former at the moment being an applicant for sanitarium care. This family—intelligent, clean, thrifty, and likable—one of thousands at the end of their rope—had had savings as a resource even a year ago, but not now.

The same situation, it was found, prevailed in regard to regular help from relatives. In the early stages of the depression a large proportion of relief families could count on this help in some form. But of our 400 families only 33 reported assistance from kinsfolk that could be counted on, and this assistance was slender indeed: A brother paid the rent to save eviction, a brother-in-law guaranteed the gas and electric bills, a grandmother, working as a scrubwoman, put in a small sum each week. Most of the relatives it was found were so hard pressed that it was all they could do to save themselves. As a matter of fact many relatives had moved in with the families and were recorded as members of the household.

In the absence of assets or income the next line of defense is credit. But most of the 400 families were bogged down in debt and retained only a vestige of credit. Take the item of rent or building and loan payments: Three hundred and forty-nine of the families were behind—some only a month or two, some for a year, a few for two or three years, with six months as the average for the group. . . .

Thus, then, the picture of the 400 families shaped itself. Gradually no income, such as there was slight, irregular and undependable; shelter still available so long as landlords remained lenient; savings gone, credit exhausted.

But what of food, the never ending, ever pressing necessity for food? In this emergency the outstanding contribution has been made by neighbors. The poor are looking after the poor. In considerably more than a third of the 400 families the chief source of actual subsistence when grocery orders stopped was the neighbors. The supply was by no means regular or adequate but in the last analysis, when all other resources failed the neighbors rallied to tide the family over a few days. Usually it was leftovers, stale bread, meat bones for soup, a bowl of gravy. Sometimes the children are asked in for a meal. One neighbor sent two eggs a day regularly to a sick man threatened with tuberculosis. This help was the more striking since the neighbors themselves were often close to the line of destitution and could illy spare the food they shared. The primitive communism existing among these people was a constant surprise to the visitors. More than once a family lucky enough to get a good supply of food called in the entire block to share the feast. There is absolutely no doubt that entire neighborhoods were just living from day to day sharing what slight resources any one family chanced to have. Without this mutual help the situation of many of the families would have been desperate.

As a result of all these efforts, what did these families have? What meals did they get and of what did these meals consist? About 8 per cent of the total number were subsisting on one meal a day. Many more were getting only two meals a day, and still others were irregular, sometimes one meal, sometimes two, occasionally by great good fortune, three. Thirty-seven per cent of all families were not getting the normal three meals a day.

When the content of these meals is taken into consideration the facts are still more alarming. Four families had absolutely no solid food whatever— nothing but a drink, usually tea or coffee. Seventy-three others had only one food and one drink for all meals, the food in many cases being bread made from Red Cross flour. Even in the remaining cases, where there were two or three articles of food, the diets day after day and week after week consisted usually of bread, macaroni, spaghetti, potatoes, with milk for the children. Many families were getting no meat and very few vegetables. Fresh fruits were never mentioned, although it is possible that the family might pick these up in the streets occasionally.

These diets were exceedingly harmful in their immediate effects on some of the families where health problems are present. In a number of cases the children are definitely reported on a hospital diagnosis as anemic. Occasionally the adults are likewise affected. The MacIntyre family for instance: These two older people have an adopted child 8 years of age. The husband is a bricklayer by trade and the wife can do outside housework. They have had occasional odd jobs over the past year but have been very hard pressed. For the three meals immediately preceding the visit they reported the menus as follows: Dinner, previous day, bread and coffee; breakfast, bread and coffee; lunch, corn, fish, bread, and coffee; one quart of milk for the little girl for the entire three meals.

Also their health problems were serious. The wife has had several operations, the husband is a possible tuberculosis case, and the child is underweight. All three have also been receiving medical attention from a hospital for the past three years. The little girl has been nervous, has fainted at times, and is slightly deformed from rickets. Being undernourished, she needs cod-liver oil, milk, oranges, and the food which was possible only when the family was on relief. She went to camp for two weeks and returned up to weight and in good spirits. But relief was cut off while she was away, and she came back to meals of milk, coffee, and bread. In the short time at home she had become fretful and listless, refusing to take anything but milk. This whole family promised to be in serious health difficulties if their situation were long continued.

The Okies in California, 1939

The most characteristic of all housing in California in which migrants reside at the moment is the shacktown or cheap subdivision. Most of these settlements have come into existence since 1933 and the pattern which obtains is somewhat similar throughout the State. Finding it impossible to rent housing in incorporated communities on their meager incomes, migrants have created a market for a very cheap type of subdivision of which the following may be taken as being representative:

In Monterey County, according to a report of Dr. D. M. Bissell, county health officer, under date of November 28, 1939, there are approximately three well-established migrant settlements. One of these, the development around the environs of Salinas, is perhaps the oldest migrant settlement of its type in California. In connection with this development I quote a paragraph of the report of Dr. Bissell:

"This area is composed of all manners and forms of housing without a public sewer system. Roughly, 10,000 persons are renting or have established homes there. A chief element in this area is that of refugees from the Dust Bowl who inhabit a part of Alisal called Little Oklahoma. Work in lettuce harvesting and packing and sugar beet processing have attracted these people who, seeking homes in Salinas without success because they aren't available, have resorted to makeshift adobes outside the city limits. Complicating the picture is the impermeable substrata which makes septic tanks

SOURCE: Carey McWilliams, testimony from U.S. Congress, House Select Committee to Investigate the Interstate Migration of Destitute Citizens, *Hearings,* 76th Cong., 3d sess., 1941, 2543–2544.

with leaching fields impractical. Sewer wells have resulted with the corresponding danger to adjacent water wells and to the water wells serving the Salinas public. Certain districts, for example, the Airport Tract and parts of Alisal, have grown into communities with quite satisfactory housing, but others as exemplified by the Graves district are characterized by shacks and lean-tos which are unfit for human habitation." . . .

Typical of the shacktown problem are two such areas near the city limits of Sacramento, one on the east side of B Street, extending from Twelfth Street to the Sacramento city dump and incinerator; and the other so-called Hoovertown, adjacent to the Sacramento River and the city filtration plant. In these two areas there were on September 17, 1939, approximately 650 inhabitants living in structures that, with scarcely a single exception, were rated by the inspectors of this division as "unfit for human occupancy." The majority of the inhabitants were white Americans, with the exception of 50 or 60 Mexican families, a few single Mexican men, and a sprinkling of Negroes. For the most part they are seasonally employed in the canneries, the fruit ranches, and the hop fields of Sacramento County. Most of the occupants are at one time or another upon relief, and there are a large number of occupants in these shacktowns from the Dust Bowl area. Describing the housing, an inspector of this division reports:

"The dwellings are built of brush, rags, sacks, boxboard, odd bits of tin and galvanized iron, pieces of canvas and whatever other material was at hand at the time of construction."

Wood floors, where they exist, are placed directly upon the ground, which because of the location of the camps with respect to the Sacramento River, is damp most of the time. To quote again from the report:

"Entire families, men, women, and children, are crowded into hovels, cooking and eating in the same room. The majority of the shacks have no sinks or cesspools for the disposal of kitchen drainage, and this, together with garbage and other refuse, is thrown on the surface of the ground."

Because of the high-water table, cesspools, where they exist, do not function properly; there is a large overflow of drainage and sewage to the surface of the ground. Many filthy shack latrines are located within a few feet of living quarters. Rents for the houses in these shacktowns range from $3 to $20 a month. In one instance a landlord rents ground space for $1.50 to $5 a month, on which tenants are permitted to erect their own dugouts. The Hooverville section is composed primarily of tents and trailers, there being approximately 125 tent structures in this area on September 17, 1939. Both areas are located in unincorporated territory. They are not subject at the present time to any State or county building regulation. In Hooverville, at the date of the inspection, many families were found that did not have even a semblance of tents or shelters. They were cooking and sleeping on the ground in the open and one water tap at an adjoining industrial plant was found to be the source of the domestic water supply for the camp. . . .

The Bronx Slave Market, 1935

The Bronx Slave Market! What is it? Who are its dealers? Who are its victims? What are its causes? How far does its stench spread? What forces are at work to counteract it?

Any corner in the congested sections of New York City's Bronx is fertile soil for mushroom "slave marts." The two where the traffic is heaviest and the bidding is highest are located at 167th street and Jerome avenue and at Simpson and Westchester avenues. . . .

. . . Not only is human labor bartered and sold for slave wage, but human love also is a marketable commodity. But whether it is labor or love that is sold, economic necessity compels the sale. As early as 8 A.M. they come; as late as 1 P.M. they remain.

Rain or shine, cold or hot, you will find them there—Negro women, old and young—sometimes bedraggled, sometimes neatly dressed—but with the invariable paper bundle, waiting expectantly for Bronx housewives to buy their strength and energy for an hour, two hours, or even for a day at the munificent rate of fifteen, twenty, twenty-five, or, if luck be with them, thirty cents an hour. If not the wives themselves, maybe their husbands, their sons, or their brothers, under the subterfuge of work, offer worldly-wise girls higher bids for their time.

Who are these women? What brings them here? Why do they stay? In the boom days before the onslaught of the depression in 1929, many of these women who are now forced to bargain for day's work on street corners, were employed in grand homes in the rich Eighties, or in wealthier homes in Long Island and Westchester, at more than adequate wages. Some are former marginal industrial workers, forced by the slack in industry to seek other means of sustenance. In many instances there had been no necessity for work at all. But whatever their standing prior to the depression, none sought employment where they now seek it. They come to the Bronx, not because of what it promises, but largely in desperation.

Paradoxically, the crash of 1929 brought to the domestic labor market a new employer class. The lower middle-class housewife, who, having dreamed of the luxury of a maid, found opportunity staring her in the face in the form of Negro women pressed to the wall by poverty, starvation and discrimination.

Where once color was the "gilt edged" security for obtaining domestic and personal service jobs, here, even Negro women found themselves being displaced by whites. Hours of futile waiting in employment agencies, the fee that must be paid despite the lack of income, fraudulent agencies that sprung up during the depression, all forced the day worker to fend for herself or try the dubious and circuitous road to public relief.

SOURCE: Ella Baker and Marvel Cooke in *The Crisis* 42 (November 1935): 331.

As inadequate as emergency relief has been, it has proved somewhat of a boon to many of these women, for with its advent, actual starvation is no longer their ever-present slave driver and they have been able to demand twenty-five and even thirty cents an hour as against the old fifteen and twenty cent rate. In an effort to supplement the inadequate relief received, many seek this open market.

And what a market! She who is fortunate (?) enough to please Mrs. Simon Legree's* scrutinizing eye is led away to perform hours of multifarious household drudgeries. Under a rigid watch, she is permitted to scrub floors on her bended knees, to hang precariously from window sills, cleaning window after window, or to strain and sweat over steaming tubs of heavy blankets, spreads and furniture covers.

Fortunate, indeed, is she who gets the full hourly rate promised. Often, her day's slavery is rewarded with a single dollar bill or whatever her unscrupulous employer pleases to pay. More often, the clock is set back for an hour or more. Too often she is sent away without any pay at all.

---

*Mrs. Simon Legree is a reference to the wife of the villain of *Uncle Tom's Cabin*. (Eds.)

Chapter 11

World War II: The Home Front

The New Deal exerted an enormous impact on American society. For the embattled farmers and workers and their families described in the previous chapter, the federal government offered relief, mortgage aid, crop payments, and even employment— programs that helped to restore the nation's flagging morale and maintain the people's faith in their government and economic system.

Yet as dramatic and innovative as the New Deal was, World War II brought even more upheavals in the lives of Americans. Nearly 15 million men and women found themselves serving in the armed forces, and the government intervened in an unprecedented way in the economy. Rationing of such products as butter, meat, sugar, and gasoline was introduced, and war contracts, initiated as early as 1939, stimulated the manufacture of millions of uniforms and the production of hundreds of thousands of ships, airplanes, tanks, and pieces of military equipment. While millions served in the army, navy, air corps, and marines, many civilians flocked to urban centers to work in the booming military economy.

William O'Neill's essay "The People Are Willing" describes numerous changes unfolding during this period, changes that enabled the United States to outproduce its enemies and win the war. But as O'Neill notes, innovations did not always come easily. What does he identify as the major challenges in uniting the American people and its economic system behind the war effort? How does he account for the many difficulties and government "bungling," especially in the early days of the war? Finally, how did the nation eventually achieve both full production and unity of purpose?

O'Neill's essay also discusses the impact of the war on particular groups. The first document is by a young man who joined the navy in 1939, nearly two years before America entered the conflict. Why did this young man leave his farm for the navy, and what does his choice indicate about the connection between the coming war and the eventual end of the Great Depression?

The essay also points to major changes in the lives of American women, among them the appearance of Rosie the Riveter, symbol of those who took wartime jobs formerly reserved strictly for men. One Rosie is represented by the second document, taken from Augusta H. Clawson's Shipyard Diary of a Women Welder. *How would you describe her reactions to her new job?*

In spite of dislocations on the homefront, most Americans found that their standard of living improved during the war years. For Japanese Americans on the West Coast, however, this was not the case. Native-born American citizens of Japanese ancestry as well as Japanese immigrants were interned in virtual concentration camps, an imprisonment ordered by President Franklin Roosevelt and sanctioned by the United States Supreme Court on the ground of national security. The last document, a government report issued in 1984 about the wartime internment of civilians, describes some of the conditions encountered by these unfortunate Americans. In 1942, Earl Warren, then attorney general of California, responded to questions regarding the civil rights of Japanese Americans by stating, "I believe, sir, that in time of war every citizen must give up some of his normal rights." Even accepting this premise, does it justify the treatment Japanese Americans received, as described in the document?

ESSAY

The People Are Willing
William O'Neill

After Pearl Harbor a flood of volunteers overwhelmed recruiting offices, especially in the South. When the entire Lepanto, Arkansas football team joined the Navy, one member attempted suicide after failing to pass his physical. "I was afraid folks would think I was yellow because I didn't get into the service," he explained. Millions who were ineligible to serve wished to know what civilians could do to further the war effort. . . .

Most Americans believed that government did not need to be overly effective because the people themselves could manage. While they overstated its benefits, voluntarism was a fact of life, and Americans were capable—within limits—of doing what elsewhere were functions of government. This attribute manifested itself immediately after Pearl Harbor. Agencies like the Red Cross and local civilian defense offices were overwhelmed with offers to help. Because many commodities would soon be scarce, scrap drives were organized that collected not only rubber items but paper, fats, bones, a wide variety of metal goods, and other essential materials.

Towns convened meetings to discuss ways of aiding the war effort. Citizens' committees sprang up. Neighborhoods organized. When a Milwaukee air-raid warden could not afford a telephone, the other families on his block agreed to donate 10 cents a month apiece so he could subscribe to the service. In Chicago 23,000 block captains were sworn in at a mass ceremony by the head of the Office of Civilian Defense. West Coast hospitals reeled before waves of enthusiastic blood donors. The hottest literary property of 1942 was the Red Cross first aid manual, which, though not considered a book and therefore omitted from best seller lists, sold 8 million copies. Farmers began plowing at night in order to put their spring crops in early. Shipyard employees in San Francisco offered to work Sundays for free. That summer an event called The National Salvage Fair was held in New York as part of a campaign to establish Salvage Sewing Workrooms in which volunteers could use mill ends and scraps of cloth to make garments for the needy and establish a clothing reserve.

Though very much in the American grain, efforts such as these suffered from the limitations intrinsic to thousands of uncoordinated local schemes, often inspired by an excess of willing hands rather than any clear sense of purpose. By summer *Life* was overflowing with complaints. Congress was

SOURCE: Abridged and reprinted with the permission of The Free Press, a division of Simon & Schuster, Inc., from *A Democracy at War: America's Fight at Home and Abroad in World War II* by William L. O'Neill. Copyright © 1993 by William L. O'Neill.

not doing a good job. Neither were the people. All the powerful interest groups continued to pursue their own agendas. Every scrap campaign had failed, the rubber drive most of all. People were still motoring frivolously. Washington was asking too little, and getting what it asked for. Everyone was living their dream of a "Hollywood war," instead of facing up to the real one in which sacrifices would have to be made.

These complaints were well founded. In 1941 when aluminum was in short supply, the call went out for housewives to turn in their pots and pans. Ten thousand tons of aluminum would build 4,000 fighter planes was what they were told. Obedient to duty's call, women stripped their kitchens and donated 70,000 tons of aluminum, apparently solving the problem. It transpired that only virgin aluminum was suitable for aircraft, so the donated cookware gathered dust until it was finally sold to scrap dealers. Then the stuff was turned into new pots and pans, women buying back what they had previously given.

More serious than bungling was government's reluctance to take full advantage of civilian support for the war effort, especially that of women. The public was encouraged to buy war bonds and practice conservation. Otherwise, it often seemed as if Washington did not want public participation in national defense, which had been the case before Pearl Harbor. In January 1941 one of Dr. Gallup's polls had revealed that 67 percent of those questioned were willing "to spend one hour each day training for home guard, nursing, first aid work, ambulance driving," and similar activities.

Though officials frequently remarked on the gravity of the world situation and the need to prepare for hardships, they seldom took their own advice. When asked what people could do, Frank Bane, Chief of the National Defense Advisory Commission's Division on State and Local Cooperation, suggested that it might be nice if women living near Army posts would help entertain the troops. They could also work as volunteers in the overburdened health and welfare programs of "war boom" towns, laudable suggestions, to be sure, but hardly a call to action.

In August the president of the General Federation of Women's Clubs— an old, large, and conservative body—complained that women were being discriminated against "intolerably" in the civil-defense program. The Office of Civilian Defense did not even have a women's division. There were only seven women in the entire federal government at the policymaking level. Women were excluded from serving in Civil Aeronautics Authority programs for training student pilots. The female Assistant National Civilian Defense Director had just resigned because Director Fiorello La Guardia disapproved of her effort to have the WPA survey and catalogue volunteer associations around the country, many of them women's groups, as possible contributors to civil defense.

Women were joining the Red Cross and other emergency related bodies in large numbers, but not because government was encouraging them to, or promising that if war came it would utilize their services. This lack of interest would not change very much after Pearl Harbor. In the age of total war the United States would make a semitotal effort, a limitation that was prefigured by government's earlier policy on civilian defense. This prejudice against women would seriously weaken the war effort.

It was obvious that vast numbers of men in uniform would be performing clerical tasks and other duties that were not gender-specific. Yet military leaders were slow to admit that women could do these jobs as well, if not better than, men, thereby freeing able-bodied males for combat. Early in 1942 the Army agreed to accept 10,000 volunteers for a Women's Army Auxiliary Corps only because a bill introduced in Congress by Representative Edith Nourse Rogers (R, MA) forced its hand. The Navy went on refusing to accept women in any capacity. There were plenty of men as yet undrafted, the military's reasoning went—which was true at the time, but this surplus did not last, forcing a change of heart. . . .

Lacking official outlets, women formed numerous paramilitary groups of their own, including the Powder Puff Platoon of Joplin, Missouri, the Green Guards of Washington, and the Women's Defense School of Boston, which taught a course in field cooking modeled on that of the Army. Some 25,000 women volunteered for the Women's Ambulance and Defense Corps of America, whose slogan was "The Hell We Can't." Its more than 50 chapters trained women to serve as air-raid wardens, security guards, and couriers for the armed forces. However, most who wished to contribute joined the Red Cross, which, with 3.5 million female volunteers, was by far the most important outlet for patriotic womanhood.

Some government agencies actually recognized opportunity when they saw it. The Office of Civilian Defense employed a number of female volunteers. The Office of Price Administration used 50,000 women in five states to conduct a three-day canvas in July 1942, during which they briefed 450,000 retailers on the new price regulations. For the most part, though, except for defense contractors who gradually warmed to the idea of hiring women workers, volunteer organizations remained the main outlets.

Of these latter groups, the most controversial was the American Women's Voluntary Services, founded by a group of Anglophile socialites in 1940 to prepare women for emergency work in a London-style blitz. It soon enrolled 350,000 members in almost every state. To refute mockers who accused them of being social butterflies out on a lark, AWVS cast a remarkably broad net for the times, organizing several units in Harlem, at least one Chinese chapter, a number of Hispanic units, and one affiliate consisting entirely of Taos tribeswomen. Defying local taboos, the New Orleans chapter bravely included Negro women. When it became evident that America was not going to be attacked by German bombers, the AWVS took on new assignments. In New York members sold $5 million worth of war bonds. In California there were AWVS "chuckwagons" that delivered food, including late-night snacks, to Coast Guard stations and remote military sites. In San Francisco AWVS women taught Braille to blinded veterans. Others organized agricultural work camps in California and Colorado. Some New York suburbs had ambulances staffed entirely by AWVS members.

Though it was the biggest, AWVS was by no means the only volunteer women's organization that made a place for itself in the war effort. At least three other women's groups provided land and air ambulance services. There were also volunteer groups of working women, such as WIRES (Women in Radio and Electric Service), WAMS (Women Aircraft Mechanics), and WOWS (Women Ordnance Workers)—the latter of whom by 1943 had a membership of 33,000 in dozens of munitions plants. As part of an elaborate recruiting campaign, Oldsmobile created WINGS (also known as the "Keep 'Em Winning Girls"), workers who were given uniforms with a torch-and-wing insignia on the front pocket. So that housewives should not feel excluded, the *Ladies Home Journal* organized WINS (Women in National Service), saying that housewives were "the largest army in the nation fighting on the home front." The outpouring of female volunteers in a host of organizations enabled women to accomplish much, and suggested how much more they might have done had there been a system in place to take full advantage of their enthusiasm. Even as it was, when in April 1942 ten thousand women volunteers marched down Fifth Avenue in New York there were so many different uniforms that no one could identify them all. . . .

While the numerous complaints about government's incompetence and neglect were fully justified, it was important to keep in mind that the mills of American democracy were supposed to grind slowly. Though this was not apparent at first, the mess in Washington would improve. Private initiatives too would become more fruitful. Scrap drives got better, the rule seeming to be that behind every successful local drive there was one especially determined person. In Seattle, which had a very big one, that man was a local jeweler by the name of Leo Weisfield.

A landmark effort was the great Nebraska scrap drive of 1942, inspired by Henry Doorly, publisher of the state's biggest newspaper, the Omaha *World-Herald*. A unique feature of his plan was that prizes worth up to $2,000 in war bonds would be given to individuals and organizations who collected the most scrap, regardless of whether it was sold to dealers or donated gratis. This was a significant feature, not just because it meant that donors could mingle patriotism with profit, but because scrap dealers had the heavy equipment required to salvage large metal structures.

The drive collected 135 million tons of scrap, the equivalent of 103 pounds for every person in Nebraska. By comparison, the previous national scrap campaign collected only 213 million tons in its first two weeks, an average of barely more than a pound and a half for each American. Many Nebraska companies donated trucks, 40 a day on average, which were employed to transport scrap. The *World-Herald* itself contributed nine tons of old press parts which a frugal foreman had been stockpiling for 30 years. In the town of Oldrege a local department-store owner and a farm-implement dealer set up a nonprofit corporation that paid $10 a ton for salvage, a dollar and a half above the going rate. To finance it they borrowed money from the local bank, and with the aid of hundreds of volunteers ended up breaking even—a feat they accomplished by sorting the scrap, which enabled them to resell it to dealers for a premium that covered their overpayments.

Rural salvage was the most rewarding because of its scale. While townspeople were turning in old appliances, the countryside yielded up treasures in the form of disused iron bridges, farm machinery, and 537 tons of abandoned track donated by the Burlington Railroad. When the prizes were given out, the individual winner was a section hand for the Burlington who brought in 97,000 pounds of scrap. The winning business was a dinette in Norfolk whose owner hired two women to run the place while he collected 81,000 pounds of salvage. The junior prize went to the Omaha Future Farmers of America, who took time out from agricultural pursuits to amass a staggering 445,000 pounds.

The most successful state drive yet, the Nebraska model was widely copied, demonstrating that the will was there and could be mobilized with inventive planning. If the weakness of democracy was inefficient government, the strength was volunteerism, especially when it exploited the national love of competition.

An example of what could be done with official support was gasoline rationing, which went into effect on December 1, 1942—tardily, of course, but as so often happened, delay was needed to convince people that the rubber crisis really existed. Americans who hated rationing, complied with the rules as a whole, despite the inevitable chiseling and the rise of black marketeers and forgers of gas-ration permits. It helped that most people walked to work (40 percent) or took public transportation (23 percent). Even the 36 percent who commuted by car ultimately accepted gasoline rationing. Though only 49 percent of all Americans saw a need for it when first proposed, by the end of 1942 the great majority of motorists (73 percent) supported gasoline rationing. The 35 mph speed limit won almost universal approval, 89 percent of car owners backing it. Fortunately, though the black market in gasoline eventually became a big business, it never grew so large as to jeopardize the war effort.

Rationing, an inconvenience to some, meant real sacrifice for others—such as small businesses that depended on the drive-in trade. Nine hundred restaurants in Los Angeles alone closed within the first two weeks after rationing took effect. Labor and other kinds of shortages would also devastate small businessmen and farmers. In Arkansas, 6,000 small businesses would fail by 1943 for lack of workers, while the state's farm population declined from 667,000 in 1940 to 292,000 by the spring of 1944.

In January 1943 pleasure driving was banned completely on the East Coast, where a genuine gasoline shortage existed, virtually emptying the streets of major cities. Compliance was encouraged by police officers, who confiscated the gas-ration books of offending drivers. If after a court hearing the accused were found guilty of frivolous motoring, the fine was in gasoline coupons rather than cash—a powerful and effective deterrent. More important than stiff fines was patriotism, since experience would demonstrate that programs with which most Americans did not agree were ultimately unenforceable.

Conversely, programs that Americans believed in could not be stopped. Victory gardens were a case in point. Food production and conservation had been strongly encouraged in the First World War, and many families that did not ordinarily grow their own produce established kitchen gardens in response. People took it for granted that food would be short this time as well. They began planting vegetables in the spring, despite the Department of Agriculture, which initially dragged its feet. By April 1942, at least 6 million gardens were being cultivated, inspiring Secretary of Agriculture Claude Wickard to call for 18 million victory gardens—a goal that was easily reached. In 1943, more than 8 million tons of produce was grown on 20 million individual plots many of them very small. In cities with populations above 100,000, victory gardens averaged only 500 square feet in size—that is, about 20 by 25 feet—but nevertheless amounted collectively to 7 million acres, an area the size of Rhode Island.

Victory gardens appeared everywhere, not only on private lots but in parks, before the San Francisco City Hall, in the yards of schools and prisons, wherever there was arable soil, and hands to do the tilling. The Agriculture Department reported that the amount of vegetables grown in victory gardens exceeded "the total commercial production for fresh sale for civilian and non-civilian use." This was all the more impressive because, after being grown, much of this produce had to be canned—hence the slogan, "Eat what you can and can what you can't," no small thing, as a mistake could result in glass canisters exploding, or even bacterial growths that were potentially lethal.

Most of the conservation burden fell on women—and children, too, who were good collectors of scrap. In the fully mobilized household there were separate holders for tins, rags, bottles, paper, and bones. Tin cans were washed and flattened. Tinfoil and rubber bands were collected in balls. Bottle caps, chewing gum wrappers, and flashlight batteries were saved for later recycling. Because it was used to make munitions, schools had "Fat Parades," enabling children to make ceremonial deposits of accumulated kitchen grease. In rural areas they collected milkweeds, whose silken fibers would be stuffed into life jackets. . . .

Secretary of the Treasury Henry Morgenthau ... wanted bonds sold widely and in such a way as to make Americans "war-minded." He believed this was even more important than helping finance defense purchases. To sell bonds was to sell the war, so bond drives were aimed at the average American rather than at wealthy investors—which meant, in turn, drawing heavily on the popular culture. Movie stars played important parts, with Hollywood organizing seven tours that played in 300 communities. Dorothy Lamour alone, the star of a series of "Road" pictures with Bob Hope and Bing Crosby, was credited with selling $350 million worth of bonds. Carole Lombard, a popular movie actress, gave her life to the cause, dying in a plane crash on her way home from a bond tour. In addition to bonds, "war stamps" costing only pennies were sold—mainly to children, though sometimes to adults, as when scantily-clad showgirls covered their flesh with 10¢ savings stamps for happy businessmen to peel off and purchase. Every form of hucksterism was employed in this cause, few managing to escape it. . . .

Despite occasional lapses, [President] Roosevelt did not truly believe in propaganda. In 1917, precisely because opinion was divided on the merits of intervention, Washington had cranked up a vast publicity machine to bolster the war effort. A Committee on Public Information was created to that end, which distributed 75 million pamphlets, issued 6,000 press releases, placed ads in leading magazines, enlisted a corps of "Four-Minute Men" who gave short, canned talks emphasizing German atrocities, and in other ways sought to promote war fever. The intellectual content of most of this is suggested by some of the war films endorsed by CPI, such as "The Prussian Cur" and "The Kaiser, the Beast of Berlin." . . .

After World War I many felt that the mixture of propaganda and intimidation had encouraged the violation of basic American rights, inflamed passions, contributed to vigilante action, stimulated xenophobia, oversimplified the issues, and aroused unrealistic expectations. FDR was not going to repeat the mistake. Public relations was one thing, a ministry of domestic propaganda another. Congress seconded his motion, conservatives fearing that government propaganda campaigns would glorify Roosevelt, the New Deal, and liberal internationalism—what Congresswoman Clare Boothe Luce referred to as "globaloney." . . .

Given Washington's lack of interest in propaganda, writers eager to aid the war effort were inspired to create their own. West Coast patriots formed the Hollywood Writer's Mobilization. Its counterpart on the East Coast was organized by Rex Stout, author of the popular Nero Wolfe detective novels, who launched the Writer's War Board two days after Pearl Harbor. Initially it helped sell war bonds, but soon grew "into a liaison office between writers and government departments, a kind of unpaid extension of the Office of War Information." Looking back, a former member described its purpose thusly. "The government was slow; we were fast. They were timid; we were bold. They used official gobbledygook; we had some wit. World War II was strangely unemotional and needed a WWB to stir things up." As this suggests, the mobilized wordsmiths put a high premium on ardor.

Members not only wrote advertising copy for war bonds, but used every known outlet to reach the public. The WWB itself might instigate a campaign; other times it responded to official requests. An example of the latter case occurred when the Air Force wanted to promote the enlistment of flight crew other than pilots. WWB's contribution included 12 short stories, 24 syndicated columns, three radio broadcasts, one novel, one handbook, and two popular songs—one of them entitled "I Wanna Marry a Bombardier." The campaign had to be terminated after it produced a surplus of volunteers. . . .

These were America's strengths, a lack of regimentation, the refusal to indoctrinate; and most of all the initiative of ordinary people organizing, conserving, collecting, recycling, buying war bonds—or if, like writers and entertainers, they had special skills, devoting them to public service. That government never found a way of fully exploiting their eagerness to help was its biggest wartime failure, and a curious one in light of the opinion polls showing a willingness to give beyond what was ever asked of civilians. . . .

Civilians contributed more to the winning of World War II than to any previous American conflict—on the homefront, but directly too in the battle against the U-boats. In this campaign the front lines were manned not just by sailors and fliers, but by civilian seamen of the U.S. merchant fleet, thousands of whom lost their lives to keep Britain and Russia going. Many more would have died had it not been for a handful of men in government and business who played key roles at critical points that were to make a tremendous difference. . . .

The war changed everything except human needs and desires. Many once ordinary tasks became fiendishly difficult to perform. Numerous goods previously taken for granted all but disappeared, were replaced by inferior substitutes, or disappeared altogether. People got by as best they could and some discovered in the war a welcome degree of excitement. Most found it possible, despite shortages and censorship, to amuse themselves, taking their pleasure in ways that tell us much about the American people and what they considered important.

It seems fair to say that life on the homefront was most difficult for married women. A 48-hour week and long commutes were the rule for all workers, regardless of gender. Because so many goods and services— including household appliances and supplies, certain foodstuffs, domestic help, and medical care—were in short supply, wives and mothers, whether employed or not, had to devote more time to such activities as housework and getting their children to doctors. Shopping was further complicated by ration books and the need to go from store to store looking for scarce products.

Like their husbands, service wives could "take it" and did not let fear for their absent loved ones keep them from shouldering what often were heavy burdens. One Illinois mother was left to care for three small boys when her husband went overseas. She worked eight hours a day in a local canning factory, yet managed to run a Cub Scout troop, keep a victory garden, and put a hot meal on the table every night—if only tunafish casserole. When the fare prompted complaints she serenely replied, as every mother did in those years, "Think of the poor, starving children in Europe."

Consumers had to return used toothpaste tubes in order to buy new ones, while tinfoil and cellophane simply disappeared—as did bobby pins, which were replaced by wooden toothpicks and thread. Mostly a drain, shopping could be adventuresome if you had the right kind of luck. In April 1945, Audrey Davis triumphantly wrote to her husband at sea:

> Honey, I'm a success. I got sheets! Such a time—went to four of the biggest stores first and was turned down cold. Finally ended up in the basement of J. C. Penney's . . . and saw some bedding so on the off-chance, I asked. The girl said, shhh, and sneaked into a back room and brought out some carefully wrapped—didn't even know what I had bought, until I got home. I felt like someone buying hooch during Prohibition.

New clothes were devoid of elastic thread and webbing, metal buttons, zippers, hooks and eyes, silk, nylon, canvas, duck, and sometimes leather. Coats could not have pleats, gussets, bellows, yokes. A "victory suit," which carried economy to the point of eliminating lapels, was ruled out. To save wool, double-breasted suits could not be vested, and no suit could come with more than one pair of pants. Cloth could not go over cloth, eliminating trouser cuffs and patch pockets. Women's skirts were limited in length and circumference and certain dyes, especially greens and browns, were sometimes unavailable. Girdles, still everyday wear for women, had to be made of bone or piano wire instead of rubber. Shoes, when you could get them, came in six colors only, three of them shades of brown. Almost anything from coffee to canned goods, half the 1943 production went overseas, could run out without notice, cigarette shortages being a particular trial for a nation of smokers.

Irritation over rationing was continuous and so sharp that in 1943 Leon Henderson, one of the most brilliant New Dealers, had to resign as head of the Office of Price Administration even though he was, according to economist Kenneth Galbraith (who worked for him), one of the "unsung heroes of World War II". . . . Urban Americans grew used to queuing up. Not only were food and clothing rationed, but the number of ration "points" required for specific items fluctuated, obliging every housewife to update her calculations on a weekly, or even daily, basis. Black-marketeering, especially in meat, aggravated shortages. For some, getting meat was a major preoccupation. One mother seems never to have written her son abroad without addressing the problem, although in the mandatory positive voice, as when she told him of her discovery that "Spam fried in butter makes a very tasty Easter dinner."

*   *   *

A striking feature of the war effort, and a source of many problems, was the enormous increase in physical mobility. Including service personnel, 27.3 million people moved from their original county of residence. In the period 1935–40, an unusually active one, total civilian mobility had amounted to 2.8 million persons a year, but during each of the peak war years it averaged 4.7 million. With automobile use restricted, most long-distance travel was by train, putting enormous stress on the rail system and also the passengers—jammed into overcrowded and poorly maintained cars which were slow and often late due to breakdowns or from having been sidetracked for high-priority troop trains.

Difficult as travel became, starting over in strange places was worse. Adolescents were particularly affected, not only because relocation is emotionally most difficult at that age, but also because so many were going to work full-time or entering the services. In 1940 the number of employed persons between the ages of 14 and 17 was 1.7 million, whereas in 1944 it came to 4.61 million, of whom 1.43 million were part-time students. During World War II the decline in child labor was temporarily reversed, as also the trend toward longer periods of education. Total school attendance for the 14–19 age group in 1940 came to 9.159 million persons, whereas by 1944 it had fallen to 7.93 million. The number of boys and girls aged 14 to 18 who were employed rose from 1 million in 1940 to 2.9 million—the number of mill girls alone rising from 271,000 to 950,000.

By May 1943 some 1.8 million boys and girls under the age of 18 were employed by farms and factories. One Lockheed plant had 1,500 boys laboring as riveters and electricians and in metal fabrication and assembly work. According to the firm, two boys in four hours could accomplish more than an adult worker during a regular eight-hour shift. For those children who remained in school full-time, life was harder, too, as teacher quality declined and class sizes went up. In Arkansas by the 1945–46 school year half the prewar teachers were gone and 72 percent of their replacements had completed less than a semester of college. During 1942–43, out of 170,000 Arkansas youngsters between the ages of 13 and 18 about 100,000 failed to attend school, some taking jobs but many because teachers were not available.

As might be expected, crime rates were strongly influenced by the physical and social changes affecting such a large number of people. Since so many young males, the principal crime-committing group, were in uniform, most crimes declined—except possibly rapes, though as they were seldom reported, the statistics are not very useful. But the number of murders, a more reliable figure, fell from 8,329 in 1940 to a low of 6,675 in 1944. Auto thefts went up in 1942 when new cars became unavailable, but the total number of reported crimes followed the same curve as murders, falling after 1940 and rising again only in 1945 when veterans began reentering civilian life. Suicides declined by a third, from about 19,000 in 1940 to some 13,000 four years later. It is an all too human irony that life seemed more worth living in wartime, the suicide rate showing this even more than the rising birthrate.

All these figures are evidence that—not to make light of its hardships—the war was more interesting than the peace had been. The war put an end to Depression America and gave meaning to ordinary lives, since all citizens were to some degree participants in the national effort. Everything changed, not always for the better, to be sure, but change of itself was often welcome after the monotonous years of austerity that followed the stock market crash of 1929. Many people were given jobs they never expected to get, saw places they would otherwise not have known, and lived richer lives. . . .

DOCUMENTS

Joining the Navy (1939), c. 1991

Well, growing up on the farm in the thirties wasn't very pleasant. I remember the banks going broke, the Depression, and then there were the dry years. I just didn't have a very good experience with living on a farm, and there weren't any jobs when I graduated out of high school, so I decided to join the navy. Part of their propaganda was "Join the navy, see the world, and learn a trade." The pay was $21.00 a month which sounded pretty good at that time. So I figured that would be a good opportunity to get off the farm.

John Zimola, Wahoo
U.S. Navy firecontrolman,
cruiser USS *Louisville*, Pacific Theater
(enlisted in 1939)

SOURCE: *Nebraska History* 72, no. 4 (Winter 1991): 169. Testimony taken 1988–1991.

Shipyard Diary of a
Woman Welder (1940s), 1944

Sunday

I am back from my first day on the Ways [staging on which ships are built], and I feel as if I had seen some giant phenomenon. It's incredible! It's inhuman! It's horrible! And it's marvelous! I don't believe a blitz could be noisier—I didn't dream that there could be so much noise, anywhere. My ears are still ringing like high-tension wires, and my head buzzes. When you first see it, when you look down Way after Way, when you see the thousands each going about his own business and seeming to know what to do, you're so bewildered you can't see anything or make sense out of it.

First came the bus ride to the Yard. Crowded as usual. I was intrigued by knowing that this time I was going to Mart's Marsh. The name has always fascinated me. I gather that it refers to bottom or marshy land once owned by a family named Mart. From the [welding] school our road led along the water where I could see several of the ships already launched and now lying at the outfitting dock to receive the finishing touches. It was easy to spot the various stages of completion; each ship gets moved up one when a new ship arrives for outfitting.

When the bus came to a stop, I followed the crowd across a pontoon bridge between rails at which stood guards checking for badges. The far side of the bridge brought us to the part of the Yard where the prefabricated parts are stored, right in the open, pile upon pile. I saw a huge building marked "Assembly Shop," another "Marine Shop," and still another "Pipe Assembly." There were lots of little houses marked with numbers. Most of them seemed to be in the sixties. And I was looking for check-in station No. 1.

I hunted and hunted without success, and finally asked someone where "new hires" check in. He immediately directed me. I showed my badge, told my number, and was given another badge to be picked up and turned in daily as we did at school. It was marked "New Hire." About then who should come along but Red-headed Marie and the Big Swede! We went together to the Welders' Office where our off days were assigned to us. I was given "C" day and told that it was the only day available. This means that I get Tuesday off this week, Wednesday next, and so on. The Big Swede said she had to have "D" day to get a ride to work and to have the same day as her husband. Although "C" day was "the only one available," strangely enough she was given "D" day. One has to learn to insist on what one wants even when told it is impossible.

The Big Swede is a real pal. She had not forgotten the patch for my overall trouser leg. She had cut a piece from an old pair of her husband's, scrubbed it to get the oil out, and brought it to me with a needle stuck in the center and a coil of black thread ready for action. "Here," she said, "I knew you wouldn't have things handy in a hotel room. Now you mend that hole before you catch your foot in it and fall." . . .

Today my book on welding came from the Washington office. I read that a welder's qualifications are "physical fitness which insures a reasonable degree of endurance during a full day of work; steady nerves and considerable muscular strength." For a shipyard welder I'd amend that to read: "An unreasonable degree of endurance during a full day of strain, plus muscular strength, plus no nerves." If you haven't the muscular strength before you start, you will have it afterward. If you haven't the nerves before, you may have them afterward, though I doubt it. By tomorrow I shall be "reasonably" acclimated, but tonight I quite frankly "ain't."

I, who hate heights, climbed stair after stair after stair till I thought I must be close to the sun. I stopped on the top deck. I, who hate confined spaces, went through narrow corridors, stumbling my way over rubber-coats leads—dozens of them, scores of them, even hundreds of them. I went into a room about four feet by ten where two shipfitters, a shipfitter's helper, a chipper, and I all worked. I welded in the poop deck lying on the floor while another welder spattered sparks from the ceiling and chippers like giant woodpeckers shattered our eardrums. I, who've taken welding, and have sat at a bench welding flat and vertical plates, was told to weld braces along a baseboard below a door opening. On these a heavy steel door was braced while it was hung to a fine degree of accuracy. I welded more braces along the side, and along the top. I did overhead welding, horizontal, flat, vertical. I welded around curved hinges which were placed so close to the side wall that I had to bend my rod in a curve to get it in. I made some good welds and some frightful ones. But now a door in the poop deck of an oil tanker is hanging, four feet by six of solid steel, by my welds. Pretty exciting!

The men in the poop deck were nice to me. The shipfitter was toothless. The grinder had palsy, I guess, for his hands shook pitifully and yet he managed to handle that thirty-pound grinder. The welder was doing "pickup" work, which meant touching up spots that had been missed. An inspector came through and marked places to chip, and the ship's superintendent stopped and woke the shipfitter's helper. . . .

As a result of all this, I feel very strongly that we'd go to the Yard better prepared if in the school we did more welding in varied positions. Even a fillet weld of two plates could be placed on the floor, and one could get down and do it there and so learn something of what will later be required in the Yard. I don't see why, too, the butterflies, the clips, and even the bolts couldn't be welded at various angles in school. We could practice some one-handed welding instead of always using two hands while sitting at a bench with plates conveniently placed. There are times when you have to use one hand to cling to a ladder or a beam while you weld with the other. I notice that the most experienced welders I have watched seldom use two hands. One large, fine-looking woman (Norwegian, I think) who has been there three months told me: "They don't teach us enough at school. Why don't they let us weld there the same things we'll do here?" I countered with, "Oh, they do teach a lot or we'd be no good here at all; but what you say would certainly help." I think she "has something," however. We do need more experience in setting our machines and recognizing when they are too hot or too cold. Struggling with an inaccurate setting and the wrong amount of heat makes a harder day than doing a lot of actual work. Yet it's hardly the fault of the training that we lack adequate experience. More and more I marvel at training that in eight days can give enough to make us worth anything on the job. And we are worth something. We're building ships.

Conditions in the Camps
(1942–1945), 1948

A visiting reporter from *The San Francisco Chronicle* described quarters at Tule Lake:

> Room size—about 15 by 25, considered too big for two reporters.
>   Condition—dirty.
>   Contents—two Army cots, each with two Army blankets, one pillow, some sheets and pillow cases (these came as a courtesy from the management), and a coal-burning stove (no coal). There were no dishes, rugs, curtains, or housekeeping equipment of any kind. (We had in addition one sawhorse and three pieces of wood, which the management did not explain.)

The furnishings at other camps were similar. At Minidoka, arriving evacuees found two stacked canvas cots, a pot-bellied stove and a light bulb hanging from the ceiling; at Topaz, cots, two blankets, a pot-bellied stove and some cotton mattresses. Rooms had no running water, which had to be carried from community facilities. Running back and forth from the laundry room to rinse and launder soiled diapers was a particular inconvenience. . . .

Others, however, found not even the minimal comforts that had been planned for them. An unrealistic schedule combined with wartime shortages of labor and materials meant that the WRA* had difficulty meeting its

SOURCE: Commission on Wartime Relocation and Internment of Civilians, *Personal Justice Denied* (Washington, D.C., Government Printing Office, 1984), pp. 159–161.
    *Wartime Relocation Administration (Eds.)

construction schedule. In most cases, the barracks were completed, but at some centers evacuees lived without electric light, adequate toilets or laundry facilities. . . .

Mess Halls planned for about 300 people had to handle 600 or 900 for short periods. Three months after the project opened, Manzanar still lacked equipment for 16 of 36 messhalls. At Gila:

> There were 7,700 people crowded into space designed for 5,000.
> They were housed in messhalls, recreation halls, and even latrines.
> As many as 25 persons lived in a space intended for four.

As at the assembly centers, one result was that evacuees were often denied privacy in even the most intimate aspects of their lives. . . . Even when families had separate quarters, the partitions between rooms failed to give much privacy. Gladys Bell described the situation at Topaz:

> [T]he evacuees . . . had only one room, unless there were around ten in the family. Their rooms had a pot-bellied stove, a single electric light hanging from the ceiling, an Army cot for each person and a blanket for the bed. Each barrack had six rooms with only three flues. This meant that a hole had to be cut through the wall of one room for the stovepipe to join the chimney of the next room. The hole was large so that the wall would not burn. As a result, everything said and some things whispered were easily heard by people living in the next room. Sometimes the family would be a couple with four children living next to an older couple, perhaps of a different religion, older ideas and with a difference in all ways of life— such as music.

Despite these wretched conditions the evacuees again began to rebuild their lives. Several evacuees recall "foraging for bits of wallboard and wood" and dodging guards to get materials from the scrap lumber piles to build shelves and furniture. . . . Eventually, rooms were partitioned and shelves, tables, chairs and other furniture appeared. Paint and cloth for curtains and spreads came from mail order houses at evacuee expense. Flowers bloomed and rock gardens emerged; trees and shrubs were planted. Many evacuees grew victory gardens. One described the change:

> [W]hen we entered camp, it was a barren desert. When we left camp, it was a garden that had been built up without tools, it was green around the camp with vegetation, flowers, and also with artificial lakes, and that's how we left it.

The success of evacuees' efforts to improve their surroundings, however, was always tempered by the harsh climate. In the western camps, particularly Heart Mountain, Poston, Topaz and Minidoka, dust was a principal problem. Monica Sone described her first day at Minidoka:

[W]e were given a rousing welcome by a dust storm. . . . We felt as if we were standing in a gigantic sand-mixing machine as the sixty-mile gale lifted the loose earth up into the sky, obliterating everything. Sand filled our mouths and nostrils and stung our faces and hands like a thousand darting needles. Henry and Father pushed on ahead while Mother, Sumi and I followed, hanging onto their jackets, banging suitcases into each other. At last we staggered into our room, gasping and blinded. We sat on our suitcases to rest, peeling off our jackets and scarves. The window panels rattled madly, and the dust poured through the cracks like smoke. Now and then when the wind subsided, I saw other evacuees, hanging on to their suitcases, heads bent against the stinging dust. The wind whipped their scarves and towels from their heads and zipped them out of sight.

In desert camps, the evacuees met severe extremes of temperature as well. In winter it reached 35 degrees below zero and summers brought temperature as high as 115°. Because the desert did not cool off at night, evacuees would splash water on their cots to be cool enough to sleep. Rattlesnakes and desert wildlife added danger to discomfort.

The Arkansas camps had equally unpleasant weather. Winters were cold and snowy while summers were unbearably hot and humid, heavy with chiggers and clouds of mosquitos. . . .

The WRA walked a fine line in providing for evacuees' basic needs. On the one hand was their genuine sympathy for the excluded people. On the other was a well-founded apprehension that the press and the politicians would seek out and denounce any evidence that evacuees were being treated generously. WRA's compromise was to strive for a system that would provide a healthy but Spartan environment. They did not always succeed, and it was usually the evacuees who suffered when they failed.

Chapter 12

Moving to Suburbia: Dreams and Discontents

World War II set off an economic boom marked by the steady growth of family and individual incomes that lasted, with few interruptions, until 1973. Never before had the nation experienced such prosperity. Never before had material products that Americans associated with "the good life"—automobiles, dishwashers, stereos, televisions, and more—become so readily available to large segments of the population.

The keystone of the middle-class dream was home ownership. During the 1930s and 1940s, the lyrics of popular ballads like "My Blue Heaven" had expressed the desire for a bungalow in the suburbs, in which husband, wife, and children would live an idyllic life. But wartime demands for the construction of military bases and for defense industries had brought private home building, already slowed by the Depression, to a virtual halt. Within a few years of the war's end, however, the building boom was under way. Kenneth Jackson's essay "The Baby Boom and the Age of the Subdivision" describes how the postwar demand for suburban housing, fueled by veterans and their growing families, was served by government assistance and enterprising builders. Among the latter, William Levitt was possibly the most ingenious; the housing tracts that he built, called Levittowns, came to symbolize post–World War II construction. Which innovations in home construction *and community planning were most likely responsible for establishing Levitt's reputation?*

Jackson describes not only the birth of postwar suburbs but also the lifestyles that characterized those communities. Although large numbers of people voted their approval of suburban life by deciding to relocate their families, the movement was not without critics. The homogeneity and conformity of housing developments were frequent targets, as illustrated by the first document, Malvina Reynolds's popular song of the early 1960s, "Little Boxes." Do the lyrics give a fair picture of the suburbs?

The second document, from the best-selling book The Feminine Mystique *by feminist Betty Friedan, singles out for attack another aspect of suburban life, which the author calls "The Problem That Has No Name." What did Friedan see as the impact of suburbanization on the American housewife? Did the problem she discusses arise because of suburban development, or because of larger cultural changes that took place in cities as well as in suburbs?*

Whether suburban life was as bleak for white women as "Little Boxes" and Betty Friedan imply is debatable. Nevertheless, white families at least had a choice, if they had the means, to live where they chose. For black Americans, suburban housing opportunities were limited. The last document, a summary of residential patterns, points to a factor to which Kenneth Jackson alludes: racial segregation. What does this report tell us about race relations in suburban America? Keep housing in mind later, when you assess the impact of the civil rights movement in the next chapter.

ESSAY
—————— •◆• ——————

The Baby Boom and the
Age of the Subdivision

Kenneth Jackson

> What the Blandings wanted . . . was simple enough: a
> two-story house in quiet, modern good taste, . . . a good-
> sized living room with a fire place, a dining room, pantry,
> and kitchen, a small lavatory, four bedrooms and accompa-
> nying baths, . . . a roomy cellar . . . plenty of closets.
>
> —Eric Hodgins,
> *Mr. Blandings Builds His Dream House* (1939)

> No man who owns his own house and lot can be a
> Communist. He has too much to do.
>
> —William J. Levitt, 1948

At 7 P.M. (Eastern time) on August 14, 1945, radio stations across the nation interrupted normal programming for President Harry S Truman's announcement of the surrender of Japan. It was a moment in time that those who experienced it will never forget. World War II was over. Across the nation, Americans gathered to celebrate their victory. In New York City two million people converged on Times Square as though it were New Year's Eve. In smaller cities and towns, the response was no less tumultuous, as spontaneous cheers, horns, sirens, and church bells telegraphed the news to every household and hamlet, convincing even small children that it was a very special day. To the average person, the most important consequence of victory was not the end of shortages, not the restructuring of international boundaries or reparations payments or big power politics, but the survival of husbands and sons. Some women regretted that their first decent-paying, responsible jobs would be taken away by returning veterans. Most, however, felt a collective sigh of relief. Normal family life could resume. The long vigil was over. Their men would be coming home.

In truth, the United States was no better prepared for peace than it had been for war when the German *Wehrmacht* crossed the Polish frontier in the predawn hours of September 1, 1939. For more than five years military necessity had taken priority over consumer goods, and by 1945 almost everyone had a long list of unfilled material wants.

SOURCE: From *Crabgrass Frontier: The Suburbanization of the United States* by Kenneth T. Jackson. Copyright © 1985 by Oxford University Press, Inc. Used by permission of Oxford University Press, Inc.

Housing was the area of most pressing need. Through sixteen years of depression and war, the residential construction industry had been dormant, with new home starts averaging less than 100,000 per year. Almost one million people had migrated to defense areas in the early 1940s, but new housing for them was designated as "temporary," in part as an economy move and in part because the real-estate lobby did not want emergency housing converted to permanent use after the war. Meanwhile, the marriage rate, after a decade of decline, had begun a steep rise in 1940, as war became increasingly likely and the possibility of separation added a spur to decision making. In addition, married servicemen received an additional fifty dollars per month allotment, which went directly to the wives. Soon thereafter, the birth rate began to climb, reaching 22 per 1,000 in 1943, the highest in two decades. Many of the newcomers were "good-bye babies," conceived just before the husbands shipped out, partly because of an absence of birth control, partly because the wife's allotment check would be increased with each child, and partly as a tangible reminder of a father who could not know when, or if, he would return. During the war, government and industry both played up the suburban house to the families of absent servicemen, and between 1941 and 1946 some of the nation's most promising architects published their "dream houses" in a series in the *Ladies' Home Journal.*

After the war, both the marriage and the birth rates continued at a high level. In individual terms, this rise in family formation coupled with the decline in housing starts meant that there were virtually no homes for sale or apartments for rent at war's end. Continuing a trend begun during the Great Depression, six million families were doubling up with relatives or friends by 1947, and another 500,000 were occupying quonset huts or temporary quarters. Neither figure included families living in substandard dwellings or those in desperate need of more room. In Chicago, 250 former trolley cars were sold as homes. In New York City a newly wed couple set up housekeeping for two days in a department store window in hopes that the publicity would help them find an apartment. In Omaha a newspaper advertisement proposed: "Big Ice Box, 7 × 17 feet, could be fixed up to live in." In Atlanta the city bought 100 trailers for veterans. In North Dakota surplus grain bins were turned into apartments. In brief, the demand for housing was unprecedented.

The federal government responded to an immediate need for five million new homes by underwriting a vast new construction program. In the decade after the war, Congress regularly approved billions of dollars worth of additional mortgage insurance for the Federal Housing Administration. Even more important was the Servicemen's Readjustment Act of 1944, which created a Veterans Administration mortgage program similar to that of FHA. This law gave official endorsement and support to the view that the 16 million GI's of World War II should return to civilian life with a home of their own. Also, it accepted the builders' contention that they needed an end to government controls but not to government insurance on their investments in residential construction. According to novelist John Keats, "The real estate boys read the Bill, looked at one another in happy amazement, and the dry, rasping noise they made rubbing their hands together could have been heard as far away as Tawi Tawi."

It is not recorded how far the noise carried, but anyone in the residential construction business had ample reason to rub their hands. The assurance of federal mortgage guarantees—at whatever price the builder set—stimulated an unprecedented building boom. Single-family housing starts spurted from only 114,000 in 1944, to 937,000 in 1946, to 1,183,000 in 1948, and to 1,692,000 in 1950, an all-time high. However, . . . what distinguished the period was an increase in the number, importance, and size of large builders. Residential construction in the United States had always been highly fragmented in comparison with other industries, and dominated by small and poorly organized house builders who had to subcontract much of the work because their low volume did not justify the hiring of all the craftsmen needed to put up a dwelling. In housing, as in other areas of the economy, World War II was beneficial to large businesses. Whereas before 1945, the typical contractor had put up fewer than five houses per year, by 1959, the median single-family builder put up twenty-two structures. As early as 1949, fully 70 percent of new homes were constructed by only 10 percent of the firms (a percentage that would remain roughly stable for the next three decades), and by 1955 subdivisions accounted for more than three-quarters of all new housing in metropolitan areas.

Viewed from an international perspective, however, the building of homes in the United States remained a small-scale enterprise. In 1969, for example, the percentage of all new units built by builders of more than 500 units per year was only 8.1 percent in the United States, compared with 24 percent in Great Britain and 33 percent in France. World War II, therefore, did not transform the American housing industry as radically as it did that of Europe.

The family that had the greatest impact on postwar housing in the United States was Abraham Levitt and his sons, William and Alfred, who ultimately built more than 140,000 houses and turned a cottage industry into a major manufacturing process. They began on a small scale on Long Island in 1929 and concentrated for years on substantial houses in Rockville Center. Increasing their pace in 1934 with a 200-unit subdivision called "Strathmore" in Manhasset, the Levitts continued to focus on the upper-middle class and marketed their tudor-style houses at between $9,100 and $18,500. Private commissions and smaller subdivisions carried the firm through the remainder of the prewar period.

In 1941 Levitt and Sons received a government contract for 1,600 (later increased to 2,350) war workers' homes in Norfolk, Virginia. The effort was a nightmare, but the brothers learned how to lay dozens of concrete foundations in a single day and to preassemble uniform walls and roofs. Additional contracts for more federal housing in Portsmouth, Virginia, and for barracks for shipyard workers at Pearl Harbor provided supplemental experience, as did William's service with the Navy Seabees from 1943 to 1945. Thus, the Levitts were among the nation's largest home builders even before construction of the first Levittown.

Returning to Long Island after the war, the Levitts built 2,250 houses in Roslyn in 1946 in the $17,500 to $23,500 price range, well beyond the means of the average veteran. In that same year, however, they began the acquisition of 4,000 acres of potato farms in the Town of Hempstead, where they planned the biggest private housing project in American history.

The formula for Island Trees, soon renamed Levittown, was simple. After bulldozing the land and removing the trees, trucks carefully dropped off building materials at precise 60-foot intervals. Each house was built on a concrete slab (no cellar); the floors were of asphalt and the walls of composition rock-board. Plywood replaced ¾-inch strip lap, ¾-inch double lap was changed to ⅜-inch for roofing, and the horse and scoop were replaced by the bulldozer. New power hand tools like saws, routers, and nailers helped increase worker productivity. Freight cars loaded with lumber went directly into a cutting yard where one man cut parts for ten houses in one day.

The construction process itself was divided into twenty-seven distinct steps—beginning with laying the foundation and ending with a clean sweep of the new home. Crews were trained to do one job—one day the white-paint men, then the red-paint men, then the tile layers. Every possible part, and especially the most difficult ones, were preassembled in central shops, whereas most builders did it on site. Thus, the Levitts reduced the skilled component to 20–40 percent. The five-day work week was standard, but they were the five days during which building was possible; Saturday and Sunday were considered to be the days when it rained. In the process, the Levitts defied unions and union work rules (against spray painting, for example) and insisted that subcontractors work only for them. Vertical integration also meant that the firm made its own concrete, grew its own timber, and cut its own lumber. It also bought all appliances from wholly owned subsidiaries. More than thirty houses went up each day at the peak of production.

Initially limited to veterans, this first "Levittown" was twenty-five miles east of Manhattan and particularly attractive to new families that had been formed during and just after the war. Squashed in with their in-laws or in tiny apartments where landlords frowned on children, the GI's looked upon Levittown as the answer to their most pressing need. Months before the first three hundred Levitt houses were occupied in October 1947, customers stood in line for the four-room Cape Cod box renting at sixty dollars per month. The first eighteen hundred houses were initially available only for rental, with an option to buy after a year's residence. Because the total for mortgage, interest, principal, and taxes was *less* than the rent, almost everyone bought; after 1949 all units were for sale only. So many of the purchasers were young families that the first issue of *Island Trees*, the community newspaper, opined that "our lives are held closely together because most of us are within the same age bracket, in similar income groups, live in almost identical houses and have common problems." And so many babies were born to them that the suburb came to be known as "Fertility Valley" and "The Rabbit Hutch."

Ultimately encompassing more than 17,400 separate houses and 82,000 residents, Levittown was the largest housing development ever put up by a single builder, and it served the American dream-house market at close to the lowest prices the industry could attain. The typical Cape Cod was down-to-earth and unpretentious; the intention was not to stir the imagination, but to provide the best shelter at the least price. Each dwelling included a twelve-by-sixteen-foot living-room with a fireplace, one bath, and two bedrooms (about 750 square feet), with easy expansion possibilities upstairs in the unfinished attic or outward into the yard. Most importantly, the floor plan was practical and well-designed, with the kitchen moved to the front of the house near the entrance so that mothers could watch their children from kitchen windows and do their washing and cooking with a minimum of movement. Similarly, the living room was placed in the rear and given a picture window overlooking the back yard. This early Levitt house was as basic to post–World War II suburban development as the Model T had been to the automobile. In each case, the actual design features were less important than the fact that they were mass-produced and thus priced within the reach of the middle class.

William Jaird Levitt, who assumed primary operating responsibility for the firm soon after the war, disposed of houses as quickly as other men disposed of cars. Pricing his Cape Cods at $7,990 (the earliest models went for $6,990) and his ranches at $9,500, he promised no down payment, no closing costs, and "no hidden extras." With FHA and VA "production advances," Levitt boasted the largest line of credit ever offered a private home builder. He simplified the paperwork required for purchase and reduced the entire financing and titling transaction to two half-hour steps. His full-page advertisements offered a sweetener to eliminate lingering resistance—a Bendix washer was included in the purchase price. Other inducements included an eight-inch television set (for which the family would pay for the next thirty years). So efficient was the operation that *Harper's Magazine* reported in 1948 that Levitt undersold his nearest competition by $1,500 and still made a $1,000 profit on each house. As *New York Times* architecture critic Paul Goldberger has noted, "Levittown houses were social creations more than architectural ones—they turned the detached, single-family house from a distant dream to a real possibility for thousands of middle-class American families."

Buyers received more than shelter for their money. When the initial families arrived with their baby strollers and play pens, there were no trees, schools, churches, or private telephones. Grocery shopping was a planned adventure, and picking up the mail required sloshing through the mud to Hicksville. The Levitts planted apple, cherry, and evergreen trees on each plot, however, and the development ultimately assumed a more parklike appearance. To facilitate development as a garden community, streets were curvilinear (and invariably called "roads" or "lanes"), and through traffic was shunted to peripheral thoroughfares. Nine swimming pools, sixty playgrounds, ten baseball diamonds, and seven "village greens" provided open space and recreational opportunities. The Levitts forbade fences (a practice later ignored) and permitted outdoor clothes drying only on specially designed, collapsible racks. They even supervised lawn-cutting for the first few years—doing the jobs themselves if necessary and sending the laggard families the bill.

Architectural critics, many of whom were unaccustomed to the tastes or resources of moderate-income people, were generally unimpressed by the repetitious houses on 60-by-100-foot "cookie cutter lots" and referred to Levittown as "degraded in conception and impoverished in form." From the Wantagh Parkway, the town stretched away to the east as far as the eye could see, house after identical house, a horizon broken only by telephone poles. Paul Goldberger, who admired the individual designs, thought that the whole was "an urban planning disaster," while [social critic] Lewis Mumford complained that Levittown's narrow range of house type and income range resulted in a one-class community and a backward design. He noted that the Levitts used "new-fashioned methods to compound old-fashioned mistakes."

But Levittown was a huge popular success where it counted—in the marketplace. On a single day in March 1949, fourteen hundred contracts were drawn, some with families that had been in line for four days. "I truly loved it," recalled one early resident. "When they built the Village Green, our big event was walking down there for ice cream."

In the 1950s the Levitts shifted their attention from Long Island to an equally large project near Philadelphia. Located on former broccoli and spinach farms in lower Bucks County, Pennsylvania, this new Levittown was built within a few miles of the new Fairless Works of the United States Steel Corporation, where the largest percentage of the community's residents were employed. It was composed on eight master blocks, each of about one square mile and focusing on its own recreational facilities. Totaling about 16,000 homes when completed late in the decade, the town included light industry and a big, 55-acre shopping center. According to

Levitt, "We planned every foot of it—every store, filling station, school, house, apartment, church, color, tree, and shrub."

In the 1960s, the Levitt forces shifted once again, this time to Willingboro, New Jersey, where a third Levittown was constructed within distant commuting range of Philadelphia. This last town was the focus of Herbert Gans's well-known account of *The Levittowners.* The Cape Cod remained the basic style, but Levitt improved the older models to resemble more closely the pseudo-colonial design that was so popular in the Northeast.

If imitation is the sincerest form of flattery, then William Levitt has been much honored in the past forty years. His replacement of basement foundations with the radiantly heated concrete slab was being widely copied as early as 1950. Levitt did not actually pioneer many of the mass-production techniques—the use of plywood, particle board, and gypsum board, as well as power hand tools like saws, routers, and nailers, for example—but his developments were so widely publicized that in every large metropolitan area, large builders appeared who adopted similar methods. . . .

FHA and VA programs made possible the financing of their immense developments. Title VI of the National Housing Act of 1934 allowed a builder to insure 90 percent of the mortgage of a house costing up to nine thousand dollars. Most importantly, an ambitious entrepreneur could get an FHA "commitment" to insure the mortgage, and then use that "commitment" to sign himself up as a temporary mortgagor. The mortgage lender (a bank or savings and loan institution) would then make "production advances" to the contractor as the work progressed, so that the builder needed to invest very little of his own hard cash. Previously, even the largest builders could not bring together the capital to undertake thousand-house developments. FHA alone insured three thousand houses in Henry J. Kaiser's Panorama City, California; five thousand in Frank Sharp's Oak Forest; and eight thousand in Klutznick's Park Forest project.

However financed and by whomever built, the new subdivisions that were typical of American urban development between 1945 and 1973 tended to share five common characteristics. The first was peripheral location. A Bureau of Labor Statistics survey of home building in 1946–1947 in six metropolitan regions determined that the suburbs accounted for at least 62 percent of construction. By 1950 the national suburban growth rate was ten times that of central cities, and in 1954 the editors of *Fortune* estimated that 9 million people had moved to the suburbs in the previous decade. The inner cities did have some empty lots—serviced by sewers, electrical connections, gas lines, and streets—available for development. But the filling-in process was not amenable to mass production techniques, and it satisfied neither the economic nor the psychological temper of the times.

The few new neighborhoods that were located within the boundaries of major cities tended also to be on the open land at the edges of the built-up sections. In New York City, the only area in the 1946–1947 study where city construction was greater than that of the suburbs, the big growth was on the outer edges of Queens, a borough that had been largely undeveloped in 1945. In Memphis new development moved east out Summer, Poplar, Walnut Grove, and Park Avenues, where FHA and VA subdivisions advertised "No Down Payment" or "One Dollar Down" on giant billboards. In Los Angeles, the fastest-growing American city in the immediate postwar period, the area of rapid building focused on the San Fernando Valley, a vast space that had remained largely vacant since its annexation to the city in 1915. In Philadelphia thousands of new houses were put up in farming areas that had legally been part of the city since 1854, but which in fact had functioned as agricultural settlements for generations.

The second major characteristic of the postwar suburbs was their relatively low density. In all except the most isolated instances, the row house completely lost favor; between 1946 and 1956, about 97 percent of all new single-family dwellings were completely detached, surrounded on every side by their own plots. Typical lot sizes were relatively uniform around the country, averaging between ⅕ (80 by 100 feet) and ⅒ (40 by 100 feet) of an acre and varying more with distance from the center than by region. Moreover, the new subdivisions allotted a higher proportion of their land area to streets and open spaces. Levittown, Long Island, for example, was settled at a density of 10,500 per square mile, which was about average for postwar suburbs but less than half as dense as the streetcar suburbs of a half-century earlier. This design of new neighborhoods on the assumption that residents would have automobiles meant that those without cars faced severe handicaps in access to jobs and shopping facilities.

This low-density pattern was in marked contrast with Europe. In war-ravaged countries east of the Rhine River, the concentration upon apartment buildings can be explained by the overriding necessity to provide shelter quickly for masses of displaced and homeless people. But in comparatively unscathed France, Denmark, and Spain, the single-family house was also a rarity. In Sweden, Stockholm committed itself to a suburban pattern along subway lines, a decision that implied a high-density residential pattern. Nowhere in Europe was there the land, the money, or the tradition for single-family home construction.

The third major characteristic of the postwar suburbs was their architectural similarity. A few custom homes were built for the rich, and mobile homes gained popularity with the poor and the transient, but for most American families in search of a new place to live some form of tract house was the most likely option. In order to simplify their production methods and reduce design fees, most of the larger developers offered no more than a half-dozen basic house plans, and some offered half that number. The result was a monotony and repetition that was especially stark in the early years of the subdivision, before the individual owners had transformed their homes and yards according to personal taste.

But the architectural similarity extended beyond the particular tract to the nation as a whole. Historically, each region of the country had developed an indigenous residential style—the colonial-style homes of New England, the row houses of Atlantic coastal cities, the famous Charleston town houses with their ends to the street, the raised plantation homes of the damp bayou country of Louisiana, and the encircled patios and massive walls of the Southwest. This regionalism of design extended to relatively small areas; early in the twentieth century a house on the South Carolina coast looked quite different from a house in the Piedmont a few hundred miles away.

This tradition began eroding after World War I, when the American dream house became ... the Cape Cod cottage, a quaint one-and-a-half-story dwelling. This design remained popular into the post–World War II years, when Levittown featured it as a bargain for veterans. In subsequent years, one fad after another became the rage. First, it was the split-level, then the ranch, then the modified colonial. In each case, the style tended to find support throughout the continent, so that by the 1960s the casual suburban visitor would have a difficult time deciphering whether she was in the environs of Boston or Dallas.

The ranch style, in particular, was evocative of the expansive mood of the post–World War II suburbs and of the disappearing regionality of style. It was almost as popular in Westchester County as in Los Angeles County. Remotely derived from the adobe dwellings of the Spanish colonial tradition and more directly derived from the famed prairie houses of [architect] Frank Lloyd Wright, with their low-pitched roofs, deep eaves, and pronounced horizontal lines, the typical ranch style houses of the 1950s were no larger than the average home a generation earlier. But the one-level ranch house suggested spacious living and an easy relationship with the outdoors. Mothers with small children did not have to contend with stairs. Most importantly, the postwar ranch home represented newness. In 1945 the publisher of the *Saturday Evening Post* reported that only 14 percent of the population wanted to live in an apartment or a "used" house. Whatever the style, the post–World War II house, in contrast to its turn-of-the-century predecessor, had no hall, no parlor, no stairs, and no porch. And the portion of the structure that projected farthest toward the street was the garage.

The fourth characteristic of post–World War II housing was its easy availability and thus its reduced suggestion of wealth. To be sure, upper-income suburbs and developments sprouted across the land, and some set high standards of style and design. Typically, they offered expansive lots, spacious and individualized designs, and affluent neighbors. But the most important income development of the period was the lowering of the threshold of purchase. At every previous time in American history, and indeed for the 1980s as well, the successful acquisition of a family home required savings and effort of a major order. After World War II, however, because of mass-production techniques, government financing, high wages, and low interest rates, it was quite simply cheaper to buy new housing in the suburbs than it was to reinvest in central city properties or to rent at the market price.

The fifth and perhaps most important characteristic of the postwar suburb was economic and racial homogeneity. The sorting out of families by income and color began even before the Civil War and was stimulated by the growth of the factory system. This pattern was noticeable in both the exclusive Main Line suburbs of Philadelphia and New York and in the more bourgeois streetcar developments which were part of every city. The automobile accentuated this discriminatory "Jim Crow" pattern. In Atlanta where large numbers of whites flocked to the fast-growing and wealthy suburbs north of the city in the 1920s, [it was] reported that: "By 1930, if racism could be measured in miles and minutes, blacks and whites were more segregated in the city of Atlanta than ever before." But many pre-1930 suburbs—places like Greenwich, Connecticut; Englewood, New Jersey; Evanston, Illinois; and Chestnut Hill, Massachusetts—maintained an exclusive image despite the presence of low-income or minority groups living in slums near or within the community.

The post-1945 developments took place against a background of the decline of factory-dominated cities. What was unusual in the new circumstances was not the presence of discrimination—Jews and Catholics as well as blacks had been excluded from certain neighborhoods for generations—but the thoroughness of the physical separation which it entailed. The Levitt organization, which was no more culpable in this regard than any other urban or suburban firm, publicly and officially refused to sell to blacks for two decades after the war. Nor did resellers deal with minorities. As William Levitt explained, "We can solve a housing problem, or we can try to solve a racial problem. But we cannot combine the two." Not surprisingly, in 1960 not a single one of the Long Island Levittown's 82,000 residents was black.

The economic and age homogeneity of large subdivisions and sometimes entire suburbs was almost as complete as the racial distinction. Although this tendency had been present even in the nineteenth century, the introduction of zoning—beginning with a New York City ordinance in 1916—served the general purpose of preserving residential class segregation and property values. In theory zoning was designed to protect the interests of all citizens by limiting land speculation and congestion. And it was popular. Although it represented an extraordinary growth of municipal power, nearly everyone supported zoning. By 1926 seventy-six cities had adopted ordinances similar to that of New York. By 1936, 1,322 cities (85 percent of the total) had them, and zoning laws were affecting more property than all national laws relating to business.

In actuality zoning was a device to keep poor people and obnoxious industries out of affluent areas. And in time, it also became a cudgel used by suburban areas to whack the central city. Advocates of land-use restrictions in overwhelming proportion were residents of the fringe. They sought through minimum lot and set-back requirements to insure that only members of acceptable social classes could settle in their privileged sanctuaries. Southern cities even used zoning to enforce racial segregation. And in suburbs everywhere, North and South, zoning was used by the people who already lived within the arbitrary boundaries of a community as a method of keeping everyone else out. Apartments, factories, and "blight," euphemisms for blacks and people of limited means, were rigidly excluded.

While zoning provided a way for suburban areas to become secure enclaves for the well-to-do, it forced the city to provide economic facilities for the whole area and homes for people the suburbs refused to admit. Simply put, land-use restrictions tended to protect residential interests in the suburbs and commercial interests in the cities because the residents of the core usually lived on land owned by absentee landlords who were more interested in financial returns than neighborhood preferences. For the man who owned land but did not live on it, the ideal situation was to have his parcel of earth zoned for commercial or industrial use. With more options, the property often gained in value. In Chicago, for example, three times as much land was zoned for commercial use as could ever have been profitably employed for such purposes. This overzoning prevented inner-city residents from receiving the same protection from commercial incursions as was afforded suburbanites. Instead of becoming a useful tool for the rational ordering of land in metropolitan areas, zoning became a way for suburbs to pirate from the city only its desirable functions and residents. Suburban governments became like so many residential hotels, fighting for the upper-income trade while trying to force the deadbeats to go elsewhere.

Because zoning restrictions typically excluded all apartments and houses and lots of less than a certain number of square feet, new home purchasers were often from a similar income and social group. In this regard, the postwar suburbs were no different from many nineteenth-century neighborhoods when they were first built. Moreover, Levittown was originally a mix of young professionals and lower-middle-class blue-collar workers.

As the aspiring professionals moved out, however, Levittown became a community of the most class-stratifying sort possible. This phenomenon was the subject of one of the most important books of the 1950s. Focusing on a 2,400-acre project put up by the former Public Housing Administrator

Phillip Klutznick, William H. Whyte's *The Organization Man* sent shudders through armchair sociologists. Although Whyte found that Park Forest, Illinois, offered its residents "leadership training" and an "ability to chew on real problems," the basic portrait was unflattering. Reporting excessive conformity and a mindless conservatism, he showed Park Foresters to be almost interchangeable as they fought their way up the corporate ladder, and his "organization man" stereotype unfortunately became the norm for judging similar communities throughout the nation.

By 1961, when President John F. Kennedy proclaimed his New Frontier and challenged Americans to send a man to the moon within the decade, his countrymen had already remade the nation's metropolitan areas in the short space of sixteen years. From Boston to Los Angeles, vast new subdivisions and virtually new towns sprawled where a generation earlier nature had held sway. In an era of low inflation, plentiful energy, federal subsidies, and expansive optimism, Americans showed the way to a more abundant and more perfect lifestyle. Almost every contractor-built, post–World War II home had central heating, indoor plumbing, telephones, automatic stoves, refrigerators, and washing machines.

There was a darker side to the outward movement. By making it possible for young couples to have separate households of their own, abundance further weakened the extended family in America and ordained that most children would grow up in intimate contact only with their parents and siblings. The housing arrangements of the new prosperity were evident as early as 1950. In that year there were 45,983,000 dwelling units to accommodate the 38,310,000 families in the United States and 84 percent of American households reported less than one person per room.

Critics regarded the peripheral environment as devastating particularly to women and children. The suburban world was a female world, especially during the day. Betty Friedan's 1963 classic *The Feminine Mystique* challenged the notion that the American dream home was emotionally fulfilling for women. As Gwendolyn Wright has observed, their isolation from work opportunities and from contact with employed adults led to stifled frustration and deep psychological problems. Similarly, Sidonie M. Gruenberg warned in the *New York Times Magazine* that "Mass produced, standardized housing breeds standardized individuals, too—especially among youngsters." Offering neither the urbanity and sophistication of the city nor the tranquility and repose of the farm, the suburb came to be regarded less as an intelligent compromise than a cultural, economic, and emotional wasteland. No observer was more critical than Lewis Mumford, however. In his 1961 analysis of *The City in History*, which covered the entire sweep of civilization, the famed author reiterated sentiments he had first expressed more than four decades earlier and scorned the new developments which were surrounding every American city:

In the mass movement into suburban areas a new kind of community was produced, which caricatured both the historic city and the archetypal suburban refuge: a multitude of uniform, unidentifiable houses, lined up inflexibly, at uniform distances, on uniform roads, in a treeless communal waste, inhabited by people of the same class, the same income, the same age group, witnessing the same television performances, eating the same tasteless prefabricated foods, from the same freezers, conforming in every outward and inward respect to a common mold, manufactured in the central metropolis. Thus, the ultimate effect of the suburban escape in our own time is, ironically, a low-grade uniform environment from which escape is impossible.

Secondly, because the federally supported home-building boom was of such enormous proportions, the new houses of the suburbs were a major cause of the decline of central cities. Because FHA and VA terms for new construction were so favorable as to make the suburbs accessible to almost all white, middle-income families, the inner-city housing market was deprived of the purchasers who could perhaps have supplied an appropriate demand for the evacuated neighborhoods.

The young families who joyously moved into the new homes of the suburbs were not terribly concerned about the problems of the inner-city housing market or the snobbish views of Lewis Mumford and other social critics. They were concerned about their hopes and their dreams. They were looking for good schools, private space, and personal safety, and places like Levittown could provide those amenities on a scale and at a price that crowded city neighborhoods, both in the Old World and in the New, could not match. The single-family tract house—post–World War II style—whatever its aesthetic failings, offered growing families a private haven in a heartless world. If the dream did not include minorities or the elderly, if it was accompanied by the isolation of nuclear families, by the decline of public transportation, and by the deterioration of urban neighborhoods, the creation of good, inexpensive suburban housing on an unprecedented scale was a unique achievement in the world.

DOCUMENTS

Little Boxes, 1962

Little boxes on the hillside, little boxes made of ticky tacky,
Little boxes on the hillside, little boxes all the same.
There's a green one and a pink one and a blue one and a yellow
   one,
And they're all made out of ticky tacky and they all look just the
   same.

And the people in the houses all went to the university
Where they were put in boxes and they came out all the same;
And there's doctors, and there's lawyers and there's business
   executives
And they're all made out of ticky tacky and they all look just the
   same.

And they all play on the golf course and drink their martini dry
And they all have pretty children and the children go to school
And the children go to summer camp and then to the university
Where they are all put in boxes and they come out all the same.

Coda (retard like a music box running down)

The Problem That Has No Name, 1963

The suburban housewife—she was the dream image of the young American women and the envy, it was said, of women all over the world. The American housewife—freed by science and labor-saving appliances from the drudgery, the dangers of childbirth and the illnesses of her grandmother. She was healthy, beautiful, educated, concerned only about her husband, her children, her home. She had found true feminine fulfillment. As a housewife and mother, she was respected as a full and equal partner to man in his world. She was free to choose automobiles, clothes, appliances, supermarkets; she had everything that women ever dreamed of.

In the fifteen years after World War II, this mystique of feminine fulfillment became the cherished and self-perpetuating core of contemporary American culture. Millions of women lived their lives in the image of those pretty pictures of the American suburban housewife, kissing their husbands goodbye in front of the picture window, depositing their station wagonsful of children at school, and smiling as they ran the new electric waxer over the spotless kitchen floor. They baked their own bread, sewed their own and their children's clothes, kept their new washing machines and dryers running all day. They changed the sheets on the beds twice a week instead of once, took the rug-hooking class in adult education, and pitied their poor frustrated mothers, who had dreamed of having a career. Their only dream was to be perfect wives and mothers; their highest ambition to have five children and a beautiful house, their only fight to get and keep their husbands. They had no thought for the unfeminine problems of the world outside the home; they wanted the men to make the major decisions. They

SOURCE: From *The Feminine Mystique* by Betty Friedan. Copyright © 1983, 1974, 1973, 1963 by Betty Friedan. Reprinted by permission of W.W. Norton & Company, Inc.

gloried in their role as women, and wrote proudly on the census blank: "Occupation: housewife."

For over fifteen years, the words written for women, and the words women used when they talked to each other, while their husbands sat on the other side of the room and talked shop or politics or septic tanks, were about problems with their children, or how to keep their husbands happy, or improve their children's school, or cook chicken or make slipcovers. Nobody argued whether women were inferior or superior to men; they were simply different. Words like "emancipation" and "career" sounded strange and embarrassing; no one had used them for years. When a French woman named Simone de Beauvoir wrote a book called *The Second Sex*, an American critic commented that she obviously "didn't know what life was all about," and besides, she was talking about French women. The "woman problem" in America no longer existed.

If a woman had a problem in the 1950s and 1960s, she knew that something must be wrong with her marriage, or with herself. Other women were satisfied with their lives, she thought. What kind of a woman was she if she did not feel this mysterious fulfillment waxing the kitchen floor? She was so ashamed to admit her dissatisfaction that she never knew how many other women shared it. If she tried to tell her husband, he didn't understand what she was talking about. She did not really understand it herself. For over fifteen years women in America found it harder to talk about this problem than about sex. Even the psychoanalysts had no name for it. When a woman went to a psychiatrist for help, as many women did, she would say, "I'm so ashamed," or "I must be hopelessly neurotic." "I don't know what's wrong with women today," a suburban psychiatrist said uneasily. "I only know something is wrong because most of my patients happen to be women. And their problem isn't sexual." Most women with this problem did not go to see a psychoanalyst, however, "There's nothing wrong really," they kept telling themselves. "There isn't any problem."

But on an April morning in 1959, I heard a mother of four, having coffee with four other mothers in a suburban development fifteen miles from New York, say in a tone of quiet desperation, "the problem." And the others knew, without words, that she was not talking about a problem with her husband, or her children, or her home. Suddenly they realized they all shared the same problem, the problem that has no name. They began, hesitantly, to talk about it. Later, after they had picked up their children at nursery school and taken them home to nap, two of the women cried, in sheer relief, just to know they were not alone.

Gradually I came to realize that the problem that has no name was shared by countless women in America. As a magazine writer I often interviewed women about problems with their children, or their marriages, or their houses, or their communities. But after a while I began to recognize the telltale signs of this other problem. I saw the same signs in suburban ranch houses and split-levels on Long Island and in New Jersey and Westchester County; in colonial houses in a small Massachusetts town; on patios in Memphis; in suburban and city apartments; in living rooms in the Midwest. Sometimes I sensed the problem, not as a reporter, but as a suburban house-wife, for during this time I was also bringing up my own three children in Rockland County, New York. I heard echoes of the problem in college dor-mitories and semiprivate maternity wards, at PTA meetings and luncheons of the League of Women voters, at suburban cocktail parties, in station wagons waiting for trains, and in snatches of conversation overheard at Schrafft's. The groping words I heard from other women, on quiet after-noons when children were at school or on quiet evenings when husbands worked late, I think I understood first as a woman long before I understood their larger social and psychological implications. . . .

If I am right, the problem that has no name stirring in the minds of so many American women today is not a matter of loss of femininity or too much education, or the demands of domesticity. It is far more important than anyone recognizes. It is the key to these other new and old problems which have been torturing women and their husbands and children, and puzzling their doctors and educators for years. It may well be the key to our future as a nation and a culture. We can no longer ignore that voice within women that says: "I want something more than my husband and my chil-dren and my home."

Segregation in the Suburbs, 1994

Roosevelt, L.I.—When Marshella Atkinson's parents decided to leave Brooklyn for Long Island, the enthusiasm of friends and teachers made her smile with anticipation.

Perhaps they pictured the swimming pools of nearby Levittown, or the shopping centers of Garden City, or the well-stocked library and spotless corridors of Plainview-Old Bethpage High School. Ms. Atkinson is not sure.

But four years later, the 16-year old does know one thing: they could not have meant Roosevelt, where boarded-up houses dot the walk home from high school and people complain that their streets are last to be plowed by the town of Hempstead, where Roosevelt is the most troubled section.

"I think they set it up so that when a black family moves here, it ends up in Roosevelt," said Ms. Atkinson, a junior at Roosevelt High School. She glanced at a hole in her classroom ceiling where tiles had been ripped away.

Graffiti scarred the walls. "I thought it was going to be a dream place," she said.

Drawn by the promise of escape from inner-city congestion and violence, more and more families like the Atkinsons are moving to America's suburbs. Like the white middle class before them, they come for a home of their own, good schools, open spaces and relative safety, everything that the suburbs symbolize in the American narrative.

But segregation is not declining as black and Hispanic people move to the suburbs, according to John R. Logan, a sociologist at the State University of New York at Albany, who has studied segregation around 10 major cities. Nationally, 1 black person in 3 now lives in the suburbs, but even those with middle-class incomes usually end up in middle-class pockets of poorer neighborhoods.

Lily-white communities tend not to become integrated but to remain largely lily-white, with the addition of well-defined minority precincts. On Long Island, 95 percent of black residents are concentrated in 5 percent of the census tracts. According to census data, the average white person in Nassau County lives in a census tract in which only 8 percent of the residents are black or Hispanic. The average white child attends a school that is just 9 percent black. . . .

"Both within cities and suburbs, Hispanics and blacks are segregated, and they're forced to locate in the least desirable communities," Professor Logan said. "And I see no evidence that any change in civil rights laws or fair housing legislation is having any effect."

Of course, some blacks choose to live in black neighborhoods. Others opted for integrated areas that white flight has since rendered mostly black. Still others can afford only the cheapest suburban housing. But a great many blacks complain they are never shown the full range of housing choices or are discouraged from buying in predominantly white communities.

Once they arrive, blacks find that the suburban landscape and the suburban way of life increase racial isolation: The tendency to restrict parks, libraries and other amenities to local residents; to rely on cars rather than on mass transit, and to emphasize home rule in government promote a segregated existence, no matter what the intent.

While the Long Island suburbs, in their postwar expansion, were providing the blueprint for an America of the automobile age, the plan accepted white prejudices of the day, typically restricting the emerging communities to "members of the Caucasian race."

Federal laws now bar discrimination, but mechanisms of segregation endure. James Thomas landed in the Suffolk County hamlet of Bellport after a thwarted attempt to buy a house in white Port Jefferson 33 years ago. Mr. Thomas's mailman, who was white, offered to sell Mr. Thomas his Cape Cod in Bellport for $10,500. "You have to take where you can get," the retired factory supervisor said.

For 20 years, Bellport remained a "solid, good community." But what he thought was steady integration turned out to be a white hemorrhage. A decade ago, Mr. Thomas realized that the people moving in were no longer working class or middle class but getting by on government aid. Bellport became as blighted as any city neighborhood, its streets lined with prostitutes and certain corners given over to drug dealing.

Mr. Thomas looked across the hedges at a house that had burned down several months before: a jungle of exposed wires and half-fallen floors. For him, the delay in razing the house, since removed, was sure proof of the Town of Brookhaven's disregard for blacks. "You can't tell me that this would be left to stand this way in a white neighborhood," he said.

Services Dwindle

Whites who bought homes in the suburbs typically began a lifelong climb up the social and economic ladder. Many blacks are forced to watch their investment decline as whites flee, poorer minorities move in and services dwindle. Homeowners like Ed Larson of the North Amityville Taxpayers Association meet to enlist police against drug peddlers, prostitutes and street crime, problems that seldom preoccupy their white counterparts.

"If the American dream is to buy a house in the suburbs, send your kid to a good school and have some grass, yes, it's the American dream," said Hugh A. Wilson, director of the Institute for Suburban Studies at Adelphi University. "If it's also to do that in an integrated setting, then for blacks, it's not fulfilling the dream."

Some blacks complain that isolation feeds a quiet acceptance of racism. Alton Williams, first vice president of the Nassau County Guardians, which represents black police officers, said he was shocked to see a white supremacist flyer on another officer's bulletin board. It showed a smiling blond child with the caption "MISSING: A future for white children in America."

Chapter 13

The Black Struggle for Equality

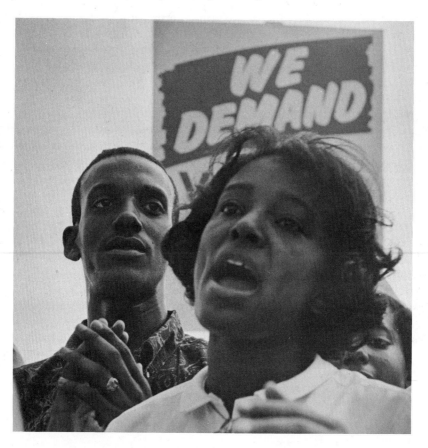

Not all groups shared in the economic boom after World War II. Blacks who had mi-grated to the North in search of a better life were often sorely disappointed at what they found. Many of those who remained in the South as sharecroppers and tenants were forced off the land by federal government programs that encouraged farmers to leave their fields fallow and by new machinery that replaced human labor. In addition, blacks in both the North and South encountered discrimination in employment, housing, schools, and public facilities. Segregation and disfranchisement proved most severe in the South, however, where local and state governments imposed and enforced them as policies.

In the mid-1950s, a struggle for racial equality and civil rights emerged. Jane Stevenson's essay "Rosa Parks Wouldn't Budge" brings to life the story of the 1955 bus boycott in Montgomery, Alabama, the event generally credited with launching the renewed crusade and the career of its great leader, Martin Luther King Jr. What factors made Montgomery's bus system an "appropriate target for the integration movement"? In what ways did the tactics employed by the boycotters illustrate King's philosophy of militant nonviolence?

Stevenson points out that plans for concerted black action against racial discrimination followed the U.S. Supreme Court's antisegregation ruling of May 1954 in Brown v. *Board of Education. The first document presents excerpts from Chief Justice Earl Warren's statement of the unanimous opinion. What were the key points in the Court's sweeping condemnation of school segregation?*

Although the Supreme Court's decision in Brown, *and later the Montgomery bus boycott cases, won widespread support among whites as well as blacks, many white Americans, particularly in the South, were determined to maintain segregation and to deny blacks political and social equality. As the civil rights movement grew, segregationist opposition became more intense and turbulent. Ironically, as television brought this violence and the contrasting peaceful resistance of the civil rights activists into homes throughout the nation, popular support for black demands strengthened. Congress finally responded, passing the Civil Rights Act of 1964 and the Voting Rights Act of 1965. The speech by Congressman James Whitten of Mississippi comprising the second document expresses sentiments typical of those who opposed the 1964 Civil Rights Act. Compare Whitten's arguments with those of Justice Warren in the* Brown *decision.*

The final document, an account of growing up black in America, is by Hosea Williams, an African-American civil rights leader. As you read his story, compare the description of black life in the South to Congressman Whitten's speech. How do Whitten's remarks strike you in light of the racism encountered by Williams and other black Americans?

ESSAY

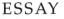

Rosa Parks Wouldn't Budge

Jane Stevenson

A neatly dressed, middle-aged black woman was riding home on a Montgomery, Alabama, bus on the evening of Thursday, December 1, 1955. Her

SOURCE: Jane Stevenson, "Rosa Parks Wouldn't Budge," *American Heritage* XXIII, 2 (February 1972): 56–64, 85. Copyright © 1972 by *American Heritage*, a division of Forbes Inc.

lap was full of groceries, which she was going to have to carry home from the bus stop, and her feet were tired from a long day's work.

Mrs. Rosa Parks was sitting in the first row of seats behind the section marked "Whites Only." When she chose this seat, there had been plenty of empty ones both in front of and behind the "Great Divide." Now they were all occupied, and black passengers were standing in the aisle at the rear.

Then two white men got aboard. They dropped their dimes into the fare box. The driver called over his shoulder, "Niggers move back." Three of the passengers obediently rose from their seats in the black section and stood in the aisle. Rosa Parks did not.

Even when the driver repeated his order and heads turned to see who was "making trouble," she sat as if she hadn't heard. The driver swore under his breath, pulled over to the curb, put on the brakes, and came to stand above her.

"I said to move back. You hear?"

All conversation stopped. No one dared move. Mrs. Parks continued to stare out the window at the darkness. The driver waited. Sounds of other traffic dramatized the silence in the bus.

It was a historic moment: the birth of a movement that was to challenge and ultimately change the social patterns that had established themselves in most Americans' minds as a way of life which was traditional and deeply rooted in the South.

Actually, that tradition of racial segregation—loosely nicknamed Jim Crow—was not as venerable as most of its adherents believed. Many segregation laws—especially those concerned with public transportation—only dated from the turn of the twentieth century, and at the start had been resisted, through boycotts, by southern blacks, sometimes successfully. But by 1906 resistance had worn itself out. And in the intervening fifty years the memory had also worn itself out. E. D. Nixon, the man who proposed the Montgomery bus boycott of 1955–56, had never heard of the successful Montgomery bus boycott of 1900–1902. In fact he did not even know that boycotts were again being tried—without much success—in a few southern cities; for example, Baton Rouge.

Nixon was a leader of the Brotherhood of Sleeping Car Porters and one of the founders of both the Alabama state and the Montgomery city branches of the National Association for the Advancement of Colored People [NAACP]. For almost a year before the night of Mrs. Parks's refusal to give up her seat, he had been trying to persuade Montgomery's black community that "the only way to make the power structure do away with segregation on the buses was to take some money out of their pockets."

Few aspects of Jim Crow life were as galling to Montgomery blacks as travel on the city's bus line, which most of them had to use to get to and from work, school, and the central shopping district. There were runs on which a white passenger was a curiosity. Yet the first four rows of seats (ten places) were permanently reserved for whites. And blacks sitting behind those rows could be told to vacate their seats if whites got on after the reserved section was filled.

Blacks also had to endure discourtesy and sometimes hostility from many drivers, all of whom were white. Some used insulting language; others picked quarrels and put blacks off the bus for real or imagined offenses. Some played a peculiarly tormenting practical joke. Since all fares had to be deposited in the box beside the driver, every passenger had to get on by the front door. Blacks then had to get off the bus and board from the rear. The game was to wait until a black passenger got outside, slam the two doors, and drive off, leaving him standing on the curb without his dime.

Resentment was wide and deep in the black community. Some whites, too, were known to disapprove of the bus drivers' harassments. And even among the die-hard segregationists, the mixing of races on a public bus was hardly the emotionally charged issue that integrated schools, or parks, or swimming pools, were. For all these reasons, in the months following the United States Supreme Court ruling of May, 1954, against segregated schools in *Brown* v. *Board of Education,* black leaders all over the South had been arguing that city bus lines were the next appropriate target for the integration movement.

In Montgomery three individual blacks, all women, had refused to give up their seats when ordered. In each case Nixon and the Montgomery NAACP had vainly tried to rally the black community to some sort of effective protest.

The most nearly successful attempt had been organized in March, 1955, after one of these three, a fifteen-year-old high school girl named Claudette Colvin, had been arrested and removed in handcuffs. An *ad hoc* committee of prominent Negro leaders had called on the manager of the bus company and on the City Commission, which governed Montgomery, to protest the way she had been treated and the whole system that led to such acts of spontaneous defiance. Three demands had been formulated: a guarantee of courtesy by drivers; a first-come first-served seating policy; and the hiring of Negro drivers on runs predominantly in Negro areas.

The proposed seating plan would not have ended segregation on the buses. It only required that when all seats were filled (blacks having seated themselves from the back forward and whites from the front backward), the next passengers to board would have to stand, no matter what the color of their skins. Such plans were in use in other southern cities, and the manager of the Montgomery City Lines was willing to go along with the idea until he consulted the company's attorney, Jack Crenshaw, who declared that the company was obligated to abide by the law, which was "clear on the principle of segregated seating."

In fact, it was not at all clear. Alabama state law did require clearly segregated white and black sections, but the Montgomery city code had a provision that no passenger could be required to give up his seat if another was not available. And there was sound legal opinion to the effect that within the city's limits the Montgomery statute took precedence over state law.

Nevertheless, Crenshaw's ruling stiffened the company's resistance. Hope of a legal challenge died when Claudette Colvin's parents refused to let her appear in court. Then community interest cooled to such a degree that the next woman who refused to move back received no organized support at all.

No one knew this background better than Mrs. Parks, who had worked with Nixon on many projects in the NAACP. She could hardly have hoped that her gesture was going to work any profound change in the status quo. She didn't move—as she explained later—because she was "bone weary" and suddenly fed up with being imposed upon. Yet circumstances would render her arrest the spark that lit the fires of resistance.

When E. D. Nixon got home that evening, his wife told him that Mrs. Parks had called from the city jail. Nixon telephoned the desk sergeant to ask about the charges and bail, and was refused the information, as an "unauthorized person." Ordinarily his next step would have been to call a young black Montgomery lawyer named Fred Gray, with whom he had worked on some NAACP cases. But Gray happened to be out of town. So Nixon turned instead to Clifford Durr, a distinguished white Alabamian who had recently returned to private law practice after twenty years in Washington, D.C. Durr had been on the legal staff of the Reconstruction Finance Corporation in the early New Deal years; later he had served as general counsel for the Defense Plant Corporation; and finally he had been a member of the Federal Communications Commission. He and his wife Virginia were part of a small group of southern white liberals who met, with black counterparts, under the aegis of the Alabama Council on Human Relations, to find ways of improving the South's racial picture. Nixon had come to know and trust them both.

"I called Mr. Durr," Nixon remembered later, "and he called down to the jail and they told him what the charge was. Bail was about $50, so I could make that all right." Then Nixon drove the attorney and his wife (who was a friend of Rosa Parks's) down to the jail. "I made the bond," Nixon told an interviewer, "and we got Mrs. Parks out. We carried her on home, and had coffee and talked."

Over coffee, Durr explained the legal alternatives as he saw them: Mrs. Parks could be defended "on the facts." She had not violated the Montgomery city code because there was no other seat available. He thought such a case could be won, but no challenge to segregation was involved. On the other hand, her attorney could challenge the constitutionality of the Alabama state law. That would mean a protracted and expensive battle, with no possible hope of victory short of a successful appeal to the United States Supreme Court. But a victory there would strike a major blow against Jim Crow.

Such a fight would need the backing of some national organization like the NAACP. Above all, it would take all the community support that Montgomery's blacks could mobilize.

Fired by the prospect Durr outlined, Nixon went home and told his wife, "I think we got us our test case at last." As he saw it, Fred Gray would take Rosa Parks's case and "do like Mr. Durr said. Go up all the way!" Meantime, he added, "What we got to do now is see about getting folks to stay off those buses Monday when Mrs. Parks comes up in Recorder's Court."

Mrs. Nixon told her husband he was "just plain crazy." "If headaches was selling for a dollar a dozen," she said, "you'd be the guy who'd go into a drug store and ask the man to put some in a bag." She didn't believe sympathy for Mrs. Parks was going to keep people off the buses "when it's as cold as this, and Christmas coming on."

There was some cause for pessimism. Montgomery's black community of fifty thousand persons was, in one observer's phrase, "as caste-ridden as any country in the world except India." No issue and no leader had yet managed to bring anything resembling unity out of its political, religious, economic, and cultural diversity. There might be strong support for Mrs. Parks in the professional group (made up in the main of faculty members from Alabama State College), but those people did not use public transportation. The working people, who did, depended on the buses to get to their jobs and on their jobs to feed and shelter their families. The risk of losing even a single day's pay was too much to ask of the head of a household already living on the edge of poverty.

But Nixon was determined to ask just that and more. Before he went to bed that night he planned a meeting of some forty people for the next day at the Dexter Avenue Baptist Church, a leaflet calling for a one-day bus boycott, and a Monday evening mass meeting to organize further action. He hoped to find a leader to carry on while he was out of town on his job.

Among the local blacks whom Nixon summoned was the Reverend Ralph Abernathy, a militant young Baptist preacher wholeheartedly in agreement with the plan and eager to get to work. There was also the Reverend H. H. Hubbard, head of the Baptist Ministerial Alliance. The Baptists were the largest denomination in the black community, so Hubbard's promise to cooperate in notifying his associates was crucial, and Nixon was elated to get it. Thus encouraged, he called young Dr. Martin Luther King, Jr., the new pastor of the Dexter Avenue church.

It was a fateful contact. Neither man could foresee that it would put young Dr. King on the road to national and historic importance, a Nobel Prize, and, ultimately, death at an assassin's hand. The future leader was then merely a recently arrived young minister of a fashionable Negro church in a southern town, well educated in the North, with a doctorate from Boston University, but with no other distinctions or activist record. Busy with his new duties, in fact, and the responsibilities to a young baby at home, he had only recently turned down the presidency of the local NAACP, and he told Nixon that while the protest organizers were welcome to meet in his church, he was not sure of his own participation. But he soon changed his mind and, with it, his destiny.

The meeting of more than forty people that afternoon quickly agreed to a one-day boycott of the city buses on the day of Mrs. Parks's trial. When it came to agreeing on demands, however, the initial unity was threatening to dissolve until someone pointed out that demands were unimportant compared to the practical problem of spreading the word quickly. There was no black "ghetto" in Montgomery. Negroes lived everywhere in and around the city. A volunteer phone committee could start work at once, but many black families were without phones—and radios or TV sets—and did not take newspapers. Leaflets, which Abernathy had wanted mimeographed immediately on hearing from Nixon, could be passed out at stores where Saturday shoppers congregated. Announcements could be made from church pulpits on Sunday, provided that every minister in town could be persuaded that the notice was important enough not to be ignored.

Transportation was a more serious problem. The first draft of the leaflet said: "... *take a car, or share a ride, or walk.*" But thousands lived too far from their jobs to walk, had no car, and knew no one with whom to share. For them some alternative way of getting to work on Monday had to be found, or the protest would not achieve the 50 per cent cut in company revenues that was the agreed target.

Someone suggested appealing to the Negro cab companies, asking them to pick up pedestrians and carry them to their destination for the ten-cent bus fare. (Segregation was so complete in Montgomery that only cabs driven by blacks and marked "Colored" were permitted to carry black passengers. The eighteen such companies and their 210 black drivers would prove a strong help in the first days of the boycott.)

By the time the meeting adjourned, assignments for phoning, distributing leaflets, and reaching ministers and the cab companies had been handed out, and morale was high. Some optimist even suggested that the passenger load of the bus lines might be cut as much as 60 or 65 per cent! Then, two events took place on Sunday that increased the chances of such success. The first was the result of a Friday encounter between E. D. Nixon and a reporter from the Montgomery *Advertiser* named Joe Azbell. The *Advertiser*, Montgomery's major journal, was seen by everyone, white and black, who read the papers in the city. It was by chance that Nixon ran into the white reporter, whom he knew to be friendly. Nixon told him he would give him a hot tip, but warned: "I don't expect to cooperate with anybody who's going to write some sort of degrading story about Negroes."

Azbell promised to write a useful story, if any. Then Nixon told him about Mrs. Parks's action and the planned boycott. Both men agreed that the story should not be attributed to Nixon, but that Azbell should "find" one of the leaflets on some city sidewalk. Sure enough, Sunday morning's *Advertiser* carried a two-column, front-page story, presumably given to the paper by an indignant white woman who had got it from her illiterate maid. The tone was properly disapproving ("Just listen to what the Negroes are up to now!"). But Azbell had kept the bargain, and as Nixon had anticipated, "every preacher in town saw it before he went into his pulpit that morning," and found it important enough to announce.

The other helpful event was a radio announcement by Montgomery's police commissioner that two motorcycle policemen would be assigned to follow every bus on Monday, "to protect anyone who wished to ride from harassment by goon squads." This, it was believed, had the effect of frightening some waverers away from the bus stops.

It was dark when the first buses began to roll on Monday, December 5. Dr. King and his wife, Coretta, who lived a few yards from a stop on one of the predominantly Negro runs, were up at dawn to see how the prospects for a 60 per cent reduction looked.

The early buses were usually crowded with black domestic workers on their way to make breakfast in white kitchens. Today, the first bus was empty. The Kings stayed at the window until the next bus passed. It, too, was empty. The third had two passengers, both white.

As the sky brightened, those of the planning committee with cars cruised the streets in different parts of town. What they saw was amazing. Sidewalks were crowded with black pedestrians. College and high school students were thumbing rides. Cars driven by blacks were overloaded with ride-sharers. There were a few old-fashioned horse-drawn buggies on the street, and one man was seen riding a mule. Youngsters waved in derisive humor at motorcycle policemen behind most of the buses. Some walkers—with up to six miles to go—sang as they trudged along. As King later wrote in his book, *Stride Toward Freedom;* "A miracle had taken place. The once dormant and quiescent Negro community was now fully awake."

At 9:30 A.M. the drama shifted to the courtroom, as Mrs. Parks's case was called. Fred Gray adhered to the line Durr had suggested. He ignored the conflict of state and local laws, and argued instead that segregation on public transportation was a violation of the spirit and letter of the United States Constitution. Without comment on Gray's argument, the judge found Mrs. Parks guilty and fined her ten dollars and court costs, which brought the total to something like fourteen dollars. Gray announced that his client would appeal the verdict, and she was released on bail. Now it was time for a third act: the mass meeting scheduled for 7 P.M, at the Holt Street Baptist Church.

But first, Nixon and Abernathy talked over the needs of the future. These included long-term plans and a permanent organization to carry out the fight. Nixon proposed to call it the Montgomery Citizens' Council, but Abernathy thought that sounded like the White Citizens' Councils that were springing up in opposition to school desegregation. His own suggestion was the Montgomery Improvement Association, and Nixon agreed to go along. They also agreed to ask the meeting to approve of repeating the demands made in Claudette Colvin's case—which fell short of total integration. And then, Abernathy raised the potentially touchy issue of leadership. "Brother Nixon, you're going to serve as president, aren't you?"

"Not unless you all turn down the man I have in mind. That's this young reverend, Martin Luther King, Jr."

Abernathy was surprised. King was not only young—not quite twenty seven years old, but very new to the area. To nominate him would be to pass over a number of other, older ministers, many of whom had good qualifications.

"I'll tell you my reasons," Nixon said. "First, there's the way he talks. Day I first heard him preach, I turned to the fellow sitting next to me and I said, 'I don't know just how I'm going to do it, but one day I'm going to hook him to the stars!'"

King's education equipped him to talk to Montgomery's white leaders in their own terms. King had a reputation for courage, too. As Nixon said, "You knew he wasn't any white man's nigger." And he had not been in Montgomery long enough to become entangled in any of the factional struggles that divided the black community.

Abernathy agreed that King was a good choice, but thought he would decline. So it was decided to nominate him without warning at a session of the "planning committee"—which would frame resolutions to present to the mass meeting. King was so astonished by the very fact of his election—it was unanimous—that he put up no resistance, confessing later that if he had had time to think, he would have almost certainly refused. Immediately afterward he received a tough assignment: presenting to the crowd not merely the routine matters of choosing a name and officers but the hard choice of whether to continue the boycott or merely threaten to renew it if demands were not met. That decision, clearly, had to be made by those who would carry it out: the thousands of humble people who had walked on this cold, gray morning. Many of them would be present at the Holt Street Baptist Church, and they would there be asked to vote on whether they could sustain their incredible initial momentum by approving a recommendation to continue.

By the seven o'clock meeting time there was not a seat empty in the Holt Street church. Loudspeakers had been installed on the roof to accommodate latecomers who might not find room inside. It took Dr. King fifteen minutes to work his way through the crowd from his car, and ten more to get to the platform after he was inside. The audience was singing "Onward, Christian Soldiers" when he joined Nixon, Abernathy, a number of other ministers, Mrs. Parks, and Fred Gray. After the ritual of prayer and scripture reading—with which all such meetings open in the South—and an ovation for Mrs. Parks, E. D. Nixon rose, glancing at Montgomery's police commissioner, whom he saw seated in one of the pews.

"Before you brothers and sisters get comfortable in your seats," Nixon began, "I want to say if anybody here is afraid, he better take his hat and go home. This is going to be a long, drawn-out affair, and before it's over, somebody's going to die."

There were loud amens, but no one reached for his hat. Nixon then delivered a rouser in favor of continuing the boycott, ending with the challenge: "We've worn aprons long enough. It's time for us to take them off!"

The next speaker was Martin Luther King, Jr. He came to the rostrum almost completely unprepared for what he knew by now would be one of the most important addresses of his life. There had hardly been time in the two hours since he had been given this task to think through the basic purpose of his speech. His analysis had gone as far as dividing it into two possibly contradictory aims: the first, to drain off the anger of those who were "tired of being kicked about by the brutal feet of oppression"—anger that might lead to violence of which he disapproved; and a second, to "keep them courageous and prepared for action." Or, as he put it in another place, the problem was to be militant and moderate at the same time. To make things more difficult, he would have to face the microphones and lights of television crews, for news of the morning's action had focused national attention on Montgomery.

King rose to the moment. Pulpit oratory, once a typical American art, is obsolete in most parts of the country today. But it lingers on in the black South, and King's sermon was a classic production. Stating the Christian case for nonviolent protest, he said: "We have been amazingly patient. . . . but we come here tonight to be saved from that patience that makes us patient with anything less than freedom and justice." Though he roused his audience at first by shouting, "We are tired. Tired of being segregated and humiliated," he brought them down to calmness again by declaring, "Once again we must hear the words of Jesus. 'Love your enemies. Bless them that curse you. Pray for them that despitefully use you.' If we fail to do this, our protest will end up as a meaningless drama on the stage of history. . . . We must not become bitter and end up by hating our white brothers." And in a final chord, he wooed them to their better selves.

"If you will protest courageously, and yet with dignity and Christian love, future historians will say, 'There lived a great people—a black people—who injected new meaning and dignity into the veins of civilization.' This is our challenge and our overwhelming responsibility."

The audience rose, cheering, and one elderly woman remembered afterward the feeling that she "saw angels standing all around him when he finished, and they were lifting him up on their wings!"

Even before Ralph Abernathy read the recommendation, the verdict was in. It was, in Clifford Durr's recollection, "a grass roots verdict if there ever was one. Some of the [black] middle-class professionals were saying, 'Well, we showed them this morning.' But the maids and the cooks, the ones who had done the walking, were saying, 'We haven't showed them a thing yet! But we're going to stay off those buses until they make up their minds to treat us decently.'"

For the first few days this unanimous determination created a euphoric optimism. In view of the unprecedented effectiveness of the boycott and the willingness of the Montgomery Improvement Association [M.I.A.] to settle for a partial victory such as first-come first-served seating through separate doors, it was generally believed that there would be a negotiated settlement. But on Thursday, December 8, when Abernathy's committee met with the City Commission, the bus company attorney, Jack Crenshaw, once more insisted that the Alabama law required continued total segregation. City officials were taking a hard line, too. It was clear that they did not want a Negro victory to stimulate further challenges. And a hint was dropped of strong action to come. The city code set a minimum cab fare of forty-five cents per passenger. Negro taxi companies might soon be forbidden to take passengers at ten cents per trip. The next day that threat did materialize. But fortunately, on Thursday evening there had been one of the twice-weekly meetings planned for the boycott's duration as a way of exchanging information, squelching rumors, boosting morale, and ratifying decisions. Anticipating the city's action, the chairman had appealed for volunteer drivers. One hundred and fifty names were handed in. Next, Rufus Lewis's Transportation Committee sat up all night, working out the details of a system which utilized the whole intricate network of black institutions that had grown up under the hothouse conditions of total segregation.

On Tuesday, just a week after the first day of the boycott, thousands of leaflets were ready for distribution, showing on a map of the city the location of forty-eight dispatch and forty-two pick-up stations, with the hours at which each would be operative. There were plenty of problems still. Dispatch stations for sending people off to work were easy to locate in Negro neighborhoods, and churches could shelter riders who had to wait in bad weather. But after-hours pick-up stations had to be in less friendly territory.

244

Without the intimate knowledge of Montgomery's white neighborhoods supplied by black mail carriers, this part of the plan would have been impossible to design. There were never quite enough volunteer dispatchers at rush hours. Cars sometimes broke down, and so, occasionally, did the tempers of passengers and drivers. But overall, the car pools worked as well as, if not better than, the old bus system. And their impact as a unifying force in the black community was incalculable.

It was expensive, but help came from two unexpected sources. As the "Montgomery Story" was spread throughout the country by the news media, contributions began coming in to the M.I.A. from cities in the North and West. Black churches took up collections to buy station wagons, which were presented to Montgomery churches of the same denominations for car-pool use.

The load was also lightened by some white Montgomery housewives, who entered into a sort of conspiracy with their black domestics. Accepting the police commissioner's fiction about "goon squads," these women began to drive their maids and cooks to and from work, "to protect them from harassment." When the mayor protested that this gave aid and comfort to the boycott, ladies wrote letters to the newspaper suggesting that he provide them with other help before telling them how to run their households.

As weeks went by without the blacks yielding, threats of violence began to be directed against the leadership of the M.I.A. King, Abernathy, Nixon, and other officers started to receive hate mail and phone calls warning them to "get out of town or else. . . ." Then, on January 30, the ugliness erupted.

On that night, while Dr. King was attending one of the regular mass meetings, a bomb tossed onto the porch of his house exploded seconds later with a shattering roar. Having heard the thud as the missile landed, Mrs. King and a visiting friend had moved quickly toward the rear of the house. They and the Kings' infant daughter escaped injury. But it looked for a time as if the chief casualty of the night would be the concept of nonviolence to which the Negroes had so far been held by their leaders.

Rushing home, King found an angry crowd milling on his lawn. As he stepped from his car, he heard one black man offer to shoot it out with a white policeman who was trying to push him back. Mayor W. A. "Jackie" Gayle and Police Commissioner Clyde Sellers were on hand, along with white reporters and the police. The mood of the crowd was so hostile that all of them later reported having felt that a race riot was a distinct and immediate possibility.

Dr. King went into his house, assured himself that his family was all right, and then came back to speak to the crowd. His voice was unusually quiet, and everyone else stopped speaking or moving, to listen.

"My wife and baby are all right," he told them. "I want you to go home and put down your weapons. We cannot solve this problem through retaliatory violence. . . . We must love our white brothers no matter what they do to us. We must make them know that we love them. Jesus still cries out across the centuries, 'Love your enemies.' This is what we must live by." Then, his voice swelling with emotion, he added: "Remember, if I am stopped, this movement will not stop, because God is with this movement."

It was another miracle of oratory, in a different style from his Holt Street speech. This time there was no applause. Simply, at his request, the crowd began to melt away, and with it, the tension. King even got them to listen quietly as the mayor promised a reward for information leading to the arrest of the bombers. But it had been a close thing. A small incident could have brought bloodshed. Calm returned, although two nights later a bomb landed—harmlessly—in the Nixons' yard.

After that climactic moment, there was a year-long struggle marked by court actions, by feats of improvisation that kept the M.I.A.'s transportation system rolling, and finally by fresh bombings.

Perhaps the most significant and least publicized action on the legal front was the petition on behalf of the M.I.A. for a hearing on the constitutionality of the Alabama segregation law before a three-judge federal court. This tactic was first suggested by Clifford Durr. About mid-April he realized that something more would be needed than Mrs. Parks's appeal, which was before the Alabama court of appeals, to carry the case to the top. The Supreme Court could not render a decision "on the merits" until the Alabama court had spoken—almost certainly against Rosa Parks. . . .

Durr therefore suggested to Fred Gray that he petition for a special three-judge federal court and ask it for an injunction against discrimination in seating, on the grounds that it was a violation of rights guaranteed in the Constitution. Such a panel was allowable in a federal action challenging a state law. And its rulings could be appealed directly to the Supreme Court.

Gray went to work at once, made contact with the New York and Washington branches of the NAACP, got some high-powered co-counsel, and filed his petition. The hearing was set for early in May. The court was composed of Richard T. Rives, at the time judge of the United States Circuit Court for the district including Alabama, who was the presiding justice; Judge Frank Johnson, an indigenous "Andrew Jackson Republican" (in Durr's words) from the northern part of Alabama; and Judge Seybourne Lynn of Birmingham.

Within three weeks, two of the three white southern judges—Johnson and Rives—outvoted their colleague and ruled in favor of Gray's petition. Rives, who wrote the majority opinion, was threatened, obliged to listen to sermons attacking the federal judiciary in the Montgomery church he attended, and had garbage dumped on his son's grave in a local cemetery. Johnson took similar abuse. But the stratagem was successful.

The federal question was raised at last. For the city of Montgomery appealed the ruling "on the merits," and the state of Alabama joined in the appeal; the matter now went onto the Supreme Court's docket. . . .

Montgomery authorities were meanwhile harassing the car pools. A car full of riders would be flagged down; the inspecting officer would find one or more violations of the state safety standards—weak brakes, poorly aligned headlights, or something else. The driver would be forced to abandon his vehicle, and a city wrecker would be called to tow it away (at the owner's expense) for repairs (also at his expense) in a city-approved shop. A similar tactic was the arbitrary cancellation of black auto-owners' insurance.

But all this was only prelude to the main attack. On October 30 Mayor Gayle directed the city's legal department to request an injunction "to stop the operation of the car pools or transportation systems growing out of the bus boycott," and to collect damages of fifteen thousand dollars for loss of tax revenues. Fred Gray's counterpetition to prevent the city's interference on behalf of the bus company was denied. A hearing was set for November 13.

There was no question in the minds of the M.I.A. leaders that this was, as King confessed to a mass meeting on the second of November, a bad moment. The city was certain to get its injunction, and to end the car pools would hopelessly undercut the boycott. He tried to rally confidence by saying, "This may well be the darkest hour before dawn. We have moved all these months with . . . daring faith. . . . We must go on with that same faith. . . ."

November 13 found the main contestants on both sides in court for the injunction hearing. The same judge who had tried Mrs. Parks a year earlier was listening to the arguments when, some time around noon, there was an interruption.

The two attorneys for the city, the mayor, and the police commissioner were all called out of the court, and there was an excited buzzing at the press table. One of the reporters brought over to the defense table a copy of a message just received over the wire service teletype machine:

> The United States Supreme Court today affirmed a decision of a special three-judge U.S. District Court declaring Alabama's state and local laws requiring segregation on buses unconstitutional. The Supreme Court acted without listening to any argument; it simply said, "the motion to affirm is granted and the Judgment is affirmed."

Legally, the struggle was over. The black-led and black-supported boycott, rising out of Mrs. Parks's spontaneous act, had resulted in the highest court's driving another nail in the coffin of legalized segregation. But life follows law slowly. It took a month more for the judicial mandate actually to reach Montgomery. In that time the injunction against the car pools was granted. So blacks, still staying off the buses, walked many extra miles when no alternative arrangements were possible.

The interval was used to prepare the black community for the first day of the new dispensation. Sheets of suggestions on how to behave "in a loving manner" were distributed. Role-playing sessions were held in black churches. Among whites reactions varied. The City Commission received front-page coverage to proclaim its "determination [to] do all in its power to oppose the integration of the Negro race with the white race in Montgomery . . . [and] stand like a rock against social equality, intermarriage and mixing of the races under God's creation and plan." But the fateful December 21, the day of official desegregation, came and went with what the Montgomery *Advertiser* called "a calm but cautious acceptance of this significant change in Montgomery's way of life." Black and white ministers sat together undisturbed in what had been the "Whites Only" section. Drivers were uniformly courteous. Most white passengers chose to ignore the innovation; those who made nasty remarks were in turn ignored by the blacks. . . .

Ahead lay many events [in the struggle for civil rights]: sit-ins, freedom rides, gunfire on the campus of the University of Mississippi, the March on Washington, the Civil Rights and Voting Rights acts of 1964 and 1965, the summers of rioting in northern cities—and then, the murder of Martin Luther King, Jr., in a Memphis motel. Perhaps it would take the decade of the seventies to discover the full meaning of the record that began with the Montgomery boycott. But in that January of 1957, as integrated buses rolled down the streets of the Confederacy's first capital, over which the Stars and Bars still flew, almost everyone must have sensed that a new page in the history of black (and white) Americans had been turned.

DOCUMENTS

School Segregation
Ruled Unconstitutional, 1954

Today, education is perhaps the most important function of state and local governments. Compulsory school attendance laws and the great expendi-

SOURCE: Chief Justice Earl Warren's majority opinion in *Brown* v. *Board of Education of Topeka*, 347 U.S. 483 (1954).

tures for education both demonstrate our recognition of the importance of education to our democratic society. It is required in the performance of our most basic public responsibilities, even service in the armed forces. It is the very foundation of good citizenship. Today it is a principal instrument in awakening the child to cultural values, in preparing him for later professional training, and in helping him to adjust normally to his environment. In these days, it is doubtful that any child may reasonably be expected to succeed in life if he is denied the opportunity of an education. Such an opportunity, where the state has undertaken to provide it, is a right which must be made available to all on equal terms.

We come then to the question presented: Does segregation of children in public schools solely on the basis of race, even though the physical facilities and other "tangible" factors may be equal, deprive the children of the minority group of equal education opportunities? We believe that it does.

In *Sweatt* v. *Painter,* . . . in finding that segregated law school for Negroes could not provide them equal educational opportunities, this Court relied in large part on "those qualities which are incapable of objective measurement but which make for greatness in a law school." In *McLaurin* v. *Oklahoma State Regents,* . . . the Court, in requiring that a Negro admitted to a white graduate school be treated like all other students, again resorted to intangible considerations: ". . . his ability to study, to engage in discussions and exchange views with other students, and, in general, to learn his profession." Such considerations apply with added force to children in grade and high schools. To separate them from others of similar age and qualifications solely because of their race generates a feeling of inferiority as to their status in the community that may affect their hearts and minds in a way unlikely ever to be undone. The effect of this separation on their educational opportunities was well stated by a finding in the Kansas case by a court which nevertheless felt compelled to rule against the Negro plaintiffs:

> Segregation of white and colored children in public schools has a detrimental effect upon the colored children. The impact is greater when it has the sanction of the law; for the policy of separating the races is usually interpreted as denoting the inferiority of the Negro group. A sense of inferiority affects the motivation of the child to learn. Segregation with the sanction of law, therefore, has a tendency to [retard] the educational and mental development of Negro children and to deprive them of some of the benefits they would receive in a racial[ly] integrated school system.

. . . We conclude that in the field of public education the doctrine of "separate but equal" has no place. Separate educational facilities are inherently unequal. Therefore, we hold that the plaintiffs and others similarly situated for whom the actions have been brought are, by reason of the

segregation complained of, deprived of the equal protection of the laws
guaranteed by the Fourteenth Amendment. . . .

Opposition to the
Civil Rights Bill, 1964

Truly . . . this is a sad day. As a student of law, and a practicing lawyer, I
never dreamed that the day would ever come when more than two-thirds of
the Congress—Senate and House—would virtually destroy the Constitution, violating every intent of the founders of our Republic.

For 10 years the executive and judiciary departments have had a virtual
partnership to set up a dictatorship. Here, today the Congress gets in on the
act, says, "Me, too," and ratifies the unconstitutional acts which have gone
before.

Present conditions are so similar to the days just preceding the Civil
War, we should pause to remember that heart-breaking conflict, which
pitted brother against brother, and father against son—today, it is section
against section, and those who need to straighten out their own sections,
cover up by going to mine.

As we look back upon those troubled times we can see that sound
leaders of both sides deplored any effort to settle the issue by armed conflict. Unfortunately, the radicals of that day prevented a peaceful solution.
Then, as now, they were not satisfied to run their own local affairs, but insisted that all other sections conform to their pattern. A terrible war resulted. . . .

Instead of forcing integration upon the Southern States, truly it would
be well for the rest of the country to learn from the States of the South that
the way for peace and harmony is to provide for separate but equal facilities
and protect each race in the enjoyment of its own way of life. . . .

You may well ask why the Supreme Court rendered the unanimous decision in the Brown integration case. It was probably argued that if we do
not bring about integration in the United States, we will lose the contest
with Russia throughout the world; and if we do not do this, Russia will
eventually conquer the world. It was said by the press, "If Russia takes over
here, the first thing they will do is set up a dictatorship. If Russia takes
over," they charged, "they will do away with the right to trial by jury."

SOURCE: Speech of Congressman James Whitten in *Congressional Record*, July 2, 1964,
15886–15887.

"Yes," they said, "if we do not integrate, Russia will force on us a system similar to Hitler's in Germany or Stalin's in Russia."

What did they do in Germany and Russia? What was the source of their absolute control of those nations? Why, they had the courts issue decrees, then they used troops and government officers to enforce the decrees.

Have we not done that here? We have seen the Supreme Court, unwilling to wait for constitutional amendment in the regular process, change the Constitution. We have seen the President send troops and Federal officials to enforce such decrees. Our Government does itself what we feared Russia might do.

We were told we have to integrate all the races of the United States or we cannot hold the friendship of the people of India, China, Japan, Africa, and all the rest. If that be true, why have China and Japan been at dagger's point throughout history? Talk about India—in spite of what you read, we know in many areas people of the same color cannot even touch each other.

The agitation is right here at home. People are using the threat of Russia here in the United States to accomplish their personal desires and actually to impose the Russian system of required conformity upon us.

My friends, history clearly shows an individual must have pride or he makes no real progress. A family must have pride or it goes down the scale. So it is with countries. So it is with race. Any race, whatever it may be, which feels it must be intermixed with another acknowledges its own lack. Such a race will not serve itself well, nor that with which it wishes to intermix.

Integration, where it has taken place, has only led to great turmoil. We all know that if you go into some sections of New York City at night you take your life in your hands; and you may be in danger there in the daytime. You can not go to certain areas of Chicago without danger to life and limb. The same is true of most of our major cities. Rape, murder, and robbery are commonplace in some areas of Washington. . . .

In recent weeks we have seen agitators deliberately go into areas of the South for the admitted purpose of violating laws of the States which have never been held to be beyond the power of such States, but rather have been held to be within the power; and then we have seen the Federal Government move its force in to protect such individuals in their avowed purpose of testing existing laws.

What if it were the law against murder they wished to test, or rape, or treason? Is there one rule in the Federal Government for laws the executive or the judiciary likes and another for the laws they do not like? . . .

I am proud that the people of my section are showing real self-restraint under trying circumstances. I hope time will show you who support this bill, that you are wrong; that those on the Supreme Court who have led this Nation down the road to state socialism are wrong; and that the present judicial dictatorship of the Supreme Court, supported by the executive branch, and here affirmed by this Congress, is all wrong and that this act will be repealed; that the rights of individuals to accumulate and control one's own property, the right to choose one's own customers, one's own companions and one's friends, regardless of color, will be reestablished. Only then . . . will our Nation endure.

Growing Up Black in the South:
A Remembrance, 1977

I was born in poverty. My mother was never married to my father, which was a stigma in the American society. . . . I was reared up in Decatur County, Georgia . . . that's southwest Georgia, and the racism of segregation was so prevalent until it was something that you had to notice, like black farmers couldn't plant tobacco. They didn't allow black men to plant tobacco, 'cause there's a lot of money in it. White people virtually owned black people . . . they'd concoct debts, like you get in jail, all the white man had to do, to come there, and the sheriff would let you out, and the white man tell the sheriff to tell you he paid a hundred dollars for you, but you didn't have to worry 'bout that hundred dollars long as you stay on his farm and work. If you ever left to go to Florida, he'd come get you, arrest you and bring you back. . . . There's a white man down there named Wonnie Miller. On the Wonnie Miller farm, all the blacks were born and worked and lived and died in poverty, and they worked like slaves from "cain't to cain't"—say, "Ya cain't see your hand before your face when you go out in the field, and ya cain't see your hand when you come in from the field," because it was dark each time. And Mr. Wonnie used to ride a big horse and never really worked, and he died a millionaire. All his children are rich. . . .

We used to walk two and a half miles to school . . . the white kids always had a bus. No black kids were allowed to ride the bus, and I guess every day of my life—it looked like to me every day, probably just my imagination—those white kids would spit on us or throw rocks at us, holler, and call us "niggers." *Every* day. Pick at us, and I just knew that was not right.

In my early life once whites tried to lynch me about a little white girl that was from a very poor family that lived up there. Her father was a bum, wouldn't work; all he did was fish and hunt all the time, just like some of

SOURCE: From *My Soul Is Rested,* edited by Howell Raines. Used by permission of Putnam Berkley, a division of Penguin Putnam Inc.

the black families. The word got around that I was havin' affair with the girl. This was a rumor, and they came to the house to lynch me . . . and my grandfather stood 'em off with a gun. We went over to white man's house, Mr. Wonnie Miller, who took the thing up and stopped the whites. . . .

The vast majority of blacks was reared in the same circumstances I was reared in. It's just hard for me to see how they can go along and take it. Then I educated myself and became a professional person. I thought you could escape black America by being educated and professional and being rich, and you just cain't do it.* . . .

I was paid well. I went right up, straight up the ladder. I was accepted, *I thought*, but what I really finally decided, I had hit that "nigger ceiling." They wasn't gonna let me go no higher. . . . I had more publication than all the white guys put together, except an old Ph.D. who had thirty years in the lab. So the assistant chief's job became open, and I thought sure they'd make me the assistant chief, because I thought they had accepted me as a scientist. And they gave the job to a white girl who knew very little chemistry, and that was a very hard pill for me to swallow. But you know the old thing 'bout how Jackie Robinson made it in baseball, the old poem, "Life Ain't Been No Christmas Day," and all this jazz, so I bought it and buckled my bed up: "After all, I'm black and she's white. My day comin'."

I remember one time after I bought this new home and new car. . . . You know, I was a social climbin', middle-class Negro. I guess I was the first black person in Savannah to have a zoysia lawn. I remember buying this grass from Sears and Roebuck, and had sodded my lawn, and I was out there one day tryin' to water it, and my hose would not stretch to sprinkle across the whole lawn. I had a big lot there. And I went back up to this new drugstore . . . gonna buy some hose connectors, an extension to a hose. . . . And I carried my two sons with me. They wasn't but about six and seven, six and eight years old then, and as we walked into this drugstore, it had a long lunch counter and these white kids were sittin' on these stools, spin- nin' around, eatin' hot dogs and drinkin' Co-cola.

And my boys started askin' me, "Daddy, let's get a sandwich and a Coke." But I always will believe what they wanted to do was play on those stools, and I said, "Naw, you cain't have a Coke and sandwich." And one of 'em started cryin'. And I said, "Well, you know, I'm gonna take you back home and Momma'll fix you a hot dog and give you a Coke," and then both of 'em started cryin'. And both of them just fell out in the floor, which was very unusual for my kids to do me like that. And I remember stoopin' down

*Williams became a chemist with the U.S. Department of Agriculture Bureau of Entomol- ogy in Savannah.

and I started cryin', because I realized I couldn't tell 'em the truth. The truth was they was black and they didn't 'low black people to use them lunch counters. So I picked the two kids up and went back to the car and I guess I made 'em a promise that I'd bring 'em back someday. So that really got me involved.

Chapter 14

The Sixties:
A Decade of Protest

The Civil Rights revolution that began in the 1950s erupted into a full-scale protest movement during the 1960s and eventually led to the enactment of the Civil Rights Act of 1964 and the Voting Rights Act of 1965, both of which greatly expanded the rights of African Americans. Largely rooted in the churches of the southern black community and appealing to black youth, the movement also attracted a substantial following among white students in the north. In the early 1960s, young men and women of both races headed south to aid in voter registration and to test segregation. They also joined protest marches to support African Americans' aspirations for equality.

 The experiences of the students heightened their awareness of injustice in America and led them to question institutions on a broad scale. In addition to those institutions supporting racial discrimination and segregation, students closely scrutinized their own colleges and universities. The University of California became a center of turmoil as students protested against the numerous restrictions on political debate and student activism imposed by the administration at that campus. In the essay from Terry Anderson's The Movement and the Sixties, *Berkeley student leader Mario Savio states that he had gone to Mississippi to struggle for civil* rights and was now engaged in "another phase of the same struggle." How would you characterize this new phase, and what do you think prompted it? Anderson also describes the free speech movement at Berkeley during the 1960s and how it escalated into a major confrontation between students and the university administration. What does Anderson consider to be the key issues during those hectic times? Anderson acknowledges that on many campuses dissatisfaction was strangely absent, that students were often "optimistic and comfortable." How was it possible for both student satisfaction and protest to exist in the same decade?

Some students were not content to limit their protests to racial discrimination and restrictions on speech on their campuses; they also objected to university rules and regulations on social behavior, such as drinking and sexual activity. Still others saw the university as only one institution in need of fundamental change. In 1962 Students for a Democratic Society (SDS) was formed. From an organizational meeting at the United Auto Workers' Port Huron center in Michigan, SDS issued the Port Huron agenda, calling for radical solutions to what they believed to be injustice in America. The first document is taken from this SDS statement. What are the main points of its critique of society? Most of these predominantly white students were privileged; how can you explain their discontent?

Terry Anderson notes at the end of his essay that unhappiness with the Vietnam War was a major factor in explaining the upheavals of the sixties, and that without the war the "sixties generation" might have taken a different shape. It is understandable why male students especially objected to the war, for they were faced with the draft and the possibility of being sent to fight, thousands of miles across the Pacific in a war in which they did not believe. But students were by no means the only Americans to oppose what many termed "Lyndon Johnson's war." Returning veterans organized the Vietnam Veterans Against the War. The second document, a statement by veteran John Kerry who would become a U.S. Senator from Massachusetts, speaks for these veterans. What was there about this war that led to such widespread disillusionment?

ESSAY

The Movement and the Sixties Generation

Terry Anderson

"Last summer I went to Mississippi to join the struggle there for civil rights," said Berkeley student Mario Savio in 1964. "This fall I am engaged in another phase of the same struggle, this time in Berkeley. In Mississippi an autocratic and powerful minority rules, through organized violence, to

SOURCE: From *The Movement and the Sixties* by Terry H. Anderson. Copyright 1996 by Terry H. Anderson. Used by permission of Oxford University Press, Inc.

suppress the vast, virtually powerless majority. In California, the privileged minority manipulates the university bureaucracy to suppress the students' political expression."

That expression had been curtailed by the University of California as students arrived on the Berkeley campus for fall semester in September. As was typical for university officials during the cold war era, a dean simply informed all student organizations that from now on they were no longer permitted to set up tables on campus to promote "off-campus" causes such as civil rights, and this ban applied to the traditional area for such endeavors, a small strip of property at the campus's main entrance where Telegraph Avenue met Bancroft Way.

Activism had long since arrived in Berkeley. In 1958 students organized Towards an Active Student Community, which later became SLATE, and a few dozen began discussing civil rights, capital punishment, and nuclear disarmament. "For us," student Michael Rossman later wrote, "the discovery was of each other. We began to realize we were not alone."

In spring 1960 they acted, holding silent vigils at San Quentin to protest the execution of Caryl Chessman and picketing the House Un-American Activities Committee investigation of Communist activities in the Bay Area, a demonstration that led to Black Friday.* Activism increased, and by the 1963–64 academic year hundreds of students had become involved in civil rights demonstrations, picketing hotels, automobile dealerships, restaurants, and other businesses that had discriminatory employment practices. At Lucky food stores, activists held "shop-ins," filling grocery carts with food, and after going through the checkout line, saying, "Sorry, I forgot my money. If you would hire some Negroes I would remember it next time." They picketed the Oakland *Tribune,* whose conservative owner was on the university's board of regents, and in March the local campaign reached a crescendo when 2000 violated a court order restricting the number of protesters in front of the Sheraton Palace Hotel; police arrested 800.

Political debate also was mounting. The Republican convention was held during June 1964 in San Francisco and the candidacy of conservative Barry Goldwater inspired discussion as he faced Lyndon Johnson in the upcoming elections. Then, in August, just weeks before students returned to classes, President Johnson declared that North Vietnam had attacked U.S. ships in the Gulf of Tonkin. He asked for and received from Congress the Gulf of Tonkin Resolution, which stimulated more student debate about America's role in South Vietnam. And as fall semester began in September approximately fifty students returned from volunteer work during Mississippi Summer.** At Berkeley and at other universities many of these students were welcomed back to campus as "civil rights heroes."

*In May 1960 a student protest against the House Un-American Activities Committee in San Francisco resulted in a violent confrontation between the police and the demonstrators. (Eds.)
**A campaign to encourage voter registration among blacks. (Eds.)

The university administration apparently was under pressure by conservatives in the state, community, and on the board of regents to curb activism when they issued the political ban. The students' response was dramatic. On September 21 campus organizations of all political persuasions united—from the Young Socialist Alliance to Youth for Goldwater—and they violated the ban. Two hundred students picketed on campus with signs such as "UC Manufactures Safe Minds," "Ban Political Birth Control," and "Bomb the Ban." To most, the issue was freedom of speech. "We're allowed to say why we think something is good or bad," said activist Jackie Goldberg, "but we're not allowed to distribute information as to what to do about it. Inaction is the rule, rather than the exception, in our society and on this campus." The movement gained support, and a week later some students set up political tables. Administrators took down names, and ordered civil rights veteran Jack Weinberg to appear in front of a dean. He did the next day, but he was followed by 500 supporters who packed into the administration building, Sproul Hall, and stayed until early the next morning. University of California president Clark Kerr suspended eight activists, but that did not stifle dissent as it would have in the 1950s. It only increased ill will and resulted in more protest. "A student who has been chased by the KKK in Mississippi," said student Roger Sandall, "is not easily scared by academic bureaucrats."

The Free Speech Movement it was called, and along with the civil rights protests the previous spring it demonstrated the emergence of a new generation. "How proud I felt," wrote Berkeley student Sara Davidson. "I belonged to a great new body of students who cared about the problems of the world. No longer would youth be apathetic. That was the fifties. We were *committed*." . . .

The role of the university in the first half of the 1960s . . . was not only to train students but to tame them to be conventional adults. To fit in, to become their parents. Students who did not play the game often were expelled or left in disgust; professors who did not teach the game usually were fired. Journalism major Phil Ochs at Ohio State was slated to become editor of the school paper, *The Lantern,* but faculty advisers rejected him because his views were "too controversial." He quit in his last year and became a folksinger. Illinois professor Leo Koch wrote in the *Daily Illini* that in his opinion premarital sex was all right for mature unmarried college students. The university president found the views "offensive and repugnant . . . contrary to the accepted standards of morality," and he fired Koch. For similar reasons St. John's University fired two dozen faculty members in 1966—none even received a hearing, for according to university rules the board of trustees could give or take away tenure at any time without explanation. *Newsweek* editorialized that "college must not abdicate its role in conserving, transmitting, and helping to mold both moral and intellectual values" of its students.

Yet many students by the mid-1960s had little desire to "be molded." This generation was different from older brothers and sisters who had been cowed by McCarthyism. That campaign was ancient history to them, hardly remembered and not taken seriously. Furthermore, these students had learned from the struggle. "If there is any one reason for increased student protest," a University of Utah journalist wrote, "it would probably be the civil rights movement. The movement . . . convinced many of them that non-violent demonstrations could be an effective device on the campus. It also served to make them more sensitive of their own civil rights." Problems in society had to be confronted and resolved, not blamed on imaginary subversives or outside agitators, and that called for student activism.

The reasons for student power were stated by the activists themselves in their campus papers and in new student undergrounds. This generation felt *in loco parentis* rules were absurd. Texas student Jeff Shero complained that campus regulations were "aimed at maintaining a 'proper image' for the University, rather than protecting girls." The young editor of *The Paper* declared "Michigan State is the Mississippi of American universities," protesting the administration's "closed-mindedness, intolerance and backwoods McCarthyism." The *New Orleans Freedom Press* proclaimed that student discontent resulted from "administrative restrictions on student autonomy," while University of Florida activists were blunt in their campus underground, *Freedom Forum:* "The American university campus has become a ghetto. Like all ghettoes, it has its managers (the administration), its Uncle Toms (the intimidated, status-berserk faculty), its raw natural resources processed for outside exploitation and consumption (the students)." Their demand highlighted the reasons for student power: "NO RESTRICTIONS MAY BE PLACED ON STUDENT DRINKING, GAMBLING, SEXUAL ACTIVITY, OR ANY SUCH PRIVATE MORAL DECISION."

The sixties generation began to confront its university administrations in 1964, politely demanding to be heard. During spring semester the administration at Brandeis consulted no one and then instituted new, stricter dorm visitation rules. That prompted several hundred students to stage a two-day demonstration, and the campus newspaper declared that such regulations "makes impossible any meaningful relationship between boy and girl." That fall semester, Syracuse University students approached their administrators with a simple request—they felt that holiday break, which began on December 23, was too close to Christmas. A few dozen students asked for more travel time to get home by Christmas Eve. After officials turned down all petitions, the students called a rally in December, and they were surprised when 2000 appeared. They demanded a speech from the chancellor, and he gave a short address, again saying no. As he ended his talk, some students jeered and booed, which shocked elders. "The students were supposed to show proper respect," a journalist wrote, "to know their place and keep it." Student activists, however, had a different interpretation. They wanted some role in the university. "If today's demonstration proves nothing else," the student paper editorialized, "we are not ones to be ignored or taken lightly."

Students at Berkeley certainly were not going to be taken lightly—they again challenged the ban on disseminating literature. On October 1, Jack Weinberg and others set up a few tables outside the administration building on Sproul Plaza and began passing out civil rights and political flyers. Before noon two university deans and a policeman approached Weinberg. "Are you prepared to remove yourself and the table from university property?" asked the dean. "I am not," replied Weinberg. After a brief discussion the official informed Weinberg of his arrest, and at this point several hundred students who were gathering for a free speech rally startled the officials by shouting, "Take us all, take us all!" Policemen drove a car onto the plaza and placed Weinberg inside, but suddenly someone shouted, "Sit down!" "I'm around the police car," recalled Michael Rossman. "I'm the first person to sit down. You will hear five hundred others who say that, and everyone is telling the truth." Students either laid or sat down around the car. They refused to move. The police could not drive their prisoner to jail as the crowd swelled to 3000. Mario Savio and many others climbed on top of the car and gave speeches, and later the crowd sang civil rights songs. They remained on the plaza all night. The next morning the area looked like a campsite, filled with sleeping bags, blankets, and even a pup tent. The crowd increased to 4000 that afternoon and President Kerr realized that the free speech issue was not going to disappear. After a thirty-hour sit-in, university administrators finally agreed to meet the activists.

To university officials, and to most citizens after the law and order 1950s, Berkeley had been reduced to chaos. Although campus rebellion would become common later in the decade, this was the first major eruption, and administrators responded forcefully. Under pressure from conservatives in the community and state government, they allowed 500 police officers to appear on campus minutes before they met activists. The police were armed with nightsticks, and the sight shocked students who never could remember a police army on campus and who felt that the incident was novel in American educational history. As police stood by, civil rights veterans taught nonviolent arrest tactics and urged those with police records or children to leave. Administrators had the support of California Governor Edmund G. Brown, a Democrat who stated that the demonstration was "not a matter of freedom of speech" but was an attempt by the students to use the campus illegally. "This will not be tolerated." He continued, "We must have—and will continue to have—law and order on our campuses."

Negotiations with Kerr continued for two hours, and then Savio and other students emerged from Sproul Hall. Savio climbed on the police car and announced that an agreement had been reached. A student-faculty committee would examine the free speech issue and make recommendations to the president. The university would not press charges against Weinberg or FSM leaders, and the eight students suspended earlier would have their case reviewed. Kerr seemed to support establishing a small free speech area at the campus's main entrance where Telegraph Avenue met Bancroft Way.

The October 2 agreement collapsed by November. The administration filled the committee with their own supporters, and then stalled for weeks. Meanwhile, Kerr took the issue to the press. Under pressure from conservative regents and politicians, the president attacked activists by raising the old bugaboos: "Reds on Campus," Kerr told the *San Francisco Examiner*. The article reported that the president "declared flatly that a hard core of 'Castro-Mao-Tse-tung line' Communists were in the crowd of demonstrators." The president then rejected political activity, provoking students to petition the regents and to set up tables on Sproul Plaza. The regents refused to hear the case, and on November 29 Kerr surprised students by announcing that the university was going to press new charges against FSM leaders Art Goldberg and Savio for their actions during the October 1 demonstrations. Charges included "entrapping a police car," "packing in" Sproul Hall, and, against Savio alone, biting a policeman "on the left thigh, breaking the skin and causing bruises."

The administration's behavior only alienated more students, irritated many professors, and fueled more protest as students and faculty began to feel that the university all along had been negotiating in bad faith. "The Administration sees the free speech protest as a simple problem of disobedience," proclaimed an FSM steering committee statement. "By again arbitrarily singling out students for punishment, the Administration avoids facing the real issues. . . . We demand that these new charges be dropped." Thousands of activists took those demands to Sproul Plaza on December 2, and Savio voiced the students' frustration by telling the crowd: "There is a time when the operation of the machine becomes so odious, makes you so sick at heart, that you can't take part; you can't even tacitly take part, and you've got to put your bodies upon the gears and upon the wheels, upon the levers, upon all the apparatus and you've got to make it stop."

"We Shall Overcome," sang Joan Baez, and others joined in as they moved toward Sproul Hall. "We'll walk hand in hand," for "the truth will make us free." The activists shut down the university administration— again they confronted the establishment.

Governor Brown responded immediately: "We're not going to have anarchy in California." He informed Kerr that force must be used to oust the students and ordered police to arrest activists who refused to leave the administration building. At about 4 a.m. some 600 policemen entered Sproul Hall and began arresting students, eventually about 770, in the largest mass arrest in California history. Some 7000 students remained on the plaza, and that morning they began picketing all entrances to the campus, handing out flyers:

IT IS HAPPENING NOW!

In the middle of the night, the police began dragging 800 of your fellow students from Sproul Hall. Sproul Hall was turned into a booking station; the University has become an armed camp—armed against its own students! . . .

Now the police take over.

Instead of recognizing the legitimacy of the students' demands, the administration is attempting to destroy the FSM. . . . The administration position is clear. It is saying "We decide what is acceptable freedom of speech on this campus. Those who disagree will be ignored; when they can no longer be ignored, they will be destroyed."

We have not been defeated by the University's troops! Our protest will continue until the justice of our cause is acknowledged. You must take a stand now! No longer can the faculty attempt to mediate from the outskirts of the crowd. No longer can students on this campus afford to accept humbly administrative fiat. Raise your voice now!

WE SHALL OVERCOME.

The faculty met, and after a long and heated discussion in their senate, they declared their position: Professors overwhelmingly voted to condemn the use of police on campus and to support the FSM. As faculty left the meeting, students cheered, and on December 4 both students and faculty held a huge rally on Sproul Plaza. Arrested activists had been released on bail, many wore a large white "V" on black shirts, and they and several professors criticized Governor Brown, the regents, and President Kerr. Students declared a strike, and that week half the classes were canceled.

With business as usual disrupted, Kerr called a special meeting for December 7 at the Greek Theater. About 16,000 students, faculty, and staff gathered, and the president condemned the sit-in but offered clemency for all acts of civil disobedience before December 2 and stated that the university would abide by "new and liberalized political action rules" then being developed by the faculty senate. The speech sounded conciliatory, and as the president left the podium Savio began walking across the stage apparently to make an announcement. Before he reached the microphone, campus police astonished the crowd by grabbing the activist and dragging him backstage. When other activists attempted to help, the police wrestled them off the stage.

"The crowd was stunned," wrote participant Bettina Aptheker, "then there was pandemonium." Students cried out "We Want Mario! We Want Mario!" Kerr, realizing that the police were ruining his efforts to reach an understanding, quickly agreed to let Savio make his announcement—a rally would be held at noon. Nevertheless, most spectators remembered the incident and its inescapable symbolism: authorities physically preventing a student committed to free speech from speaking on his own campus. As Aptheker later wrote: "That episode more than any other single event revolutionized the *thinking* of many thousands of students."

The next day the faculty met and overwhelmingly passed a motion affirming that "speech or advocacy should not be restricted by the university." While the administration and regents discussed the motion during the next two weeks, the FSM invited CORE national director James Farmer to address a rally on December 15. The administration was conciliatory, informing students that Farmer could talk on campus, but FSM activists decided to hold a legal rally off campus as a token of good faith. Farmer told the crowd that the "battle for free speech" could not be lost, for that would "turn off the faucet of the civil rights movement." When someone charged that he was an "outside agitator," he replied, "Every housewife knows the value of an agitator. It's the instrument inside the washing machine that bangs around and gets out all the dirt."

The administration eventually decided to accept the faculty's liberalized political rules. On January 4, 1965, the Free Speech Movement held its first legal rally on Sproul Plaza. The FSM was a success, Savio told the crowd, because "it was so obvious to everybody that it was right."

The FSM raised a philosophical debate that divided many students and administrators: What is the nature of a public university? While Kerr thought of himself as a liberal and had been praised for his stand favoring academic freedom, he stated the usual reasoning of cold war culture. The "university is an educational institution that has been given to the regents as a trust to administer for educational reasons, and not to be used for direct political actions." FSM advocates and many professors disagreed, arguing that the mission of higher education was much broader. "The university is the place where people begin seriously to question the conditions of their existence and raise the issue of whether they can be committed to the society they have been born into," wrote Savio. At a public institution supported by all taxpayers, activists felt that discussion should not be reserved only for campus issues but should be open to all concerns of the Republic. Art Goldberg advocated making Berkeley "a marketplace of ideas" where citizens would be exposed to "new and creative solutions to the problems that every American realizes are facing this society in the mid-60s."

That idea was not original in 1964, for actually students had initiated free speech movements earlier at a few other campuses, including Ohio State and Indiana University. In March 1963 three students at Indiana, officers of the Young Socialist Alliance, sponsored a speech by a black socialist on the civil rights movement. In May, the county prosecuting attorney charged the students with violating the Indiana Anti-Communist Act, meeting with the purpose of "advocating the violent overthrow" of the governments of Indiana and the United States. The prosecutor also demanded that the university drop its recognition of YSA. "We may all be ten years away from Senator McCarthy," wrote one professor, "but I am ten blocks away from the office of the Prosecuting Attorney." Supporters of the three established the Committee to Aid the Bloomington Students, which eventually received assistance from 50 colleges in 15 states. Over 140 faculty members signed a statement that the indictment was not "motivated by zeal for law enforcement, but by a desire to dictate to Indiana University that it shall not permit the use of University facilities for the expression of ideas repugnant to the Prosecutor." The university president agreed, and state courts found the law unconstitutional: The faculty continued supporting the students and broadly defined the university as a community where "debate, disagreement and the sharp confrontation of opposing ideas is a vital part of the attempt to come closer to the truth."

The free speech episode at Indiana differed from that at Berkeley. The Indiana administration viewed the conservative attack as a threat to the institution, and eventually the president supported the First Amendment. If Berkeley administrators had subscribed to such views, the sit-in of Sproul Hall probably would have been avoided. Flexible officials could avoid most confrontations on campus—a point remembered by hundreds of successful university presidents throughout the 1960s.

Kerr and the regents could not overcome their authoritarian 1950s mentality. They treated the students like subordinates, gave orders to tuition-payers, which only increased resentment toward authority. Activists felt that "liberal" administrators, the "power elites" who ran the university in Berkeley, seemed more interested in maintaining the status quo than changing rules, even if those regulations denied rights guaranteed by the First Amendment of the U.S. Constitution. Looking back, Kerr's position was indefensible. During the 1950s he had supported academic freedom for professors, yet in 1964 his administration curtailed freedom of speech for students. Many students wondered, if they could not hand out political statements, if freedom of speech did not exist on a public campus, then where did it exist in the land of the free?

The administration brought on the crisis, handled it poorly, and lost to students. As in the civil rights struggle, the FSM students put another dent in the idea that those in charge should be in charge, that the older generation had some monopoly on determining the proper path for the present and future in America. "Don't trust anyone over thirty," said Jack Weinberg and others, meaning that the generation who grew up in the 1950s had a different view of the world than their parents. During cold war culture the older generation "told the truth" to students, but in the 1960s students were "discovering the truth" for themselves, and their younger siblings would continue the process throughout the decade. At Berkeley, the young began to realize that the older generation had no monopoly on truth or on virtue.

Once students began to raise their voices and question policy, Michael Rossman wrote, then "the emperor had no clothes." President Kerr's decision to uphold an untenable regulation at Berkeley could be just as wrong as Chief of Police Bull Connor's enforcement of segregation rules in Birmingham.

The FSM was significant for many other reasons. Activists adopted a political style that reflected the ideas of the new left and some of the practices of SNCC.* Unlike traditional organizations or political parties, Berkeley students "worked through direct personal involvement in small autonomous interest groups. Our groups were ad hoc," Rossman recalled, "problem-orientated, flexible. They strove to govern themselves by participatory democracy, and to come to consensus on decisions." They also were pragmatic. "We were experimental social scientists, placing practice before theory. . . . We also were cheerful and funny, and made art as we went."

. . . [B]y the end of spring semester 1965 the climate on campus had shifted dramatically from the 1950s and early 1960s. "An End to Panty Raids," wrote a student at Kansas. The most important issues were civil and student rights; another continued that his generation was "fed up with their elders over such things as mass faceless education. . . . Students want to feel a sense of participation." With successes in the South and on their campuses, many students were optimistic about change, and as they became involved many began to think of themselves as part of a movement. "The thing for me right now is the movement," said Steven Block, an activist at Williams College. "That's an interesting word, if you think about it—movement. Because it is people in motion. It's not an end; it's not static. That's a very apt word for what we are doing."

The silent generation was history. *College Press Service* in December declared, "1964 Is Year of Protest on Nation's Campuses," and Professor Andrew Hacker called 1964–65 the "Year of the Demonstration." It was when compared with any time in memory.

But, more important, Hacker then placed the activists in context of the larger sixties generation. "Certainly, this year's protesters and demonstrators were not representative of their classmates, and it is instructive how quickly their ranks have tended to dwindle away after the first flamboyant outbursts. So long as a school will give an undergraduate his passport into the upper-middle-class without demanding more than . . . 15 weekly hours of studying, few are going to complain." Few indeed. Two years later, in 1967, professors Seymour Lipset and Philip Altbach flatly declared that it "should be made clear that . . . the scope of the American student 'revolution' has been greatly exaggerated by the mass media."

Newsweek confirmed such sentiments during spring 1965 when it conducted interviews and a poll of over 800 students at numerous universities.

---

*At this stage in its history, the Student Nonviolent Coordinating Committee (SNCC) employed peaceful demonstrations to achieve civil rights goals. (Eds.)

Over 90 percent expressed confidence in higher education, big corporations, and the federal government, while over 80 percent were satisfied with college and had positive views about the armed forces, organized religion, and the United Nations. When asked what students thought their lives would be like in fifteen years, most of them mimicked their older brothers: "I'll be secure, financially, married, have children, at least three," said one. Another aimed to be "upper middle class," and a third predicted, "I'll be living in a Long Island suburb." A journalist labeled the students "Flaming Moderates."

In mid-decade only a few students were activists while the larger sixties generation was comfortably moderate. A conservative student at the University of Miami wrote about the "deadly infection called student apathy" and referred to his campus as a "hotbed of apathy." Fraternities and sororities still dominated campus life, and a coed at Kansas as late as 1967 admitted that the biggest craze on her campus was "to get your boyfriend's fraternity sweater." Most college papers were similar to the *Daily Illini,* printing regular features like "The Party Line" which announced lavalierings, pinnings, engagements, and marriages. "I have respect for the ones who went to Mississippi or joined the Peace Corps, who committed themselves," said an English professor at Illinois in 1965, "but there are very, very few of them. Very few on this campus."

While some students had been provoked out of apathy by campus issues and civil rights, most of the sixties generation sitting in crowded classes during spring semester of 1965 were optimistic and comfortable— still best defined as the cool generation—mildly alienated from their parents' values and eager to sing along and "let the good times roll." *Time* surveyed the generation then and reported conformity: "Almost everywhere boys dress in madras shirts and chinos, or perhaps green Levis, all trim and neat. The standard for girls is sweaters and skirts dyed to match, or shirt-waists and jumpers plus blazers, Weejun loafers, and knee socks or stockings." At that time no one would have predicted that just two years away were the Summer of Love and the March on the Pentagon. Campus life that spring semester was cool, the good life. As the student body president of University of Texas said, "We haven't really been tested by war or depression. We live very much in the present because we don't have to be overly concerned about the future."

"There was that little conflict in Vietnam," Bob Calvert remembered, "but most of us in the movement felt optimistic during the summer of 1965." Indeed, most Americans felt that the nation was moving forward, and that mood was glowing in August when LBJ signed the Voting Rights Act. The president asked civil rights leaders to be present, and the signing ceremony included Bayard Rustin, Roy Wilkins, A. Philip Randolph, and Martin Luther King, Jr. LBJ had met with King the previous day and they discussed the remarkable advances during 1964 and 1965, not only in civil rights but also in the War on Poverty and Great Society programs—massive federal aid to education and job training, Headstart, Medicare, and Medi-caid. King spoke of the president's amazing sensitivity to the difficult problems that Negro Americans face in the stride toward freedom," and at the signing celebration the president declared, "Today is a triumph for freedom as huge as any victory that's ever been won on any battlefield." The civil rights leaders proclaimed LBJ the "greatest President" for blacks, even surpassing Abraham Lincoln.

"There was a religiosity about the meeting," recalled a presidential aide, "which was warm with emotion—a final celebration of an act so long desired and so long in achieving." Now liberals could sit back in their easy chairs and relax. In spring 1964 a new president had made his pledge, had declared his vision of the future. "This nation, this people, this generation, has man's first chance to create a Great Society: a society of success without squalor, beauty without barrenness, works of genius without the wretchedness of poverty. We can open the doors of learning. We can open the doors of fruitful labor and rewarding leisure, of open opportunity and close community—not just to the privileged few, but, thank God, we can open those doors to *everyone*. Now, just fifteen months later, it seemed that the liberals were delivering. The civil and voting rights acts had outlawed racial discrimination in public accommodations, employment, and the vote, and social programs were beginning to help the poor—white and black—to share the American Dream. On that day in August, liberalism reached its zenith in the 1960s.

Then, during the next two years, President Johnson gave the sixties generation a reason to be concerned about the future—he massively escalated America's role in the Vietnam War. The cool generation became history.

What would have happened to the sixties generation without the experience of Vietnam? Certainly, many would have continued to support and some would have demonstrated for civil rights. Five years of the struggle meant that it had become part of the generation's consciousness, and students began demanding classes on black literature and history at universities such as Stanford, Cornell, and San Francisco State. The "movement" would have been remembered as the civil rights struggle and the rise of student power. Increasing enrollments meant that the university was going to continue evolving in size and in substance, and that students would continue demanding and supporting change. In spring 1966 Stanford activist David Harris won election as student body president by calling for student control of regulations, equal policies for men and women, option of pass-fail grades, legalization of marijuana, elimination of the board of trustees, and the end of all university cooperation with the Vietnam War. The next year students challenged campus rules and regulations at Brown, Cornell, Oregon, Washington, and administrators at the best institutions were moving toward adopting the suggestion of a committee at Wisconsin that advocated "withdrawal by the University from its *in loco parentis* activities." By mid-decade it also was clear that 1950s morality was cracking and that the younger generation was revolting against the values of Ma and Pa. Most of this quest would be superficial, beer bashes and bundling at the beach as the sixties became a party decade. But for a few others, the questioning of morals would lead them to substantial changes as they became part of an emerging counterculture. Finally, the massive size of the generation alone meant that it would have modified society, and thus would have made an impact.

What would have been remembered as the "sixties" without Vietnam? The Johnson administration would have continued civil rights legislation and Great Society programs, and along with the significant rulings of the Supreme Court of Chief Justice Earl Warren, the decade would have been taught today as another major reform era in American history.

Without the war, however, one wonders if the decade would have been as dramatic—would have been remembered as "the sixties." The decade had been a turning point for blacks since Greensboro in 1960.* For white students and their parents the decade began to take shape in 1964 and 1965 as the young began to exhibit their new values and make demands on their campus administrators. Then, between autumn 1965 and the end of 1967, the Johnson administration escalated American involvement in Vietnam— and for the entire nation the decade became "the sixties."

DOCUMENTS

Port Huron Statement, 1962

Introduction: Agenda for a Generation

We are people of this generation, bred in at least modest comfort, housed now in universities, looking uncomfortably to the world we inherit.

When we were kids the United States was the wealthiest and strongest country in the world; the only one with the atom bomb, the least scarred by modern war, an initiator of the United Nations that we thought would distribute Western influence throughout the world. Freedom and equality for each individual, government of, by, and for the people—these American values we found good, principles by which we could live as men. Many of us began maturing in complacency.

As we grew, however, our comfort was penetrated by events too troubling to dismiss. First, the permeating and victimizing fact of human de-

---

SOURCE: Students for a Democratic Society, Port Huron Manifesto, 1962.
*It was in Greensboro, North Carolina that black college students began the nonviolent sit-in movement to desegregate eating facilities in southern stores and restaurants. (Eds.)

gradation, symbolized by the Southern struggle against racial bigotry, compelled most of us from silence to activism. Second, the enclosing fact of the Cold War, symbolized by the presence of the Bomb, brought awareness that we ourselves, and our friends, and millions of abstract "others" we knew more directly because of our common peril, might die at any time. We might deliberately ignore, or avoid, or fail to feel all other human problems, but not these two, for these were too immediate and crushing in their impact, too challenging in the demand that we as individuals take the responsibility for encounter and resolution.

While these and other problems either directly oppressed us or rankled our consciences and became our own subjective concerns, we began to see complicated and disturbing paradoxes in our surrounding America. The declaration "all men are created equal . . ." rang hollow before the facts of Negro life in the South and the big cities of the North. The proclaimed peaceful intentions of the United States contradicted its economic and military investments in the Cold War status quo.

We witnessed, and continue to witness, other paradoxes. With nuclear energy whole cities can easily be powered, yet the dominant nation-states seem more likely to unleash destruction greater than that incurred in all wars of human history. Although our own technology is destroying old and creating new forms of social organization, men still tolerate meaningless work and idleness. While two-thirds of mankind suffers undernourishment, our own upper classes revel amidst superfluous abundance. Although world population is expected to double in forty years, the nations still tolerate anarchy as a major principle of international conduct and uncontrolled exploitation governs the mapping of the earth's physical resources. Although mankind desperately needs revolutionary leadership, America rests in national stalemate, its goals ambiguous and tradition-bound instead of informed and clear, its democratic system apathetic and manipulated rather than "of, by, and for the people."

Not only did tarnish appear on our image of American virtue, not only did disillusion occur when the hypocrisy of American ideals was discovered, but we began to sense that what we had originally seen as the American Golden Age was actually the decline of an era. The worldwide outbreak of revolution against colonialism and imperialism, the entrenchment of totalitarian states, the menace of war, overpopulation, international disorder, supertechnology—these trends were testing the tenacity of our own commitment to democracy and freedom and our abilities to visualize their application to a world in upheaval.

*   *   *

Some would have us believe that Americans feel contentment amidst prosperity—but might it not better be called a glaze above deeply felt anxieties about their role in the new world? And if these anxieties produce a developed indifference to human affairs, do they not as well produce a yearning to believe there *is* an alternative to the present, that something *can* be done to change circumstances in the school, the workplaces, the bureaucracies, the government? It is to this latter yearning, at once the spark and engine of change, that we direct our present appeal. The search for truly democratic alternatives to the present, and a commitment to social experimentation with them, is a worthy and fulfilling human enterprise, one which moves us and, we hope, others today. On such a basis do we offer this document of our convictions and analysis: as an effort in understanding and changing the conditions of humanity in the late twentieth century, an effort rooted in the ancient, still unfulfilled conception of man attaining determining influence over his circumstances of life.

Values

Making values explicit—an initial task in establishing alternatives—is an activity that has been devalued and corrupted. The conventional moral terms of the age, the politician moralities—"free world," "people's democracies"—reflect realities poorly, if at all, and seem to function more as ruling myths than as descriptive principles. But neither has our experience in the universities brought us moral enlightenment. Our professors and administrators sacrifice controversy to public relations; their curriculums change more slowly than the living events of the world; their skills and silence are purchased by investors in the arms race; passion is called unscholastic. The questions we might want raised—what is really important? can we live in a different and better way? if we wanted to change society, how would we do it?—are not thought to be questions of a "fruitful, empirical nature," and thus are brushed aside.

*   *   *

Men have unrealized potential for self-cultivation, self-direction, self-understanding, and creativity. It is this potential that we regard as crucial and to which we appeal, not to the human potentiality for violence, unreason, and submission to authority. The goal of man and society should be human independence: a concern not with image of popularity but with finding a meaning in life that is personally authentic; a quality of mind not compulsively driven by a sense of powerlessness, nor one which unthinkingly adopts status values, nor one which represses all threats to its habits, but one which has full, spontaneous access to present and past experiences, one which easily unites the fragmented parts of personal history, one which openly faces problems which are troubling and unresolved; one with an intuitive awareness of possibilities, an active sense of curiosity, an ability and willingness to learn.

This kind of independence does not mean egotistic individualism—the object is not to have one's way so much as it is to have a way that is one's own. Nor do we deify man—we merely have faith in his potential.

Human relationships should involve fraternity and honesty. Human interdependence is contemporary fact; human brotherhood must be willed, however, as a condition of future survival and as the most appropriate form of social relations. Personal links between man and man are needed, especially to go beyond the partial and fragmentary bonds of function that bind men only as worker to worker, employer to employee, teacher to student, American to Russian.

Loneliness, estrangement, isolation describe the vast distance between man and man today. These dominant tendencies cannot be overcome by better personnel management, nor by improved gadgets, but only when a love of man overcomes the idolatrous worship of things by man. As the individualism we affirm is not egoism, the selflessness we affirm is not self-elimination. On the contrary, we believe in generosity of a kind that imprints one's unique individual qualities in the relation to other men, and to all human activity. Further, to dislike isolation is not to favor the abolition of privacy; the latter differs from isolation in that it occurs or is abolished according to individual will.

We would replace power rooted in possession, privilege, or circumstance by power and uniqueness rooted in love, reflectiveness, reason, and creativity. As a *social system* we seek the establishment of a democracy of individual participation, governed by two central aims: that the individual share in those social decisions determining the quality and direction of his life; that society be organized to encourage independence in men and provide the media for their common participation. . . .

The Students

In the last few years, thousands of American students demonstrated that they at least felt the urgency of the times. They moved actively and directly against racial injustices, the threat of war, violations of individual rights of conscience and, less frequently, against economic manipulation. They succeeded in restoring a small measure of controversy to the campuses after the stillness of the McCarthy period. They succeeded, too, in gaining some concessions from the people and institutions they opposed, especially in the fight against racial bigotry.

The significance of these scattered movements lies not in their success or failure in gaining objectives—at least not yet. Nor does the significance lie in the intellectual "competence" or "maturity" of the students involved—as some pedantic elders allege. The significance is in the fact that the students are breaking the crust of apathy and overcoming the inner alienation that remain the defining characteristics of American college life.

If student movements for change are still rarities on the campus scene, what is commonplace there? The real campus, the familiar campus, is a place of private people, engaged in their notorious "inner emigration." It is a place of commitment to business-as-usual, getting ahead, playing it cool. It is a place of mass affirmation of the Twist,* but mass reluctance toward the controversial public stance. Rules are accepted as "inevitable," bureaucracy as "just circumstances," irrelevance as "scholarship," selflessness as "martyrdom," politics as "just another way to make people do what you want, and an unprofitable one, too."

Almost no students value activity as citizens. Passive in public, they are hardly more idealistic in arranging their private lives: Gallup concludes they will settle for "low success, and won't risk high failure." There is not much willingness to take risks (not even in business), no setting of dangerous goals, no real conception of personal identity except one manufactured in the image of others, no real urge for personal fulfillment except to be almost as successful as the very successful people. Attention is being paid to social status (the quality of shirt collars, meeting people, getting wives or husbands, making solid contacts for later on); much, too, is paid to academic status (grades, honors, the med school rat race). But neglected generally is real intellectual status, the personal cultivation of the mind.

"Students don't even give a damn about the apathy," one has said. Apathy toward apathy begets a privately constructed universe, a place of systematic study schedules, two nights each week for beer, a girl or two, and early marriage; a framework infused with personality, warmth, and under control, no matter how unsatisfying otherwise. . . .

The academic life contains reinforcing counterparts to the way in which extracurricular life is organized. The academic world is founded on a teacher-student relation analogous to the parent-child relation which characterizes *in loco parentis*. Further, academia includes a radical separation of the student from the material of study. That which is studied, the social reality, is "objectified" to sterility, dividing the student from life—just as he is restrained in active involvement by the deans controlling student government. The specialization of function and knowledge, admittedly necessary to our complex technological and social structure, has produced an exaggerated compartmentalization of study and understanding. This has contributed to an overly parochial view, by faculty, of the role of its research and scholarship, to a discontinuous and truncated understanding, by students, of the surrounding social order; and to a loss of personal attachment, by nearly all, to the worth of study as a humanistic enterprise.

There is, finally, the cumbersome academic bureaucracy extending throughout the academic as well as the extracurricular structures, contributing to the sense of outer complexity and inner powerlessness that trans-

---

*A popular dance during the 1960s (Eds.)

forms the honest searching of many students to a ratification of convention and, worse, to a numbness to present and future catastrophes. The size and financing systems of the university enhance the permanent trusteeship of the administrative bureaucracy, their power leading to a shift within the university toward the value standards of business and the administrative mentality. Huge foundations and other private financial interests shape the under-financed colleges and universities, not only making them more commercial, but less disposed to diagnose society critically, less open to dissent. Many social and physical scientists, neglecting the liberating heritage of higher learning, develop "human relations" or "morale-producing" techniques for the corporate economy, while others exercise their intellectual skills to accelerate the arms race.

Vietnam Veterans Against the War, 1971

... [S]everal months ago in Detroit we had an investigation at which over 150 honorably discharged and many very highly decorated veterans testified to war crimes committed in Southeast Asia, not isolated incidents but crimes committed on a day-to-day basis with the full awareness of officers at all levels of command.

It is impossible to describe to you exactly what did happen in Detroit, the emotions in the room, the feelings of the men who were reliving their experiences in Vietnam, but they did. They relived the absolute horror of what this country, in a sense, made them do.

They told the stories [of] times they had personally raped, cut off ears, cut off heads, taped wires from portable telephones to human genitals and turned up the power, cut off limbs, blown up bodies, randomly shot at civilians, razed villages in fashion reminiscent of Genghis Khan, shot cattle and dogs for fun, poisoned food stocks, and generally ravaged the countryside of South Vietnam in addition to the normal ravage of war, and the normal and very particular ravaging which is done by the applied bombing power of this country. . . .

We who have come here to Washington have come here because we feel we have to be winter soldiers now. We could come back to this country; we could be quiet; we could hold our silence; we could not tell what went on in Vietnam, but we feel because of what threatens this country, the fact that the crimes threaten it, not reds, and not redcoats but the crimes which we are committing that threaten it, that we have to speak out. . . .

SOURCE: Hearings Before the Committee on Foreign Relations, U.S. Senate, 92nd Cong., 1st sess., 1971. Document from Bibliobase®, edited by Michael Bellesiles. Copyright © by Houghton Mifflin Company. Reprinted by permission.

I would like to talk to you a little bit about what the result is of the feelings these men carry with them after coming back from Vietnam. The country doesn't know it yet, but it has created a monster, a monster in the form of millions of men who have been taught to deal and to trade in violence, and who are given the chance to die for the biggest nothing in history; men who have returned with a sense of anger and a sense of betrayal which no one has yet grasped. . . .

In our opinion, and from our experience, there is nothing in South Vietnam, nothing which could happen that realistically threatens the United States of America. And to attempt to justify the loss of one American life in Vietnam, Cambodia, or Laos by linking such loss to the preservation of freedom, which those misfits supposedly abuse, is to us the height of criminal hypocrisy, and it is that kind of hypocrisy which we feel has torn this country apart. . . .

We found that not only was it a civil war, an effort by a people who had for years been seeking their liberation from any colonial influence whatsoever, but also we found that the Vietnamese whom we had enthusiastically molded after our own image were hard put to take up the fight against the threat we were supposedly saving them from.

We found most people didn't even know the difference between communism and democracy. They only wanted to work in rice paddies without helicopters strafing them and bombs with napalm burning their villages and tearing their country apart. . . .

We rationalized destroying villages in order to save them. We saw America lose her sense of morality as she accepted very coolly a My Lai* and refused to give up the image of American soldiers who hand out chocolate bars and chewing gum. . . .

Now we are told that the men who fought there must watch quietly while American lives are lost so that we can exercise the incredible arrogance of Vietnamizing the Vietnamese. . . .

. . . Each day to facilitate the process by which the United States washes her hands of Vietnam someone has to give up his life so that the United States doesn't have to admit something that the entire world already knows, so that we can't say that we have made a mistake. Someone has to die so that President Nixon won't be, and these are his words, "the first President to lose a war."

We are asking Americans to think about that because how do you ask a man to be the last man to die in Vietnam? How do you ask a man to be the last man to die for a mistake? . . .

We wish that a merciful God could wipe away our own memories of that service as easily as this administration has wiped their memories of us.

---

*My Lai refers to the village in which American soldiers killed many innocent Vietnamese civilians. (Eds.)

But all that they have done and all that they can do by this denial is to make more clear than ever our own determination to undertake one last mission, to search out and destroy the last vestige of this barbaric war, to pacify our own hearts, to conquer the hate and the fear that have driven this country these last 10 years and more, and so when, in 30 years from now, our brothers go down the street without a leg, without an arm, or a face, and small boys ask why, we will be able to say "Vietnam" and not mean a desert, not a filthy obscene memory but mean instead the place where America finally turned and where soldiers like us helped it in the turning. . . .

Chapter 15

The Revival of Feminism

When women gained the vote in 1920, the women's movement that had long sought this goal—dating back to the mid-nineteenth century—became dormant for several decades. Yet that victory by no means marked the end of the struggle for equality of opportunity and treatment for women. The franchise gained women entry to the voting booth, but few won elective office. Women still found most of their employment opportunities in the traditional, low-paying, "feminine" occupations, and their wages typically ranged lower than those of men with similar experience, education, skill, and responsibility. Moreover, during the Great Depression, married women discovered that many employers hesitated to hire them, insisting that men be given preference for available jobs.

    Economic discrimination had much to do with the emergence of a new wave of feminism beginning in the 1960s, but there were other factors as well. In the essay "Feminism's Second Wave: The Opening Salvos," author Flora Davis points to wide-ranging discontent among airline stewardesses during the 1950s and early

1960s. "Stewardess," rather than today's term "flight attendant," was the designation of the then almost totally feminine occupation. What were the major issues in the women's struggle with their airline employers? What tactics proved most significant in determining the final outcome? Can you think of other occupations, usually low-paid, that are dominated by women?

In 1923, a group of women led by Alice Paul had proposed an equal rights amendment (ERA) to the Constitution designed to ensure sexual equality. The idea lay quiescent for nearly half a century until the resurgence of the women's movement in the 1960s. By 1970, the ERA had again become a live issue. The first document is a statement in support of the amendment before a Senate committee by the well-known feminist writer and editor Gloria Steinem. To what extent and in what ways might the ERA affect the conditions that Steinem describes?

In 1972 Congress approved the ERA by the necessary two-thirds margin, and opinion polls indicated support for the amendment by a vast majority of the American public. Nevertheless, the amendment failed to receive ratification by the required three-quarters of the states. Opposition centered in the South, several western states, Missouri, and Illinois.

The defeat of the ERA, although a major setback, did not fatally injure the women's movement. A growing number of women ran for and were elected to office. In 1976, 21 woman held seats in the United States Congress. Twenty years later, 55 women were in Congress, and both United States Senators from California were women. In 1984, for the first time, a woman, Geraldine Ferraro, was selected as a vice-presidential candidate.

Encouraged by the spirit of feminism and aided by civil rights legislation, favorable court decisions, and government-directed affirmative action programs, increasing numbers of women entered traditionally male occupations. Since 1980 women have outnumbered men in undergraduate colleges and universities, and they have been increasing their presence in graduate schools. Women received 14.3 percent of the PhDs granted in 1970, but by 1994 the figure had reached 38.5 percent. In 1960, only 6.8 percent of physicians were women, but in the academic year 1997–1998, 42.6 percent of medical students were women, thus ensuring that they would be a strong presence in the practice of medicine in the new millenium. The change among lawyers was even more startling. In 1960 women won only 2.5 percent of the law degrees granted that year, but by 1994 the figure was 43 percent. However, as the decade of the 1980s came to an end, men continued to earn more than women, and the plight of mothers in single-parent households remained difficult, with many living in poverty.

In addition to the ERA, abortion became a highly controversial issue after 1973. The Supreme Court in Roe v. Wade (1973), parts of which are included in the second document, paved the way for the legalization of abortion in many states that had formerly imposed severe limits on the procedure. What did the justices say about the right to privacy and how it affected abortion? Did the Court suggest that abortion was an absolute right? The last document is a statement by President George Bush to a group of prolife (antiabortion) marchers in the nation's capital. What possibilities for compromise, if any, do you see on this issue?

ESSAY

—————— •◆• ——————

Feminism's Second Wave:
The Opening Salvos

Flora Davis

The women's movement, as reincarnated in the 1960s, is often called the "second wave" of feminism, to distinguish it from the "first wave," which arose during the nineteenth century and won the vote for women in 1920. The wave analogy is helpful because it underscores the fact that the women's movement didn't die after 1920, though it did lose much of its momentum. The analogy also reminds us that major social changes tend to happen in waves. First, there's a lot of intense activity and some aspects of life are transformed; then, when the public has absorbed as much as it can stand, reaction sets in. Stability reigns for a while, and if there's a strong backlash, some of the changes may be undone. Eventually, if vital issues remain unresolved, another wave of activism arises. . . .

The turbulent, affluent, optimistic 1960s provided an unusually hospitable climate for feminism. The civil rights movement had broken new ground and a number of related social movements sprang up in its wake. One of them was the women's movement. Like a brush fire in a dry season, it ignited simultaneously in two different places: among older, liberal women and among the young radicals of the New Left.

Throughout the sixties, the women's movement grew steadily, but most Americans were barely aware of what was happening. Then in the early 1970s, feminism exploded across the national scene as groups of activists cropped up almost everywhere. Often, women coalesced around a single issue, pouring their efforts into a rape hotline, a battered women's shelter, or some other highly focused project.

At the same time, a broad-based right-wing backlash began to build, fueled by white male resentment at the challenges from feminists and from the civil rights movement. When conservatives won the White House in 1980, feminists were thrown on the defensive; for the next decade, they had to fight to hang onto the ground they'd already gained. They lost some battles and won others, and overall, progress for women stalled. Nevertheless, new feminist groups kept emerging, many of them now being formed by women of color. Going into the 1990s, the women's movement was bigger, stronger, and more diverse than ever.

SOURCE: "Feminism's Second Wave: The Opening Salvos" from *Moving the Mountain: The Women's Movement in America Since 1960* by Flora Davis, p. 6, 15–25. Copyright © 1991 by Simon & Schuster. Reprinted by permission from Curtis Brown, Ltd.

Between 1960 and 1990, feminists achieved half a revolution. Laws were passed, court decisions were handed down, and sex discrimination was officially prohibited; women were elected to office, grudgingly accepted into male occupations, and promoted to positions that women had never held before. New terms entered the nation's vocabulary: People spoke of "sexism" and "male chauvinism." Probably, the movement's single greatest achievement was that it transformed most people's assumptions about what women were capable of and had a right to expect from life.

The Battle with the Airlines

The story of how airline stewardesses forced American airlines to change unfair work rules is the perfect introduction to the second wave. By throwing into sharp relief the old attitudes to women and the impact those attitudes had on people's lives, it shows just how far women have come. The activists involved were few in number, and they challenged just one aspect of the pervasive problem of sex discrimination. That was typical of the second wave and illustrates the point that social transformations, like jigsaw puzzles, are put together one piece at a time.

The battle with the airlines spanned a crucial period in the history of the women's movement. Stewardesses fought to be treated as workers, rather than as sex objects, at a time when the term "sex object" hadn't yet been invented. The work rules they challenged decreed that to keep their jobs they must remain single, and they were fired the minute they married. Many airlines fired them, in any case, as soon as they turned thirty-two, while others set the limit at thirty-five. Women much over the age of thirty were no longer considered attractive enough to fly for an airline. It hadn't even occurred to most Americans that the system was unfair, and that made changing the rules an uphill fight in a way it wouldn't have been a few years later.

The stewardess unions actually began their campaign before the second wave, at a time when few people had any interest in women's rights. When the women's movement caught up with them, union leaders used its impetus, and as they did, they quickly came to identify themselves as feminists fighting sex discrimination, not just as unionists confronting management.

At one time or another, stewardess unions at most of the major airlines joined the struggle to change the work rules. There was some communication between union leaders, but they never really made a coordinated effort. Instead, the battle was fought simultaneously on many different fronts by different groups. The women who worked for American Airlines belonged to a union called ALSSA—the Air Line Stewards and Stewardesses Association—and their campaign was typical.

The Age and Marriage Issues

In the hierarchy of "glamour" jobs open to white women in the early sixties, stewardesses ranked right after movie stars and models.* In fact, for every woman hired as a stewardess, more than a hundred applicants were turned away. Those who were chosen embodied the American image of the wholesome girl-next-door.

As the airlines saw it, these "girls" would fly for a few years, then leave the job to marry and settle down. In the midsixties, stewardesses lasted 32.4 months, on the average, less than three years. "If that figure ever got up to thirty-five months, I'd know we're getting the wrong kind of girl. She's not getting married," a personnel manager for United Airlines said solemnly in 1965.

In the early 1960s, the social pressure to marry was relentless. The average woman became a wife at age twenty, younger than in any generation since the turn of the century. Seventy percent of American women made it safely to the altar before they were twenty-four, and a woman still unmarried at the advanced age of twenty-five was considered an "old maid." She was pitied, and people wondered what was wrong with her that no man had asked her to be his wife. Most stewardesses themselves assumed when they were hired that they'd marry within a few years. In fact, at American Airlines the gold wings presented to a woman after five years of flying were known as "your failure pin," because they signified that she had so far failed to marry.

By becoming a stewardess, an adventurous young woman had a chance to travel and meet interesting people in the time warp between the end of her schooling and the beginning of marriage. And the job was said to be good experience for marriage. At the airline training schools the women learned safety procedures, but also took classes in make-up, grooming, and social skills, "the perfect course for being a perfect hostess at home," according to one stewardess. (At American, the school was known irreverently as "the charm farm.")

Although most stewardesses seemed to love their jobs, they lived with more restrictions than the most overprotected teenager. They were told how long to wear their skirts and their hair and how high their heels could be. They could be fired for gaining too much weight. Girdles were generally required and supervisors did "touch checks" to make sure employees were wearing them. In addition, the women were paid so little that home was often a small apartment shared with as many as half a dozen other stewardesses.

Almost from the beginning, most airlines expected their stewardesses to resign when they married. Age didn't become an issue until the early 1950s,

---

*Stewardesses (also called air hostesses) became known as "flight attendants" during the 1970s, as men began to be hired for the job.

when American Airlines became the first company to retire the women as soon as they reached their midthirties. To get the union to agree to the age limit, management negotiators exempted those already working for the company. They stipulated that only women hired after November 1, 1953, would be forced to retire at thirty-two.

Dusty Roads got in under the wire. So did Nancy Collins, who would become the union's master executive chairman (equivalent to being its president) in the early sixties. They led the long struggle to get the airline to lift the age restriction, because both felt a moral issue was involved.

As the 1950s wore on, more and more airlines routinely dismissed stewardesses for growing too old. By 1965, fifteen of the thirty-eight U.S. airlines were doing it. "I was twenty-eight when we fought the age issue, and I was absolutely hysterical," said Lynda Oswald, who was with American Airlines. "I was trying to prepare myself for another job, but when I tried to get into a university, they wouldn't accept me as a part-time student. The whole climate was catch-22."

Yet many stewardesses saw nothing wrong with the airlines' regulations, and union leaders found it hard to marshall support. Roads recalled that "some of our own flight attendants would say, 'I don't think you should fly when you're fat or old.'" Younger women weren't interested in the age issue. "When you're twenty, you don't believe you're ever going to be thirty-two," Roads observed drily. Older women, as their thirty-second birthday approached, often cast about desperately for a ground job with the company. Reluctant to antagonize management, most "retired" from flying without a protest. As for the marriage regulation, many women did marry and kept their marriage a secret. At one point, airline officials estimated that 30 to 40 percent of stewardesses were secretly married.

In short, the battle with the airlines was fought by a minority of activists who were willing to take risks. Most of the women who ultimately benefited from their efforts were initially too timid or indifferent to take part, or actually opposed any change in the status quo. That was the case with the first challenges to sex discrimination in many occupations.

In defending their regulations, the airlines talked a lot about the image of a stewardess as a young, single woman, and the importance of maintaining that image. However, the union's leaders were well aware that, as Collins put it, "Ninety percent of this had to do with economics." Money was usually the bottom line when employers discriminated against women. In their stewardesses, the airlines had the ideal work force. Few stayed long enough to earn more than beginners' wages, and the savings on fringe benefits must have been considerable. What other company could guarantee health insurers a group of insurees who would never be older than thirty-two?

In the beginning, ALSSA's leaders believed their problem was unique; they didn't see it as part of a pattern of discrimination against women.

Dusty Roads's eyes were opened in the late fifties. She had a good friend, Ann Cooper Penning, who was administrative assistant to Congresswoman Martha Griffiths, a Michigan Democrat. Roads recalled that "I was telling Annie about things the airlines did, and she said, 'You've got to be kidding me. I can't wait to tell this to Martha.' Eventually, I met Martha." Before that, Roads had more or less accepted the way stewardesses were treated. "But Martha was so upset about it," she said. From conversations with Griffiths, Roads came to realize that sex discrimination was widespread.

"The Old Broads' Bill"

At that point, there seemed to be two possible strategies open to the stewardesses. They could try to persuade the airlines at the bargaining table to drop the age and marriage regulations, or they could push for legislation.

Stewardess leaders tried bargaining first. However, they got minimal support from male union colleagues. All the stewardess unions were actually subunits of huge, male-dominated unions, and the union men were mostly blue-collar males who had come up the hard way. In dealing with the stewardesses, they were protective but autocratic. They had traditional ideas about a woman's role and little sympathy for women's issues.

Without the support of male unionists, the stewardesses were unable to get rid of the age and marriage restrictions. It was also clear that no airline was likely to give up these money-saving measures as long as other airlines were still taking advantage of them. Thus, in the early sixties, Collins and Roads tried to solve the problem by getting Congress to pass a law.

By that time, Roads was ALSSA's official, if unpaid, lobbyist. She was chosen for the job in 1958 because she was flying in and out of Washington, D.C., regularly, was dating a congressman, and could count Congresswoman Griffiths as a friend. Roads did her lobbying on her own time between flights. She had no trouble getting appointments with male members of Congress; she was a stewardess, and the men simply assumed that she would be young and attractive. Once through the door, she could often interest them in her union's case against the airlines.

Roads's efforts resulted in one early attempt to pass a law against the airlines' restrictions, but it was a piece of legislation few were comfortable with. Was it fair for Congress to target one industry and forbid one or two specific practices? "They didn't know how to go about this," said Roads. "To introduce a bill that would keep a company from firing anybody at the age of thirty-two was kind of preposterous. It was a very narrow attack on a very broad issue, which was age discrimination or discrimination against women. Eventually, the bill became a joke—they called it 'the old broads' bill.'"

In 1963, Collins and Roads decided to go public with their problem. They held a press conference at the Commodore Hotel in New York City.

Collins wanted stewardesses there in significant numbers, to prove a lot of them cared about the age issue, but it wasn't easy to find women who were willing to take a public stand and risk their jobs.

Once again, the aura of glamour that came with the stewardess job paid off. Many newspapers sent reporters and photographers, and after Roads pointed out that four of the stewardesses in the room were actually over thirty-two—hired before November 1953, they couldn't be fired—one photographer seized the chance to set up a picture that ultimately appeared in papers across the country. It showed nearly a dozen uniformed women, shoulder to shoulder and displaying quite a lot of leg, over a caption that in many cases invited readers to guess which of the women were over thirty-two. Columnist Art Buchwald maintained that older stewardesses were better cooks and were just as attractive—missing the point, that the women had a right not to be fired arbitrarily. Collins and Roads were willing to be patronized as long as they got the story out. The press conference produced sheaves of clippings, but there was still no progress on the age issue.

In 1964, stewardess unions filed a complaint against American and TWA with the New York State Commission for Human Rights. New York and some other states had laws against discrimination because of age, but had nothing on the books as yet about sex discrimination.

Congress, too, was concerned about just treatment for older workers. On September 2, 1965, women from several airlines appeared before a House Labor subcommittee to talk about the age issue; other stewardesses, many in uniform, were in the audience to show support. One of the congressmen on the committee seemed to think it funny that attractive women in their thirties were talking of discrimination because of age. Representative James H. Scheuer, a Democrat from New York, turned to the stewardesses and asked them to "stand up, so we can see the dimensions of the problem."

Colleen Boland, then head of ALSSA, testified that an airlines executive had explained the age regulation this way: "It's the sex thing. Put a dog on an airplane and twenty businessmen are sore for a month." Representative Scheuer gallantly replied, "I would oppose with my dying breath the notion that a woman is less beautiful, less appealing, less sensitive after thirty. . . ." Nancy Collins said, "In those days, we felt we were being patted on our little heads about 90 percent of the time."

The congressional hearing brought no visible progress, and in New York the age discrimination case dragged on through hearings and appeals. It wasn't until early 1968 that the state's five-man Appellate Court ruled unanimously against the stewardesses on the grounds that the age law was intended to apply only to those between forty and sixty-five.

Though the stewardesses' glamour image gave them advantages in pressing their case, they were very much aware of the way society devalued older women. Once a woman was no longer young and sexually appealing to men, she had lost whatever leverage she originally had.

The EEOC: Reluctant Enforcer

In 1964, as part of a landmark civil rights bill, Congress banned sex discrimination by employers and created a new federal agency, the Equal Employment Opportunity Commission (EEOC), to enforce the law. The stewardess unions were quick to seize the chance it offered them, and when the EEOC officially opened its doors in the summer of 1965, two American Airlines stewardesses were among the first people through them.

"We got there so early, we had to help unpack the typewriters; they were still in boxes," said Dusty Roads.

With Roads that day, ready to sign a sex discrimination complaint, was Jean Montague, who was due to be fired by American because she would soon turn thirty-two. The women assumed that, thanks to the section of the new civil rights law known as Title VII, the airlines would have to mend their ways. "We were naive," Roads admitted later.

The EEOC staffer who handled their complaint that day was an African-American woman. At first she couldn't see how young, educated, white women could possibly be victims of discrimination, but she soon got into the spirit of the thing. "Do they fire pilots at thirty-two?" she asked Roads. "Do they fire flight engineers?" When Roads assured her the airlines didn't, she said with relish, "Go get 'em." That's just what Roads and her union did.

However, it took almost a year before the EEOC finally held a hearing on the women's charges in May 1966. Afterward, Roads couldn't be certain how the session had gone, but it was clear that at least one of the five commissioners, Aileen Hernandez, was sympathetic. In an unexpected way, Hernandez played a key role in the stewardess story. She resigned from the EEOC in October that year, disillusioned because the Commission was so reluctant to act on women's issues. Later, she recalled that "Commission meetings produced a sea of male faces, nearly all of which reflected attitudes that ranged from boredom to virulent hostility whenever the issue of sex discrimination was raised." Hernandez noted that the EEOC's priority was race discrimination—but apparently only as it affected black *men*. She was particularly frustrated by the long delay in ruling on complaints brought by stewardesses. At the time she resigned, there were ninety-two such cases pending, and some were more than a year old.

Hernandez resigned on October 10, giving a month's notice. On the last weekend in October, a brand-new feminist organization, NOW (the National Organization for Women), held its founding conference. Afterward, the women issued a press release. Among other things, it backed the stewardesses; it also announced that Hernandez had been elected executive vice-president of NOW, subject to her consent. According to Hernandez, her election was "a charitable, but unauthorized gesture," apparently intended to express support for her decision to resign from the EEOC.*

On November 9, the day before Hernandez's resignation was to take effect, the Commission finally ruled that company policies setting age limits for stewardesses amounted to sex discrimination. Just two weeks later, the airlines won a temporary court order which blocked the ruling on the grounds that Hernandez had a conflict of interests, because presumably she was a member of NOW. In an effort to prove she was, they had a federal court subpoena Betty Friedan, NOW's newly elected president, and Muriel Fox, who was in charge of public relations, and dragged them into court in New York City on Christmas Eve, while on the West Coast Hernandez was subpoenaed in the same way. A lawyer for the airlines demanded that Friedan produce a list of NOW's members; she declined. "We had all agreed to keep the membership list of NOW secret," Friedan wrote later, "for in those early days no one was sure she wouldn't be fired or otherwise excommunicated for belonging to an organization to overthrow sex discrimination."

In February 1967, a federal district court judge issued an injunction that, in effect, erased the EEOC decision on the age question because of Hernandez's supposed conflict of interests. The Commission and the stewardesses had to begin all over again with hearings.**

Meanwhile, the unions were trying to end the marriage restriction, working on it as a separate issue from the age limit. The airlines resisted, maintaining that married women would miss work too often and would gain weight. (Some supervisors apparently believed that with marriage a woman inevitably became plump and docile.) Eventually, the unions brought marriage-regulation complaints, too, to the EEOC. In June 1968, the agency finally announced in a case involving an American Airlines stewardess that the marriage restriction violated Title VII. In the meantime, unions at other airlines had been able to resolve the marriage issue at the bargaining table.

There was still no word from the EEOC about the age restriction, and ALSSA was soon deep in contract negotiations with American with the age limit a key issue. "We were ready to roll on a strike then," said Roads. "I called Martha and said, 'If you know anyone on the Commission, call them and tell them that if they would just make a decision, there wouldn't have to be a strike.'"

Griffiths made the phone call, and on August 10, 1968, the EEOC finally released new guidelines that barred the airlines from dismissing stewardesses for being overage. The following day, ALSSA reached agreement

---

*In 1970, Hernandez succeeded Betty Friedan as president of NOW.

**NOW ultimately did help the stewardess unions a great deal by persistently lobbying the EEOC on their behalf.

with American on a new contract, and, as Nancy Collins put it, "The age and marriage issues just faded into the woodwork."

From the time the women filed their complaint with the EEOC in July 1965, more than three years had passed; it had been five years since Roads and Collins staged their press conference. However, the struggle wasn't over yet. Some stewardesses took the airlines to court, because they not only wanted to return to their jobs but they wanted back pay and accumulated seniority. There were many individual suits as well as class-action suits. The stewardess unions also challenged the airlines successfully on the question of whether a woman should be allowed to return to her job after having a baby.

Throughout the sixties, class and race were invisible elements in the struggle between women and the airlines, for the unions never addressed the fact that women of color and white women from working-class backgrounds were seldom hired as stewardesses. At the time, most white feminists saw "women's issues" solely in terms of white women's issues—and were unaware that that was what they were doing. The second wave's size and scope were limited as a result.

The Aftereffects

In tackling the age and marriage restrictions, stewardesses assaulted some of society's ingrained assumptions: that marriage was all women really wanted; that it was perfectly natural to judge a woman solely on her looks; and that men somehow had a right to the services of women—and if it could be arranged that the women doing the serving were young, single, and attractive, so much the better.

Lynda Oswald said, "I think many of us who were stewardesses during the 1960s suffered deep psychological scars. We still have a terror of age and of being discarded because our skin isn't quite smooth enough any more."

Roads, Collins, and other activists improved the lot of most women and men who were subsequently hired as (gender-neutral) "cabin crew." In 1985, flight attendants kept their job, on the average, for ten years; they were now required to retire at age seventy; and some long-term employees were making more than $40,000 a year.

There were other, less tangible gains as well. As they stood up for their rights, the stewardesses found that their image of women and of themselves changed profoundly. A story Roads liked to tell summed up the difference. A male passenger once complained to her, "I don't know why you girls should object to being called 'girls.'"

"That's because you don't know the difference between a girl and a woman," she told him. "A 'girl' is somebody who rents an apartment. A 'woman' owns a house."

In 1991, Dusty Roads and Nancy Collins were still flying. Their names weren't likely to be the first to pop into anyone's mind during a discussion of the women's movement, but their victory was typical of the second wave.

American women owed the progress they made largely to thousands of unknown activists like Roads and Collins, who tackled a small piece of the overall problem of sex discrimination. Social change advanced like an incoming tide at many different points simultaneously.

DOCUMENTS

In Support of ERA, 1970

My name is Gloria Steinem. I am a writer and editor. I have worked in several political campaigns, and am currently a member of the Policy Council of the Democratic National Committee.

During twelve years of working for a living, I've experienced much of the legal and social discrimination reserved for women in this country. I have been refused service in public restaurants, ordered out of public gathering places, and turned away from apartment rentals; all for the clearly-stated sole reason that I am a woman. And all without the legal remedies available to blacks and other minorities. I have been excluded from professional groups, writing assignments on so-called "unfeminine" subjects such as politics, full participation in the Democratic Party, jury duty, and even from such small male privileges as discounts on airline fares. Most important to me, I have been denied a society in which women are encouraged, or even allowed, to think of themselves as first-class citizens and responsible human beings.

However, after two years of researching the status of American women, I have discovered that I am very, very lucky. Most women, both wage-earners and housewives, routinely suffer more humiliation and injustice than I do.

As a freelance writer, I don't work in the male-dominated hierarchy of an office. (Women, like blacks and other visibly-different minorities, do better in individual professions such as the arts, sports, or domestic work; anything in which they don't have authority over white males.) I am not one of the millions of women who must support a family. Therefore, I haven't had to go on welfare because there are no day care centers for my children while I work, and I haven't had to submit to the humiliating welfare inquiries about my private and sexual life, inquiries from which men are exempt. I haven't had to brave the sex bias of labor unions and employers, only to see my family subsist on a median salary 40 percent less than the male median salary.

SOURCE: Testimony of Gloria Steinem, U.S. Congress, Senate Committee on the Judiciary, Subcommittee on Constitutional Amendments, Hearings, *The "Equal Rights" Amendment*, 91st Cong., 2d sess., 1970, 335–337.

I hope this committee will hear the personal, daily injustices suffered by many women—professionals and day laborers, women housebound by welfare as well as suburbia. We have all been silent for too long. We won't be silent anymore.

The truth is that all our problems stem from the same sex-based myths. We may appear before you as white radicals or the middle-aged middle class or black soul sisters, but we are *all* sisters in fighting against these outdated myths. Like racial myths, they have been reflected in our laws. Let me list a few:

That Women Are Biologically Inferior to Men

In fact, an equally good case can be made for the reverse. Women live longer than men, even when the men are not subject to business pressures. Women survived Nazi concentration camps better, keep cooler heads in emergencies currently studied by disaster-researchers, are protected against heart attacks by their female sex hormones, and are so much more durable at every stage of life that nature must conceive 20 to 50 percent more males in order to keep some balance going.

Man's hunting activities are forever being pointed to as tribal proof of superiority. But while he was hunting, women built houses, tilled the fields, developed animal husbandry, and perfected language. Men, being all alone in the bush, often developed into a creature [*sic*] as strong as women, fleeter of foot, but not very bright.

However, I don't want to prove the superiority of one sex to another. That would only be repeating a male mistake. English scientists once definitively proved, after all, that the English were descended from the angels, while the Irish were descended from the apes: it was the rationale for England's domination of Ireland for more than a century. The point is that science is used to support current myth and economics almost as much as the church was.

What we do know is that the difference *between* two races or two sexes is much smaller than the differences to be found *within* each group. Therefore, in spite of the slide show on female inferiorities that I understand was shown to you yesterday, the law makes much more sense when it treats individuals, not groups bundled together by some condition of birth.

A word should be said about Dr. Freud, the great nineteenth-century perpetuator of female inferiority. Many of the differences he assumed to be biological, and therefore changeless, have turned out to be societal, and have already changed. . . .

That Women Are Already Treated Equally in This Society

I'm sure there has been ample testimony to prove that equal pay for equal work, equal chance for advancement, and equal training or encouragement is obscenely scarce in every field, even those—like food and fashion industries—that are supposedly "feminine."

A deeper result of social and legal injustice, however, is what sociologists refer to as "Internalized Aggression." Victims of aggression absorb the myth of their own inferiority, and come to believe that their group is in fact second-class.

Women suffer this second-class treatment from the moment they are born. They are expected to be rather than achieve, to function biologically rather than learn. A brother, whatever his intellect, is more likely to get the family's encouragement and education money, while girls are often pressured to conceal ambition and intelligence, to "Uncle Tom."

I interviewed a New York public school teacher who told me about a black teenager's desire to be a doctor. With all the barriers in mind, she suggested he be a veterinarian instead.

The same day, a high school teacher mentioned a girl who wanted to be a doctor. The teacher said, "How about a nurse—"

Teachers, parents, and the Supreme Court may exude a protective, well-meaning rationale, but limiting the individual's ambition is doing no one a favor. Certainly not this country. It needs all the talent it can get.

That American Women Hold Great Economic Power

Fifty-one percent of all shareholders in this country are women. That's a favorite male-chauvinist statistic. However, the number of shares they hold is so small that the total is only 18 percent of all shares. Even those holdings are often controlled by men.

Similarly, only 5 percent of all the people in the country who receive $10,000 a year or more, earned or otherwise, are women. And that includes all the famous rich widows.

The constantly-repeated myth of our economic power seems less testimony to our real power than to the resentment of what little power we do have.

That Children Must Have Full-Time Mothers

American mothers spend more time with their homes and children than those of any other society we know about. In the past, joint families, servants, a prevalent system in which grandparents raised the children, or family field work in the agrarian systems—all these factors contributed more to child care than the labor-saving devices of which we are so proud.

The truth is that most American children seem to be suffering from too much Mother, and too little Father. Part of the program of Women's Liberation is a return of fathers to their children. If laws permit women equal work and pay opportunities, men will then be relieved of their role as sole breadwinner. Fewer ulcers, fewer hours of meaningless work, equal responsibility for his own children: these are a few of the reasons that Women's Liberation is Men's Liberation, too.

As for the psychic health of the children, studies show that the quality of time spent by parents is more important than the quantity. The most damaged children were not those whose mothers worked, but those whose mothers preferred to work but stayed home out of role-playing desire to be a "good mother."

That the Women's Movement Is Not Political, Won't Last, or Is Somehow Not "Serious"

When black people leave their nineteenth-century roles, they are feared. When women dare to leave theirs, they are ridiculed. We understand this, and accept the burden of ridicule. It won't keep us quiet anymore.

Similarly, it shouldn't deceive male observers into thinking this is somehow a joke. We are 51 percent of the population, we are essentially united on these issues across boundaries of class or race or age, and we may well end by changing this society more than the civil rights movement. That is an apt parallel. We, too, have our right wing and left wing, our separatists, gradualists, and Uncle Toms. But we are changing our own consciousness, and that of the country. [Friedrich] Engels noted the relationship of the authoritarian, nuclear family to capitalism: the father as capitalist, the mother as means of production, and the children as labor. He said the family would change as the economic system did, and that seems to have happened, whether we want to admit it or not. Women's bodies will no longer be owned by the state for the production of workers and soldiers: birth control and abortion are facts of everyday life. The new family is an egalitarian family.

Gunnar Myrdal noted thirty years ago the parallel between women and Negroes in this country. Both suffered from such restricting social myths as: smaller brains, passive natures, inability to govern themselves (and certainly not white men), sex objects only, childlike natures, special skills and the like. When evaluating a general statement about women, it might be valuable to substitute "black people" for "women"—just to test the prejudice at work.

And it might be valuable to do this Constitutionally as well. Neither group is going to be content as a cheap labor pool anymore. And neither is going to be content without full Constitutional rights.

Finally, I would like to say one thing about this time in which I am testifying.

I had deep misgivings about discussing this topic when National Guardsmen are occupying our campuses, the country is being turned against itself in a terrible polarization, and America is enlarging an already inhuman and unjustifiable war.* But it seems to me that much of the trouble this country is in has to do with the Masculine Mystique; with the myth that

---

*In 1970, many colleges were centers of the struggle for civil rights for women and minorities and the anti-Vietnam War movement. (Eds.)

masculinity somehow depends on the subjugation of other people. It is a bi-partisan problem: both our past and current Presidents seem to be victims of this myth, and to behave accordingly.

Women are not more moral than men. We are only uncorrupted by power. But we do not want to imitate men, to join this country as it is, and I think our very participation will change it. Perhaps women elected leaders—and there will be many more of them—will not be so likely to dominate black people or yellow people or men; anybody who looks different from us.

After all, we won't have our masculinity to prove.

A Woman's Right to Abortion, 1973

We forthwith acknowledge our awareness of the sensitive and emotional nature of the abortion controversy, of the vigorous opposing views, even among physicians, and of the deep and seemingly absolute convictions that the subject inspires. One's philosophy, one's experiences, one's exposure to the raw edges of human existence, one's religious training, one's attitudes toward life and family and their values, and the moral standards one estab-lishes and seeks to observe, are all likely to influence and to color one's thinking and conclusions about abortion.

In addition, population growth, pollution, poverty, and racial overtones tend to complicate and not to simplify the problem.

Our task, of course, is to resolve the issue by constitutional measure-ment, free of emotion and of predilection. We seek earnestly to do this, and, because we do, we have inquired into, and in this opinion place some em-phasis upon, medical and medical-legal history and what that history reveals about man's attitudes toward the abortion procedure over the centuries. . . .

It perhaps is not generally appreciated that the restrictive criminal abor-tion laws in effect in a majority of States today are of relatively recent vintage. Those laws, generally proscribing abortion or its attempt at any time during pregnancy except when necessary to preserve the pregnant woman's life, are not of ancient or even of common-law origin. Instead, they derive from statutory changes effected, for the most part, in the latter half of the nineteenth century. . . .

The Constitution does not explicitly mention any right of privacy. In a line of decisions, however, the Court has recognized that a right of personal privacy, or a guarantee of certain areas or zones of privacy, does exist under the Constitution. . . .

SOURCE: *Roe* v. *Wade* (1973).

This right of privacy, whether it be founded in the Fourteenth Amendment's concept of personal liberty and restrictions upon state action, as we feel it is, or, as the District Court determined, in the Ninth Amendment's reservation of rights to the people, is broad enough to encompass a woman's decision whether or not to terminate her pregnancy. The detriment that the State would impose upon the pregnant woman by denying this choice altogether is apparent. Specific and direct harm medically diagnosable even in early pregnancy may be involved. Maternity, or additional offspring, may force upon the woman a distressful life and future. Psychological harm may be imminent. Mental and physical health may be taxed by child care. There is also the distress, for all concerned, associated with the unwanted child, and there is the problem of bringing a child into a family already unable, psychologically and otherwise, to care for it. In other cases, as in this one, the additional difficulties and continuing stigma of unwed motherhood may be involved. All these are factors the woman and her responsible physician necessarily will consider in consultation.

On the basis of elements such as these, appellant and some amici argue that the woman's right is absolute and that she is entitled to terminate her pregnancy at whatever time, in whatever way, and for whatever reason she alone chooses. With this we do not agree. Appellant's arguments that Texas either has no valid interest at all in regulating the abortion decision, or no interest strong enough to support any limitation upon the woman's sole determination, is unpersuasive. The Court's decisions recognizing a right of privacy also acknowledge that some state regulation in areas protected by that right is appropriate. [A] State may properly assert important interests in safeguarding health, in maintaining medical standards, and in protecting potential life. At some point in pregnancy, these respective interests become sufficiently compelling to sustain regulation of the factors that govern the abortion decision. The privacy right involved, therefore, cannot be said to be absolute. . . .

We, therefore, conclude that the right of personal privacy includes the abortion decision, but that this right is not unqualified and must be considered against important state interests in regulation. . . .

The appellee and certain amici argue that the fetus is a "person" within the language and meaning of the Fourteenth Amendment. In support of this, they outline at length and in detail the well-known facts of fetal development. If this suggestion of personhood is established, the appellant's case, of course, collapses, for the fetus's right to life is then guaranteed specifically by the Amendment. The appellant conceded as much on reargument. On the other hand, the appellee conceded on reargument that no case could be cited that holds that a fetus is a person within the meaning of the Fourteenth Amendment.

The Constitution does not define "person" in so many words. Section 1 of the Fourteenth Amendment contains three references to "person." The first, in defining "citizens," speaks of "persons born or naturalized in the United States." The word also appears both in the Due Process Clause and in the Equal Protection Clause. "Person" is used in other places in the Constitution. . . . But in nearly all these instances, the use of the word is such that it has application only postnatally. None indicates, with any assurance, that it has any possible prenatal application.

All this, together with our observation, supra, that throughout the major portion of the nineteenth century prevailing legal abortion practices were far freer than they are today, persuades us that the word "person," as used in the Fourteenth Amendment, does not include the unborn. . . .

President George Bush Opposes Abortion, 1989

Good afternoon, ladies and gentlemen. This is George Bush in the Oval Office.* And before you begin your march today, on this first Monday of my Presidency, I wanted to take just a few brief moments to restate my firm support of our cause and to share with you my deep personal concern about our American tragedy of abortion on demand.

We are concerned about abortion because it deals with the lives of two human beings, mother and child. I know there are people of good will who disagree, but after years of sober and serious reflection on the issue, this is what I think. I think the Supreme Court's decision in *Roe* versus *Wade* was wrong and should be overturned. I think America needs a human life amendment. And I think when it comes to abortion there's a better way: the way of adoption, the way of life.

I know that this morning several of your leaders had a meeting in the White House with Vice President Quayle. I know, too, that you and hundreds of thousands with you across the country have raised a voice of moral gravity about abortion, a voice of principle, a voice of faith, a full voice that properly asserts and affirms the basic dignity of human life. I'm confident that more and more Americans every year—every day—are hearing your message and taking it to heart.

And, ladies and gentlemen—and, yes, young people as well—I promise you that the President hears you now and stands with you in a cause that must be won.

God bless you all, and God bless life.

SOURCE: *Weekly Compilation of Presidential Documents*, George Bush, January 23, 1989.

*The President spoke at 12:05 P.M. from the Oval Office at the White House via an electronic communications link with the rally site. Participants had gathered on the Ellipse for a march to the Supreme Court on the occasion of the sixteenth anniversary of the Court's decision of *Roe* v. *Wade*, which legalized abortion.

Chapter 16

The New Immigration

Sometime in the first decade of the twenty-first century, Hispanics will overtake African Americans as the largest minority in the United States. The rapid growth of the Hispanic population is mainly the result of immigration, as Mexicans, Cubans, Dominicans, and Central and South Americans have entered the United States in increasing numbers during the last forty years. They have settled primarily in California, New York, Texas, New Jersey, and Florida but can be found throughout the United States, working and living in places where their labor is needed.

In no American city can the social changes due to immigration be seen more clearly than in Miami. The essay "The Creation of Cuban Miami" tells of the impact of the wave of Cuban immigrants to that city since the triumph of Fidel Castro in 1959. The communist revolution led by Castro prompted hundreds of thousands of Cubans to flee. At first the elite of Cuban society headed for Florida, but they were followed by the middle class and then in 1980 by many working-class Cubans.

Why did so many Cubans decide to settle in Miami, even after initially going to other places in the United States? What has been the impact of these immigrants, both economically and politically, on the character of Miami?

Hispanics in the United States represent the cultures of several nations. Cubans constitute the second most numerous Hispanic group; first are immigrants from Mexico. Indeed, since 1968, Mexicans have been the largest immigrant group coming to America. Their experiences have often been quite different from those of the Cubans. They usually have arrived with less education and fewer skills than the Cubans. Moreover, because of the difficulty in obtaining an immigrant visa, large numbers have crossed the border illegally. The journey and experiences of one such immigrant, Miguel Torres, is described in the first document. Compare the reception given Torres by immigration officials to that accorded Cubans as described in the essay. How do you account for the difference?

Asians also benefited from changes in immigration laws; they represent more than forty percent of all immigrants arriving in the 1980s and 1990s. Asians have grown from less than one percent of the nation's population to four percent. With the exception of Japanese Americans, most Asians currently residing in the United States are foreign born. Some communities, such as the Vietnamese, have appeared for the first time in recent decades; others, such as the Korean and Indian, which numbered only a few thousand in 1950, each currently total over one million. As do Hispanics, Asian immigrants come from a variety of cultures that they are attempting to maintain and pass on to their children. To do this, they have established religious organizations, held language classes, and developed special programs for their youth. In recent years Hindus, Muslims, and Sikhs have run summer camps to instruct children in their parents' culture. The second document describes one such camp in Pennsylvania conducted by Sikhs. How effective do you think efforts such as this will be in the face of competition from American mass culture and the influence of the public schools that most of these youngsters attend?

As important as Hispanic and Asian immigration is, newcomers to the United States in the last four decades have come from all over the globe. More blacks have immigrated from Africa and the West Indies during the last forty years, for example, than came during the entire era of slavery. The last document, a report from the Wall Street Journal, discusses the workplace of an Illinois corporation. The plant employs 1,200 workers who speak no less then twenty languages. A similar story could be related of public schools in cities impacted by immigration. How does the plant manage such a workforce? What are the implications of such diversity for the future of American society?

ESSAY

————— •◆• —————

The Creation of Cuban Miami

Guillermo J. Grenier and Lisandro Perez

Greater Miami has experienced a quarter-century of profound changes that have transformed the city from a midsized tourist haven into a socially and economically complex metropolis. The history of Miami since the early 1960s has been driven by one particular phenomenon: immigration. Dade County's history can be divided into two basic chapters: before the immigrants and after the immigrants. . . .

The very creation of Miami hinged on the actions of northern retirees. In the 1880s, Henry Flagler, millionaire partner of John D. Rockefeller in Standard Oil, moved to Florida for his health and found a new career as a railroad and real estate magnate. A decade later he was persuaded to extend his rail line from Palm Beach to Biscayne Bay by Julia Tuttle, a widow from Cleveland who had relocated to a 600-acre tract on the northern bank of the Miami River where it flows into the bay. It is the core of downtown Miami today.

The railroad provided the necessary transportation link to fuel the local economy. In those early days, Bahamian immigrants provided the local unskilled labor, outnumbering Black Americans who came to Miami primarily from northern Florida and Georgia. When Miami was incorporated in 1896 with a petition bearing 368 signatures, only about 200 residents of the locality were White. The new city's promoters solicited the remainder of the signees among the local Black residents, primarily immigrants from the Bahamas.

The enfranchisement of Blacks did not last long. The city officials elected as a result of the process of incorporation were White. Since the Bahamians considered themselves the social equals of Whites, it was important for the new city leaders to impress upon local Black citizens the appropriate behavior standards of "southern Negroes."

Decades before Disney World, the state's laissez-faire policies gave northern entrepreneurs license to create fantasy real estate and resort ventures. Venetian and Spanish-style housing developments sprang up, while the indigenous mangrove coast was plowed away to make room for luxury hotels and wide beaches. Without the trees to hold the sand, the ocean washed it away. The hotel proprietors arranged for sand to be pumped back onto the beaches.

Miami experienced dizzying growth between 1910 and 1925. Its population grew from 5,000 to 146,000 and the development of Miami Beach began

SOURCE: Silvia Pedraz and Ruben Rumbaut (eds.), *Origins and Destinies: Immigration, Race, and Ethnicity in America*, 360–372. © 1996. Reprinted with permission of Wadsworth Publishing, a division of International Thomson Publishing.

full throttle upon completion of a causeway across the bay. By the early 1920s, the planned residential community of Coral Gables, surrounded by lush, tropical vegetation, was constructed and the doors of the University of Miami were opened.

The boom came to an abrupt end in 1926, when a major hurricane devastated the city, followed by years of financial crisis and the Great Depression. By the mid-1930s, the local economy had begun to recover and a significant influx of Jewish working-class and middle-class migrants from cities in the Northeast led to the proliferation of distinctive small hotels and apartments in what became the Art Deco district of south Miami Beach.

World War II began the next development boom that picked up steam in the 1950s. Many servicemen and women stationed in south Florida during the war decided to stay. Refugees from northern winters opted for Florida on an ever-larger scale, and the popularization of air travel brought Miami vacations within reach of growing numbers of Americans across the country. Most of the large hotels of Miami Beach (including the Fontainebleau, opened with great fanfare in 1954) date from this era. Between 1940 and 1950 the population of metropolitan Miami (Dade County) nearly doubled, rising from 268,000 to 505,000; by the 1960s it had reached nearly 1 million.

As Miami acquired the dimensions of a large metropolis, its economy began to diversify, and it took on an increasingly important role as a port city in the commerce between the United States, the Caribbean, and Latin America. Miami's image as a tropical paradise for tourists had faded by the 1960s. Eventually, tourists to Florida preferred Walt Disney World, the fantasy creation near Orlando in Central Florida. Meanwhile, those seeking sun and sea vacations increasingly found them further south in the Bahamas, Jamaica, Puerto Rico, and Yucatán.

Even before the massive arrival of Cubans in the early 1960s, the influx of northern "Anglos" (as non-Hispanic Whites are called in Miami) had slowed to a trickle, becoming negative after 1970. The next wave of Miami's development would be spurred by migration from Latin America, especially from Cuba.

Before the 1960s, Miami's population consisted largely of Black and White southern migrants and their descendants, transplanted northerners (including many Jews), and Bahamian and other Caribbean Blacks and their descendants. . . . In the past twenty-five years, however, a very large number of Latin Americans and a substantial Haitian population added to the mix with dramatic impact.

Cubans fleeing Castro's Cuba, Miami's principal immigrant group, began arriving in significant numbers in the early 1960s, following the 1959 Cuban Revolution and the failure in 1961 of the Bay of Pigs invasion. The U.S. government encouraged and aided the flow. . . . While significant numbers of Cubans settled in New York and New Jersey, Miami was the preferred destination of the vast majority, making Cubans Miami's most visible minority. Their numbers were considerably increased by the Mariel boatlift of 1980, which brought 125,000 Cubans to the United States, the majority of whom settled in Miami. In 1990, there were 953,400 persons of Hispanic origin or descent In Dade County, representing slightly more than 49 percent of the entire metropolitan population. Cubans accounted for about 59 percent of Miami's Hispanics. . . .

Southern Florida now has the highest proportion of foreign-born residents of any U.S. city. The two largest incorporated areas within Greater Miami occupy, nationally, the first and second positions in the percentage of their residents who were born in a foreign country. Hialeah, a working-class suburb of Miami that has received large numbers of Cubans since the 1960s, is by far the most populated area by immigrants in the entire nation: 70.4 percent of its population was reported in 1990 to be foreign-born. The city of Miami, second in the nation, had a proportion of 59.7 percent foreign-born.

In contrast to the growth of the foreign-born and Latin population, the White non-Hispanic population has been decreasing, in relative terms, since 1960, and in absolute terms since 1970. From a peak in the 1950s of 85 percent, it is expected to decline by the year 2000 to around 30 percent of the total, barely more than the figure for Blacks. The decline is evident throughout the metropolitan area, including the suburbs and Miami's elite residential areas.

Miami has always been a service-centered economy, but after the arrival of the Cubans, the focus of those services shifted from tourism to Latin America. Beginning in the 1960s, Miami came to displace New Orleans as the country's principal trade entrepôt with that region. By 1980, 100 multinational corporations had their Latin American headquarters in Miami and Miami stood second only to New York as an international banking center. By the mid-1980s, Miami International Airport was the ninth-busiest airport in the world in passengers and the sixth largest in air cargo tonnage. About 160,000 workers, one-fifth of its labor force, were directly or indirectly employed in airport and aviation activities. By the late 1980s, Miami's industrial profile was similar to other newer American cities in which the economy was led by services, wholesale trade, finance, insurance, and real estate.

The existence of the Cuban enclave played a pivotal role in Miami's economic transformation. Cubans frequently headed the import and export companies, the banks that financed the transactions, and the transportation and service companies that moved goods and services. Over 25,000 Hispanic businesses exist in Dade County, the vast majority of which are small enterprises that have been described as the true engines of Miami's economic growth. . . . But many of the most powerful economic corporations are also Latin-owned and operated. While Miami holds only 5 percent of

the U.S. Hispanic population, it has close to half of the forty largest His-
panic-owned industrial and commercial firms in the country. By the mid to
late 1980s, 40 percent of Miami's banks were owned by Latins..., as were
numerous Latin insurance companies, shipping firms, and innumerable import and export establishments. Some of the most important developers are
Latins, one of which became the first Latin to head the Greater Miami
Chamber of Commerce.

The city's emergence as the "capital of the Caribbean" has reinforced
these trends in immigration. Miami now is the most desired migration point
of many Latins, especially the elite and middle classes of the Caribbean
and Central America. In the late 1980s, . . . a broader, working-class flow
emerged, first from Nicaragua, then from other Central American nations as
well as Colombia, the Dominican Republic, and Puerto Rico. Meanwhile,
the frustration of democracy in Haiti increased migration pressures there,
despite U.S. policies designed to repress the Haitian flow.

This transformation of Miami's demographic profile got under way precisely when Black Americans were beginning to achieve the civil rights that
had been denied them since the city's founding at the end of the last century. The new White immigrants, the Cubans, soon received the benefits of
being a minority. While Blacks have experienced some progress, the White
Cuban immigrants leaped over Blacks, quickly garnering the political and
economic gains that still elude Black Americans. Meanwhile, the response
by many Anglos has been to abandon the city. "White flight" decreased the
number of non-Latin Whites in Dade County by 24 percent between 1980
and 1990.

Much of this decline is attributable to the decrease in the elderly population, once so characteristic of the greater Miami area. In 1980 the elderly
comprised 52 percent of the population of Miami Beach, the highest proportion for any city of comparable size in the United States. Although Miami
Beach had been founded by wealthy White Anglo-Saxons, with anti-Semitic
restrictions in housing, hotels, and private clubs that persisted for several
decades, the retirement wave made it the most Jewish of American cities as
well. By 1950, the population of Miami Beach was half Jewish; by 1970, the
proportion had reached 80 percent.

All this began to change in the 1970s, in the context of a stagnant tourist
economy and the diversion of the retirement flow to other parts of Florida.
By 1980, the Jewish component of the population had declined to 66 percent, falling even more steeply thereafter to reach 40 percent in 1990. The
decline of the elderly component of the population was just as rapid, dropping to 30 percent in 1990. . . .

. . . The rise of Cuban Miami as the largest concentration of Cubans in
the United States—and the third largest Hispanic community in this country, after New York and Los Angeles—effectively starts in 1959 with the exodus from the island that resulted from the social transformations effected

by the Cuban Revolution. Prior to that time, Miami, largely because of its youth and weak economic structure, was never the principal destination of Cuban immigrants to the United States. Sizable Cuban communities thrived in New York, Key West, New Orleans, and Ybor City, on the outskirts of Tampa, in the nineteenth century. New York was still the premier destination for migrants from the island in the period between World War II and the rise of Fidel Castro's government.

This pattern of migration started changing with the creation of rail and highway links between Miami and Key West and their extensions to Havana by way of regular ferry service. Air service between Miami, Key West, and Havana dates back to the 1920s and represents a pioneering effort in the history of passenger aviation. Those transportation links served to make Miami the principal staging area for the increasingly close relationship developing between Cuba and the Florida peninsula. In the year 1948, for example, Cuba led all countries in the world in the volume of passengers exchanged with the United States. . . .

While Miami did not have the employment opportunities Cuban immigrants required during the first half of the twentieth century, it did receive those seeking refuge from the shifting fortunes of the island's turbulent political history. Two deposed Cuban Presidents, Gerardo Machado (in 1933) and Carlos Prío Socarrás (in 1952), made their homes in Miami. A prominent Cuban politician of the 1940s built Miami's baseball stadium. Even Fidel Castro spent time in Miami in the 1950s.

As leader of the 1959 Revolution, Castro initiated a process of change that, in its rapidity and pervasiveness, alienated large sectors of the Cuban population . . . and contributed to the creation of Cuban Miami. . . .

The concentration of Cubans in Miami, starting in the mid-1970s, was first preceded by their intentional dispersion throughout the United States. The Cuban Refugee Program was established in February 1961 as a federal effort to provide assistance in handling the large influx of people coming from Cuba. One of its purposes was to ease the demographic and economic pressures that the influx was exerting on south Florida. A resettlement program was established through which families arriving from Cuba were given assistance if they immediately relocated away from Miami. According to a Cuban Refuge Program Fact Sheet . . . , 300,232 persons were resettled away from Miami between February 1961 and August 1978, approximately 64 percent of all Cubans then arriving in the United States. The bulk of the resettled Cubans went to New York, New Jersey, California, and Illinois. In 1965, 42 percent of the Cuban population in the United States lived in Dade County; in 1970, 40 percent. Resettlement reached its peak in the late 1960s. Thus, contrary to the experience of most immigrant groups for whom concentration in a city or region formed part of the process of adjustment to the United States, Cubans underwent a process of intentional dispersion early in their history of immigration.

In the mid-1970s, however, a process of concentration in Miami was well under way as many resettled Cubans decided to make their home in southern Florida. By 1980, the U.S. census found about 52 percent of all U.S. Cubans living in Greater Miami. The concentration of Cubans in south Florida increased during the 1980s as the majority of the *Marielitos* settled in Miami, where they could find employment in a familiar cultural environment. By the 1990 census, 57 percent of all U.S. Cubans lived in Dade County. The process of concentration in Miami is likely to continue in the 1990s due to the aging of the large middle-aged cohort that left Cuba during the early 1960s and were resettled away from Miami.

In the mid-1990s, the "open arms" U.S. policy toward Cuban migrants shifted dramatically. The massive exodus of rafters in the summer of 1994, initiated by the Cuban government's decision not to impede their departure, prompted the United States to intercept vessels on the high seas and send their occupants to detention camps outside the United States. The attorney general vowed that the detained Cubans would never enter this country. In May 1995, in the interest of ending the indefinite detention of more than 20,000 Cubans at the Guantánamo Naval Base, the United States announced that the detainees would be processed for admission to the United States. However, recognizing the prevailing anti-immigration sentiment, the move was balanced with an unprecedented announcement: future rafters would be intercepted and returned directly to Cuba, under the terms of an agreement reached with the Cuban government. The only way Cubans will be allowed to enter the United States from Cuba will be through the normal visa application process conducted by the U.S. Interest Section in Havana. At least 20,000 people will presumably be admitted every year through that process.

Cuban migration to the United States will continue, but the exile era has officially ended. Cubans are no longer recognized as refugees by the U.S. government. The newly established policy for their admission into this country does not differ in any essential way from the policy toward other nationalities: one enters only through the regular visa process; those attempting to enter without authorization will be returned. In effect, there has been, for the first time, a normalization of one aspect of U.S.–Cuba relations.

. . . Today persons of Cuban origin represent Miami's largest ethnic group. Cubans account for 56 percent of Greater Miami's foreign-born population and a majority of all Hispanics in the area. About 29 percent of Dade County's 1990 population was of Cuban birth or descent.

The demographic importance of the Cuban presence in Miami is evident in a myriad of ways. The "Cubanness" of the area is manifested not only in demonstrable terms, such as economic activities and cultural events, but also in its more intangible "ambience." Rieff, a New Yorker who has written on Miami, noted that Cubans have largely taken control of the "atmosphere" of the city. . . .

More than thirty years after the start of the exodus, today Cubans have a sense of "rootedness" in Miami. Miami is the capital and mecca of Cubans in the United States. As Rieff . . . expressed it, "Cubans are probably the only people who really do feel comfortable in Dade County these days. . . . Miami is their town now." Nearly 70 percent of the Hispanic population of Greater Miami, Cubans can be found throughout most of the metropolitan area. Generally the heaviest concentrations of Hispanics within the county are found along a belt running west from downtown (which is located east of Biscayne Bay) all the way to the western edges of the metropolitan area.

Since the 1960s the settlement of Cubans along this belt has proceeded from east to west, emanating largely from the area known as "Little Havana," which is located within the city of Miami, some twelve to fifteen city blocks directly west of downtown and stretching west along Calle Ocho for about fifteen city blocks.

Middle-income Cubans, and especially professionals, are now hard to find in Little Havana. As with so many other immigrant groups, their upward mobility has taken them to more suburban areas. The current residents of Little Havana are likely to be blue-collar and service workers, the elderly, the poor, and recent immigrants, including other Latin American immigrants. . . .

A strong and diversified entrepreneurial activity is responsible for the enclave's most important overall feature: institutional completeness. Cubans in Miami can, if they wish, literally live out their lives within the ethnic community. The wide range of sales and services, including professional services, available within the community makes that possible.

Three factors have been identified as promoting Cubans' economic and political activity in Miami: (1) structural factors arising from the human capital Cubans brought with them and their geographical concentration in Miami . . . , (2) the role of the U.S. government in providing aid to the arriving Cuban refugees . . . ; and (3) the creation of a collective Cuban-American political identity arising from the interplay of the U.S. state and Cuban exile counterrevolutionary organizations.

The favorable reception by the U.S. government entailed a "direct line" for Cuban exile leaders to the centers of political power in Washington. Unlike other immigrant and ethnic minorities who struggled painfully for years or even generations to gain access to the corridors of power, Cuban leaders accessed it almost from the start. This window of opportunity greatly boosted the Cubans in the 1960s and the Miami economy in general. Waves of Cuban immigrants stimulated demand and received substantial subsidies from the federal government. With a high rate of labor force participation, especially among women, the Cubans also contributed significantly to productivity growth. The 1973 to 1974 recession even had an indirect benefit for Cubans. Construction, one of the growth sectors during the boom, almost completely collapsed, spurring many American residents to flee Dade County. In the subsequent recovery of the !ate 1970s a de facto segmentation of the industry emerged, with Latins becoming the leaders in home construction and Anglos maintaining dominance in large-scale commercial construction. This division reflected an even more important development within the community, the emergence of the Cuban enclave. . . .

. . . During the 1980s Cubans in Miami were able to establish pivotal local power, exercised through an increasing number of elected officials and organizations such as the Cuban American National Foundation, the Latin Builders Association, the Hispanic Builders Association, and the Latin Chamber of Commerce. By the late 1980s, the City of Miami, Hialeah, Sweetwater, West Miami, and Hialeah Gardens all had Cuban-born mayors. The city manager and the county manager were Cubans. Cubans controlled the City Commission and constituted more than a third of the county delegation to the state legislature. After Claude Pepper died, a Cuban woman, Ileana Ros-Lehtinen, won his U.S. House of Representatives seat. Most recently, Lincoln Díaz-Balart, a Cuban-born politician elected to the state legislature in the mid-1980s, joined Ros-Lehtinen as the second Cuban American from Miami in Congress. Nowhere else in America, nor even in American history, have first-generation immigrants so quickly and so thoroughly appropriated political power.

Perhaps for this reason, no aspect of Cuban Miami attracts more national and international attention than its politics. Even after more than thirty years, Miami remains a community of exiles, largely preoccupied with the political status of the homeland. At the same time, however, Miami's Cubans demonstrated a strong participation in the U.S. political system at the local and state levels.

. . . Although the enclave favors the retention of the culture of the homeland, delaying the process of acculturation, it is unlikely that Cubans in the United States will be an exception to the usual intergenerational shift toward greater acculturation and assimilation. English is the principal language among Cubans who have lived all or most of their lives in the United States. Sharp intergenerational differences exist among Cubans in Miami, with alienation between parents and children usually found in Cuban families with interactional problems. . . . An important focus of these intergenerational tensions are the conflicting value orientations with respect to dependence and independence. . . . Cuban culture foments the continued dependence of children on their parents, even in the teenage years and beyond. Cuban children, however, are more likely to have internalized the norms of independence commonly found in U.S. society. One adaptation that reduces intergenerational tension is "biculturality," by which each generation adjusts to the other generation's cultural preferences: "parents learn how to remain loyal to their ethnic background while becoming skilled in interacting with their youngsters' Americanized values and behaviors, and vice versa." . . .

DOCUMENTS

An Undocumented Mexican Immigrant: Miguel Torres, 1977

Miguel Torres is a slight, shy youth of twenty with a pale skin and El Greco features. He works in a mushroom plant in California. He has entered the United States illegally four times in the past year, and he has been caught three times. He told his story through a trusted interpreter.

I was born in a small town in the state of Michoacán in Mexico. When I was fifteen, I went to Mexico City with my grandmother and my mother. I worked in a parking lot, a big car lot. People would come in and they'd say, "Well, park my car." and I'd give them a ticket and I'd park the car and I'd be there, you know, watching the cars. I got paid in tips.

But I wanted to come to the United States to work and to earn more money. My uncle was here, and I thought if I could come to him, I could live with him and work and he would help me.

It's not possible to get papers to come over now. So when I decided to come, I went to Tijuana in Mexico. There's a person there that will get in contact with you. They call him the Coyote. He walks around town, and if he sees someone wandering around alone, he says, "Hello, do you have relatives in the United States?" And if you say yes, he says, "Do you want to visit them?" And if you say yes, he says he can arrange it through a friend. It costs $250 or $300.

The Coyote rounded up me and five other guys, and then he got in contact with a guide to take us across the border. We had to go through the hills and the desert, and we had to swim through a river. I was a little scared. Then we come to a highway and a man was there with a van, pretending to fix his motor. Our guide said hello, and the man jumped into the car and we ran and jumped in, too. He began to drive down the highway fast and we knew we were safe in the United States. He took us to San Isidro that night, and the next day he took us all the way here to Watsonville. I had to pay

SOURCE: Joan Morrison and Charlotte Fox Zabusky. *American Mosaic: The Immigrant Experience in the Words of Those Who Lived It,* 347–49. Copyright © 1980 by Joan Morrison and Charlotte Fox Zabusky. Currently available in paperback from the University of Pittsburgh Press.

him $250 and then, after I'd been here a month, he came back and I had to give him $50 more. He said I owed him that.

I was here for two months before I started working, and then my uncle got me a job, first in the celery fields picking celery, washing it, packing it, and later picking prunes. Then, all of a sudden, one day the Immigration showed up, and I ran and I hid in a river that was next to the orchard. The man saw me and he questioned me, and he saw I didn't have any papers. So they put me in a van and took me to Salinas, and there was some more illegals there and they put us in buses and took us all the way to Mexicali near the border. We were under guard; the driver and another one that sleeps while one drives. The seats are like hard boards. We'd get up from one side and rub, you know, that side a little bit and then sit on the other side for a while and then rub that side because it's so hard. It was a long trip.

When we arrived in Mexicali, they let us go. We caught a bus to Tijuana, and then at Tijuana, that night, we found the Coyote again and we paid him and we came back the next day. I had to pay $250 again, but this time he knew me and he let me pay $30 then and $30 each week. Because he knew me, you know. He trusted me.

We came through the mountains that time. We had to walk through a train tunnel. It all lasted maybe about three hours, through the tunnel. It was short; for me it was short. We're used to walking, you know. Over in Mexico we have to walk like ten miles to go to work or to go home or to go to school, so we're used to walking. To me it was a short distance to walk for three hours. And after we got out of the tunnel, we got into a car; and from there, from the tunnel, we came all the way into Los Angeles. That was the second time. We didn't see any border patrol either time.

The second time I was here for three months. My uncle managed to get me a job in the mushroom plant. I was working there when the Immigration came. There's this place where they blow air between the walls to make it cool and I hid there. And I was watching. The Immigration was looking around the plant everywhere. There was another illegal there, and he just kept on picking the mushrooms. He'd only been back a couple of days himself. The Immigration walked over there, and that kid turned around and looked at the Immigration and said, "What's the matter? What happened?" And the Immigration looked at him and said, "Oh, nothing," and the kid kept right on picking mushrooms. Yet he was an illegal! He knew how to act, play it cool. If you just sit tight they don't know you're illegal.

Well, the Immigration looked between the walls then and he caught me again. That was the second time. They put handcuffs on me with another guy and we were handcuffed together all the way from California to Mexicali.

Altogether I've been caught three times this year and made the trip over here four times. It's cost me one thousand dollars but it's still better than what I was making in Mexico City.

It's the money. When you come back here you get more money here than you do over there. Right now, the most that I'd be getting in Mexico would be from 25 to 30 pesos a day, which is maybe $2.00, $2.50. And here, with overtime, sometimes I make $150 a week. Things are expensive here, but it's expensive over there, too. And I like the way people live here. All the—what do you call it—all the facilities that you have here, all the things you can get and everything.

The boss at the mushroom factory doesn't ask for papers. He doesn't say anything about it. The last time, he hired me back as soon as I got back here, without any questions.

I learned to hide my money when the Immigration catch me. You know, if you have a lot on you, they take you fifteen or twenty miles from the border in Mexico. But if you have just two dollars or so, they let you go right in Tijuana. Then it's easier to come back. You can just walk right down the street and find the Coyote or someone like him. A man I know was hitch-hiking along the road near San Diego and someone picked him up and it was the Immigration man who had just brought him back to Mexico! The Immigration laughed and said, "You got back faster than I did." Of course, he took him back to Mexico again then. But that man is back in Watsonville now, working in the brussels sprouts. It takes a longer time for the Immigration to catch us than it does for us to come back. [*Laughs.*]

I'd like to be able to stay here, to live here and work; but the only way now is to find someone that'll say, "Well, I'll marry you, I'll fix your papers for you." There's a lot of them who do that. I'd be willing to if I could find someone that would do it for me. You pay them, you know. You don't sleep together or even live in the same house, but they marry you. A long time ago you could fix up papers for your nephew or brother, a friend, a cousin. It was real easy then. But now it has to be close relations: mother, father, wife, son, or daughter. My uncle can't do it for me. The only way I could do it would be if I could marry an American citizen.

I'd like to learn English because it would be easier for me. There is a night school here, but I don't like to go because after work I like to go out and mess around and goof off. [*Laughs.*] Maybe I'll go later. If I could just learn a tiny bit of English, you know, I could turn around and tell the Immigration, "What's the matter with you? What do you want?" and I wouldn't be recognized as an illegal.

A Summer Camp for Young Sikhs, 1998

CHAMBERSBURG, Pa., July 11—For 70 years, daughters of the wealthy and well connected spent their summers here riding horses and playing tennis at an exclusive hilltop spread called Camp Robin Hood.

But this summer, echoing from the hilltop comes the throb of tabla drums. From the dining hall at dinner wafts the aroma of chicken curry. And bunking in the cabins are the children of a new breed of American elite, relative newcomers to this continent, whose sons wear turbans and whose daughters, on special occasions, don saris and scarves.

Camp Robin Hood is now a summer camp for Sikhs, descendants of a religious tradition born 500 years ago in the Punjab region of northern India. The parents of most of these campers are educated Punjabis who immigrated to the United States within the last 30 years. They thrived in business or in professions like medicine and engineering, and settled down where their careers led them, sometimes finding themselves the only Sikhs for miles around.

Soon they realized that their children could chant rap songs but not Sikh scriptures, could name the Ten Commandments but not the ten Sikh gurus. Concerned that the strong pull to assimilate is stealing their children's Sikh identity, Sikh parents around the country are creating summer camps like this one here in southern Pennsylvania.

"We have kids whose families have become so integrated that some of these kids have never had a Sikh friend before coming to camp," said Mandeep Singh Dhillon, 28, one of the camp's founders, who grew up in the small Sikh community in Raleigh, N.C., and whose father is a camp investor and director. "They're so isolated that they don't know any other Sikh families other than their relatives. These kids are American now. They're Americans who follow Sikhism. So we want to give them that exposure so they can understand their religion and be proud of their heritage."

Sikhs are not the only predominantly immigrant religious group organizing summer camps in an effort to stave off total assimilation. There are Hindu summer camps in states including New Hampshire and New York, Muslim camps in California, Jain camps in Texas. They rent Boy Scout centers or local fairgrounds, or, in the case of one Hindu group, buy a camp in the Poconos where Jewish parents once sent their children to learn about Judaism. . . .

The 60-acre spread of Camp Robin Hood was bought by five Sikh investors, all doctors, six years ago for about $500,000. They renamed it Lohgarh Retreat, for the first Sikh fort in the Punjab from which Sikhs defended themselves against attacking Mughals in the 1600s. Today, says the

SOURCE: *The New York Times*, July 18, 1998. Copyright © 1998 by *The New York Times*. Reprinted by permission.

camp's Web site, "the battle here and now is against the armies of ignorance and hatred, and the lure of assimilation."

The camp day is a mix of morning prayer, lessons in Sikh spiritual practice and chanting, sports, and peer group discussions. Boys get turban-tying lessons. Everyone learns traditional Punjabi dance steps. On Thursdays, after a lecture on Sikh history, all 60 campers join in an enormous pillow fight. The other day they rode the roller coasters at Hershey Park, soaking their turbans and scarves on the water rides. Some campers said it was their first time out "in public" with a large group of Sikhs. . . .

"A lot of the guys had questions about our identity," Inder Paul Singh, who is 18 and just completed his sophomore year at William and Mary, said later, "about whether we want to be Sikhs, why we have to keep our hair and tie turbans, because we are so different from everybody else."

For nearly 300 years, Sikhs have observed the mandate of their tenth guru that the faithful wear five symbols: uncut hair, a comb, a steel wrist bangle, a sword, and short breeches under their pants.

Such traditions are hard to keep in a junior high school in Winchester, Va., for example, the hometown of Inder Paul Singh (who is not related to Mandeep Singh Dhillon; in the Sikh religion, many men adopt the name Singh, meaning Lion, just as women adopt the name Kaur, or Princess). Paul said that in his early teens he was often teased about his long hair, which he wore in a bun on top of his head covered with a knotted scarf. Other boys said that they had been called "raghead," or that their turbans had been pulled off.

But many of the boys at camp have never worn turbans and have visited their share of barbers, just as their fathers may have. So, much of the discussion here, among boys and girls alike, focuses on the decision to cut or not to cut. And the pressure from parents can work in either direction.

Navraj Rai, 14, said his mother had sent him to Sikh camp because at home, in Garland, Tex., he had converted to Christianity in a Pentecostal church.

"The social status I have there is ultimate," Navraj said of the church, "Everybody knew I was a Sikh, and they were real interested in me." Yet he agreed to come to camp because, he said, he is still exploring and knows that he can never be a Sikh, and please his mother, unless he better understands Sikhism.

In contrast, Mandeep Singh Mundi, 17, said his parents, in Johnson City, Tenn., were successful business people who had forbidden him to grow his hair or wear a turban, out of fear that he would be harassed. Mandeep lied and told his mother he would be attending college registration, then drove up for a weekend at the Lohgarh Retreat. When he leaves home for college this fall, he said, he will begin growing out his hair.

"This camp has really changed my life," Mandeep said. "It turned me from the person my parents wanted me to be, this assimilated American guy, into someone who's proud of their culture."

At the end of the two-week camp, Navraj returned home to Texas to spend the rest of the summer touring with his Pentecostal choir.

For Inder Paul Singh, the evening discussions with others at camp were the first in which he had heard a rationale for Sikh customs that made sense to him. He heard Mandeep Singh Dhillon explain that having to tie a turban every morning reminded one of his identity as a Sikh, which means "disciple." And a disciple, Mr. Dhillon told the boys, is always learning, which is the essence of Sikhism.

"I kind of liked that," Paul said, adding that it had caused him to change his mind and decide not to cut his hair.

Next year, he thinks, he may return to camp—as a counselor.

Multiculturalism in the Workplace, 1998

MORTON GROVE, Ill.—Draped from the ceiling in 3Com Corp.'s sprawling modem factory in this Chicago suburb is a sign of the times: 65 different national flags, each representing the origin of at least one person who has worked here since it opened 2½ years ago.

The plant employs 1,200 people, the vast majority immigrants. They speak more than 20 languages, including Tagalog, Gujarati and Chinese. English, of varying degrees, ties them together.

"If there's a problem, I call over somebody who speaks the person's language to help," says Thai Chung, a 33-year-old refugee from Vietnam who manages Line 12, one of a dozen assembly lines.

That doesn't always work. A few days ago, Mr. Chung, a wiry man who spends much of his day striding up and down his line, wanted a janitor to clean up some grease. He spoke to him in English but obviously wasn't understood even after repeating himself slowly. He thought the man might be Polish; so he enlisted Vesna Stevanovic, one of the assemblers on his line. But she's from Serbia and couldn't speak to him, either. "I'm not even sure he's Polish," says Ms. Stevanovic, gazing over the frames of pink eyeglasses. "I don't know what he is."

The janitor eventually got the message. Nobody knows how. Stella Foy, a gruff 57-year-old Chicago native who also works on the line, says simply: "Around here, you point a lot."

SOURCE: *Wall Street Journal*, March 30, 1998. Reprinted by permission of *The Wall Street Journal*, © 1998 Dow Jones & Company, Inc. All rights reserved worldwide.

Many factories, as they hire more immigrants, are being plunged into an industrial Tower of Babel. Earlier waves of immigrants tended to have more in common, such as the East Europeans who flocked to the steel mills a century ago. Now factories, running faster and using increasingly complex equipment, might seem to need such commonality among their workers more than ever.

. . . Churning out modems around the clock, 3Com's workers could hardly be more diverse. Urbane Asians with multiple college degrees work alongside people only recently arrived from Central American villages. Serbs work with Bosnian Muslims, as well as Iraqis, Peruvians and South Africans. Managers think at least a third of their workers wouldn't mind if asked to work Christmas—as they were two years ago—because they don't celebrate it.

Overcoming language barriers is just one of the challenges. Some immigrants come from countries where you seldom say "please," and certainly not to someone you consider your social inferior. That aloofness can cause hurt feelings. The factory also has its own hierarchy, based largely on language ability and background. Those who speak the best English and are the best educated are the most upwardly mobile.

Saji Korah is one of them. "I have a bachelor's degree in economics from India and an associate's degree in computer programming," the 34-year-old says in crisp English. Yet his job today, riveting brackets onto circuit boards, could be done by someone far less educated.

It's monotonous, and he makes it clear he has no intention of doing such work for long. He is going to school part time for yet-another degree, in computer-information systems. He dreams of becoming one of the plant's roving technicians.

Asked whether he has problems communicating with less-well-spoken colleagues, he says, "Sometimes, I have trouble following their pronunciations." Standing nearby, Suresh Patel says he has trouble, too, but mainly in understanding American-born workers. "Sometimes, they talk too fast," he explains. . . .

The factory doesn't have much choice but to hire a lot of immigrants. Many native-born Americans wouldn't consider taking the often-tedious entry-level jobs. But for John Phan, a 35-year-old who came from Vietnam a decade ago speaking little English, operating a machine on Line 12 is a step up. He makes $10.05 an hour, compared with $7.50 an hour he previously earned at a plastics factory.

Mr. Phan's English is heavily accented, and he admits he sometimes can't understand co-workers. But that hardly matters; he seldom has to talk. He knows when a machine is running low on components, for instance, because a white light flashes on a pole jutting up from the top of it. One machine even talks to him: "Be careful, the feeder section may move," coos a soothing female voice, just before a big metal rack known as a feeder automatically shifts out into the corridor. "These machines are very smart," he says.

Those at the plant with good English and ambitious to advance can choose from an array of training courses beyond the basics needed for their immediate jobs. The courses cover everything from leadership skills to how to run a chip shooter. Workers can even take a course on drawing up an instructional sheet similar to those hanging over their workstations; they practice by writing one for making a peanut-butter-and-jelly sandwich. Training also relies heavily on lots of illustrations and on-the-job practice.

Hattie Curry is one of the few Americans on Line 12. A native of North Carolina, she started working for the company seven years ago, before this plant opened; the company, acquired by 3Com last year, was then known as U.S. Robotics.

Ms. Curry notes the increase in immigrants at 3Com and says working with them hasn't always been easy for her. "Before I worked here," she says, "I hadn't been around a lot of foreign people; I didn't understand their ways." As a newcomer, she thought some with more skills were reluctant to train her and tried to block her advancement. "Now, I know that's just their way," she says. "They don't mean to be mean." But she has changed her own style: "I handle them more firmly now; I've become stronger."

Yet despite all the blending of people on the factory floor, it stops in the lunchroom. From a corner table, three Indian women look over the rest of the big dining area. A table near the checkout is occupied almost entirely by African-American women. The table next to them, by Indian men. And so it goes around the room. "We share our food," says Jashwanti Bodhanwala, a mother of two who has been in the U.S. for 23 years, as if that entirely explains the apartheid-style dining.

One thing the lunch groups do is to facilitate gossip. The room is one of the few places, besides the outdoor smoking areas, where people relax and swap rumors.

Ms. Bodhanwala tugs off a piece of moist, spicy Indian flatbread, and spoons onto it a lump of homemade mango chutney from a plastic container. Asmabahen Patel, sitting opposite her, offers some mustard pickles. "Of course, if you weren't here," says Ms. Patel, gazing at a reporter, "we'd be speaking Gujarati."

PART II

Suggestions for Further Reading

Some of the changes in American society during the 1920s are covered in Lois Banner, *The American Beauty: A Social History Through Two Centuries of the American Idea, Ideal, and Image of the Beautiful Woman* (1983), and William Leuchtenburg, *Perils of Prosperity, 1914–1932* (1958). A good study on Prohibition is Andrew Sinclair, *Era of Excess: A Social History of the Prohibition Movement* (1964). On the Ku Klux Klan, see Kenneth Jackson, *The Ku Klux Klan in the Cities, 1915–1930* (1967), and David Chalmers, *Hooded Americanism: The First Century of the Ku Klux Klan* (1965). Information about the Klan and bigotry can also be found in David Bennett, *The Party of Fear: From Nativist Movements to the New Right in American History* (1988). Paula Fass, *The Damned and the Beautiful: American Youth in the 1920s* (1977), is valuable, as is J. Stanley Lemons, *The Woman Citizen: Social Feminism in the 1920s* (1973). A classic study of that era is Helen Merrill Lynd and Robert S. Lynd, *Middletown: A Study of Contemporary American Culture* (1929). On gay and lesbian history, see George Chauncey, *Gay New York: Gender, Urban Culture, and the Making of the Gay Male World, 1890–1940* (1994), and Lillian Faderman, *Odd Girls and Twilight Lovers: A History of Lesbian Life in Twentieth-Century America* (1991).

On the Great Depression, a good introduction is Robert S. McElvaine, *The Great Depression: America, 1929–1941* (1984). Also of use are Caroline Bird, *The Invisible Scar: The Great Depression and What It Did to American Life, From Then Until Now* (1966); Donald Worster, *Dust Bowl: The South Plains in the 1930s* (1979); and William Leuchtenburg, *Franklin Roosevelt and the New Deal* (1963). For women during the 1930s, see Susan Wave, *Holding Their Own: American Women in the 1930s* (1982). On blacks, see Nancy Weiss, *Farewell to the Party of Lincoln: Black Politics in the Age of FDR* (1983). A good picture of life in one American community can be found in Robert Lynd and Helen Lynd, *Middletown in Transition: A Study in Cultural Conflict* (1937). Information on workers during the Great Depression and after can be found in Robert H. Zieger, *American Workers, American Unions, 1920–1985* (1986). Another good book on the Great Depression is James Goodman, *Stories of Scottsboro: The Rape Case That Shocked 1930s America and Revived the Struggle for Equality* (1994). Especially good are Lizabeth Cohen, *Making a New Deal: Industrial Workers in Chicago, 1919–1939* (1990), and Neil Foley, *The White Scourge: Mexicans, Blacks and Poor Whites in Texas Cotton Culture* (1997).

America during World War II has received increasing attention. For introductions see William O'Neill, *A Democracy at War* (1993), and Peter Lingeman, *Don't You Know There Is a War On?* (1970). Another general work is Richard Polenberg, *War and Society* (1972). On Japanese Americans, see Peter Irons, *Justice at War* (1983), and Roger Daniels, *Concentration Camps,*

U.S.A. (1970). On women during the war, see D'Ann Campbell, *Women at War with America: Private Lives in a Patriotic Cause* (1984); Maureen Honey, *Creating Rosie the Riveter: Class, Gender and Propaganda During World War II* (1984); Leisa D. Meyer, *Creating GI Jane: Sexuality and Power in the Women's Army Corps During World War II* (1996); and Ruth Milkman, *Gender at Work: The Dynamics of Job Segregation During World War II* (1987). The experience of gay men and women is told by Allan Berube, *Coming Out Under Fire: The History of Gay Men and Women in World War II* (1990), while the battle experience is covered in Gerald F. Linderman, *The World Within the War: America's Combat Experience in World War II* (1997). A revisionist account of the war is Michael C. Adams, *The Best War Ever: America and World War II* (1994).

For changes during the war and after, see Kenneth Jackson, *Crabgrass Frontier: The Suburbanization of the United States* (1985), and Gavin Wright, *Old South, New South: Revolutions in the Southern Economy Since the Civil War* (1986). On suburbs, see Herbert J. Gans, *Levittowners: Ways of Life and Politics in a New Suburban Community* (1982); Gwendolyn Wright, *Building the Dream: A Social History of Housing in America* (1981); and William Dobriner, *Class in Suburbia* (1963). Elaine May, *Homeward Bound: American Families in the Cold War* (1988), attempts to trace the impact of the Cold War on families. Also useful are Arlene Skolnick, *Embattled Paradise: the American Family in an Age of Uncertainty* (1991), and Donald Katz, *Home Fires: An Intimate Portrait of One Middle-Class Family in Postwar America* (1992). For a view of city life in contrast to suburbia see Thomas J. Sugrue, *The Origins of the Urban Crisis: Race and Inequality in Postwar Detroit* (1997).

The civil rights movement is covered in Harry Ashmore, *Civil Rights and Wrongs: A Memoir of Race and Politics, 1944–1994* (1994). Another overall view is Harvard Sitkoff, *The Struggle for Black Equality, 1954–1992* (1993). On the background of the *Brown* v. *Board of Education* decision, see Richard Kruger, *Simple Justice: The History of Brown vs. Board of Education: Black America's Struggle for Equality* (1976). A moving biography of Martin Luther King Jr. is Stephen Oates, *Let the Trumpet Sound: The Life of Martin Luther King* (1982). The process of ghettoization is discussed in Nicholas Lemann, *The Promised Land: The Great Black Migration and How It Changed America* (1991), and Arnold Hirsch, *Making the Second Ghetto: Race and Housing in Chicago, 1940–1960* (1983). A controversial book about black progress is William Wilson, *The Declining Significance of Race: Blacks and Changing American Institutions* (1978). Wilson's *The Truly Disadvantaged: The Inner City, the Underclass, and Public Policy* (1987) centers on poverty. An attempt to look at black progress is Reynolds Farley, *Blacks and Whites* (1984), while the National Research Council publication *A Common Destiny: Blacks and Whites in American Society* (1989) is filled with information. Two newer accounts of the civil rights movement are Robert Weisbort, *Freedom Bound: A History of the Civil Rights Movement* (1989), and Taylor Branch, *Parting the Waters: America in the King Years, 1954–1963* (1988). For women and the civil rights movement, see

Belinda Robnett, *How Long? How Long? African American Women in the Struggle for Civil Rights* (1997). A view of race relations at the end of the 1990s is David K. Shipler, *A Country of Strangers: Blacks and Whites in America* (1997).

For the 1960s, the standard treatment of the Vietnam War is George Herring, *America's Longest War: The United States and Vietnam, 1950–1975* (1996). See also Lauri Umansky, *Motherhood Reconsidered: Feminism and the Legacies of the Sixties* (1996); David Burner, *Making Peace with the 60s* (1996); and Paul Berman, *A Tale of Two Utopias: The Political Journey of the Generation of 1968* (1996).

For American women in recent years, the best introduction is William Chafe, *The American Woman: Her Changing Social, Economic, and Political Role, 1920–1970* (1972). Jacqueline Jones, *Labor of Love, Labor of Sorrow* (1985), is also useful, as is Alice Kessler-Harris, *Out to Work* (1982). Also helpful are Sara Evans, *Personal Politics: The Roots of Women's Liberation in the Civil Rights Movement and the New Left* (1979); Carol Stack, *All Our Kin: Strategies for Survival in a Black Community* (1974); and Susan Estabrook Kennedy, *If All We Did Was to Weep at Home: A History of White Working-Class Women in America* (1979). Jane Mansbridge, *Why We Lost the ERA* (1986), centers on the ERA; Susan Hartman, *From Margin to Mainstream: American Women in Politics Since 1960* (1989), discusses politics. A useful history of American women is Sara Evans, *Born for Liberty: A History of Women in America* (1989). Susan Faludi, *Backlash: The Undeclared War Against American Women* (1991), covers recent developments, especially in the media.

On recent immigration, Ronald Takaki, *Strangers from a Different Shore: A History of Asian Americans* (1989); Robert Daniels, *Asian America: Chinese and Japanese in the United States Since 1850* (1988); and Peter Kwong, *The New Chinatown* (1986) are useful regarding Asians. General information can be found in Alejandro Portes and Ruben G. Rumbaut, *Immigrant America: A Portrait* (1990), and David M. Reimers, *Still the Golden Door: The Third World Comes to America* (1992). On Miami, see Alejandro Portes and Alex Stepick, *City on the Edge* (1993). On Hispanics, consult Roberto Suro, *Strangers Among Us: How Latino Immigration is Transforming America* (1998). On Mexican women, see Vicki L. Ruiz, *From Out of the Shadows: Mexican Women in Twentieth Century America* (1997). A general account of immigration since 1920 is Elliott Robert Barkan, *And Still They Come: Immigrants and American Society, 1920–1990s* (1996).